ADOLESCENCE

The Farewell to Childhood

by Louise J. Kaplan, Ph.D.

A TOUCHSTONE BOOK
Published by SIMON & SCHUSTER, INC.
NEW YORK

First Touchstone Edition, 1985

Published by Simon & Schuster, Inc.
Simon & Schuster Building
Rockefeller Center
1230 Avenue of the Americas
New York, New York 10020

TOUCHSTONE and colophon are registered trademarks of
Simon & Schuster, Inc.

Designed by C. Linda Dingler

Manufactured in the United States of America

10 9 8 7 6 5 4 3 2 1 Pbk.

Library of Congress Cataloging in Publication Data

Kaplan, Louise J.
Adolescence, The Farewell to Childhood.
Includes Bibliographical references and index.
1. Adolescence.   2. Adolescent psychology.   I. Title.
HQ796.K286   1984   305.2'35   84-5486
ISBN 0-671-60463-5 Pbk.

The author gratefully acknowledges permission to reprint the following:

from *Life and Confessions of a Psychologist,* by G. Stanley Hall. Copyright
1923 by D. Appleton & Co., renewed 1951 by Robert G. Hall. Reprinted by
permission of E. P. Dutton.

from *The First and Second Discourses,* by Jean-Jacques Rousseau, ed. by
Roger D. Masters and trans. by Roger D. and Judith R. Masters. Copyright © 1964
by St. Martin's Press, Inc. Reprinted by permission of the publisher.

from *Emile, or On Education,* by Jean-Jacques Rousseau, trans. by Allan

(*Continued at back of book*)

ACKNOWLEDGMENTS

I thank Aaron H. Esman for his generous recommendations and enthusiastic response during the initial phase of my research for this book. To Peter Blos I am immensely grateful, not only for his thoughtful suggestions but also for his formulations on the evolution of the adult ego-ideal, formulations that had a considerable influence on my version of the moral transformations of adolescence. However, neither Dr. Esman nor Dr. Blos, psychoanalysts who themselves have written extensively on the adolescent experience, are responsible for my interpretations, which sometimes go in directions quite different from theirs. I also wish to thank Dean Elizabeth Coleman of the New School for Social Research for her collegiality and encouragement during the years I was writing this book. I am especially grateful to the Seminar College students for never consenting to my theories on adolescence if they went against the grain of their experience and for giving me their ardent approval when the theories struck home.

To my children, Ann and David

CONTENTS

TO THE READER

I regard the Notes for this book as an essential adjunct to the main narrative and not merely as a bibliography or reference list in the customary scholarly tradition. I strongly recommend them to your attention. There are numerous passages that a reader is likely to question: "How do we know this?" The reader will also recognize that some descriptions of adolescents are composites that were derived from several sources. The Notes cite the sources that support these passages, and occasionally a fuller amplification of the specific details is also given.

In the Notes I also express my indebtedness to the many psychoanalysts, psychologists, social workers, biologists, anthropologists, historians, philosophers, poets, novelists, lyricists, and social critics whose writings influenced the substance of the book you are about to read. Like myself, most of these writers are informed by the sexual and moral perspectives of modern Western civilization. Certainly some of the statistics and specific adolescent behaviors I present are even more narrowly restricted to middle-class, urban, nuclear family settings. Nevertheless the sexual and moral transformations I describe are a *prototypical* process and characteristic of our species. My over-all intent was to convey the central dynamic spirit of the *human* passage from childhood into adulthood.

Finally, in *Oneness and Separateness,** my earlier narrative on the first three years of life, I followed the convention of referring to the child with the pronouns "he" and "him" for clarity—in order to distinguish the baby from the mother. The convention in writing about adolescence is also to refer to all persons otherwise unidentifiable as "he." This convention I did not find reasonable or acceptable. Nor did

---

* New York: Simon and Schuster, 1978.

I wish to burden the reader with an endless stream of "he or she"s. Thus you will find the adolescent generally referred to as "she," occasionally as "he or she," and when appropriate, as "he." Most often I continue to refer to the infant as "he," but not always. When I do refer to the adolescent as "she," the reader can assume that the topic being discussed is the same or similar enough applied to boys. When this is not so, the necessary qualifiers will be found in the text itself or in the Notes. When other writers, such as Rousseau and G. Stanley Hall, refer to the human species as "man" and "mankind" I have retained their usage.

INTRODUCTION

More than birth, marriage, or death, adolescence entails the most highly elaborated drama of the passage from one realm of existence into another. It is that critical point in a human life when the sexual and moral passions come to fruition and attain maturity. And it is then that the individual passes from family life into cultural existence. This book is a narrative of how a once powerless and morally submissive child becomes caregiver and lawgiver to the next generation.

Some notions of adolescence conceive it to be merely an awkward age, a time characterized by rebellious destructiveness or a passive and painful transition between childhood and adulthood. Recently it has become fashionable to regard it as an arbitrary social invention hardly worth examination. It will be my contention that in the adolescent's personal struggle to reconcile genital sexuality with the moral authority of the social order, the cultural and moral aspirations of our species are born anew. As each generation of adolescents stands poised to take over the reins of the social order, it brings with it new hopes and new possibilities.

Though they themselves might be as surprised as their parents and teachers to hear it said, adolescents—these poignantly thin-skinned and vulnerable, passionate and impulsive, starkly sexual and monstrously self-absorbed creatures—are, in fact, avid seekers of moral authenticity. They wish above all to achieve some realistic power over the real world in which they live while at the same time remaining true to their values and ideals. Among the several legacies that adults inherit from their adolescent years is the urge toward ethical perfectibility.

In its main arguments this book illustrates the manner in which each individual constructs the narrative of his or her life history and the place of adolescence in this construction. From the standpoint of life-history chronology, adolescence acts as the conjugator of childhood and adulthood. A life-history narrative is a great deal more than a sequence of scenes, events, characters in which past, present, and future are linked by a linear story line. Adolescence is a time of active deconstruction, construction, reconstruction—a period in which past, present, and future are rewoven and strung together on the threads of fantasies and wishes that do not necessarily follow the laws of linear chronology. The adolescent phase of life is not a mere space of time that stands between the past of infancy and the future of adulthood. As the anthropologist Bruce Lincoln interpreted the scarification designs in certain puberty rites, the time of adolescence "is not a hairline between 'was' and 'yet-to-be' but a totality filled with history and potentiality."

Another related argument of this book, one that crops up in various guises, is that adolescence is a kind of emotional battleground on which the past and the future contend for mastery over the adult mind that is about to emerge. In this battle between past and future the adolescent poses a considerable threat to the present adult generation, a threat countered by all manner of defensive maneuvers, from open warfare and suppression to more insidious methods, such as denial, trivialization, even imitation and appropriation of youthful prerogatives. This resistance to recognizing the profound cultural and moral possibilities of adolescence is to be expected—it is probably why we adults still feel less than confident about the psychological dimensions of this phase of life. It is an odd fact that what we now know of the mental and emotional life of infants surpasses what we comprehend about adolescents, these older children of ours who could—given the opportunity—speak so eloquently about their sexual and moral dilemmas. That they do not confide in us is hardly surprising. They use wise discretion in disguising themselves with the caricatures we design for them. And unfortunately for us, as for them, too often adolescents retain the caricatured personalities they had merely meant to try on for size.

When Freud announced his discoveries of infantile sexuality and the infantile Oedipus complex to a reluctant and disbelieving scientific community, one of his specific intentions was to demonstrate that the sexual life of human beings does not commence with puberty, or sexual maturity. He sought to illuminate the connections between the developmental events of infancy and the mental life of adulthood, but with no intention of diminishing the impact on adult mental life of the unique sexual and moral changes that occur at puberty. Freud knew that the route of developmental transition from infancy to adult sexual and moral functioning was not a direct one; that between infancy and adulthood were many transformations, many backward and forward movements; and that puberty represented a crucial turning point in the complex relationships between infantile and adult mental life. Nevertheless Freud's revolutionary emphasis on the influences of the infantile past has had the long-term effect of obscuring the monumental changes that occur during the adolescent years, changes that may, in fact, have a more decisive and immediate impact on the evolution of the human mind than do the events of infancy.

Certainly there have been psychoanalysts who continued to stress the vital significance of the adolescent years. The contributions of Erik Erikson and Peter Blos, for example, went a long way toward amplifying the special dilemmas and solutions of adolescence. Yet it would seem that there is still considerable resistance, renewed resistance, to treating adolescence as a unique phase of human life, one that plays a part at least the equal of infancy in the formation of the adult mind.

My personal experiences with this resistance are relevant here. Shortly after the publication of *Oneness and Separateness* I encountered among many of my colleagues a peculiar hesitancy to regard adolescence as a phase of development in its own right. Almost overnight, it seemed, it had become the custom to think of adolescence as a recapitulation of the separation-individuation of infancy. I was familiar with Ernest Jones's widely cited paper "Some Problems of Adolescence" (1922), in which Jones had proclaimed that adolescence was a recapitulation of the infantile sexual scenarios leading up to the Oedipus complex, but I had not been aware of how firmly entrenched the recapitulationist notion was in psychoanalytic circles. In my writings and in my discussions at professional meetings I repeatedly asserted that despite the numerous apparent similarities between adolescence and separation-individuation, adolescence was not a repetition of that phase of infancy or, for that matter, of any earlier phase of development. My position on these issues was particularly uncomfortable because *Oneness and Separateness* was often quoted as evidence for the recapitulation theory of adolescence, and I was therefore expected to uphold and amplify that point of view. I began to wonder why adolescence had become the stepchild of psychoanalysis and why it was that so many clinicians of various theoretical persuasions were so insistent on regarding adolescents (and sometimes even adults) as though they were larger, more sexually active infants who needed once again to "separate" from their parents.

As I set about to investigate the history of this misinterpretation of the adolescent years, I found myself happily enmeshed in several other issues. Quite naturally, historical themes of various sorts began to impose themselves on the attempt to formulate my own narrative of adolescent life—the relatively recent history of some of our common views on adolescence, the personal history of the two so-called "inventors" of adolescence, the history of the recapitulationist notion in psychoanalysis, the patterns that govern the evolutionary history of the human species, the biological history from the initiation of pubescence to the termination of puberty. Although this book touches only briefly on most of these topics, my investigations into them enhanced my appreciation of the special kind of historical logic that regulates the mental life of adolescence. Repeatedly my research was to impress upon me that adolescence, far from being a passive recapitulation of the past, was a time of life devoted to a vigorous and immensely active revision of infancy and

childhood. I came to realize that when we disregard the manifold ways in which infantile scenarios are transformed and revised in the course of the adolescent passage, we are bound to be left with the misleading idea that the childhood past lives on in the adult in its original form. Adolescence is no more a repetition of the past than it is a mere way station between childhood and adulthood. It is a space filled with history and potentiality.

The more I immersed myself in these investigations, the more frequently I found myself nostalgically longing for the innocent, less abstract, comparatively nonhistorical years of infancy. I longed especially for the lyrical simplicity of the infant-mother dialogues that had inspired the writing of *Oneness and Separateness.* In this very basic and personal manner I came to appreciate why it has proved so tempting to think of adolescence as a repetition of these earliest human dialogues.

Fortunately, what the more abstract mental life of adolescence lacks in concreteness and simplicity it amply compensates for in intellectual richness and moral complexity. The variety alone of opinions and attitudes that the topic of adolescence manages to arouse in social historians, philosophers, biologists, psychologists is itself a source of wonderment. On the role of adolescence in human life, opinions range from considering adolescence a disposable social invention to regarding it as a "second birth" in which the highest moral attainments come to fruition. This latter perspective was shared by Jean-Jacques Rousseau and G. Stanley Hall, who are designated by most social historians to be the discoverers, if not the "inventors," of adolescence. That these two men, so vastly different in their own sexual and moral attitudes, should have arrived independently at a number of very similar views on the relationship between sexual puberty and moral enlightenment struck me as worthy of some detailed consideration. Moreover, certain aspects of Rousseau's moral philosophy turned out to correspond to an idea central to what I had learned—the critical role of adolescent narcissism in promoting the ethical sense.

Rousseau speaks of how in the second birth of adolescence "love of oneself" is transformed into "love of the species."

And so I decided to devote the first part of this book to the major historical issues surrounding the significance of the adolescent phase in the evolution of human morality. The lives of Rousseau and Hall are outlined, with emphasis on the relationships between their own adolescence and early manhood and their later writings on adolescence. Both men are brought in not only for their ideas on the intrinsic meaning of adolescence but also as minor characters whose very lives were dramatic examples of some of the dilemmas and resolutions of adolescence. Their views on matters of sexuality and morality also appear in subsequent chapters.

The second part is concerned with the unique dilemmas and innovative solutions of adolescence as informed by the vast psychoanalytic literature on adolescence, childhood, and infancy. Though the recapitulationist fallacy is still lively in the minds of some clinicians and theoreticians, with very few exceptions (such as Ernest Jones), the classical psychoanalytic papers and recent publications specifically addressed to the adolescent years reveal a far more subtle and complex view of the developmental events leading up to adult sexual and moral functioning. As in *Oneness and Separateness,* I have tried to substitute ordinary language for technical terms. Nevertheless some terms—"libido," "narcissism," "superego," "ego-ideal," "regression"—all of which have come to have some currency in ordinary usage, became indispensable to a faithful rendition of the complexities of adolescent mental life. For the cumbersome term "object relations" I have substituted the not entirely accurate but more emotionally resonant phrase "love dialogues," which should be understood to include not only love but also hostility, envy, jealousy, shame, grief.

My primary consideration was to arrange the psychoanalytic literature in such a way as to present the adolescent as an active reviser of the infantile past. Accordingly, the narrative does not follow the linear chronology of adolescence but rather a thematic logic that reveals the adolescent's construction of his or her life history. And since many of the emotional scenarios of infancy and childhood do play a considerable role in the working out of the adolescent dilemmas, they interweave with the book's predominant story of adolescence.

The logic of the life-history approach directs us along the path suggested by the psychoanalytic method in which various themes interweave and influence one another: fantasy and reality; past, present, and future; internal life and external actuality. Here the concept of adolescence as a kind of emotional battleground on which past and future contend for their respective rights is elaborated. In bidding farewell to childhood each adolescent must make decisions, largely unconsciously but also consciously, as to how much of the past and which of its aspects will be allowed to prevail into the future. These decisions are not arrived at overnight. Before the future can make itself felt, many backward movements occur. Adolescence represents an inner emotional upheaval, a struggle between the eternal human wish to cling to the past and the equally powerful wish to get on with the future. The purpose of adolescence is not to obliterate the past but to immortalize what is valuable and to say farewell to those items of the past that stand in the way of a full realization of adult sexual and moral potentials. Saying farewell entails considerable grief and longing. In that regard the adolescent is like a mourner, but a mourner who at first only dimly realizes what it is she is losing. What the adolescent is losing, and what is so difficult to relinquish, are the passionate attachments to the parents and to those dialogues that had once been the center of infantile existence.

The last two chapters of this part on dilemmas and resolutions concern the transformations of adolescent narcissism. One such transformation entails sexuality, from autoeroticism to genital love for another person. The initial love affairs of adolescence are essentially narcissistic or self-serving; thus the *ars erotica* of adolescence contributes, albeit indirectly, to the eventual moral transformation of love of self to love of the species. In another transformation the adolescent reaches back to the earliest moments of his or her infantile past when bodily omnipotence was the primordial experience of love of self. Such narcissistic omnipotence expressed in an adolescent appears as dreams of glory and the sense of living forever in the realm of infinite possibility. These dreams must be transformed into the life of feasible possibility and, one hopes, into an adult capacity for moral dignity, cultural aspiration, and ethical ideals— into love of the species. Here we encounter the age-worn moral paradox of identifying self-interest with the interests of all other selves, the idea that if one is true to oneself one is thereby true to others. But as we know, moral authenticity does not follow from self-interest as easily as Polonius' night follows day.

One of Freud's basic tenets was that "What has belonged to the lowest part of the mental life of each of us is changed through the formation of the ideal into what is highest in the human mind by our scale of values." This provocative sentence is subject to several interpretations. One that many contemporary psychoanalysts adhere to is that the ego-ideal—that aspect of the human conscience that comes to maturity during adolescence—originates in the infant's primary narcissism. Though analysts often interpret Freud's proposal in this way, the process by which this immense transformation occurs is rarely explicated. On this issue I have introduced my interpretation of primary narcissism— an interpretation that is supported by current observational and experimental studies of infants and in other writings on the mental life of infants. I have equated primary narcissism with infantile omnipotence.

The route from infantile omnipotence to adolescent dreams of glory can be delineated fairly well if one is familiar with the growth processes and fantasy life of young children. Yet the transformation of adolescent dreams of glory into adult moral and cultural aspirations, though probably the most significantly human outcome of the adolescent passage, is also the one that requires significantly more investigation and understanding. We know that it happens, but how it happens is still something of a riddle. In this sense adolescence is like a work of art about which we are privy only to the final solution; we must endeavor through interpretative efforts to derive the process that led to the solution.

One aspect of the transformation from adolescent narcissism to social and ethical ideals has to do with the adolescent's homoerotic passions for the same-sexed parent. Another, even less well understood, concerns the love of oneself that some of us believe is never converted into love for another person. I speak of that "true self" that we strive to preserve no matter how much we eventually bend the life of desire to the authority of the social order in which we live.

If there were no adolescence, no time allowed to grow up to sexual and moral maturity, if human beings, like other animal species, simply marched straight ahead from childhood to adulthood, we would be dutiful citizens of the social order, forever childlike in our sexual and moral attitudes. In those individuals or during those social moments when the adolescent phase of life cannot, for one reason or another, exert its full influence on the remodeling of a life history, that is, in fact, what occurs.

The third and concluding part of the book considers a few of the reasons for such deflections of the adolescent process, both from the perspective of individual history and that of the social order. To illustrate the quality of some individual divergences on the way to womanhood and manhood, I decided to use two emotional disorders that can flourish during the adolescent years when the love dialogues of infancy are too insistent and refuse to relinquish their hold on the present. Though these two emotional disorders are exceedingly rare in their primary form, there are variations of them common to us all.

The solutions represented by these two unusual disorders, both of them associated with reconciling oneself to the finality of gender differentiation during puberty, are prototypically "feminine" and "masculine." Anorexia nervosa is an eating disorder seldom found in males. "The Impostor" is a condition that in its full-blown form is believed never to occur in females. But, as with eating disorders, imposturous tendencies of various sorts are more prevalent in both sexes than is generally recognized.

Some of the dilemmas of becoming caregiver and law-giver are personal ones and are to be understood on the basis of personal life history. Others concern the social order that waits to receive these sexual and moral change-lings. And so I close *The Farewell to Childhood* with a chapter on the social and moral dilemmas of modern civili-zation. Despite the enormity of these dilemmas, parents and educators, religious and political leaders have it within them, as the legacies from their own adolescent years, to sponsor the hopes and aspirations that might be born anew in the next generation of caregivers and lawgivers.

Near the conclusion of this narrative on the sexual and moral transformations of adolescence I state the following: "When adolescence is over, the young adult's character is etched with the inner struggles she has undergone. The changing woman has not been a passive recapitulator of in-fancy; she has been an active reviser. Her strategies, her losses, her defeats, her triumphs, her new solutions leave their imprint on the adult form." In much the same way, the intellectual dilemmas I have encountered in my own life and my personal way of solving them are etched on the book you are about to read. Another psychologist might have re-lied more on cognitive development and less on elabora-tions of the fantasy life. It is entirely possible that others would have continued to stress the indomitable hold of the infantile on adult mental functioning; still others might have insisted on the absolute discontinuity between infancy and adolescence and therefore might have given very little, if any, attention to the influences of the infantile past on adolescent emotional and mental life.

I suppose that it is also inevitable that no matter how faithfully a writer tries to convey the spirit of an intellectual tradition to which she is devoted, if she chooses not to be a dutiful repeater of the past, then the narrative she does construct will turn out to be something of a revision. Any venture beyond acceptance entails a process of reinterpretation. Never is it a totally new solution, always it is a reposing of the ancient human dilemmas.

PART ONE

RETROSPECTIVES
Images of Adolescence

1

ADOLESCENCE
Trivializations and Glorifications

Between the closing moments of childhood and the yet-to-be of womanhood and manhood is that ambiguous time of life we have come to refer to as adolescence. In contrast to the factual clarity of a word such as "puberty"—the biological condition of having acquired mature genitals and the functional capacity to reproduce—"adolescence" embodies all the connotative uncertainties of emotional and social growth. There is little controversy about the existence of puberty. Even the experts who question the existence of adolescence agree that the average girl arrives at puberty between ages fourteen and sixteen and the average boy between fifteen and seventeen, give or take a year or two. Adolescence, on the other hand, is a widely debated concept. It—if indeed "it" exists at all—may last anywhere from a week to the decade or so typical in contemporary Western societies.

On the subject of adolescence about the only affirmative declaration specialists will agree to is that it is a psychological process somehow associated with puberty, a process that will vary from person to person, family to family, society to society, and from one epoch, era, century, decade to the next. When consensus is desired they omit the word "psychological." Anyone who has ever embarked on a search for some unified theory of adolescence knows that the safest strategy is to take refuge among the folds of this agreeable social relativism. The manifest behaviors of adolescents are contradictory and overwhelming in their diversity. But when one decides not to go along with the fashionable doubt about the feasibility of a meaningful concept of adolescence, then soon enough the seemingly contradictory data are no longer unfriendly antagonists. Diversity becomes simply an expectable characteristic of the issues of adolescence, an invitation for exploration.

The facts of puberty provide a reliable anchor. Girls and boys do become women and men. Girls begin menstruating and soon after produce fertile ova. Boys begin ejaculating and in a few years the ejaculate will contain mature sperm. That girls and boys themselves attach psychological significance to these dramatic events, and that the adults around them respond to such changing physical status we can be certain.

As it turns out, human beings respond to the approach or advent of puberty in a characteristically human way. All the more remarkable for its sturdy resistance to changing circumstances, one response repeatedly asserts itself. In every period of human history some recognition is accorded to the potential threat to society of this transition period. Both changing child and adult world make an effort to harness an emerging genitality to the prevailing social norms and to the moral order—whatever these may be. Sexuality and morality always mature in tandem, and everything else grows up around them.

As remotely different from our modern ways of dealing with adolescence as they appear to be, the puberty rites of hunter-gatherer peoples reveal the same themes, dilemmas, plights, and resolutions.

In hunter-gatherer societies the rites of initiation into adulthood involve mutilation of the body, among them, depending on the society: pulling out a tooth, cutting off the little finger above the last joint, cutting off the earlobe or perforating the earlobe or nasal septum, tattooing, scarifying the face, chest, back, legs, and arms, excising the clitoris, perforating the hymen, subincising the penis, cutting off the foreskin. The human body is treated like a piece of wood whose surfaces can be trimmed, broken through, written on, whose irregular projections can be carved away or shaped into whatever a society designates as womanly or manly.

The scarifications etch the body with a permanent record

of the dilemmas of existence. They posit such contrasts as male/female, line/circle, lineage/age group, ancestors/descendants, and, most important, past/future. The oppositions are resolved in the scars. In the last opposition, that of past and future, the scar represents the emergence of a present moment that is capable of drawing on the past as it creates the future. The present is not thought of as a hairline between "was" and "yet-to-be" but as a space filled with history and potentiality.

The scarifications, amputations, excisions, and perforations are permanent body transformations. They are marks of membership in a community of peers, signs of incorporation into adulthood. Most directly they signify the irreversible differences between woman and man. The ritual initiations into manhood and womanhood also typically include a few temporary body transformations, such as paring the nails, pulling out the scalp hair or cutting off a few locks, painting the body with clay, menstrual blood, semen, or saliva, or wearing special garments, masks, jewelry. Whether permanent or temporary, the body transformations are meant to divest youthful sexual vitalities of their social threat and transform them into a source of social rejuvenation.

Usually a girl's puberty rite is closely linked to her actual physiological pubescence, which in one respect at least is inescapably noticeable. In many societies it is thought that a girl becomes a woman when she menstruates. There are no comparably definitive changes to suggest the attainment of manhood. With boys it is not uncommon for the rites to take place several years before or after the onset of the physical changes leading to manhood. In some instances the official puberty rite occurs every four or five years, so that boys of different ages and degrees of sexual development undergo initiation together.

Regardless of the age assigned for becoming adult, the over-all significance remains the same. An individual is separated from the asexual world of childhood and initiated into adult sexuality and adult moral responsibility. Permission to be a sexually functioning adult is granted under conditions of initiation into the moral order. In all rites of passage, but particularly in those associated with puberty, the sexual and moral realms intertwine.

The ceremonies for boys are frequently derived from some idea of separation from the world of women and children. At one or another moment over a period of time the boy is required to give up his emotional attachment to his mother—who weeps for him. He becomes attached to all men. He abandons his boyhood sports and games along with his domestic ties to his mother. After the ceremony of severing the bonds of childhood the boy is instructed by a designated sponsor or group of teachers in the duties and moral responsibilities of his community.

In some tribes the boy will be considered dead for the period of his novitiate. He is separated from his usual environment and secluded, either alone or with a group of same-sexed peers. He undergoes a physical or mental weakening, which is meant to eradicate all recollection of childhood. He is subjected to flagellation and other physical ordeals. Intoxication with palm wine, tobacco, or peyote induces anesthesia and amnesia. His former personality is erased. Toward the end of this trial period come the transition rites, which may include body mutilations and painting of the body. During the transitional period, sometimes referred to as the "sacred time," the child-adult speaks a special language and eats special foods. After weeks or months or years he is deemed ready for instruction in the tribal law, totem ceremonies, recitations of songs and myths.

In many societies women are likened to children. They are regarded as closer to nature, more controlled by nature and on more intimate terms with it than men. As she approaches puberty a girl's rupture with childhood need not be as definitive as a boy's. However, a woman's intimacy with the mysterious forces of nature requires that her pubescent physiology be brought under control as soon as possible. The female rites of passage tend to have the effect of binding a girl to a home place, which more often than not is the home of her childhood. Whereas boys are initiated into the public sphere, girls are initiated into the domestic sphere.

At menarche, nettles and grass may be inserted into the vagina to "cause" the bleeding and impel the girl into womanhood. The young girl will be instructed by older women in the patterns of behavior her society assigns to menstruating women. The feminine tribal lore takes the form of rules for the prevention of defilement—the cooking and sexual taboos associated with menstruation.

The onset of menstruation is the commonest occasion of a girl's initiation, but it is not the only one.* A girl may be considered ripe for initiation when her breasts begin to form, a development that precedes menstruation by a few years. The girl's breasts are rubbed with fat. A circle of red ochre is painted around each nipple. In some societies a girl whose breasts are beginning to develop is instructed to enlarge her labia by pulling and stroking or placing vegetable irritants, herbs, or leaves into her vagina. The lips of her vulva may be enlarged by an older woman who stretches them and lightly punctures the vaginal tissue in several places. A woman with thick vaginal lips is considered beautiful.

The molding of the girl into womanhood is meant to control her physicality but also to change her inner qualities. She is a beautiful and good woman if she is kind, cheerful, friendly, unselfish, strong, capable of enduring much.

The growing of the girl, though it does not involve a violent severing of her ties with childhood, impresses on her the necessity for subduing her physical self in order to attain feminine virtue. Her body is scarified and molded. She is enclosed in a designated space within her own household or village, in a hogan or seclusion chamber, surrounded by a

---

* Here I remind the reader to consult the notes not only for the original sources of all the data in *Adolescence* but also for the fuller explications of certain details. For example, the puberty rites I am describing are sometimes composites derived from several societies and sometimes concern only one or two specific societies.

mound of earth, buried from her waist down in a pit of sand. Her separation from childhood does not require a removal in actual space. Like a caterpillar that must be enclosed in a cocoon and undergo a quiet, unseen metamorphosis to then emerge from the chrysalis as a butterfly, the girl undergoes transformation to maturity, but by way of imaginary adventures. These acts may take the form of an identification with a mythic heroine or the undertaking of a cosmic journey. Often the metamorphosis entails both mythic patterns. However far-reaching the imaginary journey, it takes place in a cocoon—the family nest or nearby hut.

Through her identification with a mythic heroine, the initiand abandons the historical moment in which she lives. She enters the primordial, atemporal zone. Her acts are eternal in duration, ever renewed, ever repeated. Like the heroines she impersonates, the girl is infinitely creative and virtuous. The gifts she acquires are never solely for herself. She appropriates for herself the personal qualities of the mythic heroine: fruitfulness and courage. She reappropriates for her society the gifts of civilization: grain, agriculture, medicine. Her personal initiation benefits society as a whole and, beyond this, the entire cosmos. Though at the close of the ritual she must reenter historical time, the girl retains her creative powers. Thereafter her existence partakes of divine virtue.

When the girl undertakes a cosmic journey she is *symbolically* liberated from the limitations of her household or village. She is freed from the restrictions of the safe world of childhood. Her journey is an ordeal, a descent into the underworld or beneath the sea or above through the dark cosmos, a confrontation with all manner of demonic powers. The girl returns from her journey utterly transformed. She is no longer an immature child whose field of activity is restricted to domestic matters. She is a mature woman who is expected to transcend the boundaries of the mundane existence to which she is henceforth consigned, a cosmic being who contains within herself the universe at large. Though she reenters the household and village of her childhood, she retains forever the virtues and cosmic powers of all those who have undertaken the sacred journey. The women and men who have accompanied her on her journey or have listened to her tale or sung the songs or danced the dances with her will see once again through her eyes all they once knew so well and then forgot.

Whether they undertake their passage into adulthood in actual time and space or enclosed in a domestic cocoon, pubescent boys and girls are considered neophytes. The neophyte is a blank slate on which is inscribed the wisdom of society. A neophyte is without gender, anonymous as a piece of wood or bit of clay or mote of dust, mere matter whose form will be impressed on it by society. In some instances the neophytes act as though they are newborns who have forgotten how to walk or eat. They pretend that they must be retaught all the gestures of ordinary life. As they relearn the ways of the world, they are becoming adult. Just before becoming adult the boy or girl participates in a dramatization of the encounter between the generations. The masculine scenario is a fight or competition that stresses the discontinuity between childhood and adulthood. The feminine scenario entails a confrontation with cosmic forces. The novitiate takes on a new identity and frequently a new name. The dead child has been resurrected into adulthood.

All rites of passage embrace a double series of separations with a transition between. Puberty rites begin with a separation from childhood, a separation that is at the same time an incorporation into a sacred environment. The sacred world is a transitional realm, a margin, both exit and entrance, a cocoon, a mound of earth, a gateway, a passage, a journey between childhood and adulthood. In the sacred realm the individual is suspended, perhaps above the earth or below the sea or in the underworld, temporarily isolated from the anchorage of everyday life. Here the past is put away in preparation for the future. Here the child learns that access to adult sexuality requires a revision of the moral life of childhood—a moral life that has been based solely on family attachments and peer camaraderie. The passage through the sacred realm endows an individual with qualities she did not possess as a child.

Although she may not remember what occurred, she will retain forever an aura of the experience of the hunger, fear, grief, loneliness associated with her separation from the world of childhood. The youngster learns that her family is no longer her sole refuge, protection, security. The ceremonies of the sacred realm are a cultural means for deflecting emotional energies away from the childhood past in order that they may be invested in emotional identifications and anchorage within the larger social group.

Later there must be a second separation, this time from the "unreal" sacred realm, which is then followed by a ritual of reincorporation in which the emotions associated with the physiology of sexuality and reproduction are divested of their antisocial qualities.

There is a pretense that society has controlled the natural processes, that the rites have prevented the natural world from usurping the social order. An appearance of orderliness is imposed on disorderly events—on unruly nature and socially incompatible desires. The ceremonies of reentry assert the authority of tradition. The rite of reentry stresses obedience to prescribed ways of performing sex, giving birth, teaching children. There is an assignment to the individual of circumscribed domestic, social, and religious roles. Permission is granted to be an active participant in the rites of birth, marriage, puberty, burial. Thus at the conclusion of the ceremonies of puberty, order is restored; a child has become caregiver and lawgiver. The message is that although there has occurred a drama of threatening emotional intensity, nothing new will happen.

But the rites also proclaim that there is something larger than the personal or the social. By participating in the passage from one realm of existence into another, even the most wretched human is witness to the dilemmas of the omnipotent gods, who though they rule the cosmos must also reckon with their powers to create and destroy. The mortal being encounters the eternal dilemmas of virtue, sin, and ethical responsibility. The self has been enlarged to accommodate the divine. The individual has become a participant in the system that rules the cosmos.

"In all times and in all places"—in Constantinople, northwestern Zambia, Victorian England, Sparta, Arabia, the Machado tributary of the Amazon, Hispaniola, medieval France, Babylonia, the Kidepo Valley, Carthage, Mohenjo-Daro, Patagonia, Kyūshū, Nouakchott, Dresden—the time span between childhood and adulthood, however fleeting or prolonged, has been associated with the acquisition of virtue as it is differently defined in each society. A child may be good and morally obedient, but only in the process of arriving at womanhood or manhood does a human being become capable of virtue—that is, the qualities of mind and body that realize the society's ideals.

In classical thought the virtues of prudence, courage, justice, temperance were thought to be forms of conduct that could be imposed on human nature through training and discipline. In Christian theology, faith, hope, and charity were virtues assumed to be innate dispositions residing in all humans, potential in the infant and child but actualizable only in women and men. By the fourteenth century the classical and early Christian virtues were combined as the seven cardinal virtues, which were meant to stand in opposition to the seven deadly sins: prudence could tame covetousness, courage conquer lust, justice regulate anger, temperance overcome gluttony, faith defeat sloth, hope diminish pride, charity assuage envy.

The Latin word *virtus,* which means "manliness" or "valor," makes explicit the association between moral excellence and male sexual power. *Virtus* is a reminder also that virtue, like the process of adolescence, is often a privilege granted only to special persons. In its original renderings *virtus* was restricted to supernatural or divine beings. Through identification with some divine figure a human might acquire the power of virtue. Virtue is a constant, but interpretations of it fluctuate. Chastity is frequently considered a virtue in young women but a failure of valor in young men. An unchaste woman is said to be "of easy virtue."

While virtue and ethics are not synonymous, implicit in the concept of virtue is that when these ideal qualities reside within the person, that person is capable of reflecting on human behaviors and evaluating the consequences of those behaviors for other persons, whether they are family members, neighbors, colleagues, or society at large, and then acting according to that evaluation. Nevertheless we cannot presume that the ethical sense automatically follows from virtue as night follows day. As we know, ideals of virtue have been promoted in one class or sector of a society as a way of excluding or dominating others.

Clearly the social order does not bestow all the advantages or impose the identical moral trials on all those growing up into womanhood and manhood. Some children are encouraged to pass through to adulthood tranquilly and unobtrusively. Or, if they must be raucous and sow a few wild oats, they are expected to do so as quickly as possible and then simmer down to a conventional adult life—with or without virtue or the ethical sensibilities.

The growth changes of pubescence can and often do take place without any recognizable rite of passage. Not all hunter-gatherer societies have puberty rites. In some, only the boys are initiated into adulthood; in others, only the girls. In Western societies, as in some hunter-gatherer societies and in all the ancient civilizations, the time to *adolescere,* or "grow up into adulthood," was originally granted exclusively to young men of the upper classes and to a few intellectual, religious, artistic, or otherwise gifted girls and boys. Until the emancipation of the working class and the advent of the youth movements in the early twentieth century the term "youth" was generally understood to imply a young man of mental or financial advantage, one who could be counted on to benefit from the conveniences and inconveniences of virtue. The underclasses, like the majority of women, were treated as obedient children who reflexively proceeded without benefit of transition into an obedient and dutiful adulthood. Whatever moral strengths they had acquired during childhood would suffice for the uneventful, uncomplicated adult lives they were about to lead. A husband's virtue could protect the wife, the lord's his serfs, a knight's his pages and his damsels.

Now the benefits and trials of adolescence are technically available to every person between the ages of thirteen and twenty-three. It is a characteristic of modernization that the privileges of adolescence became rights granted to all youth. Adolescence was enmeshed with Romantic ideology: revolution, naturalness, spontaneity, idealism, emancipation, liberty, sexual freedom. It is not surprising that such apparently easy availability of liberty and sexual freedom should be regarded doubtfully by parents, educators, theologians, philosophers. One response to such doubt has been to regard adolescents with tolerant condescension. We can think of them provisionally as innocent victims who are powerless and naïve. Sooner or later, however, they begin to be perceived as victimizers—sinister, amoral, hostile invaders of adult territory.

Now that adolescence is accessible to the multitude and not restricted to gentlemen and lords, many adults are taking alarm at what seems to be a barbaric horde of scruffy girls and boys out to dismantle the structures of society. It is hard to see any virtue in it all. What the grown-ups see in its stead is considerable evidence of pride, covetousness, anger, gluttony, envy, sloth, and a great deal of lust. On occasion, not long ago, the enmity between adults and adolescents erupted into real warfare, with guns, knives, rocks, and tear gas. More usually, however, the generational antagonisms are masked and more insidious.

A characteristic unique to the human species is immense mental agility, especially when it comes to coping with fear. One technique is straightforward denial. Our minds look away and pretend that nothing is happening. A trickier version of denial is trivialization of what we fear. And so we invent "teenagers," the Val girls, the Atari addicts, the army of soporific sloths whose classroom thoughts are intent on one matter—getting home to watch the soaps. Another favored trivialization of youth is the image of the illiterate, greasy-haired, leather-jacketed "hood" with the heart of gold. He may not know much about grammar or history, but put him on the dance floor and he is transformed into a divine being. He's got rhythm. And what's more, he goes to church.

By far the most popular image is the teenager ensconced in his or her armchair, feet up on a desk, jabbering for hours on the phone, surrounded by a cozy mess of unopened textbooks, gym clothes, hair dryer, teddy bear, and tennis racket, half-eaten pizza and hot dog, Coke bottle, posters of Jagger and Blondie and other superstars plastered across every inch of wall space, including the doors and closets. Annoying and frustrating, these silly kids. But they'll soon grow out of it.

Another technique for reducing anxiety is to become as much like the object of fear as possible. The method, identification with the aggressor, comes naturally to little children, who fear and envy the extraordinary power they attribute to parents, dentists, policemen. So they roar like ferocious lions; they dress up like monsters, as they soberly administer injections to dolls, toy soldiers, stuffed animals, and trucks.

Grown-ups, when they feel intimidated by adolescent barbarisms, can get fairly rambunctious themselves. Besides, sometimes those enviable teenagers seem to be having a lot of fun. After a generational truce during World War II, when young men between the ages of seventeen and twenty-six were too busy soldiering to be a challenge to their elders, the generational antagonisms took a surprising turn. The grown-ups began to emulate youth. Middle-aged parents revived their sexual appetites. They donned gaudy T-shirts, jeans, jumpsuits, psychedelic jewels. They pranced at the discos. They vied with their teenagers for youthful sexual partners.

Not to be outdone by youth, the adults simulated Woodstock. A common sight at professional meetings was groups of psychologists, philosophers, ministers, college professors, doctors, social workers, and lawyers, sandaled or barefoot, decked out in feathers, ethnic skirts and shirts, jeans, Indian beads, headbands, plunking guitars, chanting mantras, grunting like the Dead, sprawled in the lobbies, on the lawns, or along the poolsides of the various Hiltons and Sheratons. But soon the Age of Aquarius was over. In hindsight many of these sobered, gray-haired, burned-out elders have begun to lament the caricatures of youth they had allowed themselves to become.

All along, throughout the turmoil and generation confusion, the academic presses kept rolling. In their personal habits and in the lobbies of hotels some academics may have imitated the adolescent generation they feared and envied, but on campus everybody managed to get on with the business of teaching, delivering lectures, writing, doing research. Biologists, social historians, psychologists were inquiring into such matters as circadian rhythms, sleep, fourteenth-century manners, womanhood during the Reformation, Jane Eyre's descendants, evolutionary biology, genetic recombination, headaches, ulcers, intelligence tests, power, love, infancy, childhood, adolescence. Though there was a lot of bending over backward to protect their work from bias, it was unavoidable that the methods scientists employed in conducting research and the ways in which they reported their results would be influenced by political and personal considerations.

On the subject of the psychology of adolescence the result has been an exotic amalgam of defunct Aquarian politics and conservative backlash. The denial, trivialization, and identification are just below the surface. Only now word is out that adolescence might not exist. Or if it does exist, it's not at all what we had supposed. Once adolescence caught on, a lot of people decided they would like nothing better than to abolish it. As we now move into the last decades of the twentieth century, adolescence has become more than annoyance. It seems to have become a menace.

In July 1981 the science section of *The New York Times*

headlined: "Adolescence Appears Far Happier Than Adults Usually Imagine." Four days later the *Times* followed up with an editorial, "Goodbye, Holden Caulfield." The editorial stated: "Adults have been swaddled in the saga of the anguished adolescent and believe every word. But the kid carrying the Rocky Road to a Superman movie knows better." The report was that 85 percent of all normal teenagers are happy. Adolescents are not at all the emotionally stressed revolutionary firebrands we had grown accustomed to imagining. They are not covetous or slothful. They are honest and energetic. They are not frightened by the changes in their bodies. In fact they rather like the changes. Parents like the kids. And the kids harbor no bad feelings toward the parents.

The *Times* report was a popular gloss of the findings of Daniel Offer and his research team. He and Eric Ostrov and Kenneth I. Howard had just published *The Adolescent: A Psychological Self-Portrait*. In this book, which is an expansion of their earlier published research, Offer et al. analyze a self-image questionnaire that they had administered to over fifteen thousand adolescents. The researchers realized that a questionnaire that invited teenagers to confide their secrets by responding to such items as "Dirty jokes are fun sometimes" and "I believe I can tell the real from the fantastic" might be disparaged. In a telephone interview with the *Times* reporter Dr. Howard explained: "We were studying the ways kids see themselves; that was our focus. Of course, somebody looking at *unconscious* conflicts wouldn't do it with a questionnaire."

Nevertheless Offer et al. are confident as they render the latest image of adolescence. According to them the *Sturm und Drang* of adolescence we are used to is simply a myth constructed by discontented adults who have foisted their fears, dreams, fantasies, and wishes on the adolescent. Most teenagers, the writers claim, are confident, happy, self-satisfied. As one reviewer of their work commented, the teenagers "sound like clones of the researchers' own evidently staid selves." Most adolescents, Offer continues, meet the formidable challenges of becoming adult in an accepting, even-going fashion. The mood swings and rebellion are the characteristics of disturbed adolescents, not of the normal variety. Normal adolescents undertake the passage to adulthood with equanimity. They get along nicely with parents, siblings, peers. They are content with the workings of the social order and do not want to change anything.

Offer, Ostrov, and Howard are not alone in this revision of the adolescent image. In fact, several years before *The New York Times* reported the news, the earlier Offer research had already become the basic premise of other investigations on adolescence. This sort of rapid proliferation of a research finding is not uncommon. A gratuitous observation from a not remarkably reliable or valid study can begin to be regarded as the authoritative and final word, particularly when the observation represents a dramatic reversal of a previously held position.

By now the notion that adolescence is a fiction generated by an antiquated breed of psychologists and psychoanalysts has acquired around it a mythology of its own. Some researchers are more deeply steeped in the mythology than others. There are those who, like Offer, stick pretty close to the surface. They are content with a simple demonstration (usually in the form of a questionnaire sampling of the opinions and attitudes of teenagers) that the misguided psychologists, parents, novelists, teachers, philosophers have exaggerated the extent and depth of the emotional stress that accompanies the move into adulthood.

Others probe more deeply. They base their conclusions on more sophisticated methods of investigation, such as clinical interviews or observations of actual behavior. These researchers are contending that American and European teenagers, especially those of the middle and upper classes, are cynical, self-seeking, uncommitted politically, sleepy-eyed conformists and not at all the political idealists depicted in romantic novels and similarly outdated naïve, philosophical, and psychological treatises.

Advancing the argument a notch or two are those who

declare that the technical term "adolescence" is merely a social artifact. It was invented to buttress the habits of mind and customs of child rearing that are congenial to our urban-industrial societies. Support for this sweeping generalization, the "invention theory of adolescence," is easily found through a search of the literature. Almost invariably the dictionary is enlisted. We are told that until 1940 the German language had no word for adolescence and that the word "puberty" sufficed to cover the biological realities and the emotional manifestations. Since the English word "adolescence" can be traced only as far back as the fifteenth century, the invention must have occurred then.

The etymological proofs are followed up by a chain of reasoning bent on demonstrating the intimate relationships between the invented term "adolescence" and the economic necessities of our industrial and postindustrial societies. Along the way there is the obligatory tribute to Margaret Mead's descriptions of the tranquil coming of age in Samoa. A popular reference is F. Musgrove's study *Youth and the Social Order,* which contains a chapter entitled "The Invention of Adolescence." Musgrove attributed the invention to the naïve political and educational idealism of Jean-Jacques Rousseau. And many unquestioningly follow Musgrove's example.

Some adherents to the invention theory are social idealists who want to call attention to the paradoxes inherent in our legal arrangements for children and adolescents. They claim that compulsory education for children from ages six to eighteen, child-labor laws, the concept of juvenile delinquency—all of which were ostensibly designed to protect youngsters from the exigencies of adult responsibility—have produced instead an underworld of disenfranchised children and youths, who now view themselves as prisoners of a social system that promises success, power, income in exchange for delaying adult sexual and legal status but in fact delivers very little of these advantages to most children.

Taken on their own merit, the arguments that link the

artificial prolongation of childhood with some of the inequalities of our social system have something to be said for
them. By exposing such relationships, researchers sensitize
us to the disquieting discrepancies between our professed
aim to protect children and our insidious suppression of
them. They are quite right to point out that marked concern
for the safety of young persons can be a disguised method
for thwarting their moves toward independence. Adolescents themselves are quick to detect the hostility behind the
solicitude, which is why they sometimes react so violently
when we are "simply trying to protect them." However, by
enlisting their well-meaning commentaries on social inequality to legitimize the trivialization of adolescence,
these critics of the social order are inadvertent spokesmen
for some of the more conservative, if not reactionary, positions on the relationships between human nature and society.

The unwholesome affinity of the desire for social equality
and reactionary views of human nature is exemplified by
Philippe Ariès' *Centuries of Childhood*. The book has become the most frequently cited text in support of the invention theory of adolescence. With the same passion both social reformers and reactionary moralists have seized upon
Ariès' research as conclusive documentation that prior to
the seventeenth century, adults had hardly any notion of
infancy and childhood, let alone a concept of prolonging
childhood beyond the seventh year of life.

But then, Ariès never claimed, as those who cite him invariably do, that childhood and adolescence did not exist prior
to the fifteenth century. Ariès is well aware of the medieval
penchant for dividing the life of man into stages, such as
childhood, adolescence, youth, old age. Moreover, though
he dismisses the "ages of man" tradition as having little
connection with what people actually understood as human
growth, he traces the tradition back to the Ionian philosophies of the sixth century B.C., and he lets us know, albeit in a
few brief sentences, that he is similarly acquainted with the
meaningful age groupings of Neolithic times and the Hellen-

istic *paedia,* which "presupposed a difference and a transition between the world of children and that of adults, a transition made by means of an initiation or an education."

In order to enhance his colorful and provocative thesis that the coddling of and devotion to children during the Enlightenment presaged the imprisonment of children and their banishment from real life to the stifling confines of classroom and family cocoon, Ariès underplayed the disastrous quality of life in the centuries between the fall of the Roman Empire in A.D. 476 and the beginnings of the Renaissance in the fifteenth century. In view of what we know about the Middle Ages, Ariès' cheery descriptions of those centuries before the so-called invention of childhood and adolescence are bizarre.

The early Middle Ages in western Europe were the dimmest if not the darkest ages yet known to the common man, whose lot in civilized societies had never been very bright. After the ninth century, with the advent of feudalism, the Holy Roman Empire, the rise of Christendom, the Crusades, the Hundred Years' War, the general quality of life improved somewhat. On the other hand, the holy Crusades into the lands of Jerusalem, Egypt, and Constantinople led to the wholesale pillage of the Holy Lands and the Byzantine Empire. Plague, pestilence, ignorance, extraordinary poverty, drudgery, starvation, perpetual warfare were balanced by the code of chivalry, a fusion of Christian and military virtues: piety, honor, loyalty, valor, and the chastity of the youthful knight and the virgin or married lady whom he courted. The outward trappings of chivalry remained constant throughout the later Middle Ages, but courtly love rapidly deteriorated into a glorified excuse for adultery and promiscuity, while valor was put in the service of barbarous warfare. Except for the irrepressibility of certain cultural aspirations, those metaphors of human existence that rose above the personal and the social brutalities to make life more bearable—Gothic architecture, the university, troubadour verse, *The Divine Comedy*—the Middle Ages represented a violent rupture of human progress which otherwise nearly obliterated the philosophical, artistic, scientific, and moral advances of the ancient civilizations that preceded them.

Yet to hear Ariès tell it, life during the Middle Ages was a marvelous pageant. "People lived in a state of contrast; high birth or great wealth rubbed shoulders with poverty, vice with virtue, scandal with devotion. Despite its shrill contrasts, this medley of colours caused no surprise. A man or woman of quality felt no embarrassment at visiting in rich clothes the poor wretches in the prisons, hospitals or streets nearly naked beneath their rags. The juxtaposition of these extremes no more embarrassed the rich than it humiliated the poor."

Ariès' colorful medley of vice and virtue, scandal and devotion neglects entirely the ethical dimensions of life in medieval society. He extols spontaneity and freedom of social movement as though the moral obligations of one person toward another could be discounted, as though the poor were much better off when they did not embarrass the rich with their wretched existences. In a later essay, a commentary on the relationship between modern family history and urban history, Ariès contrasts the open spaces and freedom of domain in the medieval world with the closed, fortress-like separation of private and public spaces characteristic of our modern cities. In the free-for-all, open spaces of the late Middle Ages the average child after the age of seven could participate in all the entitlements of adult life. When a young boy left his mother's apron strings, "like an animal or bird, he had to establish a domain, a place of his own, and he had to get the community to recognize it." Natural talents counted for more than knowledge. "It was a game in which the venturesome boy, gifted in eloquence and with a dramatic flair had the advantages." The rest, we must suppose, could be relegated to a state of marginal and harrowing subsistence.

The fabric of medieval society, Ariès continues, was loose and left plenty of room for play and freedom of movement. Feelings also were unbound. They could be diffuse, "spread out over numerous natural and supernatural objects including God, saints, parents, children, friends, horses, dogs, orchards and gardens." As he had earlier suggested in *Centuries of Childhood,* until the Enlightenment the child, like the Little Prince, was free, "free of that weight of human relationships which impedes movement, those tears, those farewells, those reproaches, those joys, all that a man caresses or tears as he sketches out a gesture, those countless bonds which tie him to others and make him heavy." From the seventeenth century on, the solicitude of family and church would inflict on the carefree, bondless child "the birch, the prison cell—in a word, the punishments usually reserved for convicts from the lowest strata of society."

But as Ariès surely knows, until the Enlightenment mad kings and naughty princes, those recipients of the best of all possible care, were cured of their "illnesses" by being chained, beaten, blistered, starved, threatened. Unless he was one of the eloquent ones, the average child, who was free as a bird to move wherever he chose, had no opportunity to improve his lot through education. He had a slim chance of survival into his twentieth year. Life was short and brutish, Ariès allows. But it was sweetly alive.

To be sure, a few of Ariès' contentions about the effects of overly scrupulous child care are borne out by the history of childhood since the seventeenth century. The more the child was coddled and idealized as an object of supreme value, the more she was invested with the intense, ambivalent attitudes of her parents, educators, and religious mentors. In the nineteenth century the shadow of Calvinism haunted family life, each child an innocent when she obeyed, sin incarnate when she temporarily fell from grace. As we know, the Victorian-Calvinist child grew up into an adult burdened by an overidealization of filial piety, plagued by the dichotomies of absolute good and absolute evil, and haunted by a conscience of ever-watchful eyes.

By the twentieth century, as individuality and self-fulfillment ascended as the reigning values, conscience relaxed its vigilance and was partially replaced by public opinion, general consensus, and pragmatic morality. The contemporary child and adolescent upon whom this child-centered society has invested so much value carry the combined burdens of an uncertain conscience and a sense of grandiose self-entitlement—a chimerical combination that leads to despair, cynicism, and disenchantment.

The family cocoon that was originally thought to shelter the individual against the indignities of the industrial machine age became an iron cage that sheltered its inmates by closing the door on the social realities outside the cocoon. And the more the family isolated its members from the community, the more society surreptitiously but steadily invaded the cocoon. As Christopher Lasch has observed, in the end the family did not serve as a refuge. More and more it came to resemble the harsh world outside. "Relations within the family took on the same character as relations elsewhere: individualism and the pursuit of self-interest reigned even in the most intimate of institutions."

Ariès was not altogether off the mark in what he tells us about the indignities of modernization. His writings have shed considerable light on how the emergence of childhood in Western consciousness might be regarded as a symptom of the shock of modernization. He laments the inner deadness and spiritual alienation of modern urban life, industrial expansion, conscious social policy, the division of labor, and all those newly invented social institutions that were meant to compensate for the shattering of traditional forms: the modern family unit devoted to consumption, leisure, and child rearing; formal education; the mental hospital. Ariès counters the calculation and cold abstractions of modernity with the magical and the sacred, sympathy and community, spontaneity and instinct.

Where Ariès is finally unconvincing is in his interpretation of the psychological and moral effects of daily life in medieval society. In the easygoing companionship of children and adults which led to all members of the community playing the same games and pursuing the same vices and virtues and sexual freedom, Ariès allows that adulthood might seem to us now as rather puerile. Ariès' passing admission suggests that the blurring of the transition phase between childhood and adulthood is just as likely to produce grown-ups who remain childish as children who advance to immediate adulthood. As the tribal elders and psychoanalysts recognize, an infantile sexual life has correspondence to an infantile moral life.

Ariès' rhetoric extolling freedom and classlessness smacks of right-wing agrarian politics, a pastorale to the happy-go-lucky serf, the good old days on the plantation. Those social critics who deny the universality of the adolescent phase of life are usually, like Ariès, misled by the divisions within modernity itself, divisions that often impart a spurious quality to the political categories of left and right. In the modern social and artistic debates the Western image of childhood figures prominently, sometimes as a reflection of the lost medieval community of spontaneity, spirituality, and instinct, at other times as the herald of social progress with its touchstones of rationality, equality, and individuality.

Some critics who identify with the politics of the left are social idealists who zealously uphold the belief that social forms exclusively can create the child's personality and mold the adult into a proper citizen. For them human nature is infinitely pliable. All one need do to expand psychological potential is modify social structures. These reformers are offended by matters biological. They regard with suspicion such phrases as "human nature," "the laws of nature," "biological imperatives." They contend that in the dialogue between nature and society it is society that enforces its template on nature. At other historical moments the ideals of the left do an about-face. Then the virtues of an alleged natural innocence and freedom of movement are extolled. Society is then the enemy.

At the other extreme are the controllers of the right, who wish at all costs to maintain the status quo. Nothing new must happen. Every potential change must be directed, channeled into the pathways of tradition. The strains within the individual life must never be allowed to disrupt the cogwheels of social machinery. Biology is a fetter, an inconvenience that interferes with social indoctrination. But sometimes other slogans prevail, particularly when any segment of the society is about to shake off the yoke of tradition. Then we hear that "nature is all good" and "instincts are immutable and God-given."

The possibility of an inherently valuable tension between the natural and the social, a tension that could protect the individual from a tyranny of either, is considered a reactionary aberration by the so-called left and an unsettling intimation of the overthrow of authority by the right. From the fact alone that both sides these days are indistinguishable in their congeniality to the idea that adolescence is a fiction of modernization, a mere invention, we can infer that something about this transition between childhood and adulthood has become immensely threatening.

A child's arrival at sexual puberty is a biological fact. What remains obscure and therefore potentially menacing are the relationships between sexual maturity and moral maturity. In all the controversy over the existence of adolescence there is some consensus that puberty represents a conflict with the structures of society. In order for the adult generation to deal with the challenge of persons about to become the next generation, they invariably invent some social form that institutionalizes and regulates pubertal sexuality. What is more remarkable than the supposed homogenization of childhood-puberty-adulthood during the Middle Ages is that even in those desperate times a form of adolescence, or growing up into adulthood, was institutionalized in the chivalric code, in which a young boy might progress from page at age seven to squire at age fourteen to virtuous knighthood at age twenty-one. Similar progressions were observed in the initiation of novitiates into the church and in the progression from apprenticeship to journeyman to master craftsman in the guild system.

Every human society endeavors to preserve itself by inventing the adolescence it requires. Yes, to put it another way, we could say that every society invents the adolescence it deserves and then regards that invention as monstrous, saintly, or heroic. Adults are prone to create myths about the meaning of adolescence. Whatever their political or personal inclinations, whether they glorify nature or revere society, whether they are identified with youth or they are detractors of youth, most adults find it imperative to defuse the awesome vitalities of these monsters, saints, and heroes.

2
THE "INVENTORS" OF ADOLESCENCE
Jean-Jacques Rousseau and G. Stanley Hall

When writers credit Jean-Jacques Rousseau with the invention of adolescence they usually imply that adolescence as a distinct phase of life did not exist until the late eighteenth century or that *modern* adolescence was an imaginative construction of Rousseau's which gradually permeated Western consciousness and then went on to become an unfortunate mythology that adults impose on growing children. In fact, Rousseau did not invent adolescence. He discovered for the modern world the distinctive human plight that arises when a child assumes the sexual and moral responsibilities of adulthood. The plight was there to be discovered and had already been accorded cultural recognition by the hunter-gatherer and ancient civilizations that preceded the Enlightenment.

Much of the misunderstanding about Rousseau's discovery comes from the long-standing custom of confusing Rousseau the person with the true spirit of his moral philosophy. At the turn of the twentieth century G. Stanley Hall, the American psychologist, was to rediscover adolescence and find there the same sexual-moral tensions that had been described by Rousseau some hundred and fifty years earlier. Hall, a conservative man brought up on puritan ethics, also failed to distinguish Rousseau's philosophical ambiguities from his exotic personality. He was unaware that his own discoveries of adolescence bore an uncanny resemblance to those of that pagan firebrand Rousseau.

Rousseau, a figure who polarized a whole intellectual movement during his lifetime (1712–78) and thereafter, has been thought of variously as "the mastermind of the French Revolution," "the architect of Democracy," "the true son of Plato," "the father of Kant's moral philosophy," "the spirit of Romanticism," "the Laureate of Nature," "the glorifier of the Noble Savage," "the defender of Passion against the domination of Reason and Divine Revelation." Or, as Mme. de Staël wrote of Rousseau, "He invented nothing but he set everything on fire."

In keeping with the Rousseauean attributions, the image of adolescence that has dominated Western consciousness ever since the eighteenth century embodies revolution, social and moral idealism, romanticism, naturalness, nobility, savagery, passion: in sum, "fiery youth."

As much as his writings are thought to convey the spirit of adolescence, so has Rousseau's own personality come to epitomize the naïve idealism and storm and stress ascribed to the adolescent years. The tendency to associate Rousseau with adolescent excess has made it plausible to consider Rousseau as an emotional force rather than a serious thinker and to assume an identity between his unconventional, impetuous, vagabond, bohemian way of life and the intrinsic merit of his writing. Like the European nobility and wealthy *bourgeoisie* (a type scorned by Rousseau) who were first captivated by his striking phrases, epigrams, passionate moral overtones, moods, and sentiments, most readers rarely bothered to reflect on the meaning of his texts alone. It was said that the inner contradictions of his writings were a direct reflection of his contradictory personality. Then, in the same breath, Rousseau's critics would call attention to the glaring discrepancies between his professed doctrines of human dignity and the deplorable way he conducted his life.

Immanuel Kant may very well have been the only eighteenth-century thinker to appreciate the philosophical substance of Rousseau's writings. Until the 1930s, when Ernst Cassirer began to assess the dynamic subtleties in Rousseau's thought, it was acceptable critical practice to treat Rousseau in much the same way that many adults treat an unruly, perplexing adolescent—with awe, certainly, and then, depending on personal susceptibilities, either with derision or idealizing reverence, a combination of reactions that could result only in trivialization.

Following Cassirer's lead, recent interpreters have rescued Rousseau's writing from the tempestuous life that furnished its materials and inspiration. There is no doubt that his works represent a heroic effort at self-analysis and self-cure, that the sexual and moral conflicts he could not solve in his own life were rectified by the dedication of virtue expressed in his work. Rousseau is now said to have been one of the first victims of modernity, a man alienated from both his self and his society. His divided personality prefigured the divisions within modern consciousness. He alone among the Enlightenment philosophers realized that the faculties that distinguished humans from the beasts were imagination and the striving for self-improvement or perfectibility. These faculties were, he declared, the ineluctables of human existence and the source of our basest impulses and highest virtues, destroying as they create, corrupting as they civilize. In the adolescent phase of life, when sexual puberty might fuel moral aspiration, lay the hope of reconciling the contradictions inherent in human imagination and the wish for perfectibility. The paradoxes and ambiguities of Rousseau's work convey his profound appreciation of the moral plight of the human species, of all of us in our striving toward a perfection that we inevitably must recognize as unattainable.

Rousseau was born in Geneva on June 28, 1712. Both his parents were Protestants and belonged to the respectable *citoyen* class. On his father's side Rousseau's genealogy is traced to his great-great-grandfather, who emigrated from Paris and settled in Geneva during the earliest days of the Reformation (1529). His father, Isaac, a watchmaker, is said to have maintained certain characteristics of the French. He was gallant, romantic, and loved his pleasures. Of Rousseau's mother, Suzanne, we know only that she was the daughter of a clergyman and that she was a sensitive, intelligent romantic who died nine days after giving birth to Jean-Jacques. An only brother, seven years older than Jean-Jacques, was learning the father's trade. But having first lost his mother and then been much neglected by his bereaved father, this boy eventually ran away and was not heard from again.

In spite of his extraordinary grief Isaac was immensely attached to Jean-Jacques, who reminded him of his wife. Jean-Jacques was beloved and idolized. His father's sensible and kindly sister was scrupulously protective. Until he left his father's house at the age of eight, Rousseau was attended by his aunt and his nurse, Jacqueline, both of whom spoiled him considerably. They coddled him and did not allow him to play or run about with the neighborhood children.

After supper Isaac would read to Jean-Jacques from the mother's library of sentimental romances and historical novels. Later on, when Jean-Jacques had learned to read and the mother's library had been exhausted, the fare turned to Plutarch, Ovid, Nani, Fontenelle. Jean-Jacques' favorite was Plutarch.

A brother of Suzanne Rousseau, Gabriel, had married one of Isaac's sisters. So Jean-Jacques had what he called a couple of "double first cousins." Because his father had been forced to leave Geneva due to a legal dispute, Jean-Jacques was dispatched to his Uncle Gabriel when he was eight. Gabriel quickly sent him, along with his own son of the same age, Bernard, to live with a pastor, M. Lambercier, in the country village of Bossey.

Rousseau recalled his two years at Bossey as idyllic. The bond of affection between him and Bernard was powerful. They obediently studied their Latin and catechism and "all that sorry nonsense as well that goes by the name of education." The pastor's sister, Mlle. Lambercier, who treated the boys with a mother's love, often exercised a mother's authority, at first with threats and then by inflicting various punishments. On a few occasions she beat Jean-Jacques soundly, but soon gave up this form of punishment. Rousseau most likely provoked the beatings, for he enjoyed them thoroughly. It was from them that he discovered "in the shame and pain of the punishment an admixture of sensuality which left me rather eager than otherwise for a repetition by the same hand."

Then at last, after the two boys were "unjustly" punished for some petty household infraction, they grew to dislike the Lamberciers. The earthly paradise of Bossey lost its glow. The boys began to be secretive, to rebel, to lie. When Uncle Gabriel came to remove them from the Lamberciers' care, there were no regrets on either side.

Two years later Bernard and Jean-Jacques began their separate apprenticeships. They were heartbroken at having to part from each other. Jean-Jacques was apprenticed to an engraver, who "managed in very short time to quench all the fire of my childhood, and to coarsen my affection and lively nature; he reduced me in spirit as well as in fact to my true condition of apprentice." When he neared the age of sixteen, Rousseau resolved to become a tramp. Not surprisingly, since he was a man whose entire life would come to epitomize adolescence, Jean-Jacques's actual adolescence was faithful to the image.

Jean-Jacques's first sexual arousals had been generated by Mlle. Lambercier's motherly beatings. This childish perversity was to determine his sexual tastes and desires for the rest of his life. Jean-Jacques did not have any knowledge of sexual intercourse. With awe he had witnessed animals copulating. He did know the ambiguous thrill generated by his beatings. So his sexual thoughts were informed by what he had seen and by what he had felt. Yet his horror of fulfilling what he imagined kept him physically pure even after puberty. "The heat in my blood incessantly filled my mind with pictures of women and girls. But not knowing the true nature of sex I imagined them acting according to my own strange fantasies."

Jean-Jacques was restless, absentminded, dreamy. He wept and sighed. He longed for a pleasure he could not comprehend. In his heated confusion he began to haunt dark alleys and lonely country spots in order to display his penis to unsuspecting girls. At last, after an "involuntary outbreak," Jean-Jacques discovered "that dangerous means of cheating Nature, which leads in young men of my temperament to various kinds of excesses, that eventually imperil their health, their strength and sometimes their lives. . . . It allows them to dispose, so to speak, of the whole female sex at their will, and to make any beauty who tempts them serve their pleasure without the need of first obtaining their consent."

Consummation brought guilt and shame. In his sexual reveries Jean-Jacques longed for a pure voluptuousness that might combine gratification and innocence. At moments he suffered feelings of unworthiness. Suddenly he would be overcome with fantasies of omnipotence and dreams of glory. Jean-Jacques was tormented by the contradictions between his lustings for sexual intimacy and his longings for solitude and fantasy. All this Rousseau reveals to us in his *Confessions,* written in England in his late fifties after he had been banished from France and then from his "motherland," Geneva.

At sixteen, after he had run away from the engraver and his homeland, Jean-Jacques wandered penniless about the Swiss, Parisian, and Italian countrysides. He prowled the streets of Turin, served as a lackey in the villa of a count, loafed about Annecy, stole, begged, exposed his penis, resisted the sexual seductions of the various men and women he encountered on his tramp through Europe. Once, in a burst of religious enthusiasm, he converted to Catholicism.

Between the ages of twenty and twenty-nine he lived on and off at Les Charmettes, the French country house of Mme. de Warens, a woman twelve years his senior, who had been seduced away from her husband by a count and then had been the lover of a number of men. From their first meeting it was understood that Jean-Jacques was to be her "little one" and she his "mamma." In Mme. de Warens' household Rousseau studied musical composition, geometry, Latin, astronomy, philosophy—Plato, Locke, Aristotle, Descartes. Mamma also determined to save her little one from the temptation to cheat Nature. She decided to introduce him to real manhood. She went about her mission in a spirit of calm instruction. And so in his early twenties Rousseau found himself for the first time in the arms of a woman. Was he happy? "No; I tasted the pleasure but I knew not what invincible sadness poisoned its charm. I felt as if I had committed incest and two or three times as I clasped her rapturously in my arms I wet her bosom with my tears." Finally, at the age of twenty-nine, after a much prolonged and eventful growing up into adulthood, Rousseau turned toward Paris, where he hoped to win distinction and fortune in the world of music.

His sole resources when he arrived in Paris were a copy of his opera-comedy *Narcissus,* his personal scheme of musical notation, and fifteen louis. He was introduced to musicians and academicians and noblemen, all of whom rejected his new system of musical notation. It was not long before Rousseau was again destitute. Just as he was down to his last sou he received some words of advice from a Jesuit father who had befriended him: "Since musicians and theorists will not sing in unison with you, change your string and try the women." Rousseau's rustic manner and his extraordinary bashfulness were not in accord with the Parisian mode. But he managed to attract the fancy of a noblewoman, who obtained for him a position as secretary to the newly appointed ambassador to Venice. During his eighteen months in Venice, Rousseau was exposed to every corruption of diplomatic life, an experience that would influence heavily his subsequent political treatises.

Rousseau returned to Paris in 1743 a chastened and sober man. He quickly resumed his bohemian ways and took up with a humdrum servant girl, Thérèse Le Vasseur, who was to become his mistress and remain his faithful companion to his last days. Over the course of her years with Rousseau, Thérèse bore him five children. In light of Rousseau's idealistic views on the natural way to raise children, on the duty of parents to educate their own children, on the necessity for breast-feeding, his critics make much of the fact that all five children were sent away to be raised in foundling homes, never to be seen again by their parents.

Some critics contend that these acts of abandonment are proof of Rousseau's moral hypocrisy. Others regard them as evidence of Rousseau's dishonesty. They say that the "five children legend" was merely a boastful lie by a conceited man who wished to hide the fact that he was impotent. Rousseau's comment on the whole matter was: "I will be content with the general statement that in handing my children over to the State to educate, for lack of means to bring them up myself, by destining them to become workers and peasants instead of adventurers and fortune hunters, I thought I was acting as a citizen and a father, and looked upon myself as a member of Plato's Republic."

Thérèse could barely read. Despite Rousseau's initial efforts to improve her mind, she never could tell time or recite the twelve months of the year or count money. With all her limitations, "her stupidity, if you like," Rousseau lived as pleasantly with his Thérèse "as with the finest genius in the world." Rousseau was soon recognized as a rising star in the worlds of music and literature. One of his operas was performed at Versailles. With his first major political essay he achieved instant fame.

Now in his mid-thirties, Rousseau plunged into the life of the French salon, bursting with the innocence of his heart, the purity of his ideas—truly an image of raw youth, exposed and vulnerable in an atmosphere of cynical adults. He was ill at ease, clumsy, halting with the spoken word, careless in his dress (he had tried to imitate the Parisian dress code but soon gave up), with manners entirely at variance with the conventions of the salon. He was tolerated, even admired, but was regarded as a curiosity.

Rousseau, of course, was no longer an adolescent when he began to write his celebrated treatises on social and educational reform. He was a morbidly sensitive, immensely intelligent, spiritually courageous adult, but with little sense of proportion about his beliefs and absolutely no capacity for humor. He could not abide the artificial conversational style, the pandering to the nobility of the *philosophes,* who were his intellectual peers.

The *philosophes* of the French Enlightenment—among them Montesquieu, Diderot, Voltaire—were not ivory-tower philosophers. They were men of action, pamphleteers and propagandists. Their revolutionary ideas were meant to have a direct impact on the social and religious beliefs of their day. Except for Diderot, the *philosophes* did not much care for Rousseau. Though Rousseau shared with them a world view that involved the reevaluation of all religious, ethical, and political systems, and the premise that truth resided in the laws of nature and the use of reason, Rousseau's personality and his approach to human nature were offensive to their fundamental beliefs.

By temperament Rousseau was an isolate who preferred solitude and rural surroundings to the society of men and city life. As his immense popularity proved, Rousseau's impatience with artificial manners was to constitute the spirit of the ensuing decades. In England, Germany, Italy, and France, inspiration and sentiment, a taste for unspoiled nature and informal gardens, became the fashion. In these respects Rousseau marched ahead of the other *philosophes,* who generally represented the "rational" aspects of the Enlightenment. It was Rousseau who urged the Enlightenment into the Romantic age.

Among the *philosophes* Rousseau was the outcast. Even Diderot eventually broke with him. Diderot was an atheist. He disapproved of Rousseau's persistent deism, his faith in the works of God. But finally it was Rousseau's seeming primitivism that offended him.

In 1749, while he was still Diderot's close friend and colleague, and when he still had high hopes of gaining the respect of his peers, Rousseau won the prize of the Academy of Dijon for his *Discourse on the Sciences and Arts.* He was famous despite his messsage, which was an attack on the arts and the sciences: ". . . our souls have been corrupted in proportion to the advancement of our sciences and arts toward perfection." This *First Discourse,* as it came to be known, was conceived in a sudden inspiration, like a religious conversion. Rousseau's description of his inspiration contributed to his reputation as the perpetual adolescent:

All at once I felt myself dazzled by a thousand sparkling lights; crowds of vivid ideas thronged into my mind with a force and confusion that threw me into unspeakable agitation. I passed half an hour there in such a condition of excitement that when I arose I saw the front of my waistcoat was all wet with tears, though I was wholly unconscious of shedding them. Ah, if ever I could have written a quarter of what I saw and felt under that tree, with what clearness would I have brought out all the contradictions of our social situation; with what simplicity I should have demonstrated that man is naturally good, and that by institutions only he is debased.

Several years later Rousseau applied for the second prize of the Academy. This time he did not win. His *Second Discourse (On the Origin and Foundations of Inequality),* a much misunderstood treatise, which came to be regarded as a paean to the noble savage, was in fact an attack on the abuses of private property and a history of the human species. Here Rousseau painted the picture of the savage as an innocent whose needs could be gratified through instinct and simple family and tribal life. With the growth of private property, war, murder, and wretchedness ensued. The evils unknown to the savage now became the universal lot of mankind.

For all his nostalgic yearnings, Rousseau never lost sight of the fact that man could never return to his natural state. Rousseau despised the social order as it existed, but he always insisted that nature does not turn back. His writings are a lament on the cleavage between nature's highest dispositions and the social order. He portrays the civilized human soul as a kingdom divided against itself—false to its own true nature and useless to society. A man who is no longer true to himself (love of oneself, *amour de moi*) cannot be a true citizen of the earth.

Acknowledging his receipt of the essay on inequality, Voltaire thanked Rousseau for his "new book against the human race," adding that the essay made him "want to walk on all fours, but since I lost the habit more than sixty years before, I feel that it is unfortunately impossible."

Emile, or On Education, the book that precipitated Rousseau's exile, is universally acclaimed as "the most influential treatise on pedagogy ever written." To this tribute some educators and philosophers hasten to append the words "and the worst" or "and the most impractical." It was in *Emile* that Rousseau "invented" the adolescent phase of life.

In order to bypass the censorship of the Parisian authorities Rousseau had *Emile* and *The Social Contract* published in Amsterdam. But then, early in 1762, a number of copies were smuggled into France, and soon both books were being avidly read by the Parisian upper classes. No sooner did *Emile* arrive on the Paris bookstalls than it aroused a storm. *The Social Contract* and *Emile,* both written during the previous four years, were of the same philosophical cloth. But *The Social Contract* was to produce only a few minor tremors, whereas *Emile* rocked the foundations of Europe. The fury against the book came as a shock to Rousseau.

A Parisian decree of May 8, 1762, was directed against the author of *Emile* and the entire volume, especially its unorthodox profession of religious faith. The Archbishop of Paris condemned *Emile*. It was also condemned by the Sorbonne and the Parliament of Paris. All available copies were confiscated and burned. Death and/or incarceration were recommended for the author. But Rousseau was permitted to "escape" to Geneva.

What Rousseau could not comprehend was that it was precisely the widespread appeal of *Emile* that had made it dangerous. The simplicity and sweet sentimentality, the bucolic view of human nature, the allegorical style, the tantalizing epigrams and paradoxes were precisely right to capture the imaginations of the European ruling classes and wealthy bourgeoisie. It was an offense to the mainstream of thought of the *philosophes,* who saw themselves as the champions of reason and the scientific method. The fundamental premise of the Enlightenment was reason, and Voltaire was thought to epitomize that aspect of the century. It was said that "Italy had a Renaissance and Germany a Reformation, but France had Voltaire." Voltaire also had the reputation of being a petty, spiteful, vindictive snob who, when it suited his purposes, could be outright dishonest. He was envious of any competitor for public attention. Rousseau was bound to offend him in every way. It is believed that Voltaire convinced the other *philosophes* to cooperate with the state censor in denouncing *Emile* and branding Rousseau a heretic. Voltaire's *Sentiments des Citoyens,* an attack on Rousseau, was the low point of his career. He described Rousseau as an anti-Christian, a seditious, violent madman who deserved capital punishment. Reason and revelation joined hands to cleanse the French soil of irrationality and passion.

Voltaire himself was twice imprisoned in the Bastille and later lived in exile rather than denounce his beliefs. Diderot spent some time in prison. Almost every writer of the Enlightenment had the experience of seeing his articles and books suppressed or burned. Even publishers and booksellers could be sentenced to imprisonment. What was unusual about the case of Rousseau was that he managed to offend every party, not only the orthodox religious party, which included the nobility, but also the *philosophes,* who, some say, instigated the persecution.

Geneva, Rousseau's motherland, turned out to be a cruel stepmother. Here *The Social Contract* was interpreted as an attack on the Genevan political system. Within a week after his arrival a Genevan decree banished Rousseau and condemned *The Social Contract* and *Emile,* thus assuring Rousseau's reputation as a hero and a martyr. After some months of wandering around Switzerland with Thérèse, Rousseau accepted the invitation of David Hume to live with him in England. On his way to England Rousseau had to pass through Paris to join Hume. Instead of being molested as he had feared, Rousseau found himself lionized and adored. Hume remarked, "Voltaire and everybody are quite eclipsed by him."

Emile is an allegorical novel, organized as five books and structured along several thematic facets. The topics treated correspond to the first five books of *The Republic*. Rousseau's theories of nature and nurture at once pay homage to the Greek classic and reply to the social and moral inequities of Plato's doctrines. Emile, the person, is likened to the ideal city described in *The Republic*, his childhood and adolescence an ideal of the possible but unattainable perfection of the human being.

By studying man as a creature who develops, Rousseau was proclaiming the centrality of history for understanding the species, society, the individual. The historical principle was to be crucial to the political philosophy of such diverse thinkers as Hegel and Marx, de Tocqueville, Comte, Spencer, Mill, and of course Darwin and Freud. The *Second Discourse* is a history of the human species and the development of society. *Emile* is the history of individual man, his first five developmental stages from birth to late adolescence, with a prescription for the educational methods appropriate for each stage. With *Emile*, Rousseau intentionally avoided the traditional form of a metaphysical or moral treatise. *Emile* is explicitly addressed to fathers and mothers and implicitly to all those concerned with improving the education of children.

Book I, on infancy (birth to age two) is for mothers. Rousseau's passionate exhortations to women to nourish their babies instead of using wet nurses created an instant craze for breast-feeding among upper-class women. "But let mothers deign to nourish their children, morals will reform themselves, Nature's sentiments will be awakened in every heart, the state will be repeopled." Rousseau also advocated the abolition of swaddling bands and recommended that walking and talking be learned in their own time, never forced.

With his characteristic flair for inconsistency, Rousseau promulgated these practical reforms in the Platonic mode. Thus the same Rousseau who exhorts mothers to breast-feed their infants assigns Emile's upbringing not to a mother and father but to a tutor, a young man of "boyish tastes," who will desire (even without pay) to take charge of his pupil for twenty-five years. As for the pupil, Rousseau suggests that he be of good family, robust health, ordinary ability, rich, born in a temperate climate—preferably France and an *orphan* (italics mine). The tutor will select a nurse to assist him, a woman of good character, gentle, patient, and clean, who is willing to remain with Emile as long as he needs a nurse. Then, applying the ideal to practical life, Rousseau declares that a father and mother should act as a natural tutor and nurse. Like these ideal persons, parents must concentrate all their efforts on developing the nature of the child. The bosom of the family is the only place for a child's early education. And, after that, it is a father's duty to rear and educate his children himself.

When he is twelve, Emile the orphan sometimes gets letters from his mother and father. And he replies to them. These Rousseauean inconsistencies bothered none of his adoring readers, while his detractors built careers on detecting such errors. Rousseau, who was well aware of the inconsistencies and paradoxes of his writings, warns the readers of *Emile:* "Common readers, pardon me my paradoxes. When one reflects, they are necessary and, whatever you may say, I prefer to be a paradoxical man than a prejudiced one."

In Book II, on the child (ages two to twelve), Emile learns only what is available to his five senses. His moral education is limited to what is practical in daily life, such as not harming others and appreciating the meaning of private property. In Book III, on boyhood (age twelve to puberty), Emile is taught how to learn. Rousseau continues to inveigh against all book learning. There is one exception, *Robinson Crusoe,* which Rousseau felt was essential reading matter for young boys. The tutor engenders in Emile a love of learning for its own sake. Emile is given no education in the sciences, but he learns how to appreciate the value and the character of the various arts. He also learns a trade, carpentry, so that he will be capable of working and supporting a family when the time comes. "It is clean, it is useful; it can be practiced at home. It keeps the body sufficiently in shape; it requires skill and industry from the worker; and while the form of the work is determined by utility, elegance and taste are not excluded."

It was Rousseau's intention that Book IV, devoted to the period of adolescence proper (ages fifteen to twenty), would contain his crucial moral and educational theories.

Book V, the final stage of Emile's education (ages twenty to twenty-four), concerns his courtship of Sophie, the travels and political studies that prepare him for the best life of man, his marriage to Sophie. The beginning of Book V, entitled "Sophie, ou la Femme," is a description of the ideal education for women. The principles for Sophie's education are radically different from those proposed for Emile. Rousseau was especially critical of Plato's solution in *The Republic* proposing that men and women should receive identical educations. "Having removed private families from his regime and no longer knowing what to do with women, he found himself forced to make them men." Plato's attempt to abolish the family and to remove eros from the political realm is countered by Rousseau's passionate argument: ". . . as though there were no need for a natural base on which to form conventional ties; as though the love of one's nearest were not the principle of the love one owes the state; as though it were not by means of the small fatherland which is the family, that the heart attaches to the large one; as though it were not the good son, the good husband, the good father who make the good citizen!"

"Sophia" in Greek means "wisdom." And it is Sophie's

wisdom and her virtue that she is not free, that she does not exercise independent judgment, that she accepts constraints, that she obeys public opinion. Furthermore, since the human species lacks instinctive limits on sexual activity, it is the woman who must be entrusted to restrain the sexual excitements of the man. To justify these apparent inequalities between the sexes Rousseau declares that the fundamental differences between male and female are "a law of nature." And then, exploiting his talent for tantalizing paradox, he asserts that he intentionally preserves the natural inequalities in order to free men and women from the artificial variations that often arise from social institutions.

In its practical application Sophie's education is designed to enhance family morality and to bring the natural sentiments of the child into connection with the social order. By nursing and teaching their own infants women initiate the moral education of the race. In this earliest bond between infant and mother the "love of oneself," which is natural to all humans, is joined for the first time to a longing for community with others.

The fourth stage of Emile's education is the decisive one. Book IV is divided into three sections: the stage before sexual maturity, the Profession of Faith of the Savoyard Vicar, and the stage immediately after puberty. Rousseau's design here is to put off Emile's sexual consummation until he has acquired the rudiments of ethical sensibility and virtue. According to Rousseau, the preadolescent has no moral sentiments, only primitive sentiments connected with love of himself, his own preservation and pleasure.

Until adolescence "Emile has only natural and purely physical knowledge. He does not know even the name of history or what metaphysics and morals are. He knows the essential relations of man to things but nothing of the moral relations of man to man." The acquisition of social life, the virtues associated with it, and the capacity to reason about nature are not possible until adolescence. At puberty, youth is first capable of sexual passion and thus of appreciating the moral passions that will bring him into a relation with his species. Adolescence is the time to enlarge the natural sentiments of pity, friendship, and generosity, the time to develop an understanding of human nature and the varieties of human character, the time to gain insight into the strengths and weaknesses of all men and to study the history of mankind. At this point Emile is deemed ready for moral education.

By removing Emile from the influence of books and religious training until adolescence, Rousseau's pedagogical philosophy understandably was perceived as undermining both reason and the authority of the church. But it was the Profession of Faith that most offended the *philosophes* and the church. For some of the *philosophes* the heresies of the Vicar's proposals consisted of the affirmation of God and the Vicar's downgrading of materialist doctrines. For the church the heresies were more serious. Rousseau's God sounded too perilously akin to nature, and the Vicar's Articles of Faith encouraged freedom of thought—including the possibility that some virtuous men might even choose not to believe in God. As if that weren't enough, love of God, "the author of one's being," seemed perversely contaminated with narcissism and sexual passion.

Rousseau did believe that reason and conscience could not harmonize until the maturation of the sexual passions. The impulsive goodness of a child is not sufficient for the higher moral sense, and so, until puberty, the child's potential for virtue cannot flourish.

The laws of nature, says Rousseau, postpone sexual maturity in order to elevate the moral sensibilities. And even then, after puberty, the sexual instincts should not immediately be linked to a sexual object. "The first sentiment of which a carefully raised young man is capable is not love; it is friendship. The first act of his nascent imagination is to teach him that he has fellows; and the species affects him before the female sex." Rousseau's plan was to harness eros as the facilitator of the education of the natural sentiments, especially pity for one's fellow humans.

Whereas previously the tutor could let nature have its

way, using only gentle persuasion to curb Emile's childish passions, with the approach of sexual maturity the tutor must become a firm helmsman. He must muster all his strength and wisdom to guide Emile through the treacherous waters. Rousseau pictures the approaching crisis of puberty as a ship at the mercy of powerful and potentially overwhelming waves. He cautions that now the tutor must never leave the helm. At the point when most formal educations end, Emile's positive education in morality and reason begins. Before he achieves manhood Emile must himself learn to be a helmsman—an educator and a lawgiver. "Up to now you were only apparently free. You had only the precarious freedom of a slave to whom nothing has been commanded. Now be really free. Learn to become your own master. Command your heart, Emile, and you will be virtuous." The virtuous man living in society is freer than he would have been in a state of nature, for now he is capable of true or moral acts of freedom. He lives according to self-legislation.

The relations between sexual passion and virtue rest on Rousseau's distinctions between love of oneself (*amour de moi*) and self-love (*amour-propre*). "Love of oneself is a natural sentiment which inclines every animal to watch over its own preservation and which directed in man by reason and modified by pity produces humanity and virtue." Self-love, on the other hand, is "artificial and born in society, which inclines each individual to have a greater esteem for himself than for anyone else, inspires in all men the harm they do to one another." In the state of nature self-love does not exist.

As soon as youth reaches sexual maturity and the capacity for sexual love, the vices inherent in *amour-propre* must be reckoned with—envy, jealousy, and hatred. In an innocent state of nature, love of oneself can exist without contradiction. But such innocence is not virtue. The truly virtuous man or woman is one who can reconcile the contradiction between innate love of oneself and socially bred self-love. The inequities born of self-love might be tempered, Rous-

seau thought, by the reciprocities of sexual love—that special love between a man and a woman that tolerates the
differences between them without envy, jealousy, or hatred.
Thus the adolescence of Emile is "a second birth." During adolescence man is "truly born to life," and "nothing
human is foreign to him." The sexual passions of adolescence propel him beyond love of himself to love of mankind. The advent of the sexual drive is the true foundation
of man's relations with his species and "all the affections of
his soul."

The idea that adolescence is a second birth was first proposed to the American public at the turn of the present century in *Adolescence, Its Psychology and Its Relations to
Physiology, Anthropology, Sociology, Sex, Crime, Religion and Education.* G. Stanley Hall, the author of that
exhaustive two-volume treatise, was the first president of
Clark University. It was Hall who invited Freud and numerous other European scholars to address American audiences,
professional and lay persons, on the scientific and intellectual matters that were then lively on the Continent. Thus it
was that, in 1909, Freud carried the message of psychoanalysis across the ocean to the New World. Hall had a reputation for looking to the future.
Hall described adolescence as the "last great wave" of
human growth, a wave that "throws the child up on the
shores of manhood or womanhood relatively helpless as
from a second birth." For Hall, as for Rousseau, adolescence
was to be the point of departure for a higher stage of humanity: "for those prophetic souls interested in the future of our
race and desirous of advancing it they must seek to find both
goal and means. If such a higher stage is ever added to our
race, it will not be by increments at any later plateau of
adult life, but it will come by increased development of the
adolescent stage which is the bud of promise for the race."
It is evident from Hall's treatise that he thought of adolescence as much more than a scientific topic worthy of investigation. He believed that the results of such investigation

could be extensively applied to all realms of social existence. Like Rousseau, who proclaimed that the adolescent second birth culminated in the birth of virtue, Hall said: "Adolescence is a new birth . . . for the higher and more completely human traits are now born." And again like Rousseau, Hall concluded that it was the adolescent phase that could lift the individual to a higher level of moral relations—that of love of the entire human species and the animals below on the *scala naturae*. Both Hall and Rousseau struggled to reconcile sexuality with the way of life they regarded as the highest and most noble expression of human virtue.

To these considerations on the relations between adolescence and human destiny Hall brought the flavor of puritan ethics. Though he himself was thought to be hopelessly romantic on the subjects of childhood and adolescence, he lamented the then popular sentimental views of adolescence, which were extensively informed by the usual misinterpretations of Rousseauean doctrines. Hall would have been astonished, possibly shocked, by the commonalities between his views and those of Rousseau. In *Adolescence,* Hall scarcely refers to Rousseau except to point out his adolescent excess. He deplored Rousseau's careless educational reforms. He admonished him for "his premature sensations of erotic voluptuousness, but *without any sin*" (italics mine). "A neurotic vein of prolonged ephebeitis pervades much of his life." He suspected that with Rousseau there was "a spice of conscious flattery" in his portrayal of youth. Emile tried too hard for those affected and artificial phrases that would placate the eighteenth-century adult tastes. Hall also indicates his disapproval of Rousseau's glorification of the noble savage. In short, like so many other readers with a concrete view, Hall did not take Rousseau seriously. He confused the man and his work. He had not bothered to explore the dynamic conflicts at the core of Rousseau's moral philosophy, conflicts that were in fact not altogether unlike his own.

That these two educational-moral philosophers should

have arrived at a number of similar conclusions concerning the role of adolescence in human life is of course no testimony to the validity of their theories. What is compelling for a contemporary reader is not whether they were right or wrong on this or that aspect of adolescence but rather that, through a personal struggle to reconcile sexual passion with moral sensibility, both men came to appreciate the importance of the adolescent phase for modifying the direction of a human life—as well as its potential for bringing the human race to a higher level of moral development. They intuitively grasped the dynamic tensions inherent in puberty rituals. They presaged some of the recent psychoanalytic inquiries into the relationship between narcissism and ethics. The idea that what is earliest in human life—primary love, primary narcissism, the beginning of a sense of self—might be transformed during adolescence into what is highest—the ego-ideal, the desexualized conscience that allows us to preserve the species as we once preserved our own narcissism—is a thesis present but not fully elaborated in a number of contemporary psychoanalytic writings.

Along the vast spectrum of human possibilities—in genetic predispositions, childhood and upbringing, ways of living a life and dying—these two men who share credit for the "invention" of adolescence are ostensibly at opposite ends. But in the way they came to express the inevitable plight of every human life, with its crucial turning point at adolescence, they spoke in the same voice.

Hall, like Rousseau, determined near the close of his life to write his confessions. *The Life and Confessions of a Psychologist,* written in his late seventies and published in 1923, the year before his death, begins with Hall's pedigree. He was born February 1, 1844, at his maternal grandfather's farm in Ashfield, Massachusetts. On his mother's side his great-grandmother was Abigail Alden, a direct descendant of John Alden, one of the signers of the Mayflower Compact. "Thus," says Hall, "I am one of the descendants in the eighth generation of John Alden and Priscilla." Hall does not stop here. His mother's name, Beal, is traced back to John Beal, who died in England in 1399. On philological bases, Hall muses, the name goes back to the ancient "Baal," meaning "lord." Or perhaps to William the Conqueror or the Druids. On his father's side the name Hall is traced through nine generations to John Hall, who at the age of twenty-one came from Coventry to Charleston, Massachusetts, in 1630. Ten generations take Hall's paternal ancestry back to James Gorham, born in England in 1550. Hall concludes: "Reckoning back nine generations (two parents, four grandparents, eight great-grandparents, etc.) would give me theoretically in the ninth generation 512 progenitors, all of whom would have contributed equally with those that can be traced above to my psychogenic makeup. Of the rest nothing is known." These unknown progenitors, Hall speculated, might have been criminals or wastrels or, on the other hand, personages of royal blood.

His mother, Abigail, was the fourth child and youngest daughter in a family of seven children and the only girl to seek a higher education. She was the favorite of her father, a pious deacon. She was emotionally and intellectually closer to him than was her mother, a worldly woman quite out of touch with religious life. The man Abigail married, Granville Bascom Hall, was altogether different from the father she had revered. Granville reserved his religion for Sunday. He led the frugal life of a poor farmer. Like all of Stanley's male ancestors on his father's side, who were farmers, sailors, or carpenters, Granville worked with his hands and was "content with simple ways, and virtuous, whether with or without piety." Stanley's father was quick-tempered, unaffectionate, narrow-minded, with little tolerance for fancy extras in manners or piety. He did believe, however, in "brains," which he insisted should be put into work—inventing machinery, devising new methods of farming. Brains should also be developed by reading and advanced education.

Both parents were ambitious for their three children to receive the educational advantages that they had failed to attain. Aside from the running of the farm, the center of Granville and Abigail's interests was the children. Stanley's brother became a pastor, his sister a teacher of higher education.

At the age of fourteen Stanley climbed to the top of the nearby Mount Owen. Inspired by the grandeur of his position 1,500 feet above the surrounding countryside, Hall stormed about, raged, and threw himself face downward on the grass. He resolved then and there that he would not become a farmer. He would amount to something in the world. He vowed never to visit that mountaintop again until he had made a name for himself. "It was resolve, vow, prayer, idealization, life plan, all in a jumble. . . ."

Throughout his childhood Stanley regarded his father with awe and during adolescence with some degree of resentment. He turned to his gentle mother for sympathy and warmth. She was his confidante in nearly everything, and Stanley counted on her to soothe his father's irascible temper. Abigail had a sunny, even temperament and a dread of disharmony and disagreement. She acted as a "balance-wheel" on the father's impetuous and rough ways. Stanley's parents always addressed each other with utmost dignity as "wife" and "husband."

As Stanley Hall looked back on his life he proudly asserted, "On the whole I would not exchange my boyhood for that of any boy I know." Speaking of his parents he confesses, "Hard as it was for them I think it was most fortunate for me that they were poor, humble and hard up against the stern realities of life." As for his pubescent antagonism toward his father, this, Stanley believed, was the foundation for his later independence of authority. On the other hand, Stanley's strivings for freedom of thought and his impatience with restraint were held in check "by the prevalent and ambivalent feelings of respect and even awe for him." If we are to judge from Hall's *Confessions,* his parents had a deep affection for each other and a loving devotion to all their children.

But the atmosphere of puritanism in the Hall household

chilled all manifestations of affection, joy, and certainly sexuality. At the Halls' the only name for the genitals was "the dirty place." When Stanley went to the village primary school he was shocked by the obscenities of "townie" children, who not only freely talked about these parts of the body but showed them, compared them, and experimented with homosexuality, fellatio, onanism, and relations with animals. Once in a while, against his will, Hall was made privy to the secrets of French cards, innocent transparencies until they were held up to the light. On the farm Stanley was daily exposed to the sexuality of animals. One of his jobs was as the "accountant" for their reproductive activities. He saw how the hired bucks had their parts painted red with madder, and Stanley's task was to count up until every ewe had had her parts reddened by the bucks. Another farm duty was to assist his uncle, who was the neighborhood expert in the castration of pigs, lambs, calves, and colts.

During his adolescence Hall was as obsessed with sexual thoughts as was Rousseau. The combination of overexposure to matters sexual and the puritanical morality that pervaded his boyhood home drove the young Stanley to a preoccupation with the sinfulness of sexuality. Onanism and erethism, the excitement of the organs of the body—in this case the genitals—were to become major subjects of Hall's scientific investigations. But during his adolescence, so great was Stanley's dread of masturbation that in his earliest teens he "rigged an apparatus and applied bandages to prevent erethism." The minister's Sunday-morning sermons had impressed on Stanley that all who indulged in this unpardonable sin could be smitten with some loathsome disease—most likely, Stanley imagined, leprosy, which would eat away his nose; perhaps even idiocy.

Except for teenage kissing games, which Hall found singularly unappealing, he never spontaneously kissed a girl until his Antioch professorship, when he was twenty-eight years old. As Hall tells it: "I was always rather a boy's boy and a man's man, for during my social life at Williston and later at Williams and professional school in New York I never called on a young lady or even had more then the most passing acquaintance with one."

Hall maintained his sexual purity and his idealizing distance from women until his second visit to Berlin, when, in his mid-thirties, he fell in love one after the other with two *Mädchen.* "They awoke capacities hitherto unusually dormant and repressed and thus made life seem richer and more meaningful. If passion was aroused, the power to moderate and control it was also gained and I have never had regret but only a sense of enlargement of soul from it all." With the awakening of eros, Hall speculated, he acquired a deeper appreciation of both sin and virtue. He became an ardent proponent of the theory that sexual passion was essential for the attainment of true virtue.

Shortly after his first erotic encounters Hall married Cornelia Fisher, an intelligent, sensitive woman, very much like his mother. They had two children, Robert Granville and Julia Fisher. About ten years later, when Hall was president of Clark University, Cornelia and Julia were killed in their sleep by a household accident. A gas lamp was inadvertently turned on without being lit. In his *Confessions* Hall would reveal his heart on all manner of subjects—masturbation, eros, his religious devotion to science, his relations with his parents, his political humiliations at Clark. On the tragic deaths of his wife and daughter he is silent.

Hall remained a puritan. But once his dormant paganism had surfaced in the Gemüt of Berlin café life, it never slept again. Whatever pulsated and transcended ordinary moods or heightened the senses was good, be it euphoria or erethism (two of his favorite words).

Even by the puritanical standards that then prevailed, Hall would have been considered retarded in his full appreciation of eros. But by the age of eighteen his passions for philosophy and scholarship were already evident. At Williams College, Hall studied with Mark Hopkins, who introduced him to aesthetics, logic, psychology, philosophy—Locke, Berkeley, Descartes, John Stuart Mill, Kant. Though Hopkins' scheme of life and his theories on man's destiny had an evolutionary ring to them, he had absolutely no use for Spencer and Darwin. Eventually Hall was to disagree with Hopkins on almost every point of his views on human nature. Yet Hall always treasured the intellectual attitudes he had acquired from Hopkins, especially that "the highest study of mankind" is the study of man.

When he left Williams, Hall made an earnest effort to fulfill his mother's hope that he pursue a career in the ministry. He entered Union Theological Seminary. Fortunately Henry Ward Beecher, who had become acquainted with Hall during his stay in New York, detected Hall's lack of enthusiasm for formal theology and also his considerable gift for philosophy. With Beecher's blessing and one thousand dollars from a wealthy benefactor friend of Beecher's, braving his family's bewilderment, Stanley set sail for Germany to study philosophy. There he exposed himself freely to what he called his "wild electives"—theology, physiology, surgical anatomy, Aristotle, Egyptology. After a few months Hall managed to calm his scholarly erethism. He settled down to concentrate on Aristotle, Hegel, and Lutheran theology.

While in Germany, influenced by positivist philosophy, Hall had become convinced that the metaphysical-theological stage of man's thought would have to be transcended. "But, the only whole-hearted scheme of things which I had accepted with ardor and abandon was that on evolution which applied no whit less to the soul than the body of man. This was bedrock. Darwin, Haeckel, and especially Herbert Spencer seemed to me to represent the most advanced stage of human thought."

In his forties and fifties Hall became one of America's most influential psychologists, second perhaps only to William James. He began his career as a professor of high rank at Johns Hopkins, where he established the first American laboratory devoted to experimental psychology and founded the American Psychological Association and the *American Journal of Psychology*. Eight years later he became the first president of Clark University. While at Clark he invited

Freud and numerous other European psychologists and philosophers to lecture to American audiences.

He resumed the scientific studies of children's thinking that he had initiated some ten years earlier at Johns Hopkins. The first child study to come from Clark was in 1894 on the subject of anger. From then until 1915, at least 194 child and adolescent research reports were published by Hall and his students on such diverse topics as dolls, fears, habits, sacred music, puzzles, moral defects, tickling, truancy, worship, heat and cold, humor, unselfishness, flowers, light and darkness, the moon, affection, the monthly period, superstition, the soul, stubbornness, envy, jealousy, ambition, shame, justice, joy, sorrow, conscience.

Throughout his research career Hall flourished on the "wild elective" style of scholarship with which he began, a quality of mind for which some dubbed him "the playboy of Western scholarship" and others "an incorrigible *enfant terrible* in psychology." To these criticisms Hall replied: "I would rather be a fool of the Parsifal order stumbling along paths wiser men would fear to tread than a partisan who could not see impartially the real good being done by all who make positive additions to any part of Mansoul which has so many chambers and so many ways of entrance."

Because of his interest in psychoanalysis and his urgings that there be more frankness regarding adolescent sexuality, an *odium sexualis* was attached to his writings and to his person. An austere man, who remained cool and reserved in his personal relations, Hall was reproached for all sorts of imagined sexual exploits. A deeply religious man, whose 1917 book *Jesus the Christ in the Light of Psychology* revealed his tenderness toward the sufferings of Christ and all humankind, Hall was condemned even at his funeral for having depreciated the Christian church. Shortly after the publication of the Jesus book a close friend told him frankly that it would have been better had he died rather than write such a blasphemous treatise.

Hall also acquired a reputation as the "Darwin of the Mind," an attribution he felt he did not deserve but that he proudly accepted. In his ecstatic devotion to the mysteries and beauties of evolution Hall had found his escape from the rigidities of puritan ethics. "As soon as I first heard it in my youth I think I must have been hypnotized by the word 'evolution,' which was music to my ears and seemed to fit my mouth better than any other." Hall remained faithful to his found religion. The university became his church. Scientific research was the very highest vocation of man, the most intense pleasure of which "noble souls are capable."

Hall's version of adolescence was an expression of evolutionary biology laced with puritanism. And his version of Darwin was strongly influenced by the recapitulationist theories of evolution then popular in Europe and America. As a recapitulationist Hall was convinced that each stage of human development—infancy, childhood, adolescence—repeated a stage in the evolution of humankind. The infant and the child hark back to the remoter past; the adolescent represents the later acquisitions of the race. During adolescence, development is suggestive of "some ancient period of storm and stress when old moorings were broken and a higher level attained."

Since adolescence occurred last in ontogeny, it would embody the latest advances of human phylogeny. Hall was also a Lamarckian who believed that characteristics acquired during adolescence could be passed on to the next generation through the soma. According to Hall, adolescents were the great revealers of the past of the race and the great predictors of the future. In their sentiments they long for a lost idea almost "as plants dream of the sun." But in their ideals and aesthetic sensibilities they predict "the superanthropoid that man is to become." Hall's pedagogical strategies were based on these evolutionary principles. It is essential, he claimed, to prolong the adolescent phase so that the race might profit from the infusion of the highest forms of intellect, religion, and ethics.

This meant, in practical terms, the postponement of "ev-

ery nubile function." Like Sir Galahad, youth was to aspire
to a rigid chastity of "fancy, heart and body." In these restraints lay true personal virtue and the ascendancy of the
race. "The apex of individuation must be attained before
genesis." Hall fully appreciated the intensity of the adolescent sexual drive. He stressed, therefore, the intimacy
between erotic and divine love. The excitements of the one
(the erotic) could, by "contagion," be an inspiration for the
other. Youth is the ideal time for religious conversion.

As the pagan, Hall deplored the romanticization of the so-
called noble savage, who was not at all the innocent described by Rousseau. As the puritan, Hall wrestled with the
immorality of the "higher races" toward the "lower ones."
The university curriculum he designed included mission
work and the psychology of the lower races, who were in
most respects children or, "more properly, adolescents of
adult size. . . . Their faults and their virtues are those of
children and youth." If adolescents were the seeds of the
future, so might some savage race be the breeding ground
for the "superanthropoid."

The last chapter of Hall's *Adolescence* considers the pedagogy of "the adolescent races," who then occupied two-
fifths of the land surfaces and comprised nearly one-third of
the human race and were in subjugation to the few civilized
nations. Hall compared the relations between civilized and
savage men to the extinction of the great auk, the bison, the
wild ass, the mammoth, the woolly rhinoceros, the Irish
elk—by which man became the lord of the animal world
and thereby wiped out his line of ascent. By viewing the
lower races as weeds that must be "plucked from the human
garden," man destroys the most precious thing in the world,
"stocks and breeds of men of new types and varieties, full of
new potency for our race."

Hall was convinced that the brightest pages of the human
race had not yet been written. The adolescent races might
be, he thought, "the heirs of all we possess, and wield the
ever-increasing resources of the world for good or evil

somewhat perhaps as we now influence their early plastic stages, for they are the world's children and adolescents." So concludes Hall's mighty treatise on adolescence.

Like most scientists at the turn of the twentieth century, Hall mistakenly equated the savage mind with the child's mind, an equation that was familiar to Western mentality long before the notion that ontogeny repeats phylogeny lent it scientific authority. Though Hall must be discredited for his patronizing attitude toward the savage mind, he consistently demonstrated an ethical concern for the human species (and for that matter, all animal species). And when he specifically addressed the unique contributions of adolescence toward the progress of the human species he actually rediscovered the universal dilemmas explicitly described by Rousseau and implicit in the so-called "primitive" puberty rites. The reconciliation of genital sexuality with the moral authority of the social order during adolescence is the occasion for the awakening of the highest moral potentials of the human species.

Most Western developmental psychologists continued to uphold the theory that ontogeny recapitulates phylogeny. They believed, for example, that the human infant repeats the phylogeny of the race by growing up from little primate to little savage during the first three years of life. These antiquated notions of human evolution and individual development are still pervasive in some academic circles, including that of psychoanalysis, where it has had the lamentable effect of obscuring the distinctive contributions of adolescence toward advancing the moral life.

3
THE STEPCHILD OF PSYCHOANALYSIS
The Recapitulationist Myth

These days many grown-ups tend to think of adolescents as moral barbarians or as "mindless teenagers" who will soon grow out of their awkward and annoying ways. Others are convinced that youthfulness is tantamount to godliness and therefore emulate the mighty gods they fear and envy. Modern social historians tell us that this whole business of so-called adolescence is simply an invention of those two romantic idealists Jean-Jacques Rousseau and G. Stanley Hall.

It would appear that some psychoanalysts are just as much in awe of adolescents as everyone else. Denial, trivialization, and identification are not the exclusive devices of ordinary parents and elitist social historians. As regrettable as some of the popular views of adolescence are, what is even more lamentable on a practical level is that most therapists, given the choice, would prefer not to deal with adolescents at all. Sometimes the rationalizations are disguised as technical issues: "It's best to leave them alone until they've worked things out. They'll only act out and drop out." Or we might hear similes that come right to the point: "It's like running next to an express train," or "adolescence is like an active volcanic process, with continuous eruptions taking place, preventing the crust from solidifying." These same therapists are quite comfortable treating little children and adults. Something must be going on that frightens therapists away from the adolescent.

It is certainly true that adolescence has become the stepchild of psychoanalysis. When Freud announced his discoveries of infantile sexuality and the infantile Oedipus complex to a reluctant and disbelieving scientific community, it was partly to demonstrate that the sexual life of human beings did not commence at puberty or sexual maturity. It was far from Freud's intention to diminish the impact on adult mental life of the unique sexual and moral changes that occur at puberty. Nevertheless Freud's revolutionary emphasis on the influences of the infantile past had the long-term effect of obscuring the monumental changes that occur during the adolescent years, changes that may, in fact, have a more decisive and immediate impact on the evolution of the human mind than the events of infancy.

Freud himself, because of his adherence to certain widespread misinterpretations of Darwinian theory, became an unwitting participant in the psychoanalytic neglect of adolescence. In all likelihood, when Ernest Jones bestowed on Freud the title "Darwin of the Mind," he was unaware that American scholars had already conferred the honor on G. Stanley Hall more than thirty years before. With this gesture toward Freud, Jones was calling attention to the evolutionary strains that had been lively in psychoanalysis from its inception. Actually, the two evolutionary themes that left their mark on psychoanalysis, the thesis that acquired characteristics could be inherited and the biogenetic law ontogeny repeats phylogeny are not strictly Darwinian. The former theme was, of course, Lamarck's. The terms "ontogeny" and "phylogeny" had been coined by Ernst Haeckel, the nineteenth-century German zoologist, who also perpetuated the Lamarckian thesis among his students. Most European and American scientists, including Freud and Hall, had studied either with Haeckel or one of his disciples. In practical terms, Haeckel was more influential than Darwin in spreading the doctrine of evolution and therefore had a more decisive effect on the form in which it would be spread.

Jones contends that it was Freud and not Darwin who finally was able to resolve the doctrine of evolution with religion and morality. Those theologians who were friendly to the theory of evolution had arrived at what they considered to be a strategic compromise. Man's body may have evolved over millions of years; not so his soul. In order to distinguish man from the other creatures, the Deity decided to add the soul to man's body. Freud argued that it was unnecessary to evoke the supernatural in order to reconcile morality with evolution.

In place of the supernatural Freud evoked Lamarck. Freud recognized that the experiences of the ego could not be passed on to the next generation. And the id, which is the repository of all that is capable of being inherited and is the core of the unconscious, cannot be reached by the external world except through its contact with the ego. In spite of these restrictions, Freud maintained that experience can be inherited when certain conditions obtain: "when they have been repeated often enough and with sufficient strength in many individuals in successive generations, they transform themselves into experiences of the id, the impressions of which are preserved by heredity. When the ego forms the superego out of the id, it resurrects these ancient experiences. Thus, the loftiest religions and moral aims of mankind retain their links with the archaic past."

What is pertinent to our narrative on the moral transformations wrought by adolescence is not Freud's insistence on the inheritance of acquired characteristics but rather his unique conception of the development of individual conscience. His remarks suggest that conscience (ego-ideal, superego) is formed out of the innate core of the self and is then taken over by the experiencing self (ego) to be transformed into moral authority. "What has belonged to the lowest part of the mental life of each of us is changed, through the formation of the ideal, into what is highest in the human mind by our scale of values."

Here our thesis is in harmony with the spirit of Freud's thought. As I have earlier indicated and will be elaborating further on, what was earliest "love of oneself" evolves during adolescence into what is highest, "love of the species."

Of far greater impact than Lamarck's tenet was the Haeckelian doctrine of recapitulation, which served as the organizing principle in embryology, physiology, morphology, and paleontology from the middle of the nineteenth century through the 1930s. The theory that ontogeny recapitulates phylogeny also left its mark not only on psychoanalysis but on literature, art, history, education, anthropology, nuclear physics, criminology.

One of the more unfortunate offshoots of recapitulation-ism has been to equate the child with the primate, the primate with the savage, the savage with the ancient primitive, the primitive with the child. The equations tend to overlap in stunning confusion. Children of the higher races are passing through stages of the savage races. Adults of the lower races are like white children. The lower modern races are like the primitive stages of the white man. Infants of all races are like adult primates, and so on. The equation is often extended to certain criminal types and to women:

. . . the child is naturally by his organization, nearer to the animal, to the savage, to the criminal, than the adult.

. . . the atavism of the criminal when he lacks every trace of shame and pity, may go far beyond the savage even to the brutes themselves.

. . . perhaps all men can recall a period of youth when they were hero-worshippers when they felt the need of a stronger arm and loved to look up to the powerful friend who could sympathize with and aid them. This is the woman stage of character.

Many of Freud's followers were and still are entranced by the biogenetic law of recapitulation. In 1917, commenting on the wholesale adoption of evolutionary biology by psychoanalysts, one zoologist generously put it this way: "In nothing is the courage of the psychoanalysts better seen than in their use of the biogenetic law. They certainly employ that great biological slogan of the nineteenth century with a fearlessness that makes the timid twentieth century biologist gasp."

The influence of recapitulationism on Freudian developmental theory and clinical practice is still pervasive, if often subtle. For example, one of the guiding principles of analysis is that through the transference relationship with the analyst the patient will repeat, remember, and work through, and thereby rectify, the traumas of infancy. The transference *does* reactivate elements of infancy and childhood, and interpretations of these reactions of the past in the present can affect profound therapeutic gains. Unfortunately the idea of repetition is often taken over literally. Some therapists assume that an adult patient is reliving her actual infantile past. The present transference activations are interpreted as exact replicas of the infantile past, as though no historical transformations had intervened between the ages of four and twenty-four.

There is an almost unshakable conviction that what matters above all in the treatment of adult patients is the manner in which the infantile past comes to be reflected in the present. Until recently case reports rarely if ever mentioned a patient's adolescence. The reports left an impression that the adult in question had passed directly from infancy to adulthood. When, in the clinical situation, the adolescent years were attended to, they were regarded as repetitions of infancy.

The recapitulationist mythology was given the stamp of approval by Ernest Jones, one of the most influential purveyors of the psychoanalytic doctrine. Brilliant and scholarly though it is, Jones' three-volume biography of Freud tends to enshrine certain aspects of Freud's thinking which should have been subjected to a critique. Sometimes Jones would cogently interpret the spirit of Freud's writing; at other times there was a failure of interpretive response and Jones became overly literal.

In his paper "Some Problems of Adolescence" Jones incisively enumerates the several characteristics that distinguish adults from children: adults direct their sexual impulses away from the parents and toward strangers; in adults the capacity to love is stronger than the desire to be loved, "especially in the male sex"; the adult mind works more as an integrated whole, bringing about a greater degree of coordination between the various components of the mind; there is an intensification of such character traits as enterprise, responsibility, initiative, self-reliance, once again "distinctly more pronounced in the male sex." How did Jones account for these profound alterations of childhood ways of loving, thinking, and behaving? Recapitulation is the principle:

But before these important changes can be brought about the transitional stage of adolescence has to be passed through and this is affected in a highly interesting manner. *At puberty a regression takes place in the direction of infancy, of the first period of all and the person lives over again, though on another plane, the development he passed through in the first five years of life.* As this correlation between adolescence and infancy is the most distinctive generalization to which I wish to call your attention in this paper, I should like to dwell on it at some little length; it is one to which I would attach considerable importance as affording the key to many of the problems of adolescence. Put in another way, it signifies that the individual recapitulates and expands in the second decennium of life the development he passed through during the first five years of life, just as he recapitulates during these five years the experiences of thousands of years in his ancestry and during the pre-natal period those of millions of years. [Italics mine]

Elaborating on his thesis, Jones does say that recapitulation would not mean an identical repetition of the former development. Yet in the end he arrives at a description of adolescence that retains the recapitulationist form: "adolescence recapitulates infancy and the precise way a given person will pass through the necessary stages of development in adolescence is to a very great extent determined by the form of his infantile development." Jones is referring to the stages leading up to a young child's attachment to the opposite-sex parent, from autoerotic to anal erotic to narcissistic to homosexual to heterosexual. To be sure, regressive events of this sort do infiltrate adolescence. However, as we shall see, the pathways of regression and progression are not so evenly or neatly marked out as Jones' commentary would lead a reader to believe.

Furthermore, Jones speaks of the repetition as though it

occurs reflexively—a fact of life, as it were. He does not explore the specific dilemmas or motives that would lead an adolescent to revert temporarily to a psychological past. We are left with the rather unsatisfactory inference that the way one gets from childhood to adulthood is to simply repeat the stages of infancy, which are a replica of embryonic development, which is a replica of the history of the race. True, Jones throws in the caution "though on another plane," but this is simply a concession to the obvious facts: something new is going on in adolescence.

In view of their increasing sophistication in theoretical, developmental, and clinical matters, it is quite remarkable that many psychoanalysts persist in the belief that adolescence is a recapitulation of the events of infancy. By the 1950s it was evident that adolescence had become the stepchild of psychoanalysis and that the misleading Haeckelian notions may have been only rationalizations for deeper resistances.

In the treatment of adult cases it was always customary to reconstruct the patient's infancy. But analysts seldom if ever succeeded in reviving adolescent experiences. A few analysts began to investigate this perplexing phenomenon. They discovered that analysts were encouraging the patients' own tendencies to resist "growing up" by allowing them to cling to the helpless infant-omnipotent analyst dynamics. As one highly respected analyst commented: "The patient brings us a wealth of infantile material, more and more, in different forms and associations, even when the childhood history has already been fairly well reconstructed and reexperienced. He clings tenaciously to infantile material." Why are psychoanalysts so inclined to follow the patient in this flight toward infancy? "One can smile at a little child's direct form of aggressive behavior, but an adolescent's aggression is clothed in a much more irritating, tormenting and sometimes intolerable shape."

In contrast to the infant and the little child who idealizes the parents and conceives of them as perfect, omnipotent creatures, adolescents know that adults are not omnipotent.

They feel that they might even be as vulnerable as themselves. This realization, which shakes an adolescent's belief in her own self-worth, is one of the major factors in taming her conscience and leading her toward a more flexible and humane evaluation of herself and others. Until this crisis of moral authority, a youngster's love of her own self is largely predicated on sharing in the power of her parents. In early adolescence the narcissistic injury of recognizing her parents' vulnerabilities is countered by attempts to revive the image of an omnipotent mother and father. This is why young adolescents, with their characteristic inconsistency, will reproach adults as being absolutely worthless and impotent, only to become intensely anxious when their denigrations finally manage to provoke these same adults to primitive counterreactions. One day the youngster condemns her parents for their less than perfect behavior; the next day she sees them as all-powerful: "They are invulnerable, so I can scold, torment, and act out every aggression without having to feel guilty or reproach myself." It is no wonder that therapists would not encourage in an adult patient a full revival of her adolescent emotions.

In theory most psychoanalysts would agree with these assessments of the stepchild status of adolescence. By now the issue has been brought up at international meetings, on panels, and in theoretical and clinical papers. Analysts admit that their therapeutic efforts would be vastly enhanced if they paid more attention to the adolescent revision of childhood. The need for more deliberate efforts to appreciate the role of adolescence is clearly recognized. Yet the emotional resistance persists. Adolescence continues to be viewed as a holding pattern, a way station between childhood and adulthood, or a recapitulation of infancy.

Within the last three decades, inspired by Margaret S. Mahler's discoveries of the progressive stages in the mother-infant relationship during the first three years of life, the recapitulationist strain in psychoanalysis has been given a further boost, much to the detriment of Mahler's theory of separation-individuation and to the psychoanalytic appreciation of adolescence. Now the recapitulationist slogan is "Adolescence is a second separation-individuation," a repetition of the first three years of life, though of course "on another plane."

Here an excursion into Mahler's findings is worthwhile for a few reasons. Her work is of vast and current concern among therapists and thinkers of every psychological persuasion, but it is increasingly misapplied as a model for understanding the adolescent stage of development. This is lamentable because, properly applied, Mahler's theory promises a richer account of adolescence and a more creditable version of the psychoanalytic principles of development than the recapitulationist version. The narratives of a life history always consist of the *interweaving* legends from infancy, early childhood, latency, adolescence, adulthood. Therefore I shall be making reference to the stages of separation-individuation as they infiltrate and affect the dilemmas and solutions of adolescence.

Mahler's studies of normal separation-individuation grew out of her theory of the symbiotic origins of human attachment. Her work with certain severely disturbed children who seemed unable to establish a satisfactory symbiotic bond or to make effective use of a mothering person and who then also could not take the necessary steps toward separating from mother led Mahler to investigate the steps by which normal infants emerge from the state of symbiosis.

Part of the evolutionary inheritance the average human newborn brings into the world are sensations and responses that enable him to tune in or out, to move toward or away from arousing events. Even before a newborn forms the symbiotic attachment to the person who will care for him and teach him the ways of the world, he is capable of selecting which stimuli he will respond to and which he will ignore. For the first six weeks or so the primary interest of a human newborn is what's going on inside his body. He is only attentive fleetingly to what's happening in the outer world. But during these moments of alert attentiveness the newborn can be amazingly discriminating. He shows decided preferences for certain visual displays and sounds. At the trilling murmur of his mother's voice a hungry four-week-old might even stop nursing and search around with his ears, eyes, nose to find the source of that wondrous sound, the sound that will soon become more marvelous and exciting to him than the sensualities of his sucking lips and tongue on the nipple or the exquisite filling-up sensations in his alimentary canal.

As he moves out from the limbo between fetalness and humanness the infant begins to mold his body to the body of his mother. Her devoted ministrations and his yearnings for contact with her have lured him into his first human dialogue. From the infant's point of view there are no boundaries between himself and mother. Mother and he are a unit of symbiotic oneness, floating together within a common boundary—a womblike membrane of emotional relatedness. In molding oneness the infant's experience is absolute bliss, a communion with the universe. Why would anyone be tempted to leave this state of perfect harmony?

The very same sort of innate sensations and responses that enabled the fetallike neonate to experience absolute power over his inner and outer environment continue to urge him to search out, to move toward the sights and sounds, to seek distance from mother, to discover the world outside the mother-infant membrane. This primary sense of oneself (primary narcissism), which exists before there is any relating to others, keeps the infant from simply falling asleep at the breast and never awakening to the world outside his skin. From the beginning moments of life, the urges for each of us to become a self in the world are there—in the liveliness of our innate growth energies, in the vitality of our stiffening-away muscles, in our looking eyes, our listening ears, our reaching-out hands. Thus after the initial two phases of limbo and oneness, which were relatively inward in their focus, the separation-individuation process that Mahler discovered gets under way. It lasts from about three months of age to about two and half to three years. The stages of this process are what analysts and other psychologists refer to when they speak of the adolescent recapitulation of separation-individuation.

Separation-individuation consists of two continuously interweaving strands: the strand of individuation, which has to do with growth, sensation, muscular power, memory, the sense of reality, autonomy, speech, intellectual power, the sense of self; and the separation strand that entails the infant's emotional attachment to his mother—approaching her, distancing from her, setting boundaries between them, learning the conditions of loving and hating, transferring some of his inborn power to her in exchange for the experience that he is safe, loved, and valued, discovering that he is separate from her and learning to accept this most difficult fact of life.

From the dialogue of symbiotic oneness the infant gradually becomes aware of his mother's existence as a presence out there—in the world. At four to five months the infant begins to differentiate from mother. Her presence lights his way to the small familiar world outside their shared psychological membrane. *Differentiation* is the first stage.

In his wary curiosity with strangers, in his creeping away, crawling away to unfamiliar territory and then scurrying back to his mother's lap for some emotional refueling, in the way he checks back to her face for reassurance when he's about to do something adventurous, the eight-month-old is letting us know he is still quite cautious about separating. In this phase, *early practicing,* the infant's individuation energies keep on urging him to use his inborn powers while his emotional attachment to his mother keeps him in check and prevents him from running away with himself.

By twelve months, moves away from mother are much more courageous. The junior toddler stands up and walks away. So begins the *practicing proper* subphase. With these steps—as he walks away on his own two feet—the toddler's body-mind has reached its moment of perfection. The world is his and he the mighty conqueror of all he beholds. The toddler has a love affair with the world and can temporarily forget all about his mother—unless she leaves him alone for too long, in which case his exhilarated mood is replaced by low-keyedness, a silent, mournful imaging of the ideal state of self that went out the door with mother. As long as mother sticks around in the wings, the mighty acrobat confidently performs his tricks of twirling in circles, walking on tiptoe, jumping, climbing, staring, naming. He is joyous, filled with his grandeur and wondrous omnipotence.

However, at the height of this joyous period of life an infant is still not able to comprehend that he and mother are separate beings. His exhilaration is partly based on the illusion that the world is mother—that her presence pervades the world. Not until he is around eighteen months, when his body-mind is joined by an imperfect thinking mind, will the child achieve full awareness that his mother has an existence apart from his own. Then he confronts the crisis of *rapprochement.*

He is thrown into turmoil. The elated mood of the previous months is replaced by letdown, anger, and sadness. Whining explosions of "No" and "Mine" dominate the household. The eighteen-to-twenty-four-month-old expects his mother to be everywhere, yet he pushes her away when she comes to hold him. Stormy temper tantrums and intense mood swings, from hyper-elation to grief, supplant the confident exhilaration of the love affair with the world. With the awareness of separateness the mighty omnipotent conqueror of the universe experiences himself as small, vulnerable, impotent, entirely helpless. The normal prevailing tendency to perceive the frustrating mother as all bad and the gratifying mother as all good is intensified. Similarly, depending on his mood, the rapprochement toddler invests his own self with qualities of absolute goodness and absolute badness. What's more, the bad, no-good side often gains the upper hand and predominates during this phase. It becomes almost impossible for the toddler to retain a coherent self-image or a consistent representation of his mother or his father.

The toddler would want to return to the unconditional

bliss of symbiotic oneness, but now he cannot relinquish his sense of separateness, his overwhelming desire to claim his body and mind as his own. He begins his quest to comprehend the conditions of actual love. He meets with many defeats, humiliations, and setbacks. But eventually he learns that it is possible to be a separate self without giving up his sense of goodness and wholeness, that he can lay claim to his own mind and his own body and still retain the love of his parents. By three years of age the average child will have achieved his initial sense of separateness and identity.

On the way toward this crucial developmental outcome, each phase of separation-individuation makes certain positive contributions to the shaping of a child's personality and character. Among these contributions are the organization of the oral and anal components of sexuality, the patterning of a child's sensorimotor responses and language acquisition, the expansion of his emotional range, the enrichment of his mood and affect predispositions, the establishment of a beginning sense of right and wrong. When separation-individuation occurs in a more or less average way, the long-term effect is a facilitation of the sexual and moral transformations of later developmental phases, like adolescence. When, on the other hand, the dialogues of separation-individuation are inadequate, they will infiltrate and distort later developmental solutions. But, as we shall see, even in these less favorable outcomes, what occurs is not a recapitulation of separation-individuation.

Nevertheless, one can see why professionals fell on Mahler's narrative as a key to understanding the supposed adolescent repetition. Manifestly, the stages of the adolescent passage from childhood to adulthood seem to duplicate the phases of the first journey from oneness to separateness. The temptation to analogize from infant to adolescent was irresistible.

The adolescent hunger for the ecstasies of perfect love are reminiscent of symbiosis. The adolescent tendency to wander away, explore the world, and then return to home base for a bit of emotional refueling does remind us of the early

practicing phase. The older adolescent's self-centered elation and exaggerated perceptions of the environment and
his own powers sound very much like the practicing-proper
love affair with the world. The erratic moods, negativism,
grief reactions, and temperamental displays of adolescence
seem to replicate the behaviors of rapprochement. And so:

The dynamics of adolescent individuation are strikingly parallel to the process described by Dr. Mahler and her associates . . .
it is not unlikely that the massive structural modifications that
take place in adolescence repeat the process of the original
structure formation.

. . . early adolescence is a second stage of omnipotence—a
young person of this age feels he can do anything, the self is all-
good . . .

. . . the low-keyedness which Mahler and her associates have observed in the later practicing toddler as he senses the mother's
absence is frequently mirrored by the adolescent's oft described
moodiness, and irritability, as he seeks to deal with the relative
objectlessness and self-depletion that result from his efforts at
detachment.

Granted, of course, that we cannot speak of the normal latency or
pre-adolescent child and his parents as being involved in a symbiotic state akin to that of the first months of life, it remains true
that there are distinct behavioral parallels between the adolescent process (in our culture at least) and the normal separation-
individuation and its several sub phases, as Mahler has described
them.

Peter Blos, the psychoanalyst who first spoke of adolescence
as a "second individuation," was careful to warn that
though genital maturity stimulates a renewed quest for identity and an upgrading of the moral life, these adolescent-
specific mental and emotional events should *not* be thought
of as a replica of the first *separation*-individuation. Like
Mahler, Blos was precise in maintaining the distinction
between the word "separation" and the word "individuation." Individuation, an ongoing growth process from birth
to adulthood, undergoes two major spurts, one during the

first three years and another during adolescence. Adolescent individuation, which involves the reconciliation of genitality with morality is altogether different from the separation-individuation of infancy. Separation-individuation occurs once and only once, during the first three years of life; it refers only to an infant's gradual recognition and acceptance of the boundaries between his own self and those of the mother.

Like tribal elders, biologists, social historians, and all the rest of us, some psychoanalysts are more at ease when they can say of adolescence, "although there has been a drama of great intensity, nothing new is really happening."

Swayed though he was by his inclinations to idealize what is natural and by his romantic visions of the noble savage, Rousseau knew that nature does not turn back. In the *Second Discourse,* written a century before *The Origin of Species,* Rousseau already took an evolutionary view of human nature that was extraordinarily modern. There are those who, like Claude Lévi-Strauss, would say that Rousseau's descriptions of the passage from nature to culture pose the central dilemmas of present-day anthropology. Yet, because he had no firsthand knowledge of the animal species or savage races that he wrote about, he was forced to draw on the sixteenth- and seventeenth-century African voyages and on the writings of the scientific figures of his own period. Thus Rousseau exaggerated the moral and intellectual innocence of the "savage races." Similarly, his knowledge of child development, though considerably advanced for the eighteenth century, was based essentially on his personal recollections, his experiences as a tutor, and his scrupulous readings of Locke's educational reforms, which by and large he opposed because of Locke's emphasis on restraint and reason as the guideposts to child rearing. Thus Rousseau underestimated the raw quality of infantile morality and the complicated narcissistic structures that arise in conjunction with the infant's relationship to the parents. Nevertheless he was the first Western philosopher to recognize that the advent of puberty brought man to a *new* birth, in which the antagonisms between self-interest and social duty might be reconciled. With the awakening of the genital passions, morality could surpass an unquestioned submission to the laws of reason.

Even Hall, recapitulationist par excellence, when he spoke of the second birth was alluding to the appearance during adolescence of hitherto unexpressed genetic characteristics, which, if they were reconciled with pubescent sexuality, could evolve into what was highest and most advanced in human nature.

Freud also, misled as he was by the Haeckelian theories of evolution, when he wrote about puberty, highlighted the distinctive mental and emotional advances generated by the maturation of the internal and external genitalia. Until puberty the leading erotogenic zones, in addition to the still immature genitals, are the skin surfaces, the eyes, the mouth, the anus. After puberty the infantile erotic zones must become subordinated to the primacy of the genitals. These erotogenic areas of the body and the fantasies associated with them become the contributions of forepleasure. The excitements they generate add up to erection in males and lubrication of the vagina in females. Freud emphasized the tragic moral dimension of this subordination of infantile sexuality. He frequently wrote of the inverse relationship between civilization and the free development of sexuality. At the conclusion of adolescence the incapacity of sexuality to yield the complete satisfactions we long for and remember from infancy becomes a fact of life—an inevitability of civilization. Yet the adolescent reconciliation of genitality with moral aspiration also produces noble cultural achievements.

Though Freud often spoke like a true Haeckelian, equating primitive, savage, infant, and neurotic mentalities, there were occasions when he distinguished between the infantile and the primitive in mental functioning: "the primitive mind is, in the fullest sense of the word, imperishable." The primitive mind does not restore the past in the form of a replication of the original immaturities but rather recreates in present fantasies those long-standing desires that have been disguised, attenuated, revised by subsequent developmental events. Dreams, for example, do not consist of immaturities but rather of primitive modes of thought that persistently infiltrate the present with the many layers of the past. The infantile, by contrast, is always under revision.

When it came to the narratives of human existence, Freud always stressed that the direction is never a direct road forward to a finite conclusion. Mental progression is a tenuous business that always entails some backward movement. Freud's clinical accounts of the interactions between forward movement and backward movement were far more ingenious and complicated than mere repetition or recapitulation.

As psychological life proceeds, and particularly to those junctures at which old ways of organizing experience must be revised in conjunction with the new issues that arise, temporary backward moves are always to be expected—in fact, desired. New ways of thinking, feeling, imagining, acting are not acquired fully formed. Just as we do not expect to wean a toddler overnight, we do not expect the adolescent to relinquish childhood without a struggle, without grief, without anxiety, without some relapse into the past. Success is gradual and fraught with relapse, trial and error.

During adolescence what occurs is not a wholesale regression of the entire personality. In some respects the adolescent can seem quite primitive, in others merely more immature and childlike, in still others she can be more grown-up and responsible than ever before. Some features of psychological life—for example, the earliest parent-child love dialogues—exert extremely powerful regressive pulls. These pulls can be strong enough to rouse *primitive* modes of loving and hating, especially when the past scenarios were not adequately resolved or when there were traumas that could not be overcome at that earlier time. Yet even here the adolescent is not behaving like an infant, who after all was only acting in those immature ways appropriate to infancy. An infant in the throes of the rapprochement crisis is behaving not in a primitive manner but like a normal child attempting to solve a normal developmental crisis. When an adolescent seems to be acting like a rapprochement toddler, she has regressed to a primitive mode of functioning. She is not reinstating the past as it was; the past is infiltrating the present, and the adolescent has enlisted a primitive mode of functioning to solve and work through a present crisis.

In some aspects of mental life the adolescent regression is less dramatic. It may be annoying to parents and teachers, but it is far less frightening to everyone, including the adolescent. In these instances only the most recent developmental achievements are temporarily lost. What happens here is that many of the civilizing trends just lately acquired during childhood are temporarily dissolved; such rote and concrete forms of intellectual mastery as memorizing, collecting, categorizing that once gave parents and child much pleasure seem to vanish, as do honesty, obedience, fairness, neatness, filial piety. But these dutiful forms of intellect and goodness that are based on a childlike submission to authority are being brought up for revision—not obliteration. In a decade or so, if all goes well, these intellectual and moral attributes will have been subsumed under the aegis of the more abstract intellectual and moral capacities of the caregiver and lawgiver to the next generation of infants and children.

The major advantages of these backward movements is a loosening of controls and a freeing of the mental life. Old desires, fantasies, wishes are brought forth from their recesses in the mind. Why is this desirable? When the past becomes available again in the present it can be transformed and reinterpreted. Adolescence provides the possibility of selecting what is to be continued and what is to remain in the past. The adolescent revision helps to assure that adult existence will not be consumed by repeating the past. We respect the past and give it its rightful place alongside the present and the future, but we do not allow it to dominate or assert its sovereignty over the new.

During adolescence, as at all major transitional phases of human life, we expect a clash between the past and the future. As the scarifications in puberty rites signify, there is an opposition of past and future; the scar represents the emergence of a present moment that is capable of drawing on the past as it creates the future.

In order to advance to adulthood, the adolescent makes excursions into the past. But these excursions are not linear, any more than the forward moves are straight ahead. Adolescents dip into the past because the sexual and moral dilemmas they now confront require a relinquishing of those aspects of the past that would impede movement into adulthood. The major impetus of the adolescent rebirth is to get on to the future, but this is not possible until the past is revisited, remembered, revised.

From a psychological point of view adolescence is the second birth that Rousseau and Hall discovered. After leaving the womb an infant undergoes the first psychological birth and emerges as an individual, with a coherent sense of selfhood and separate identity. In the second psychological birth, now into adulthood, are those innovative solutions that represent our strivings toward human perfectibility. If we judge by surface appearances alone, we miss entirely the dramatic revision of the inner life—which is what adolescence is all about. The underlying sentiments are decipherable only if we have access to a method that translates surface into essence. Such a method of investigation must concern itself with the interweavings of appearance and substance in order to reveal how each individual constructs, revises, and then reconstructs the narratives of his or her life history. Psychoanalysis is such a method, for it gives an account of the interplay between the sexual and moral life, fantasy and reality, past and present.

Initially, in the 1890s, Freud made his clinical observations of the adult psyche and discovered there the markings of infantile life—infantile sexuality and the infantile Oedipus complex. Freud worked with adults and discovered infancy. Some of his followers investigated infancy and came to understand much more about adulthood. The relationship between the version of a life history constructed retrospectively, as Freud did it, and a life history seen prospectively, as in the recent discoveries, is still not clear. The riddles are a source of consternation and considerable controversy among psychoanalysts. Adolescence is the conjugator of childhood and adulthood. As we trace the sexual and moral outcomes of this phase of life we come closer to understanding the perplexing logic of the narratives of human existence.

4

THE RETARDED PRIMATE

BIOLOGICAL INTERLUDE:
The Onset of Pubescence

Human evolution and human individual development proceed according to evolutionary principles entirely different from those promulgated by Haeckel and then so enthusiastically adopted by legions of anthropologists, criminologists, poets, and psychoanalysts. Retardation and not recapitulation is the quintessence of human evolution.

Among animals we are an eminent breed. We belong to that order of mammals, the Primates, distinguished by its propensity for repeated single litters, intense parental care, long life-spans, late sexual maturity, and a complex and extensive social existence. The feature of this common primate heritage that distinguishes humans from all the other primates is an *unusually* slow and prolonged development. It is retardation, or slow development, that has allowed us to progress furthest up the *scala naturae* and to gain dominion over every other living creature. Our protracted biological and psychological helplessness, which extends well into the third year of life, intensifies the bond between infant and parents, making possible a sense of generational continuity. In contrast to other primates these bonds are not obliterated after sexual maturity.

The postponement of final brain differentiation and sexual maturity until the second decade of life allows humans to benefit from a prolonged childhood apprenticeship that equips us for civilization. Because we learn how to behave over many decades rather than simply to react to the environment via preset instinctual codes, we are less rigidly dependent on an unvarying environment. We can manipulate our environments, even change them radically, in order to advance our emotional and intellectual interests.

Another potentiality of our irrepressible juvenility is a capacity to maintain until the onset of senility an active creative interaction with our environment. We persist in exploring, investigating, inventing, discovering. In these respects humans of all eras, in all societies, all ages of life, are more like baby chimps and not at all like the sedate and rigidly conforming adult chimpanzee, who hasn't changed much since she was five or six years old. Human infants aren't at all like adult chimps, as the recapitulationists thought, but human adults are like baby chimps. Like a baby chimp, who for a few years at least enjoys the benefits of delayed development, we have a hunger for learning new things. Our minds are flexible and we are very curious. We cannot resist exploring novel events, running around, looking here and there, poking our fingers into every nook and cranny of our universe. The baby chimp, after her adventurous and flexible beginning, rapidly grows to maturity. Her face will lose its humanlike juvenile proportions. She will acquire the skull proportions of an adult chimpanzee: a relatively small, backward-tilting braincase and a large, protruding jaw and snout. She will soon find a mate and become a parent. The chances are, with the exception of her feeding and holding gestures and her tolerant encouragement of her baby's exploratory lust, she will have severed all emotional connections with her own mother. Her baby will repeat everything she once did, in almost exactly the same ways. Each generation returns to the beginning. Nothing changes.

We humans undergo two major growth spurts: one during infancy and another from eleven or twelve until fifteen or sixteen—pubescence. Between the two is a relatively quiescent growth period in which most of the body takes a rest from growing while the brain continues to mature. This period of life is generally referred to as childhood or, sometimes, latency.

Biphasic growth and its concomitant of delayed sexual maturity are directly related to the exceptionally long time allowed for the human brain to mature. In those mammals in which the brain matures to its final form rapidly, such as rodents and felines, sexual maturity follows directly after a few weeks, months, or years of infancy. It would be an evolutionary disadvantage for any creature to produce young before its brain and nervous system had progressed to the level required for the social and parental functions of that species.

In the human the parts of the brain responsible for advanced intellectual functioning necessary for human social life have a chance to grow and develop before the parts of the brain that initiate pubescence are given the biological "signal" to commence functioning on an adult level. It could be said that nature's design intended that the intellectual and sexual capacities should grow in tandem in order to preserve the continuity of social life necessary for each species, from the lowly rodent to the potentially virtuous human. The special biphasic growth in human girls and boys provides an opportunity to learn to cooperate in family and group life and to be educated in the ways of society before being forced to negotiate the complex demands of genitality, sexual competition, reproduction, and the prolonged parenting requirements of the human species.

The physical manifestations of pubescence—the rapid growth of the skeletal and muscular systems, the maturing of the genitalia, the appearance and development of the secondary sex characteristics such as pubic hairs and breasts— have been observed and sometimes accurately described in most ancient civilizations and some hunter-gatherer cultures. Yet throughout the ages the biological underpinnings of the pubescent spurt to maturity were shrouded in mystery.

Toward the end of the nineteenth century Western biologists discovered that the so-called sex hormones estrogen and testosterone were involved in the maturation of the sex organs and the secondary sex characteristics. However, they did not understand what caused these hormones to begin secreting when they did, nor did they know what factors might account for the timing and sequences leading to sexual maturity. Only within the past three decades have scientists apprehended the complex hormonal interactions that regulate the onset of pubescence, its sequences, and duration. And even now puzzles remain. The precise "trigger" of the hormonal changes that set in motion the events of pubescence has not been identified. And we are almost completely in the dark with regard to how or why puberty terminates when it does.

Shamans and tribal elders have to do the work of "growing-up" the child without benefit of all the details. We are enlightened. The central physiological components that control the timing and sequences of pubescence and puberty are within our grasp. But our knowledge is still flawed and inadequate. Our present language for describing the onset of pubescence exposes shadowy regions. Negative and positive feedback loops with "signals," "switches," "triggers," "thermostats" are the language model. Scientists speak presumptuously about "instructions from the cortex" that "trigger the hypothalamus," not really knowing much about the nature of these events. But it's the best they have for now.*

Basically, this is how the feedback relationship works. Throughout infancy and childhood the hypothalamus is exquisitely sensitive to the suppressive effects of the small amounts of hormones secreted by the yet immature testes and ovaries. The gonads themselves cannot proceed to maturity until they are stimulated by special hormones secreted by the pituitary. During infancy and childhood the hypothalamus inhibits the pituitary from secreting these

---

*In recent years the pituitary hormone, cortical androgen stimulating hormone (CASH), was hypothesized as a regulator of adrenal androgens, which in turn could be the trigger that alters hypothalamic sensitivity. Another more generally accepted discovery has been the melatonin secretions of the pineal, a tiny gland buried at the center of the brain. Melatonin synthesis decreases as children age. It is thought to suppress pubescence by inhibiting gonadal hormones. The drop in the secretion of melatonin might be the trigger that sets pubescence in motion.

gonadotropic hormones. Upon receiving a "signal" that the child's body and brain have matured far enough to allow the pubescent transition from childhood to adulthood the hypothalamus gives the go-ahead to the pituitary.

The Onset of Pubescence

The marching orders for pubescence come from the *hypothalamus*—the part of the brain that lies under the cerebrum, behind the optic nerves, at the end of the brain stem. The hypothalamus regulates the vital functions of the human body. Despite its crucial importance in the functioning of the human being, the hypothalamus accounts for only 1/300th of total brain weight and is about the size of an almond.

Through its nervous and cellular connections to the cerebral cortex above and to the pituitary below, the hypothalamus acts as an integrator of the nervous and endocrine systems. The main control of all endocrine secretions is based on a negative feedback situation, in which an increased level of hormone in the blood has a depressant effect on further secretion of that hormone. Hypothalamic releasing factors responding to nervous stimuli elsewhere in the body can rapidly adjust this state of equilibrium.

When it receives the "message" that the child is ready to become adult the hypothalamus turns down its gonadostat and becomes less sensitive to the suppressive effects of estrogen and testosterone. It then synthesizes LRF, luteinizing releasing factor, a hormone that "instructs" the pituitary to permit sexual maturation to proceed.

The *pituitary,* called the master gland because all other endocrine glands are stimulated by its secretions, is the only gland that is part of the brain. It is a tiny oval consisting of two lobes. The posterior lobe, which is continuous with the tissue of the hypothalamus, does not have any direct effects on pubescence. The anterior lobe is regulated by the hypothalamus through a vast blood-cell network. This lobe synthesizes and secretes at least seven hormones, four of which are intimately involved with the events of pubescence: growth hormone (GH), follicle-stimulating hormone (FSH), luteinizing hormone (LH) [in the male LH is known as interstitial cell-stimulating hormone (ICSH)] and ACTH, which controls the secretions of the adrenal, an endocrine gland that also plays an active role in pubescence.

In the female, FSH stimulates oogenesis and the production of estrogen. LH is related to ovulation and the production of progesterone, the other "female hormone." In the male, FSH stimulates spermatogenesis. ICSH activates the cells that lie between the sperm-bearing tubules of the testes to produce testosterone, the "male hormone."

ACTH activates the adrenal gland, which produces about thirty hormones, among them androgens and estrogens in both sexes. The adrenals are two inches long and are located above each kidney. Adrenal androgens stimulate the growth of pubic and underarm hairs in females as well as males. The small amounts of estrogen secreted by the adrenals stimulate certain feminizing changes, such as breast mound development in pubescent girls and boys. The major feminizing and masculinizing changes of pubescence will derive from the ovarian estrogens and the testicular androgen, testosterone. However, there will be a constant interaction and balancing with the estrogens and androgens from the adrenals. The adrenal androgens and estrogens have the primary responsibility for the pubescent growth spurt in both sexes. In that sense the so-called sex hormones can act as growth hormones, depending on the tissue cells they influence.

The male gonads are two organs that develop within the abdominal wall and gradually descend on either side of the penis, where they will be suspended extra-abdominally by the scrotum and spermatic cords. The descent of the testes is usually accomplished before pubescence. Within the testes are eight hundred coiled tubules, whose linings contain the cells that will be developing into sperm-producing (Sertoli) cells under the stimulation of FSH. Lying between these cells are the interstitial, or Leydig, cells, which will produce testosterone under the regulation of ICSH. In infancy and childhood small amounts of testosterone from the immature testes and androgens from the adrenals stimulate descent. After the onset of pubescence these secretions increase and stimulate the growth of the penis, prostate, and other male reproductive organs, masculinization, and the male secondary sex characteristics.

The female gonads are homologous with the testes of the male. In the fetus the ovaries are situated in the abdominal cavity near the kidneys. They descend gradually into the pelvis but, in contrast to the testes, they remain inside the body. Moreover, they increase in size only slightly during pubescence. Each ovary is about the size of an almond and has an outer rind, or cortex, rich in the follicles that contain the primordial germ cells. About 500,000 egg-containing follicles are believed to be present at birth. Follicles in their immature form are numerous in the ovary of the young girl. Many of these immature follicles never attain full development. They shrink and disappear. At puberty the follicles that remain become capable of adult functioning. The ova they contain become capable of fertilization.

Three or four years before the ovulatory cycles become regularized, the ovaries begin to secrete appreciable amounts of estrogen. Ovarian estrogens in cooperation with adrenal estrogens stimulate the growth of the clitoris, vulva, uterus, and other female sex organs, feminization, and the female secondary sex characteristics. In interaction with LH, ovarian estrogens and progesterone will begin to regulate the monthly cycle of ovulation and menstruation.

We presume that the adult feedback circuit of hypothalamus, pituitary, and gonads will not be activated until such time as body weight and size, metabolic rate, brain differentiation, and other growth factors "trigger" the "signal" that the child is ready to progress to adulthood.

Upon receiving the readiness "signal," possibly from elsewhere in the brain or perhaps from a pituitary hormone acting on the brain, the hypothalamus will synthesize LRF and secrete it to the anterior lobe of the pituitary. Shortly afterward the gonadal hormones begin to regulate the ensuing events of pubescence that will lead to sexual maturity and final gender differentiation. And the gonadal hormones in cooperation with adrenal androgens and estrogens and pituitary growth hormone initiate the growth spurt that will take place in almost every organ, bone, tissue of the body.

Once set in motion, the processes of physical growth that bring the child to adult stature, genital maturity, and final gender differentiation are irreversible except in rare circumstances, such as brain tumors, anorexia, or certain hormonal disorders. The outlines on the maturational blueprint, which were there in the womb, to be modified only slightly in the first months of extrauterine existence, come to light. The physical adult we were meant to become emerges. We all become adult in specifically human ways, with the human proportion of braincase to jaw, trunk to leg length, with human genitals and secondary sex characteristics, and with the individual varieties of adult stature, pubic-hair distribution, breast shape and size, shoulder width, fat distribution, metabolism, and heart rate that result from the interaction of biological givens with environmental factors.

The psychological self that will finally materialize is more obscure. In this determination neither biological givens nor social influences nor the emotional scenarios of infancy and childhood will play exclusive or decisive roles. In human psychology the direction of causality is not linear. Past and present overlap. Present conditions can and often do determine the effects of the past. How much and in what ways the preconditions of infancy and childhood will exert their influence on adulthood is largely contingent on the solutions that emerge during the adolescent passage.

Because we humans are so immensely flexible and inventive, our universal dilemmas and plights can be expressed by a variety of fascinating and disarming behaviors. The guises of adolescence are as diverse as the vast *comédie humaine*: the protected hunter-gatherer whose cosmic journey into adulthood takes place in her family hogan, the erotically precocious Rousseau, the retarded Hall, the chaste Galahad, the leather-jacketed divinity of the dance floor, the teenager surrounded by posters of her superheroes and superheroines, the sleepy-eyed conformist, the carefree muncher of pizza slices and Rocky Roads, the rebel without a cause, the mindless Val girl, the flower child. As different as they appear to be, all children who are given the opportunity to *adolescere,* to grow up, will confront the same dilemmas. They must solve them before they become adults. If they are to arrive at psychological adulthood, all adolescents must face the loneliness and heartbreak of bidding "farewell to childhood." To arrive at an adult identity, all adolescents must reconcile their newly awakened genital desires with the moral authority of the society in which they live. And if in the bargain some adolescents find a way to modify the moral heritage of infancy they will have created some new solutions to the eternal human debate between desire and authority. In doing so they will have moved us all further into the light. Not everything remains the same. We do not ever quite return to the beginning.

The maturational blueprint of human pubescence assures the future. It opens the pathways of innovation. As G. Stanley Hall understood it, during adolescence "The floodgates of heredity seem opened . . . it is a crucial period for recomposition of the hereditary forces. Passions and desires spring to vigorous life but with them normally comes the evolution of higher powers of control and inhibition." Infancy is the preserve of the past. Adolescence introduces new possibilities and new solutions. Paraphrasing Paul Ricouer's considerations on the distinctions between dreams and art, we might put it this way: Infancy is the realm conveyed to us in dreams which look backward to the past. Adolescence, more like a work of art, is a prospective symbol of personal synthesis and of the future of humankind. Like a work of art that sets us on the pathway to new discoveries, adolescence promotes new meanings by mobilizing energies that were initially invested in the past.

By ensuring that the average human newborn is equipped to participate in a love dialogue with a caregiving person, the maturational blueprint of infancy preserves the continuity of the human race. This dialogue will assert itself, sometimes against enormous odds, whenever there is an average baby born into some average version of a human family. The mother-infant love dialogue transforms a psychologically helpless infant, a child who knows only the boundless experience of love of oneself, into a social being. A human infant is lured out of the self-contained bliss of primary narcissism into the love partnerships that become the safety net of her existence. Love dialogue becomes vital to her, more longed for and satisfying than food or warmth. The inordinate force of moral authority derives from the conditions of the first psychological birth, when an infant's physical and psychological survival depended entirely on the protection and approval of her parents. Dread of loss of dialogue can make cowardly, submissive infants of us all—which is why the human conscience is so largely an instrument of the status quo. It is ruthless in its opposition to change. It preserves the past.

Adolescence provides the opportunity to remodel the archaic conscience, which is constituted of the residues of the infantile love dialogues—watchful eyes, prohibiting voices, demands for perfection. At the conclusion of the adolescent passage the watchful eyes might seem a bit friendlier, the no-saying voice less harsh. But the most significant change wrought by adolescence is the taming of the ideals by which a person measures herself.

One outcome of this taming process is that the adolescent learns to forgive her parents for being less powerful than she had once imagined them to be. Another is that the exaggerated personal narcissism of the adolescent, especially her omnipotence and dreams of glory, might be impersonalized and transformed into social ideals. Love of oneself becomes love of the species. Conscience is pointed to the future, whispering permission to reach beyond the safety net of our ordinary and finite human existence. The struggle to revise the past entails an upheaval of the inner life. Each phase—pubescence, puberty, youth—makes a distinctive contribution to the resolutions of an adolescent's inner dilemmas. How can I reconcile genital desire with the commandments of conscience? How can I preserve the marvelous love dialogues and exquisite passions of infancy and still affirm my genital vitalities and commitment to the future?

The drama unfolds. Pubescence is Act I. Biologically it is a process of arriving at puberty. It covers the years (eleven to fourteen) between the first signs of an adult body, such as pubic hairs and breast mound, and the capacity to produce mature ova and sperm. Socially it proclaims the necessity for bidding farewell to childhood. During puberty (fifteen to eighteen), the second act, the biological changes that transform a child's body into the body of an adult are completed. The individual acquires an irreversible gender identity. Also, she is expected to accomplish an irreversible displacement of sexual desire away from her family and toward the larger social group. She must give up her idealizations of the parents, those very idealizations that once enabled her to feel safe, powerful, and absolutely adored. The drama reaches a peak.

Youth (eighteen or nineteen and onward) is the denouement. This last act is less directly influenced by physiological events and more susceptible to cultural interpretation than either pubescence or puberty. Nevertheless, whether youth is prolonged into the fourth decade of life or compressed into the final segments of a rite of reincorporation, some resolution of the debate between personal desire and moral authority must take place. The physiology of genital sexuality and reproductive capacity is divested of its antisocial possibilities and attached to components of the social order.

These temporal sequences are a convenient framework for appreciating the basic plot. Chronological time, however, does not do full justice to the complexities of the underlying narrative. As with any narrative, exclusive attention to the manifest story line can obscure the understructures that reveal meaning. In fact, with regard to adolescence, all three psychological dilemmas—the farewell, the displacement of sexual desire, the reconciliations of desire and authority—are reverberating from the minute the curtain lifts until the last words are spoken. Even though each act highlights one of these dilemmas, the three themes interact throughout adolescence, according to principles that defy linear logic.

Our route requires us, first of all, to trace some significant constants in human experience: desire, love dialogue, and authority. Human love dialogue is born of desire. And once there is love dialogue, desire must be rationed. Authority supplies the rules of rationing. Lawfulness comes into play. We soon discover that narcissism imposes itself on the life of desire and cannot be ignored. How to bend desire to the hunger for love dialogue and still preserve narcissism is the quest of infantile existence. The adolescent revision entails transformations of infantile desire, infantile moral authority, *and* infantile narcissism.

How does love of oneself—"the source of all our passions, the origin and principle of all the others, the only one which is born with man and never leaves him so long as he lives"—enter into the revision? What of that inborn form of narcissism that precedes the life of desire and seems to evolve according to its own rules? Is it on the side of desire? Of authority? Could it be that love of oneself is the nourishing stream of the ethical life? Possibly. But, as Rousseau understood, love of oneself does not alone produce an ethical person. It is a source of virtue only in the context of desire's great debate with authority.

The legends of finding love dialogues, of losing them, of mourning their loss, of refinding and immortalizing them is one pathway of adolescent existence. The other pathways will take us through the realm of narcissism and the uniquely human contradictions between love of oneself and *amour-propre*. And as we follow along these circuitous pathways we ask, "Will the drama end like *Hamlet*? Will the upheaval of an individual life conclude, as in the tragedies, with the remnants of the new generation cleaning up the mess and restoring law and order? Or will it end, as in the life-celebrating comedies, with the lovers and the jesters having the last words?"

PART TWO

DILEMMAS AND RESOLUTIONS

5
LOVE DIALOGUES I:
DESIRE'S GREAT DEBATE
WITH AUTHORITY

BIOLOGICAL INTERLUDE:
Pubescence

A burst of growth propels the adolescent toward the future. A wave of fresh vitality that expands every appetite and interest will unlatch the structures of the past, opening the way for new solutions. Despite these inexorable forces thrusting her forward to what is to be, the adolescent is at the same time drawn back to what once was. Infancy will not allow itself to be discarded. It will impose its archaic desires and demand that they continue to reign.

Yet at puberty, precisely when genitality could at last serve the archaic desires of infancy, the adolescent encounters the incest taboo, which compels a remodeling of sexual desire. Until this point the parents are the primary objects of a child's sexual hungers and longings. Until this point the parents, however partially and imperfectly, are a child's sanctuaries. They protect her. And through their power the child experiences herself as powerful. After puberty these parents must be relinquished as objects of desire. The infantile idealizations that enshrined their power must also be given up.

The irrevocable giving-up of the love relationships of childhood entails an extended and painful emotional struggle. The struggle is intensified by the arbitrary demands of what is still an immature sense of what is permissible, of the differences between right and wrong, of the punishments that accrue to moral transgression. At the beginning of adolescence, conscience has not grown up. It is still absolute in its conditions. It commands continued obedience to the idealized parents upon whom its own extraordinary power has been founded. It insists on total sexual renunciation. If she obeyed the messages of her schoolgirl conscience, the adolescent would continue to be bound to her childhood loyalties, and there would be no place to direct her genital desires. To become an adult the adolescent must eventually gain permission to be a person with mature genitals and reproductive capacity. She must recognize that her parents are not the omnipotent gods she once imagined them to be.

Sexual puberty therefore instigates a displacement of sexual desire outside the family and a revision of moral authority. Whenever a passion must be deployed from one realm to another, whenever there is a reordering of moral priorities, whether in the social order or in the individual, the event always begins on a variation of violence. The question is whether the revolution that takes place will be a revolution of annihilation or of transformation.

When a child becomes an adult, society is always at risk. The elders are fearful. And for good reason. The adolescent strains against personal limits, and the personal risks she takes are threats to tradition. Adolescents, with their towering physical and psychological presences, are also constant reminders of fecundity and new life. Not we but they are the germinators of future generations. Will they leave us behind as we did our parents? Will they forget us? Consign us to neatly paved retirement villages? Trample us in the dust as they go flying out to their new galaxies? We had better tie them down, flagellate them, isolate them in the family cocoon, carve their bodies into our kind of manhood and womanhood, indoctrinate them into the tribal laws and make sure they kneel before the power of the elders.

How soon we forget our own adolescence. Adolescents are not so determined to abolish the past as we imagine. Furthermore, the influences of the past are not as weak as we suppose them to be. Every vigorous thrust away, every rejection of them is countered by passionate longings to go back, to become reabsorbed into the passions of infancy. The tenacity of our earliest love dialogues resists any movement into the future. Adolescents cannot generate new worlds until they find a way to reconcile the past with the future. The struggle to retain what is valuable from the past and yet to resist infantile modes of loving churns up the inner life.

The love attachments of childhood exert a constant pull on the present. Just as the adolescent is suddenly and joyously free and independent of the smothering past, the past will tug at her heartstrings, beg, demand, seduce, all without consciousness of what is happening. The adolescent's exhilaration is followed by a perplexing feeling of grief.

We humans, once we have become emotionally invested in a homeplace, a prized personal possession, or, especially, in another person, find it immensely difficult to give them up. We will sacrifice self-interest; we will endanger our lives rather than leave behind what we have once loved. We would rather remain on the slope of a live volcano or on a delta of land where the annual life-destroying typhoon is a fact of life than give up this risky dwelling we call home. Because they were made at a time of life when we were utterly dependent on them, the love attachments of infancy have inordinate power over us, more than any other emotional investment.

At that juncture of generational time—infancy—when the child is most vulnerable, it is only natural that those who cherish and protect her would become her most intensely desired others. Simple satisfaction of hunger and pleasure of discharge rapidly become interwoven with a hunger for relating to others, the sexual hunger we call *libido*.

Libido does not exist at birth. It develops in the context of infant-mother dialogue. Human love dialogues are born of desire, of the ever-recurring cycles of appetite, anticipation, and consummation. Unless there is an attachment to a loved one, there is no way to gratify human desires. And once there is attachment, there also must be rationing, frustration, disappointment, disruption, separation, lawfulness—the where, when, and how of gratification.

It is a human circumstance that when we are born we have not yet come into existence. We are lured into our special human existence by a mothering presence that gratifies our innate urges to be suckled, held, rocked, caressed. But that same gratifying presence puts limits on desire and rations satisfaction. In this sense the mother is also the first lawgiver. Perhaps it would be easier on the infant if the situation simply required trading satisfaction for obedience. The situation, however, is more complicated.

The infant cannot control or possess this all-powerful lawgiver upon whom her existence depends. The mother comes and goes as she pleases. She allows intrusions from the outer world. She interrupts the marvelous love dialogues, which are more important than a full stomach. The infant is reminded that she is not always held, that she can fall away into nothingness and nonbeing.

And so begins desire's great debate with authority. From dialogue to absence, from nursing to weaning, from oneness with mother to separation from her, from the first awakenings of genital longings to the humiliation of Oedipal defeat, infancy is a legend of finding love objects, losing them, and refinding them.

Loving another person entails conditions. We obey the conditions because we apprehend the extent of our limitations, dependency, helplessness, vulnerability. Other-love, with all its frustrations and limitations, is the safety net of human existence. For better or worse, the ones we first hunger for are also our primary representatives of authority. From the beginning they are the agents of delay, of law and order. They are the watchful eyes, the prohibiting voices. They are the checkers of desire, who regulate consummation according to principles that are mysterious to the child. But because these powerful authorities are also the safety net of her existence, because her hunger for dialogue with them is more vital than food or warmth, the child will submit to their demands. But not without a struggle. Not without efforts to protect her own self—that vague and as yet amorphous someone that she regards as the center of her being. And not without some resentment for having to sacrifice a part of her self.

The decisive chapter of infantile love dialogue concerns the fate of Oedipal desire. What happens is that the two-person, dyadic love dialogues of infancy become subplots of a far more complex scenario.* The toddler certainly experiences moments of hatred and envy of both her parents and moments of intense love. But not until the advent of Oedipal desire does the child find herself involved in a love-hate triangle that forces her to reckon with sexual lust, jealousy, ambivalence, guilt. She compares her own small and pitifully inadequate body with the grandness and virtuosity of her parents' bodies. She confronts the humiliation of Oedipal defeat. Always for her own protection and for the protection of family life, the drama must terminate with the defeat of the child's Oedipal desires. For the first time in the child's experience desire is not rationed or dosed. It is entirely forbidden. Heretofore the urges to suck, swallow, be held, caressed, rocked were granted, even if in terms of "only so much," "in this place," "at that time." Similarly, the sexual hungers and aggressive intensities associated with the child's urges to expel or hold onto her urine and feces encountered the training procedures and reciprocating approval or disapproval of the parents. However, the appetites connected with erotic sensations from her immature clitoris, vulva, and inner genital organs find no outlet, no reciprocating permissions, no love object to attach themselves to. The young child's mysterious genital appetites can adhere only to fantasy images of herself and her parents. The actual sexual dialogues that these fantasies represent are totally outside her experience. Desire is cut off from any reciprocity. It resides only in the form of fantasies.

Finally, at the close of the infantile period, the fantasies

*The scenario also occurs in the negative, or homoerotic, form. See Chap. 7.

have been so thoroughly disguised that they also seem to have been banished from consciousness. The law and order of family life has declared that when it comes to genital desire, the child is an outsider. The most telling humiliation of childhood is the devastating recognition that no matter how skillful, obedient, lovely, or clever she might be, she must not and *cannot* partake of the mysterious pleasures, sounds, smells, body probings, looking and being looked at. The delicious intensities of desire that she imagines to be going on behind those closed doors are forbidden to her. Nor can she be anything but a miserable onlooker at those more open exchanges of grown-up tenderness—the kissing, hugging, touching, exchanges of looks—from which she is also excluded.

The Oedipal scenario is the culmination of the infantile legends of losing libidinal objects. It does, however, produce a gain of sorts. In exchange for her loss the child acquires as her own some inner authority to rule over her own desires. This new acquisition is the most significant precipitate of the infantile debate between desire and authority. It is the part of human mental life that derives its force from absence, weaning, separation, withdrawal of love dialogue; it is the agency of authority that represents the lawfulness of family life. It establishes itself as that aspect of a child's inner life that we call superego or conscience. The child submits to its commands. She restrains her desires and renounces her genital appetites in favor of enlarging her ties and identifications with her parents. In exchange for the advantages of sharing in the grandeur and omnipotence of her parents' authority, the child brings her desires into harmony with social order. This internalized authority will remain relatively unchallenged until puberty.

We would expect the developing ability to limit desire to be an ally during adolescence, an instrument for resisting the pull to the infantile past, a worthy opponent of the adhesiveness of sexual hunger. But this is not the case. The functions of *observation* and *conscience,* as well as the infantile forms of *idealization,* which make up the superego, will chain the adolescent to the past as powerfully as the infantile forms of desire.

With the function of *observation* the superego reveals its watchful gaze—the precipitate of having been watched and criticized with condemning looks. *Conscience* invariably reveals the severity and cruelty of a no-saying voice, primitive reproaches, verbal condemnations and prohibitions. Even the infantile *idealizations* born of infantile narcissism and then transferred to the safety net of other-loving, the ideals by which the ego measures itself and whose demands for perfection it strives to fulfill, even this function carries with it elements of submission and surrender that hearken back to the infantile history of helplessness and vulnerability.

Assuredly the development of a moral sense is an inescapable human necessity. In order to participate in social life a child must rein her desires. Yet, at heart, childhood morality is an offshoot of desires. The superego devours, scrutinizes, probes, tempts, torments. It appears in our dream thoughts as threats of defilement, castration, starvation, exile—as the dread shadow of the God of Job, who demands submission above all else.

Childhood morality reflects the child's first identifications, those that arose at a time when her sense of self and capacities to judge or decipher the world around her were still feeble. At that time the infant projected onto the images of the parents her own untamed fierce desires. The infantile superego is a reservoir of infantile desires and infantile anxieties. It matches in harshness the intensity of the desire it limits.

Furthermore, although its manifest contents are social prescriptions, the excessive severity of the superego commandments do not follow a real model—parental or social. The contents of a young child's superego are modeled primarily on the parent's own superego, only a small portion of which has grown into adulthood. The superego is the vehicle of tradition and of the time-resistant judgments that propagate themselves from generation to generation. Far from being regarded as a promise for the future, the super-ego is often referred to as an anachronism of the human mind.

During adolescence the legend of losing love objects and refinding them takes on a new momentum and urgency. In the process of giving up the old love dialogues and finding new ones the adolescent adds a chapter to the history of the great debate between desire and authority. The most signifi-cant outcome of adolescence will be the taming and reor-dering of infantile desire under the aegis of adult genitality. The other outcome will be the taming of the infantile super-ego. Desire and authority have an intimate partnership. They are the two poles of human existence. As one is trans-formed, so will be the other.

In the latency between infancy and adolescence, desire is held in abeyance, so that the child is able to absorb herself in acquiring the skills and knowledge, the rules and man-ners of the social order in which she lives. She moves out-side the family nest into a world of teachers and peers. The forms of civilized living in the world are transmitted to her. She perfects her memory, her perceptions of reality, and her judgments about the meaning of reality. Her methods of testing the differences between fantasy and reality are re-fined. During latency the defenses that simultaneously ap-pease authority and guard the life of desire gradually achieve more wholesome compromises between limitation and expression. The defenses become more flexible, more amenable to new influences. But the voice of authority re-mains essentially a prohibiting, no-saying one and exercises a constant surveillance over the life of desire. Latency-age children are concerned with conformity and obedience. They thrive on order and regularity. Individual passion is surrendered to the impersonal loyalties of group life. Chil-dren in this stage are the dutiful citizens of a well-ordered utopia.

It may come as a surprise to find the conformity of the schoolchild linked with a utopia. We are accustomed to

thinking of the adolescent as the constructor of ideal societies. True, adolescents are the visionary ones. It is they who
prefer the hypothetical and abstract to the real and the concrete. Even the sleepy-eyed middle-class conformist who
likes the world just as it is will be more concerned with
ideals and possibilities as an adolescent than she had been as
a young child. Why, then, this association between utopian-
ism and the latency years?

Utopias themselves are a peculiar amalgam of visionary
possibility and societies built on conformity. The word
"utopia," which means "nowhere," was first used in connection with an ideal society in Thomas More's *Utopia,*
written in 1515. More's book gave its name to a whole
genre of literature.

The actual tradition of utopian fantasies goes back in Western literature to Plato's *Republic.* Plato's society was built
on a hierarchical class system. More's society was classless.
Nevertheless Plato was the main source of More's inspiration and all subsequent western European utopian writings.
The creators of these imaginary societies are critics of an
existing social order. The ideal communities the authors
construct are usually designed as correctives of the existing
order: *The Republic, Utopia,* Rousseau's *Social Contract,*
Thoreau's *Walden,* Skinner's *Walden II.*

Or the fantasies might take the form of satiric exaggeration of societies the authors deplore, such as the antiutopian
utopias of Zamiatin's *We,* Huxley's *Brave New World,* Or-
well's *1984,* Burgess' *Clockwork Orange.* These so-called
"disutopian" novels are also sly pokes at the entire utopian
genre. They call our attention to the underlying totalitarian-
ism of the "good" utopias. Though the intentions of Plato
and More were passionately visionary, the societies they
envisioned were oppressively restrictive and passionless.

The visionary aspects of *Utopia* derive from the intellectual climate of More's day. The idea that one could work
with the imaginary and the nonexistent as a way of solving
real problems was an innovation of the sixteenth century.
This trend could be observed even in mathematics, in which

field, for the first time, philosophers conceived of negative, irrational, imaginary *numeri ficti*—fictitious numbers. Hence the title, *Utopia*—nowhere.

In its content, however, More's vision of the imaginary future is a harking back to the past. More, who was essentially a deeply religious man with an ascetic bent, constructed his ideal society along monastic lines. His utopia is a looking backward to the medieval ideal, a kind of enlarged monastery based on the Rule of Saint Benedict. Everyone spends the day doing good deeds. The population lives in a cooperative fellowship that very much resembles a Boy Scout troop. There are no time-wasting and corrupting activities such as "gaming" or "dicing." Clothes are simple and the same for everyone—uncannily like the garb of Franciscan monks.

Utopias, whether modeled on the ideal city of Plato or the imaginary island community of More, are *chimères*—dreams, longings. In application, though, they turn out to be exaggerated versions of the emotional life of the latency-age child. Even those eternal religious utopias of the lost-pilgrim type, which ostensibly aspire toward a refinding and realization of the authentic self, are in their institutional arrangements pledged to subduing the personal *passions* while preserving and elaborating the forms of civilization and group life. Rousseau, whose writings are profusely laced with utopian visions, was well aware of the tensions between the ideal of individual self and the ideal of communal self. The Rousseauean paradoxes are a posing of the utopian ambiguities. "What happens to individuality in the communal utopia?" "How can we reconcile our yearning for personal authenticity with our longing for community?"

Rousseau knew that personal passions were not necessarily antagonistic to civic responsibility. "Our passions," he declared, "are the principal instruments of our preservation." During adolescence Emile's sexual passions could turn his heart toward the rest of humanity. "So long as his sensibility remains limited to his own individuality there is nothing moral in his actions. It is only when it begins to extend outside of himself that it takes on, first the sentiments and, then, the notions of good and evil which truly constitute him as a man and an integral part of the species." Rousseau, whose own utopian visions were a combination of Platonic idealism and pastoral romanticism, took issue with the passionless quality of life in *The Republic.* He was critical of Plato's efforts to do away with family attachments and gender differences as methods of ensuring good citizenship and group loyalties.

With rare exceptions, whether in the good utopias or the bad ones, the individual passions are portrayed as the enemies of group life. Family life and the passions it generates are rightly seen as undermining influences in a well-designed utopia. In *Brave New World,* individual love is opposed by a decree enforcing promiscuity. The idea of the decree is that during specified hours everyone couples with whoever comes along next. As a wise and absolutely essential underpinning for this indiscriminate sexuality, the mother-child relationship is abolished. Babies are produced out of test tubes or snatched away to be raised in an environment uncontaminated by mother love.

In the Soviet novel *We,* children are produced artificially. Citizens wear identical uniforms, numbers replace names. The teachers are robots. Poets and anyone else who does not celebrate communal life are liquidated in a machine controlled by "Well-doer," the supreme ruler. Sexual hours are permitted, but romantic love is forbidden.

In the good utopia of *The Republic* the rulers are encouraged to manipulate sexual relations in order to improve the race. Children are to be brought up by the community. All connections between child and parent are erased. Those ruled by the passions and physical excitements, such as laborers, farmers, merchants, and artisans, are confined to the lowest orders. The philosophers rule, because the best part of humanity is the part invested in wisdom and learning.

Education and reeducation are prominent themes in utopian fantasies. More's *Utopia* is founded on the daily inculcation of moral lessons. The manner of the teachers is kindly and gentle. In bad utopias, such as *1984,* the educational methods are stringent. The heroes are subjected to torture when they do not produce the right answers. Operations are performed to excise imagination. Whatever the method—gentle persuasion, brainwashing, torture, or body mutilation—the educational authorities exercise constant surveillance over the learners. Citizens are watched by philosopher-kings, gentle teachers, Big Brother, telescreens, robots. The educators are eternally vigilant. A high value is placed on acquiring knowledge. But censorship of lite ature, especially poetry, is a major support of utopian soc eties. Shakespeare's works are locked up. Poets are exiled.

Utopias are legends of what it means to become civilized. Though they are portrayed as visions of the future (or anti-visions), utopias actually reflect the past. They commemorate that real event of childhood when the child was commanded to surrender the personal passions of family life in order to become an obedient member of society. The event is not the adolescent farewell to childhood, a heroic effort to revise the childhood conscience and de-animate the passions and romances of infancy. The event is the Oedipal banishment and the entrance into the larger social world. The taboos against romantic love, the value placed on education and the role of the teacher, the feeling of constant surveillance, the suppression of individuality, the censorship of literature, the banishing of poetry are not fanciful utopian visions. The severity of the utopian order accurately depicts the immature conscience of childhood.

Even in the most benevolent of school and home environments the latency child creates her own prison. The child invents routines and compulsive rituals in order to silence desire. The oppressive surveillance that plays so large a role in the utopian fantasy conforms less to actual teachers and parents than to a child's relationship to her own conscience. The all-seeing, all-knowing qualities of the robots and Well-doers are the residues of the infantile versions of authority that now reside in the latency child's inner conscience. The schoolgirl's conscience haunts her with afflictions of arrest, capture, torture, exile, annihilation, mutilation.

Schoolchildren make up their own rules and enforce their own conformities. They feel safest when leisure time is rationed and dosed. They like to wear uniforms, and they frown on personal idiosyncrasies. Deviance is the mark of the outsider.

Schoolyard games invented by children and passed on from generation to generation extol the conventional and cement the loyalties of group life. By banding with others as their equals and noticing how others observe the rules the latency child is helped to soften her implacable conscience. The peer bonds of childhood are the bonds of ritual and conformity, not the bonds of passion, as in adolescence. "I am not alone." "I belong to a group." "Together we obey the rules." Games are impersonal and run on well-known tracks. The plots are codified. The roles are frozen.

Utopias are versions of what life might be like if we marched straight ahead from childhood to adulthood. Philippe Ariès' pastoral to the medieval homogenization of society does sound very much like life in the schoolyard—except that in his version the adults never left it. If we never left the schoolyard we would have civilization without culture. We would be obedient to conventional rules, frozen plots, traditional forms, impersonal loyalties. Our feelings would be diffusely and equally spread out over parents, friends, dogs, orchards, and the supernatural. And as social planners know, utopias are most efficiently maintained if family life can be abolished before school age. At birth is best—or before, if at all possible. If desire were never to be born at all, the work of authority would be simplified.

Isn't this all a somewhat "utopian" version of the childhood years? As most parents, teachers, and anyone who has ever peeked through the gates of the schoolyard knows, the school-age child is not entirely the creature of pliability and conventionality she often appears to be. Her passions may have been repressed and socialized, but they have not been abolished. The latency child valiantly defends herself against the breakthrough of desire. Nevertheless, at times she is consumed with rankling envy. She is overcome with vengeful hostility at reminders that she is the outsider ejected from the Garden of Eden. Moreover, she secretly nourishes her infantile longings. One reason why conventions and defenses are so rigidly maintained during latency is that desire continues to press forward for expression. Once born, desire fights for its rights. The Big Brothers and the Well-doers know exactly what they are up against.

Desire can be reined and muted, but it is always there, a continual presence that must be reckoned with. It asserts itself in ingenious ways by changing its form and modes of expression. Desire is devious. It learns to speak softly, disguise itself, turn itself into its opposite, become temporarily forgotten, pretend that its longings come from someone else. Desire will appease authority through absolute obedience, if only in order to rebel in new and surprising ways. Indeed, obedience can become a variety of defiance. Desire is hiding, waiting for the opportunity to erupt, break through, rush in, take over. If the desire to look is prohibited, desire will settle very nicely for being looked at. Or looking and being looked at will be given up entirely for the self-admiration of being able to say "I am better and stronger than those who need to look. I don't even care. There is nothing I wish to see or know."

In the not-looking, in the silent wishes, in the daydreams, in the night dreams, in the realm of fantasy, desire makes its presence felt. Although children obey the rules in the classroom and on the playing field, in their fantasy life they are busily at work rectifying the humiliations of Oedipal defeat. They even invent a family romance that reinstates the love dialogues of infancy and revises the unhappy conclusion. In this romance the child imagines that she has been abducted from her true family and placed temporarily in the home of some ordinary, workaday, not-so-clean, impatient, quarrelsome, but kindly peasants. Her true mother and father, to whom she will one day return, are noble, grand, strong, magnificent, gratifying, shining with perfection. They are far superior in every way to the humble parents with whom she is forced to live. It is these ordinary, supposed parents who exclude her from the adult pleasures. It is they who disillusion her by their moral infractions and less-than-perfect control of passion and desire. It is they who conspire against her to hide and misrepresent the facts of sexuality and childbirth.

But her own true mother and father, the parents from whom she was abducted as an infant, would love only her. They would admit her to all the magical secrets. They would reveal to her the magic words. They would be perfect and all-knowing. They would transmit to her the radiance of their omniscient and omnipotent powers. Her earthly mother and father are adequate for bandaging scraped knees and cooking dinner, but the child longs for the heavenly parents she once knew. The hope remains alive that she will start life all over again in the nest of her true family. One day she will be restored to the Garden of Eden, where she was an angel baby on the lap of a madonna, where she was the adored baby of the rulers of the empire.

The latency child has not really accepted her banishment to the drab and colorless existence she now leads. Like Cinderella, she awaits the day when she will don the silvery raiment of the princess she really is. The young boy imagines he will defeat the bad king, escape the clutches of the witch, subdue the dragons, puzzle out the confusing mazes that will lead him from the dungeon of his passionless existence.

In their family romances and daydreams schoolchildren reveal the powerful attractions of the desires and idealizations of infancy. If it were not for adolescence, we would remain perpetual schoolchildren who harbor secret romance lives that continually fan the flames of infantile desire. We would be like those dutiful citizens who must be kept under constant surveillance.

The relative quiescence of desire during latency allows children a few years in which to perfect its modes of expression, disguises, ways of appeasing authority. As pubescence proceeds, some of the restraints of latency will be undone. But desire will have been tamed and modified. The child will have mastered most of the social and intellectual skills of the social order in which she lives. She will have come to appreciate and value her loyalties outside the family nest. As the changes of pubescence and puberty announce the imminence of adulthood, the adolescent will be able to call on every advanced way of living that she acquired during the latency years. She will negotiate the adolescent passage, more or less, like a civilized person.

Pubescence

Pubescence refers literally to downy hair, the soft hairs that grow on the leaves and stems of blossoming plants and certain parts of animals—especially insects. With respect to human growth, the word *pubes* may refer to the pubic hair or to the region of the body that becomes covered with pubic hair. *Pubis* indicates the portion of bone that forms the outer wall of the pelvis. *Puberty* refers to sexual maturity, the time when fertilization becomes possible. The initial signs of an adult body occur four to five years before there are fertile ova or sperm.

In girls pubescence announces itself with changes in the mammae, or breasts, and with the first finely textured, downy pubic hairs. At around age ten and a half to eleven, just preceding these more noticeable signs, a slight elevation of the nipples is detectable.

Breast budding proper consists of elevation of the breast and nipple together as a small mound. At this time there is also a slight enlargement of the areolar circle that surrounds the nipple. The pink color of the nipple and areola gradually deepens to a darker hue, and fat accumulates in the body of the breast. Finally, the nipple projects from the areola and breast and grows firm. The nipple then becomes especially sensitive to tactile and other sensory stimulation.

During pubescence the breasts grow from ½ inch across and $\frac{1}{16}$ inch in thickness to an average of 4½ inches wide and ½ inch thick. The distance of the breasts from each other increases in proportion to the curve of the thorax. There is a wide range of individual variation in this distance and in the shape and final size of the breasts.

The most commonly referred to alteration of the male sexual organs is the doubling in length and thickness of the penis, which will grow during pubescence from an average of two inches to nearly four inches. Actually, the enlargement of the testes is the first outward sign and always occurs about a year preceding the beginning of penis growth.

Testicular growth is due primarily to the increase in size of the eight hundred coiled seminal tubules that make up the major bulk of the testes. Before pubescence these tubules are small, lined with a single layer of undifferentiated cells, and interspersed with a few nonactive spermatogonia—sperm cells. When the boy is around ten or eleven, the lining of the tubules begins to increase in thickness and the cells differentiate to become Sertoli cells—adult sperm cells. As the seminal tubules enlarge and the spermatogonia start to multiply, the testes will increase in size and weight to about three times their prepubescent status. A few years later the Sertoli cells will begin to produce active sperm.

The other cells of the testes, the interstitial, or Leydig, cells also increase in size and number. Though the Leydig cells will not reach full maturity for several years, when the boy is around twelve they begin to secrete testosterone and, in cooperation with the adrenal androgens, initiate the growth of the penis, scrotum, prostate, seminal vesicles, and Cowper's glands.

The scrotum, which surrounds the testes, will expand to twice its prepubescent size. At first the skin of the scrotum will redden and change in texture from smooth and tight to wrinkled and flaccid. As puberty progresses, the scrotum darkens still further to a brownish hue.

Pubic hairs usually appear simultaneously with the initial growth of the male genitalia. Occasionally they appear a bit earlier or a bit later. In females the pubic hairs appear simultaneously or occasionally before the budding of the breasts. Hair develops in the pubic region at around twelve in boys; in girls it develops at around eleven, generally preceding the first menstruation by about a year or two.

The first pubic hairs are slightly pigmented, usually tawny in color. They are straight or only slightly curled. They make their appearance as a sparse growth chiefly at the base of the penis and along the outer lips of the vulva. As the hairs become considerably darker, coarser, and curlier, they spread over the pubic region. The pubic hairs will gradually become adult in texture and color, but the area covered is considerably smaller than in the adult. Spread may go as far as the inner surface of the thighs, but not up the pelvic midline or elsewhere above the base of the inverse triangle. In general, until puberty proper the pubic hair distribution is along the horizontal or "feminine" pattern, in both sexes.

Around a year after the pubic hairs first appear, hairs begin to grow around the anal region. These are called circumanal hairs, and they are generally finer in texture than the pubic hairs. Shortly thereafter axillary, or underarm, hairs will crop out, at first sparse and thin but then becoming dense, curly, and somewhat coarse.

Coinciding with the appearance of axillary hair is the initiation of the sequence and patterning of facial hair; first at the corners of the upper lip, then across the upper lip, next at the upper part of the cheeks and at the midline below the lower lip. In males the sides and lower border of the chin are the last sites of facial-hair growth. These hairs will combine with cheek and lower-lip midline hairs to form the beard. In females the facial-hair sequence usually extends no farther than the corners of or across the upper lip.

Beard growth in males is seldom completed until the final stages of pubic-hair development. In these final stages male pubic hair will spread and form a line toward the umbilicus. Scalp hair will spread along the ears. Body hairs begin to grow around the breast and along the legs, arms, chest, and back. Body hair may continue to develop in males well into the fourth decade of life.

The most obvious manifestations of pubescence are the pubic and axillary hairs in both sexes, breast development in girls, and scrotum, testicle, and penis growth in boys. In girls there are less obvious but definitive sex-characteristic changes in the size and physical structure of the labia, vagina, and clitoris. In boys there is an attenuated breast development, which then recedes as pubescence progresses.

Boys will develop more body hair, become larger, acquire broader shoulders, stronger muscles, and a deeper larynx. In girls the pelvic diameter will enlarge and fat will be deposited on the hips, thighs, calves, and breasts. Like pubic, axillary, and body hair, these features are considered secondary sex characteristics in the sense that they are stimulated by sex hormones or sex-differential hormone secretion but are not essential to sexual or reproductive functioning. They do contribute significantly to erotic appetites and to the arousal of genital desire.

Sexual maturity awakens a hunger for genital love dialogue. Simultaneously the repressed Oedipal fantasies of infancy return in various guises and clamor to reassert their sovereignty. The incest taboo, which originally had protected the young child from premature exposure to adult sexuality, establishes itself in the mind of the adolescent.

Whereas earlier it was endured passively, now the taboo *actively* obstructs the fulfillment of genital desire. It poses some dilemmas every adolescent must solve. "Shall I renounce genital desire and remain faithful to the past or shall I direct my genital love-desires away from my family and give up my childhood loyalties and idealizations?" In the choice between remaining bound to their parents in a nongenital, infantile way or affirming genital vitality and their commitment to ongoing life, most adolescents will decide in favor of giving up the past.

The decision, however, is not an all-or-nothing affair that can be accomplished at once. The struggle to detach libido or sexual hunger from the parents is long and difficult. Desire will seize on every opportunity to reattach itself to the old scenarios. The past does not willingly or easily allow itself to be given up.

On the other hand, the message of reality is abundantly clear. It is brought home forcibly in the physical realm. The growing body, with pubic hair, enlarging genitalia, seminal ejaculation, and menstrual flow heralds adult sexuality and the possibilities of procreation. The message is announced in the vast upheaval of the endocrine system—the hormonal awakenings that encourage adult genital desires as well as genital erotic fantasies. The social order, which must defend itself against the danger that its own interests might be swallowed up by the enduring passions of infancy, subtly but definitively proclaims that it does not tolerate violations of the incest taboo.

At every reassertion of the old wishes and fantasies, reality insists that sexual hunger be withdrawn from the parents. Reality subverts the idealizations created by the love dialogues of infancy. Throughout adolescence the demands of reality will continue to meet with considerable opposition. But in the average course of the passage from childhood to adulthood, respect for reality slowly but surely gains the day.

6

LOVE DIALOGUES II:
MOURNING THE PAST

BIOLOGICAL INTERLUDE:
The Growth Spurt

For an adolescent to complete the passage from childhood into adulthood, a special kind of displacement of desire is required. In contrast to the usual displacements present in both dreams and waking life, which consist of shifting from one feeling to another, one person to another, one time frame to another—a shifting hither and yon of all sorts of emotions and conflicts that are temporary and easily reversible to the original time/place/person—the displacement at adolescence involves incestuous desires exclusively, goes in one direction only—away from the parents—and is *irreversible*. This special form of displacement has been given the awkward label "removal" in order to stress that once the adolescent detaches libido from her parents, the sexual hunger will have been removed once and for all and placed somewhere else, usually in a person of the opposite sex who is not a member of the immediate family. Removal entails more than displacement. The quality of the sexual hunger is converted from incestuous longing to adult genital desire.

What is removed in *removal* is the sexual hunger that had once been attached to the infantile images of the parents. Removal has two aspects: genital desire *and* the loved person to whom the desire adheres. Eventually the adolescent must come to terms with her genital longings. The decisive element in gaining access to genitality, however, will be her success in detaching sexual hunger from the images of her parents (and siblings). Until she can be sure that her parents will not become the objects of her genital longings she must ward off the eruption of desire. As she arrives at puberty proper, the adolescent is driven slightly mad by the paradoxical imperatives of the incest taboo. Failure to defend against genital desire could result in actual incest. And yet if a child is ever to become an adult, sooner or later genitality must gain expression.

From the adult point of view, an adolescent does seem like a wild creature driven mad with desire. What is hard for adults to appreciate is that "adolescent madness" is the result of an all-out unconscious warfare against all forms of desire. Some of the more outlandish and bewildering behaviors of the adolescent years are overt manifestations of this underground warfare. To aid her in her warfare on desire the adolescent employs a number of strategies. These strategies, or defenses, are unique to the adolescent years, and they refer directly to the problem of removal.

Bodily asceticism is one way to rein desire. Ordinarily the warfare proceeds with alternating rhythms of abstension and yielding. Refusals to eat and idiosyncratic dietary abstentions will alternate with bouts of gluttony or elaborate mealtime rituals. Refusals to sleep will alternate with lying in bed for days on end. Refusals to care for the body will alternate with a consuming interest in body adornment, face lotions, new soaps, hours before the mirror inspecting the body, tweezing body hairs, applying acne creams.

Sometimes asceticism takes over. There are adolescents who for weeks, sometimes months, eat "just enough," refusing meat, poultry, fish, eggs, milk, desserts, potatoes, and pasta and managing to thrive on the purest and least appealing foods they can find—beans and wheat germ, for example. They sleep only one or two hours a night, dress in the equivalent of sackcloth, and either never bathe or become preoccupied with scrubbing away body dirt and body odors. These adolescents are uncompromising in their war on bodily pleasure.

Many adolescents will manifest their total warfare on desire in the less obvious way of becoming uncompromising in their thinking and attitudes. What goes on in the mind is thus protected from the ugly temptations of the body. What is ideal is kept apart from the contaminating influences of practicality or necessity. One either loves or hates. The possibilities of blending opposites or assenting to possible harmony between opposing points of view are intolerable.

Some variations of these uncompromising antidesire defenses are to be expected during adolescence. Balance between pursuit of pleasure and restraint, harmony between opposing desires, cooperation between mind and body, concession of pure ideals to practical necessity are goals never fully achieved by any human being. Yet for one to become adult these compromises must be tolerated. Eventually they become the intellectual and emotional aims that an ethical person will strive toward, with full knowledge that the aims may never be fulfilled.

There is a poignancy to the adolescent's warfare on desire. The vitalities of growth and genital awakening announce that nothing human is alien. They inspire the adolescent to act all parts in the vast human comedy. Yet there are other voices, those of infancy and latency, which demand renunciation, sacrifice, obedience. In order for her to expand beyond the confines of the schoolyard, with its dreary shoulds and oughts, in order for her to partake of the experiences that life now holds open to her, desire must be victorious. Yet no matter how consciously committed to ongoing life and the future an adolescent might be, until removal is accomplished she must continue her warfare on desire.

The adolescent does not rely solely on antidesire warfare. Much of her behavior is a reflection of another category of defensive strategies, one aimed at loosening the child's passionate attachments to her parents. The first major strategy in this category is transferring sexual hunger outside the family.

The detachment of libido from the parents can take the gradual course of a piece-by-piece relinquishment of the past. But when the anxiety aroused by incestuous desire becomes overpowering, the adolescent is unable to tolerate

such a slow and potentially hazardous method of detachment. She must, under these circumstances, take recourse to
more dramatic and immediate tactics. Sadly, the quick
methods, while they alleviate the anxiety, rarely succeed in
the long run.

The most straightforward method of transferring incestuous desire elsewhere is flight. The adolescent abruptly
removes herself from the family setting. She runs away, either literally or figuratively. The flight away from family
love-desire, however, leaves the adolescent with an unbear-
able longing for love partnership. So, as soon as possible
after taking flight, she will become enmeshed in an intense
and passionate love relationship. Because this kind of precipitous falling in love simply transfers—but does not eliminate—the incestuous longings, the old desires and love dialogues will remain as insistent as ever. They are acted out
in other bedrooms with persons who might appear to be
diametrically opposite to the parent in appearance and social values but who are in fact disguised parent substitutes.

It is not necessary to remove oneself from the household
in order to take flight from the anxieties of incestuous desire. More usually, as they attempt to transfer libido elsewhere, adolescents will find some way to keep their bodies
at home. While somewhat more temperate and subtle in
their methods of transfer, these adolescents may be as desperate as those who actually do run away. They may be as
committed to an immediate transfer of sexual hunger as
their counterparts who had no other recourse but to flee
from the family nest. They also find themselves hungry for
love partnerships, and they rush headlong into love affairs
with parental substitutes. The adolescent in flight is endlessly resourceful. She may transfer desire to idealized
leaders or to heterosexual love affairs with contemporaries
or to a consuming love allegiance with a same-sexed friend.
The peer group can become the target of her love-desires.
Very often flight takes the form of a "crush" on a woman
who is somewhere in age between the mother's generation
and the girl's own.

Each time the adolescent succeeds in transferring love-desire away from the family, she can comfortably ignore her parents' values and disclaim everything they stand for. She is free at last of "their smothering love." She has stripped them of all importance. She consents to stay on at home as a nonpaying, rude and inconsiderate boarder.

Emotional transfers of love-desire might be expressions of the more typical gradual detachment. Or they might be signs of pathological short-circuiting of the incest dilemma. The degree to which passionate attachments outside the family are way stations on the road toward the necessary and appropriate removal or are symptomatic of pathology is difficult to gauge. When the new love alliances are abrupt, extreme, overemphasized, and appear to be diametric to everything parental—values, appearance, social class—the transfer is assumed to be an expression of a too-hasty retreat, an avoidance of the prolonged sorrows and anxieties of gradual detachment.

When the defensive flight from the parents is extreme and not temporary, it can have further negative consequences, especially for the adolescent's ongoing battle with desire. Once the parents and their authority have been stripped of value, all the formerly forbidden desires are given permission. This free rein of desire may lead to sexual promiscuity or the various forms of criminal behavior we label "juvenile delinquency." If the adolescent in flight has had the good fortune or unconscious wisdom to attach herself to benevolent persons or groups with noncriminal social ideals, she may survive her hasty withdrawal from family life without too much harm to the rest of her personality. Nevertheless the threat of incest will remain. The conflicts and anxieties associated with incestuous desire will persist into adult life, casting their shadows on marriage, parenthood, and work relationships.

Another way to "remove" the parents is to turn love-desire and infantile dependence into hatred, contempt, derision, revolt. By reversing her emotions into their opposites the adolescent can suppose that she is no longer dependent on her parents for love or protection. She is free of them at last. But these frantic reversals will actually entangle the adolescent more tightly in the threads of the family web. Flight has the advantage over emotional reversal by at least enabling the adolescent to derive some pleasure from love partnership. With the reversal of love-desire into hatred and compulsive disobedience, nothing remains but hostility, suffering, and pain for all concerned. Reversal perpetuates the need for constant reinforcement of the defenses against the anxiety of incest. Moreover, the strategy of reversal eventually entails more painful and pathological elaborations.

Even the most hostile adolescent will be unable to tolerate her destructive wishes toward her parents. She begins to imagine instead that her parents hate her. She feels that they are out to destroy her. She views them as persecutors and oppressors. Soon the entire adult world and everything it represents may become imagined as persecutory. The adolescent retreats from the world. She retires more and more into the web of family hatred, making herself less and less available to a transfer of love-desire outside the family.

Another possibility for the eventual outcome of the reversal-into-hatred is that the destructive wishes directed toward the parents become turned around toward the self. Instead of the expectable periods of grief and despair associated with normal detachment, the adolescent will be overcome by more extreme and prolonged depressive reactions. Self-denigration and severe forms of self-abasement and self-injury are common outcomes of the reversal series: love-desire reversed into hatred becomes intense self-hatred. Suicidal thoughts and fantasies are typical aspects of this overall picture of self-hatred, and are sometimes carried into action, not out of a wish to be done with life but as an escape from a deeper form of self-hatred.

The most pathological strategy of adolescence is total emotional surrender to the parents. Emotional surrender, as pitiful as it is, can become an adolescent's last stronghold against incestuous desire. Here the incest dilemma is solved by regressing to the earliest stage in the history of desire, to the stage of love dialogue, when there were no boundaries between the self and other. The adolescent surrenders her soul, all her unique, hard-won characteristics, all the items of selfhood that she regards as the center of her being. She gives up her own personality and becomes a caricature of mother, or father, or an amalgam of both. Essentially, she merges with some infantile version of what they are. She no longer exists as a separate person. Although such a reinstatement of symbiosis has the effects of freeing the body of genital desire and releasing the mind from all the conditions and conflicts inherent in loving another person, it signifies the obliteration of human emotional connections and loss of sanity. An adolescent will defend herself by every available means from such total dissolution of her personality. Given the impossible choice between incest—which signifies exile from the human community—and emotional surrender—which signifies a falling away into nothingness—suicide can seem a benevolent option.

In the more usual course of the adolescent passage, at various times, in various combinations, bodily asceticism, uncompromising ideation, transfer of love-desire, reversal of love into hate will be employed to ease the anxiety of incest. Suffering from bouts of self-hatred, the average adolescent is frequently rejecting of everything her parents represent. And there are moments when she would wish to escape from her conflicts by handing her body and soul over to the parents. At some time or other, frightening thoughts of suicide will creep into her mind. And even the average adolescent will occasionally entertain the notion that her parents are persecuting oppressors.

Optimally, the adolescent will eventually succeed in retaining what is valuable from her family love dialogues and reject just enough of them to leave room for a few new possibilities. Her mate will represent something old and something new. Or, in those somewhat less than optimal solutions, the final selection of wife or husband might be made on the basis of absolute similarity or dissimilarity to the parental prototype. In these instances the stereotype has become a requisite for genital love. Such partial removals constitute an average range of adult love choices, lying midway between the optimal and the failed attempts at object removal.

An important characteristic of optimal solutions and those that fall in the midrange is that they enable a person to accept her sexual desires and to maintain her inner moral convictions even if she might be deprived of her role in the society. Not so with the failures of removal.

Failures of removal are usually signaled during adolescence proper by the suddenness, intensity, and exaggerated form of the special adolescent defenses. The varieties of failed removal fall along three axes. The least pathological of these is determined when the adolescent has so successfully waged her war on desire that almost all sensual and erotic tendencies are eradicated. Only tender and affectionate impulses are allowed to survive. Now that desire has been defeated, she can remain comfortably attached to the familiar past. Incest has been avoided. But in the unconscious, which has hardly been altered at all, incest claims the day. There the former loved ones and the former libidinal desires are triumphantly reunited. All that remains of the adolescent struggle is an innocuous attachment to the mother and/or father. In extreme instances of this type of failed solution the opportunity to find new sexual love or to perform sexual intercourse with anyone is lost. The person accentuates the altruistic and affectionate aspects of her personality. Although she has forgone procreation, she may be a creative person. She may become a schoolteacher, a chef, a nurse, a psychologist, a poet, a painter. The unconscious triumph of incestuous desire, like all other unresolved or poorly resolved infantile scenarios, might serve as an incentive for certain social roles.

Human societies preserve themselves by trying to provide a variety of acceptable roles for nearly all adult members. Society also sets up structures for elaborating these roles and for defining the rules of conformity to them. If certain personal solutions of a deviant nature become prevalent, society accommodates to them by normalizing the deviance. It is not difficult, therefore, for adults to hide their less than adequate adolescent solutions in a social role. We cannot discern from the outside which dancer or psychologist maintains her adult façade only by conforming to the stereotype of her social role. When a person is rigidly possessed by a social structure, she begins to look deviant only if that structure slips or if her role is no longer acceptable or if it becomes obsolete.

More seriously hampered in adult functioning are those who have vanquished both genital desire and love attachment. The reversal of love into hate has triumphed. By making certain that nothing is left—neither sexual hunger nor the objects it might adhere to—removal has been forgone and incest avoided. These unfortunate souls live out their remaining existence in bitter emotional isolation. They are kept away from any sort of genuine love relationship, both the sensual kind and the tender or altruistic kind. Only a few will become actual hermits. The force of their inordinate hatred and persecutory fantasies can serve as an incentive for achieving power over other human beings. And though bitterness and rankling envy will show through in whatever they go on to accomplish, these emotionally barren adults may also contribute to the social order. They might settle with relative comfort into the role of banker, general, corporate executive, judge, politician, philosopher, astronaut. Still, some philosophers, if deprived of their books and their positions in the academy, might become actual hermits or religious fanatics. A general without his elaborate social structure and his army might look like a paranoid maniac.

The third axis of failed solution is seen when there have been no defenses against desire or any effective strategies for loosening the passionate attachments to the parents. Then the incest possibility can easily become a reality. This solution is not accommodated by the social order. In those subgroups of society in which incest is prevalent the families involved have been placed above or outside the domain of ordinary social existence. They might be kings or queens, who maintain their absolute power through in-breeding. Or, more usually, they are social outcasts, who have marginal social roles and who are regarded as deviants by society at large. When incest does occur in less exceptional or less marginal family situations, the child usually is a victim of the parent's sexual abuse. The dread of incest is embedded in the human mind. It takes an extraordinary set of family circumstances to normalize it. Again, from the outside we have no way of discerning the emotional distress, the inner price a person pays when incest gains the day.

The embattled position of the adolescent and the elaborate strategies she requires to protect her from incest anxiety make it eminently clear that there is an immense difference between the repression of an infantile love dialogue and its true disappearance. At the conclusion of infancy the Oedipus complex is repressed. But it remains extant in the unconscious, deferred to puberty when the complex is reawakened for its permanent resolution. Until puberty, Oedipal desires are not transformed into socially meaningful scenarios. All other infantile desires have been given meaning through the reciprocating parental gestures of return and absence, feeding and weaning, the approvals and disapprovals of toilet training, the admiring and frowning looks directed toward the child's exhibitionism, the parents' bodies hidden and then revealed. But there are no parental gestures that reciprocate or interact with the infant's genital desires. During early childhood and the latency years all other infantile desires are transformed into such socially harmonious behaviors and traits as knowing how to eat in public, neatness, cleanliness, intellectual curiosity, dressing appropriately, kindness, displaying one's skills and talents in games and performances. The articulation of genital desire with social form, however, remains obscure throughout childhood. Only after puberty, when the child arrives at genital maturity, can her genital desires be articulated with the requirements of the social order.

From the point of view of society, which must protect itself from being swallowed up by the passions of family life, the essential modification wrought by adolescence is the complete and irreversible ridding of the incestuous desires connected with both parents. What happens to the life of desire or just exactly how an individual solves the incest dilemma is of little concern to society, which cares only that its own interests be preserved.

The definitive resolution of the Oedipus complex during adolescence has the potential for expanding the superego into something more humane than watchful eyes, prohibiting voices, and submission to a demand for perfection. In the process of solving the incest dilemma the adolescent usually tames her conscience at least enough to gain permission to be a genitally functioning adult. If in the bargain she also extracts permission to aspire toward values and ideals that go beyond moral obedience and sexual gratification, it is the result of her personal inner struggle, a struggle that cannot be ordained by any social order.

Society cares only that individuals become civilized, that they leave the family nest to procreate new families, that they work at their assigned jobs and obey a few simple moral commandments. If parent-infant love attachments are necessary to preserve the social order, then society will do what it can to protect the family.

Society does not arrange itself so that some individuals may acquire an ethical conscience through which moral dignity counts for more than self-interest or moral obedience. However, in saying farewell to childhood, some adolescents are on their way to becoming adults more concerned with expanding the boundaries of human existence than with preserving the social order as it is.

The adolescent solution to the paradoxical imperatives of the incest taboo is a slow, painful process. The orders of reality cannot be carried out all at once. Bit by bit, at a great expense of emotional energy, every single one of the memories and expectations that had bound the libido to the parents must be brought up, reexperienced, and reinterpreted. This arduous piece of emotional work is the prototype for mourning the death of a loved one. Through this special version of giving up the past, the adolescent recognizes for the first time the *irreversible* nature of loss. The adolescent is not a true mourner, but by giving up the past in this gradual way, she is acquiring the capacity to mourn.

A true mourner is more or less aware that her moods are connected with the loss of a loved one. The adolescent, however, does not know why she is so suddenly overcome with sadness, despair, anxiety, nostalgia. She has no way of consciously realizing that her ever-changing moods and seemingly capricious emotions are attributable to the loss of her infantile past. In contrast to a true mourner, who has suffered an irrevocable loss of a real person, the adolescent suffers from the loss of an infantile form of desire. Her actual parents are still there.

Similar to a mourner who will divert all aggression away from the memory of the lost one, who is then idealized, the adolescent idealizes the lost past and directs the aggression elsewhere—usually toward her parents and other family members. Parents can be demoralized by the outbursts of hostility and devaluation that are directed at them. Though they are bewildered and hurt, they manage to survive. Parents try to soften for the adolescent the inevitable disappointments and despair. They anguish along with the adolescent, fearfully wondering about the final outcome. The fate of the entire family seems to hang in the balance.

Sooner or later both the true mourner and the adolescent are released from their preoccupation with the past. Everyone is relieved that the emotional turmoil has subsided. The young adult begins to treat her parents with respect and tenderness. But both she and her parents know that something sweet has gone away. It will never return. The new respectful love, although welcomed, can be particularly hard for parents, who are facing the end of life and the waning of desire. The young adult has been set free to find genital love outside the family.

For parents the grown-up child's leave-taking from the family nest is a time for reexamining their own lives. They recall the day they met, their courtship and marriage—the sweet moments they had together and the bitter. They reminisce about the birth of this marvelous child, her first smile, her first words, her first steps, her first days at school, her graduations and performances, her first date. They look back with longing and regret to the "golden" days of their own infancy, to their mothers and fathers as they seemed then— so strong, so marvelous—to the schoolyard games, to the springtime of youth when the energies of growth propelled them into the future and everything still seemed possible.

The Growth Spurt

Except for the brain, which reaches its maximum growth and differentiation before the initiation of pubescence and the involution of lymphatic tissue growth, every muscular and skeletal dimension of the body takes part in the pubescent growth spurt: the wrist, the pelvis, the heart, the abdominal viscera, the thyroid, the face.

The chief element initiating the spurt for both sexes is increased secretion of adrenal androgens. Adrenal estrogens and growth hormone from the pituitary also influence the growth spurt. The sex-differential effects of growth, such as broader shoulders and greater bone width in the male calf, greater fat accumulation on the hips and thighs in the female, are presumed to be caused by testosterone and the ovarian estrogens, respectively.

Throughout pubescence the muscle cells and tissues of the heart, the stomach, the kidneys, the liver, the spleen, the intestines are increasing in size. These size increases are not dramatic, but they do contribute to the inner sense of expansiveness.

The most dramatic growth changes are those of the long bones of the legs, arms, and trunk. It is this growth that is as apparent and prominent as the growth of the pubic hairs, secondary sex characteristics, external genitalia, and the internal reproductive structures. Long-bone growth directly accounts for the rapid increase in stature during pubescence. It is referred to as the height spurt. The height spurt can begin in girls anywhere between nine and a half and fourteen and a half, and in boys between ten and a half and sixteen and a half.

Long-bone age is considered a better criterion of developmental status than chronological age. According to the skeletal maturity criterion, some individuals may have completed puberty while others have scarcely begun. In girls skeletal age is more advanced than in boys from fetal life onward—until adulthood. By the time of puberty there is a two-year disparity. Throughout infancy, childhood, and adolescence, girls are considered more advanced than boys in developmental age and in psychosocial maturity. They arrive at physical maturity before boys. The height spurt terminates about two years earlier, and the differentiation of sexual characteristics is also completed about one or two years earlier in girls. Boys grow for a longer period of time and they are usually taller than girls when puberty terminates.

The sequence of the height spurt is the same in both sexes. Leg length reaches its peak first, followed by hip width and chest breadth. Trunk length and chest depth are the last to accelerate. The foot bones mature before the calf or thigh. The forearm has its peak velocity around six months before the upper arm. The two major constituents of stature are leg length and trunk length. Whereas in childhood leg length accounts for most of the increases in stature, the pubertal stature spurt is primarily due to the acceleration in trunk length. The childhood proportion of leg length to trunk length is reversed during pubescence.

Growth of parts of the skeleton, of the jaw and face, or of some vertebrae will not cease after puberty. But the epiphyses, or extreme ends, of the long bones will close completely, and after that those bones can never grow again.

The long bones fuse, not all at once but in a definite sequence. The first epiphyses to close are at the elbow. The knee epiphyses close a year or two later, at seventeen in early maturers and not until twenty-four in late maturers. The last epiphyses to fuse— several years after most other long bones have closed—are at the midline end of the clavicle. It has been estimated that the height spurt ceases at around eighteen for boys and sixteen for girls, after which there is only about a 2 percent increase in stature.

The closing of the vast majority of long bones usually signifies the termination of puberty. The precise sequence of the closing of the epiphyses was determined by analyzing the skeletal structure of American soldiers between the ages of seventeen and twenty-eight who had been killed in battle.

Inasmuch as most adults have forgotten the painful emotions associated with becoming adult, they tend to imagine the adolescent years as brimming with opportunity. They see the adolescent as having infinite possibilities for love relationships, friendships, interests in dance, music, clothes, learning, work. They do not always understand why the new loves and friendships, the passionate new interests, usually prove to be unstable, transient, and heartbreakingly disappointing.

The adolescent is in a constant search for new forms of love, but she is still bound to the past. Inevitably she will try to transform potentially new experiences into some disguised replay of the past. Her first loves often resemble her father or brother in some aspects. She frequently acts out with peers a role that aims at rectification of infantile humiliation. In dance or music she temporarily recaptures the intoxication and elation of having been an adored infant at the center of the universe. These experiments with trying to retain the old in the guise of the new, while they succeed in diverting sexual hunger and aggressive energies outside the family, usually end up leaving the adolescent emotionally depleted. Disillusionment is profound.

For periods of time the outer world becomes devoid of its former attractions and interests. It cannot be invested with desire. When there is no place for desire to go, no other person to love, no ability to divert sexual hunger into friendship or activity, then depressive moods and feelings of hopelessness take over. Occasionally the adolescent becomes aware of a vague sense of loss, followed by grief of an intensity unknown at any other previous period of life. Moreover, when libido is suspended, with no one to attach itself to, the dread of loss of dialogue can overwhelm the adolescent. This anxiety resembles the falling away into nothingness characteristic of the earliest months of infancy.

The depressive moods, grief reactions, and profound anxiety states so typical of adolescence are manifestations of the inner struggle to relinquish the past and at the same time never let it go. As an expression of this struggle a new, bittersweet emotion comes into existence. During adolescence the child can for the first time experience nostalgia for the lost past *and* a sense of the irreversibility of time. What has once been is gone. It cannot be brought back—except in memory.

A younger child, even an infant, will occasionally yearn for the past. When longing for an absent mother, an infant turns her emotional focus inward. She is trying to restore the sensations of well-being and safety, the serenity, bliss, wholeness, harmony, of the lost world of oneness-love, when mother's presence was everywhere. This inward mood of infancy is called "low keyedness." It resembles adolescent nostalgia. The infant, however, does not consider the past irrevocably lost.

A few years later, when most young children can get along without mother for longer periods of time, they are still comfortable enough with the idea that they can return to the baby days. And they frequently do so by whining, clinging, crawling on all fours, sucking a thumb, having a temper tantrum, showing off, wetting their beds. The past can be brought back. Time is not irreversible.

School-age children, being much wiser and more controlled, will consciously repudiate everything connected with baby life. They disclaim the passions of babyhood and exert every effort to leave the past behind them. Pride in new accomplishments and the ability to make friends outside the family help the latency child to resist the past. Yet these yearnings continue to gain expression in the school-yard games, where life can begin again with each new turn, and in a secret romance life that reinstates the loves that once were. Time is still reversible; what has been can be brought back and done over.

It is only after the adolescent has experienced the full sense of all she is leaving behind that an appreciation of the longed-for past can develop in conjunction with the conviction that it will never come again. The young woman is unaware of the deepest meanings of her nostalgia. She does not realize that her conjuring refers to infancy and to infantile versions of herself and her parents.

The idea of infancy as the golden age of humankind has its origin in adolescent nostalgia. Adolescents particularly, but also many adults, perpetuate the fantasy that the infancy years were pure and innocent. No matter how frightening or humiliating infancy might sometimes have been, we fantasize much of it as the glorious time.

The heartbreak and grief of the adolescent years are difficult to bear. By arousing memories of a delicious and joyous infantile past, the disappointments of the present are mitigated. The family rivalries and jealousies revived by the adolescent passions are screened out by memories of having been an infant or child who was once perfect and absolutely adored. In a nostalgic mood it is always the romance of infancy that is revived, never the frustrations and defeats. The adult romancers would have it that "Heaven lay about us in our infancy," or that infancy was "The happy highways where I went/And cannot come again."

Nostalgia softens grief. It takes the sting out of the sense of loss. Grief empties the soul. Nostalgia replenishes. Our quiet tears remind us of lost innocence. Just thinking about the goodness that was engenders a feeling of inner worthiness. Time is irreversible, but the goodness that was serves as incentive for aspiration. Longings for a lost state of perfection can heighten the adolescent's social awareness. Occasionally nostalgia evokes some musings on how to improve the lot of humanity. The idealizations of the past are transformed into social ideals.

The popular songs of adolescence express the sense of loss even as they gently screen out the intensely personal nature of that loss. What we hear are the lyrics of disappointed love:

> *August die she must*
> *The autumn winds blow chilly and cold;*
> *September I'll remember*
> *A love once new has now grown old.*

The camaraderie of the school years:

> *Goodbye to Rosie, the Queen of Corona*
> *See you, me and Julio down*
> *by the schoolyard.*

The halcyon days that were:

> *Time it was and what a time it was*
> *It was a time of innocence*
> *A time of confidences.*
> *Long ago it must be,*
> *I have a photograph,*
> *Preserve your memories*
> *They're all that's left you.*

> ...

> *Kodachrome*
> *They give us those nice bright colors*
> *They give us the greens of summers*
> *Makes you think all the world's*
> *A sunny day.*

The heroines and heroes who embodied perfection and are gone:

> *Where have you gone, Joe DiMaggio?*
> *A nation turns its lonely eyes to you.*

The nation we dreamed of and lost:

> *They've all come*
> *To look for America*
> *All come to look for America.*

• • •

We come on the ship that sailed the moon
We come in the age's most uncertain hour
And sing an American tune
But it's all right; it's all right
You can't be forever blessed

And, then, sometimes, as the comparison between what
might have been and what is becomes too much to bear,
nostalgia, with its undercurrents of good things yet to come,
yields to dread:

We work out jobs
Collect our pay
Believe we're gliding down the highway
When in fact we're slip slidin' away

• • •

The words of the prophets are written on
*   the subway walls*
And tenement halls
And whisper'd in the sounds of silence.

The adolescent is vastly innovative. However much she
may silently mourn, daydream, long for the past that was,
her powerful individuation strivings keep thrusting her
forth into the world of others. In order to find out who she
really is and who she is not, the adolescent fervently engages friends, lovers, cohorts, peers. She extends herself,
reaching out to her environment, commanding from it those
responses that will advance her cause. Retarded primate that
she is, she is capable of manipulating her natural and social
environments, even changing them radically. For it is another characteristic, unique to the human primate, that we
can alter our internal environment—our fantasies, wishes,
hopes, sense of self—by temporarily engaging the external
world and shaping it to comply with these fantasies and
hopes. In this way even the deepest recesses of our inner
life, through its many layers of cumulative revision, can
once again be revised and transformed.

he more an adolescent can assimilate what the external environment offers her and put it to her own uses, the better are her chances of modifying the direction of the rest of her life. Out of the materials her social environment presents she creates a special personal environment. She does not actually change the social environment. In this instance she uses it for the sole purpose of changing herself, for enhancing her own inner life and advancing its emotional causes.

Usually the inner life of the adolescent is not available for scrutiny. Nor do we always have access to the ongoing and ever-changing connections between her internal life and her actions in the real world. What we can observe is her intense hunger for emotional relatedness. And we are amazed, at times infuriated, by the fantastic use she makes of friends, lovers, teachers, sisters, parents, idols, crushes—by her self-absorbed preoccupation with making use of other people for her own purposes.

She has peculiar effects on those who know her. For some months we find ourselves reacting to her as though she were a saint, more audaciously virtuous and altruistic than any human ought to be. Suddenly she seems to her family and friends an obnoxious monster, the embodiment of evil. Her hair is unkempt, her face contorted with spite, her voice growling and harsh. The very same week she will astonish us by rescuing her little brother from the bullies on the street corner. The monster's face shines in the aura of her bravery and heroism. She seems to have it within her to be all things. But she can't get together a consistent picture of who or what she really is. Inside she feels divided and confused.

Fortunately for most of us and for the adolescent, this inner divisiveness can be expressed in arenas other than the household or classroom. Since for an adolescent a peer group is the most plausible and natural environment, it is also natural that she should try to make considerable use of her peer milieu to express these divided feelings and incoherent images of who she is. Which is one of the reasons why an available peer environment is crucial to adolescent sanity. She "creates" peer groups in accordance with her own emotional needs in order to bring about a more wholesome integration of self-experience. She has no interest whatsoever in changing these groups or the world. She may, for example, join a group whose aim it is to advance the cause of women's liberation. The divided adolescent, however, is more interested in self-liberation. The peer groups she creates are in her mind. They are what they are, and may or may not resemble the images in which they are created. As we observe her behavior in these groups we begin to comprehend what might be going on inside her.

It is typical of the divided adolescent that she wanders from group to group without feeling committed to any of them. In each group she wears a different mask. In this group she seeks power by being brilliant and all-knowing. In that group she dominates by attacking the weaker members. Here she is silent and thoughtful, there loud and obnoxious, in still another group contemptuous and demeaning. Sometimes she joins a particular group in order to be demeaned or attacked. Wherever she goes she seems to be able to elicit from her peers just the kinds of responses she needs. She is able to get the peer group to respond to her like an all-bad, frustrating, humiliating mother or father or like an all-good parent who bestows unconditional love, undivided attention, and total acceptance. The absence of any genuine emotional relatedness in these peer group experiences makes the adolescent feel lonely and terribly shut off from the kinds of dialogues she would like to have. She has no idea what she's doing.

Eventually these peculiar enactments can bring about a greater sense of continuity and coherence. What the adolescent is doing is revising the past by reenacting it in the present. She is acting out those items of the past that should fade into the background of her adult life, almost as though they had never existed at all. These are the love dialogues of the past that could most impede her progress into the future.

What once actually happened between an infant and her parents in a real external environment has been transformed into aspects of a child's own self—her conscience, her fantasies, her daydreams, her ways of thinking and feeling. The past has become immortalized by being internalized, not as it actually happened but in these varied modes of thinking and feeling.

During adolescence the dynamic relationship between the internal life and the external world is often reversed. By reexternalizing certain aspects of her now internalized psychological environment the adolescent is able to bring the past out into the open—perhaps now things might come out a little better. Through reenactment adolescents are, quite unconsciously, attempting to remedy some of the humiliations and deprivations of infancy.

When an adolescent reenacts the past in the present, her actions are not a replica of how she or her parents actually behaved in the past; rather, the reenactments reflect the ways in which these earlier relations became represented in her mind. The adolescent is not recapitulating the past. She has been pressed toward reenactment because something about her personal adolescent dilemmas *resembles* some dilemmas of infancy. These resemblances rouse that imperishable past which is always ready to infiltrate the present when a current trauma has elements in it that correspond to a trauma of the past. Primitive modes of thought and feeling are aroused.

The inevitabilities of normal infantile mental life leave a heritage that can be activated at any point later in life. It is the activation in the present that makes these modes of functioning *primitive*. The infant is not behaving in a primitive manner; neither is the adolescent who reenacts the past behaving like an infant. The retrograde pulls of the earliest love dialogues are especially likely to rouse primitive modes of functioning during adolescence, when the personality is undergoing such dramatic and sometimes overwhelming changes. The eruption of primitive fantasies and thoughts is extremely frightening to an adolescent. She feels even more confused and overwhelmed than usual. Sometimes, then, in order to wrench free of the past, the adolescent finds it imperative to act out rather than work through her dilemmas internally. Her unsuspecting friends or temporary group allegiances become the props and personae of her drama of rectification. Some of the residual traumas of infancy are revised by way of such exotic reenactments.

One of these inevitable traumas of infancy is the crisis of separation, when the child realizes that she and mother are not one. A mother usually maintains a coherent experience of who she is even when her infant is raging from frustration, irritable from inner discomforts such as hunger or teething, humiliated by the recognition of separateness, grieving over the unpredictable comings and goings of the mother, trembling with that awesome dread of loss of dialogue. But in the infant each of these unpleasurable emotional experiences evokes an image of the mother as some sort of biting mouth, sharp and penetrating object, devouring witch, growling monster. When the infant is content after a good feed or enwrapped in the soft, good-smelling warmth of her mother's arms or confidently exploring the world around her, then the mother seems to be an all-good mother who never frustrates, never disappoints, never interrupts the marvelous love dialogue by coming and going whenever she pleases. At these blissful, elated moments the infant feels that she herself is an all-good baby filled up with loving, blissful wholeness.

In addition to these transitory alterations of self-other experience, each phase of infancy brings its own different experience of who the mother is, who the father is, who the self is, with its own varying qualities of loving or hostile significance. The phase of *symbiotic oneness,* for example, carries with it an over-all experience of goodness and trust with inevitable and occasional overtones of fearfulness and rage. In contrast, during the crisis of *rapprochement,* when the infant is forced to reckon with the incontrovertible fact of her separateness from mother, the mother becomes endowed with all-bad, hostile qualities. The anxieties of separation intensify the infantile propensity for viewing the parent as a different parent, depending on whether she gratifies desire or frustrates it. The mother who understands perfectly and gratifies is all-good. The mother who misunderstands the child's wishes or otherwise frustrates her is all-bad and hostile. During the crisis of separation the father is sometimes viewed as the rescuing knight in shining armor, sometimes as the satanic cohort of the witch, and sometimes as the despicable villain who intruded on the mother-infant love dialogue and demolished it. Moreover, when the infant's awareness of separateness is at its height, her raging, irritable, humiliated, grieving, trembling reactions make her feel that she is an all-bad child who could destroy the world and everything in it.

As the crisis of separation comes to its resolution the child normally acquires the ability to maintain a consistent image of herself, an image that is relatively independent of her varying emotional states. Correspondingly, she is able most of the time to hold onto a positive image of her mother or father as a whole human being she loves and admires. The tendency to "split" into all-good/all-bad diminishes sufficiently to allow the child to enter the culminating phase of her infancy with a more or less constant picture of who she is and who her parents are. By the time she has to reckon with the humiliations and dilemmas of the Oedipal triangle, the previous dyadic love dialogues of infancy will have diminished in importance. They become mere subplots, minor dialogues in the more elaborate Oedipal drama. The dyadic dialogues will contribute to the emotional quality of the five-year-old's more advanced identifications with her parents and to the tenor and force of her superego. But the solution to the infantile Oedipal triangle brings about a *synthesis* of the entire experience of infancy, a synthesis that immortalizes all the love dialogues of infancy and endows the child's personality with a sense of coherence and unity.

During adolescence this sense of coherence is threatened. Inevitably, the demand for removal brings about a certain degree of desynthesis of the Oedipal solutions, which in turn reactivates the "splitting" mechanisms of the infantile period. Splitting is quite different from the adolescent's normal propensities for polarizing the world into good and bad, her uncompromising attitudes, her intolerance for qualification or blending of opposites. In order to accommodate to her changing body and deal with her desires, the adolescent tends to see herself and everybody else as either gorgeous or ugly, exciting or boring, stupid or brilliant, generous or greedy, friendly or hostile. These attitudes are aspects of the defensive strategies that accompany removal. In contrast to these expectable adolescent attitudes, which may be annoying to the rest of the world but quite comfortable to the adolescent, the reinstatement of splitting leads to extreme vacillations in the way the adolescent experiences her self—a frightening fragmentation that pressures her toward acting out. She becomes and also elicits from others the split renditions of her parents and herself that could not be adequately synthesized at the culmination of the infantile period.

If the earliest phases of infancy were contaminated by too much hostile aggression, too little individuation aggression, uneven forward movement of the libidinal dialogues (before the infant had the chance to enjoy the experience of oneness she was confronted with the dilemmas of separation), peculiarities in the maturational sequences of sitting up, crawling, walking, and talking, inappropriately timed or overly stressful weaning and toilet training, excessive exposure to the anatomical differences between the sexes, sexual seduction of any kind, we can expect the tendency for desynthesis during adolescence to be exacerbated.

Even the most benevolent infancy, however, is bound to leave residues of infantile stress that will press themselves to the forefront during adolescence. Adolescence is an occasion for ameliorating the infantile injuries. Or the extraordinary regressive pull of these traumas can lead to premature closure—to flight, hasty retreat, emotional surrender, psychosis, suicide. Some adults spend their lives trying to rectify the past. Ordinarily the adolescent vitalities will unlatch the structures of the past and open the way for more coherent syntheses.

Side by side with her exotic peer reenactments, the ordinary adolescent is involved with the more genuine peer relationships that we are accustomed to think of as characteristic of adolescence. Usually she has one or two special girl friends with whom she shares her passions, secrets, and anxieties. Then there are the outsiders whom she and her friends view as stupid, mean, hostile, ugly. She also belongs to a group from school or the neighborhood which she regards as her home-base peer group; this group she counts on to be there for her always, especially when she returns from her lonely excursions into the all-good, all-bad past. Later in life she will scarcely remember anything at all of her reenactments—neither her odd behaviors nor the reactions she elicited. These spurious and transitory group relationships are immortalized in the changed, more coherent person she eventually becomes. In contrast, her genuine friends and home-base group are cherished forever as the important relationships that helped her to become something more than what she had been. She immortalizes them in the changed, more coherent person she becomes. And she immortalizes them also in memory.

The reenactment arena, however, vanishes as soon as it has served its purpose. The reenactments prove to be temporary, and if they have succeeded in rearranging the emotional priorities of the dyadic and Oedipal love dialogues, they will not carry forth into adult life. The dialogues are transformed, not obliterated. What remains is a more advanced and wholesome synthesis of the infantile legend. It is almost as though the psychological solutions of human infancy have been left in a state of incompleteness so that the adolescent revision can leave its imprint on the adult form. The generational continuity of the human species requires an intense and prolonged infant-parent bonding. On attaining sexual maturity, the adhesiveness of these bonds must be loosened sufficiently to allow the adolescent to leave the family nest and become an adult member of the society at large. The survival of civilization requires in addition that what was learned during infancy and childhood be preserved and passed on to the next generation.

Infantile love dialogues are never really lost. However much they are transformed, they will continue to exert their influence on the present, reflected in that unchanging fundamental wish to retain the attachments of infancy. Adolescence can free the individual to participate fully in new knowledge and experience. It can liberate the adult to continue the quest for human perfectibility. What we hope for at the conclusion of the adolescent passage is that not too much of adult life will be consumed by reenacting and repeating the past in the present.

But for all of us there will be those irreconcilable injuries and humiliations that persist and infiltrate into adult existence. They may become the seeds for despair, for those monotonous repetitions of hurting others and getting hurt ourselves. Or, as so often happens, the leftover traumas can be incentives for innovation and change. As the old passions force themselves into the present, we still have the opportunity to rewrite the scripts, introduce a few new characters, get rid of one or two, perhaps even change the ending, and free the lover and jester inside us all.

7

THE BRIDGE BETWEEN LOVE DIALOGUES AND NARCISSISM

Love for the Parent of the Same Sex

Adolescence entails the deployment of family passions into those sexual and moral passions that bind individuals to new family units, to their social community, to their species. In the choice between remaining bound to the family in a nongenital, infantile way or affirming their genital vitalities and commitment to ongoing life, most adolescents will decide in favor of giving up the past. Sooner or later the adolescent will begin to direct the erotic components that have been invested in the parent of the opposite sex toward a person exempt from the incest taboo. In the process the rivalrous and aggressive passions that had been invested in the parent of the same sex are transformed and also directed outside the family into work and sexual competition with peers, and into the energies of parenting and community participation.

Side by side, and subtly interwoven with these more recognizable deployments of family passion, are those transformations that involve the homoerotic passions for the parent of the same sex. There is more to manhood and womanhood than the transfer of heterosexual libido. And there is a great deal more to the relationship with the same-sex parent than rivalry, jealousy, and competition. Normally the erotic components of a child's relationship to the parent of the same sex remain in the background. What we see is identification with that parent's behavior and traits, affection, loyalty, and considerable evidence of a narcissistic wish to become what one loves and admires in the parent. With the onset of pubescence, however, every child is confronted with the dilemmas of what to do with the erotic and narcissistic passions invested in the parent of the same sex.

The crucial sexual and moral issues are to preserve the tender and affectionate ties to the parent of the same sex, to de-eroticize the passions that are attached to that parent and transfer them elsewhere, and to humanize the exalted idealizations that had been attributed to that parent. These issues cannot be resolved by simply transferring the erotic and narcissistic investments to a relationship with a person of one's own sex who is exempt from the incest taboo. Even homosexual love choices are not made solely on the basis of such transfer. Whatever their eventual sexual orientation, all adolescents must confront these issues. They are part of each adolescent's problem in making a lasting choice for his or her love life. Each adolescent must come to terms with his or her homoerotic strivings—strivings that were first aroused in the context of infantile family life.

Alongside his erotic strivings toward his mother and rivalrous feelings for his father, the little boy wishes to get from his father the sexual pleasures he imagines the mother is getting from the father. A little boy also wishes to give to his father the sexual pleasure he imagines the mother is giving to the father. Just as the little boy is aroused to his feminine strivings, so the little girl is aroused to masculine strivings. She wishes to give to her mother what she imagines the father is giving to the mother and to get from the mother what she imagines the father is getting from the mother. These wishes necessarily engender envy of the parent of the opposite sex—the one who has the wished-for powers of gratification, the one who has received the longed-for sexual gifts. On the other hand, a young child's narcissism is protected and enhanced by the exalted idealizations he or she attributes to the parent of the same sex. The little boy loves in his father what he wishes to be. The little girl loves in her mother what she wishes to be.

In childhood, boys and girls can tolerate the coexistence of their masculine and feminine strivings. Sexual maturity, however, demands some final resolution of gender identity. At stake are not only the kind of man or woman one becomes and the choice of sexual attachment but also a definitive coming to terms with the narcissistic core of the love for the same-sex parent—that parent begins to be seen as she or he actually is, and not as an omnipotent god who can mirror the child's wish for perfection.

The central dynamic issues, then, are *not* whether the adolescent makes a homosexual or a heterosexual adjustment, but how she arrives at that adjustment and the relative balance between self-love and a capacity to love others. Is the person able to commit herself to lasting love relationships? Are the relationships dominated by the narcissistic longing to see mirrored in the other what one wishes to be oneself? Does the person have the sexual and moral capacity to be caregiver and lawgiver to the next generation? As we have seen, heterosexuality is no guarantee of sexual or moral maturity. Social conventions make it possible for a heterosexual adult to hide his or her less-than-adequate solutions in a social role. A philosopher deprived of her position in the academy might become a hermit or a religious fanatic. A general without his elaborate social structure and his army might look like a paranoid maniac. Unless they are pressured into the role of deviant by social conventions, homosexuals also have available to them a variety of successful or failed solutions to the incest taboo.

Insofar as every adolescent's homoerotic passions are concerned, the dilemmas are: What does the adolescent do with the erotic strivings toward the parent of the same sex? Also, when the parent of the same sex is de-idealized, how is the self-esteem that was derived from the idealization attributed to that parent maintained? What will become of the idealizations that had been invested in the images of the same-sex parent?

These dilemmas are further complicated for *both* sexes by the longings and passions associated with separation-individuation, those mother-infant dialogues that exert in memory a pull toward the early nongenital forms of sexuality. Almost every prominent form of behavior of adolescence is marked by the conflict between surrendering to infantile sexuality and asserting genitality. Masturbation, for example, familiarizes the adolescent with her genital longings and with the excitement that leads to genital discharge. But the fantasies associated with autoeroticism can also heighten the wish to be a passive, eternally-cared-for infant. The wish is to play at life rather than live it. The problems of gender choice can be postponed. One need not assume adult sexual and moral responsibility. The major problem that arises with homosexual love choice is that it always entails some relinquishment of genital vitality. The homosexual love act necessarily encourages the ascendancy of infantile sexuality and therefore a certain degree of surrender to the past. Thus, for the homosexual the temptations to linger in the never-never land of genital ambiguity, to play at life rather than live it, are apt to be extremely difficult to resist. Nevertheless, surrender is not inevitable. And, as with any struggle to resist the past, any attempt to rectify the humiliations and traumas of infancy, the scenarios can represent a monotonous repetition of hurting others and getting hurt ourselves or they can be incentives for cultural innovation and moral aspiration.

Whatever their eventual love choice, all adolescents must struggle with their homoerotic strivings. And for every boy and girl, the attractions of the mother-infant dialogues will be complications in this struggle. The homosexual-narcissistic passions of a girl's relationship to her mother, of a boy's relationship to his father, are always infiltrated by the persistent wish to surrender one's body and soul to an all-giving, ever-present, magical caregiver, who will mirror everything one wishes to be. The persistent and tormenting wish to submit to the past is countered by adolescent boys and girls with all the energies and vitalities at their command.

If they are to become caregivers and lawgivers, boys and girls have to find a way to preserve the tender and affectionate relationship to the same-sex parent. The erotic aspect must be desexualized and the idealizations must be humanized so that they can be invested in one's own children, a calling, a profession, in social and ethical ideals. Even more than with the deployment of the heterosexual family passions, the transformations of the homosexual passions of childhood have the effect of extending the individual into social units that reach beyond the domestic domain. And as with any deployment of passion from one realm to another, the event begins on a variation of violence.

The prologue to male pubescence is a violent turning away from females. Accompanying the rampant messiness and obstreperous invasiveness of the eleven-to-thirteen-year-old boy is an alarming range of aggressive forms of behavior: incessant drawing of military objects and scenes, fidgeting, restlessless, foul language, vandalism, theft, gang conflicts, assaults on "gays" and other sexually threatening types. Boys of this age seem determined to banish eros. They consider girls bitchy, cheating, untrustworthy witches. They revel in tormenting female and aesthetic male teachers.

What eleven-to-thirteen-year-old boys fear is passivity of any kind. When they do act passively we can be fairly certain that it is an act of aggression designed to torment a parent or teacher. While his mother is rushing to go to work and get the kids off to school, the boy suddenly becomes too helpless to tie his own shoelaces. While his teacher is explaining to him the homework he missed, the boy yawns, gets dreamy-eyed, and stares out the window. The reminder of being dependent, or the temptation to surrender to caresses, affection, endearments, tender sentiments, sets off the alarms. Mischief at best, violence at worst is the boy's proclamation of masculinity. Everything would be perfect if being masculine didn't have to include contact with the entrapping girls and women, whose very existence is a constant threat to manhood.

At this age, in contrast to the later years of puberty proper, adolescent boys usually have a pleasant, easygoing relationship with Father. Father is the ally, the comrade-in-arms against Mother, who is plainly and simply a castrating bitch. Since she is so often tormented and provoked by her son, the mother can be turned into the half-crazed demon her son imagines her to be. There are times when the alliance between son and father can be exasperating to a mother. Knowing that her "little boy" is merely on the brink of manhood, she worries about his risk-taking and delinquencies. But Father, male teachers, even the policemen who might occasionally appear at the front door, exchange the tolerant winks of male bonding: "Boys will be boys."

The underlying scenario to this prologue to male puberty is the boy's desperate flight from the caregiving mother of infancy, the adored and powerful one who first caressed his body, nursed him, rocked him, told him what, how, and when to eat, regulated the time and place for urination and bowel movements, and seemed to own his body, mind, and soul. Ironically, the physical changes of early pubescence are not altogether reassuring to the boy. In comparison to girls of the same age, eleven-to-thirteen-year-old boys are often shorter, physically less well developed, and less proficient academically. The boys are plagued by unconscious fantasies that it might be rather nice to have breasts and babies, fantasies that are bound to increase their sense of inferiority in comparison to the "weaker" sex, who actually achieve such envied characteristics. To add insult to injury, during prepuberty the genital area often symbolizes the female breasts, as the testes are the area in which the boys are growing most dramatically and vividly.

The testes increase in size from 4 grams at age nine to 17 grams at age fourteen to 20 grams at seventeen. Now that the testes are growing, and the boy has this slightly larger, sometimes erect and uncontrollable penis, with its mysterious seminal emissions, also a few pubic hairs and a small but distressing breast mound, the boy feels he has to muster all his masculine resources to ward off the emotional surrender he equates with femininity. Any surrender at all is tantamount to becoming the passive, receptive infant he sometimes secretly wishes to be. The clamoring insistence on being a man's man is a massive mobilization, an all-out, no-holds-barred, preemptive first-strike defense of the boy's still fragile, merely incipient masculinity. The exhibitionistic risk-taking acts—brazen, right out in the open, catch-me-if-you-can, defiant—are a declaration of masculinity: "I can do anything. Nothing can happen to me. *My* body is impervious to damage."

During this phase the boy's idealization of his father is at its height, and so he manages to deny everything about his father that might contradict the image of a strong and powerful man. To all others the father might seem a different sort of man, one who submits to wife and boss like a Milquetoast. But to the son, Father is the best and the greatest. Later on, from about fifteen to seventeen, as the devaluing of the father sets in, much of the boy's aggression that had been directed toward Mother and the caregiving environment at large—including buildings, subways, public monuments, parks—will shift to Father. Father and son become open rivals. On both sides the competition and envy gain momentum. It is then that the erotic overtones of the father-son relationship are potentially threatening. The boy steps up his denigrations of the father precisely at those moments when he might be seduced by some feelings of tenderness for him.

As for Mother, she begins to lose her image as an overpowering, devouring witch. But the imperatives of the incest taboo will keep the boy at a cautious distance from her. Until removal is completed, the adolescent boy will continue to regard his mother with some degree of suspicion and fear. Not surprisingly, when at last he has a girl friend or two, relations between son and mother are more cordial and friendly. And occasionally, as he is engaged in wild controversy and stubborn arguments with his father, the boy may even turn to Mother for solace and understanding.

As his masculine characteristics become more pronounced and certain, the boy can begin to admit that the characteristics of the opposite sex have some allure. Though the boys still shy away from the tender trap, girls become for them fascinating and tempting creatures. In their first approaches to the girls, the boys band together. They are rowdy and predatory. But unrelenting eros is now more friendly and sponsoring. The boy is possessed by feelings of tender desire for the girl of his dreams. His coarse and vulgar approaches are toned down into an awkward approximation of civilized courtship. Romance and affection intermingle with the purely erotic. The boy is enthralled. His friends are mocking and disparaging. But he is overcome, swept away. And delightedly so. Slowly and surely eros has triumphed over another willing victim. Surrender enables the gift of love.

The girls, on their side, while they have had romantic inclinations from the early pubescent years onward, have no less a time of it coming to terms with their femininity. With the first downy hairs and barely detectable elevation of the nipples, girls may be less threatened by bisexuality than boys are, but the backward pull to the mother-infant love dialogues is also a complication for them. A girl, whose original struggles to become a self separate from Mother were more dramatic, violent, and fraught with conflict, must on this score fight even harder than a boy. During adolescence the emotional dissension between mothers and daughters can assume wild proportions. The struggle, a result of personal, unique inner conflicts, is always exacerbated by the subtle social message that girls are better off if they remain childlike.

Because of her still-lingering temptations to cling to Mother and to be cuddled and caressed—temptations that are considered "feminine" and therefore socially acceptable—a fourteen-year-old girl might be inclined to take surprising flight from Mother. One way to flee is to become precociously heterosexual. Female juvenile delinquency is most often an outcome of sexual promiscuity. What the girl is searching for in the men or boys to whom she flees is cuddling and caretaking. In the girl's fantasies she is a nursling at the breast. Sexual intercourse for her has less to do with penises and vaginas than with reinstating a nursing situation. The typical female delinquencies are shoplifting, lying, spreading rumors, and similar "secret" crimes that symbolize her compromise between getting the maternal love she longs for and her resentment for not getting it.

Many girls do not have to take flight from Mother. They do not rush into precocious sexuality. Their secret crimes are on the petty side of law and order. They do not inflict damage on themselves or the world at large. In subtle ways, however, they may try too hard, too fast, to become the epitome of sexy womanhood. The exaggerated makeup, weird hairstyles, and outlandish "whory" dress they adopt are caricatures of grown-up femininity. There is a transvestite quality to their womanly arts that succeeds in frightening off the boys, who do not need much to be frightened off.

There are, of course, the "good" girls, the ones who share all their secrets with Mother, rarely if ever yield to the temptation to masturbate, never get into trouble, never steal or dress extremely. They are, and usually remain, carbon copies of an idealized version of Mom—imitating the way she combs her hair, dresses, eats, talks, walks. "We were never as close as we are now," brags her proud mother. For this mother-daughter couple the adolescent seas are clear and unruffled. No storm. No stress. Everything floats back to the beginning, just as it was before the girl began to become a woman. Even after she is married, her best friend is Mom. Mom is her confidante, her ally against her husband. No man can come between this mother-daughter intimacy. In many traditional societies and in ethnic groups in which girls are expected to do no more than simply exchange one domestic hogan for another, the options for growing up into womanhood are prescribed and limited, and this sort of mother-daughter intimacy can pass as normal to themselves and to others. When varieties of womanhood are more numerous, we expect more inner stress and overt conflict between mother and daughter, even in the intimacy just described, which is more rigid and defensive than the easygoing intimacy of traditional societies.

Whereas the prepubertal boy is mortified by signs of femininity in his body, some eleven-, twelve-, and thirteen-year-old girls will actually do everything they can to accentuate their masculinity. The girl is brazenly tomboyish, almost as though she were deliberately trying to avoid her move into womanhood. Pubescent girls, some more consciously than others, hold onto a magical belief that they can still decide whether to be female or male. At moments they become aware of the tantalizing question "Am I a boy or a girl?" The transformation of the exuberant, rowdy, "horse-crazy" girl-boy into the eternally self-grooming, sentimental, moping fifteen-year-old, which seems to happen overnight, has been brought about by a gradual and imperceptible undermining of the girl's illusions of total narcissistic self-sufficiency: "I don't need boys. I can do it all by myself."

The recognition that she is not immune to the *ars erotica* of males produces some fleeting reactions of self-scorn in the tomboy. She counters her genital yearnings by going through a vulgar phase, using as many dirty words as the guys, and emulating their strutting walk, Apache hairstyles, and silver-studded, leather jackets. This transitory masculine protest soon yields to the insistence of her feminine eroticism. But despite her near-decisive turn to the opposite sex for libidinal gratification, a girl continues to struggle, even after puberty, with her wishes for emotional and physical contact with Mother. When a girl is not permanently molded into womanhood by a rite of passage or distinct social convention, the options of whether to be a grown-up woman or a genitally ambiguous girl-woman remain open until the adolescent passage is completed—though sometimes its completion extends far into adulthood, and sometimes it is unending.

As puberty proceeds, a girl's sensitivity to her gradual feminization—enlarging breasts, rounded hips and thighs, erect nipples, the cycles of menstruation that alert her to the "inner secrets" of her uterus and ovaries—is as likely to summon up homosexual yearnings as heterosexual ones. It takes a few years for the girl to achieve a permanent removal of libido from her mother. The temptation to creep back into Mother's lap is always lurking in the background of her thoughts and fantasies. A woman's aggressive, rivalrous feelings toward her mother will always have an admixture of erotic, libidinal yearnings—sometimes to be the passive, cared-for baby, sometimes to be the active lover who can satisfy all her mother's desires.

Bouts of yearning followed by bouts of disparagement begin to dominate the scenario of the adolescent girl's relationship to her mother. The girl's fascination with her own breasts and thighs revives the longing for Mother, whose breasts, arms, thighs, lap, caresses, and mirroring admiration were once the elements of the most powerful love affair the girl has yet known. In this now-revived infantile scenario the father was the voice of law and order, the one who played the role of intruder, the one who eventually proclaimed his authority over the mother: "Mother is mine, not yours. Enough of this cuddling, toileting, wooing, and showing off for Mommy. Besides, you do not have what it takes to satisfy Mother. I have something Mother desires that you do not have." The father, who remains in the girl's mind as the symbol of power and authority, usually does not become the target of the adolescent girl's provocative denigrations. Perhaps later in life, when the very idea of masculine power fills her with bitter envy and resentment, she will make a few men pay for the humiliations of her infancy. But right now, during puberty, it is Mother who pays.

As the homoerotic yearnings well up, they are also the signals to dredge up the familiar grievances against Mother, to ruminate on Mother's shortcomings and give her F's for beauty, wisdom, strength, valor, justice, temperance, prudence. These stringent measurements counteract the erotic pull. But by tearing down the woman she had once idealized and then identified with, the adolescent girl is measuring her own self as worthless and powerless.

Having a special girl friend, a chum with whom to share secrets and fantasies, helps to divert the passions away from Mother. Identification with the special and marvelous friend also goes a long way toward bolstering the girl's self-esteem. The two girls are bound to each other heart and mind. They

depend on each other for emotional and intellectual suste-
nance. They dress alike, talk alike, eat the same foods, read
the same poets, daydream about the same boys, idolize the
same idols, despise the same enemies. The kind of woman
the girl will become is strongly influenced by her identification with this special friend. The friendship is energized by
the mutual curiosity about the sex life of grown-ups. Together they puzzle out the meaning of their own physical
changes for adult sexuality. Most of the action consists of
intrigue and romance: imagining the love affairs of others,
concocting love triangles complete with secret meetings,
exotic passions, jealousy, and betrayal. The shared fantasies
are a blend of the stereotypes from television soaps, comic
books, ladies' magazines, and are spiced with events from
Anna Karenina, the fate of Janis Joplin, and nostalgia for
the good old days of infancy. The girls might carry the action into real life. They become participants in a love triangle by competing for the favors and attentions of another
girl or boy. Often the friendships survive these Oedipal-like
upheavals. But such passions can get out of control. The
breakup of a special friendship can be as devastating as any
other love affair. Between friendships the girl is bereft. And
Mother, as usual, pays the price.

One of the most significant diversions from the emotional
intricacies of the mother-daughter relationship is the adolescent girl's wholehearted "crush" on another woman—a
teacher, camp counselor, next-door neighbor. The crush
typifies a feminine solution to growing up. Boys have their
homosexual intrigues, and they can become deeply involved in idealizations of older boys and men. But for reasons we shall see, these masculine solutions usually do not
have the emotional intensity of the feminine crush.

Crushes are one-way affairs. The revered woman who is
the object of the crush may or may not be aware of it. She is
likely to be in her late twenties or early thirties, somewhere
in age between her secret adorer and the age of the adorer's
mother. Wittingly or otherwise, the chosen woman becomes
a mentor. She guides the girl through the stormy seas. She

embodies positive alternatives to the disparaged values and attitudes of the mother. She helps the girl convert her homosexual passion into some passing or enduring absorption—in the poetry of Tennyson, the French language, the game of soccer or basketball, the politics of Camus, the music of Vivaldi, the manners of exotic cuisine. The homoerotic passion is thereby raised to the sublime, is sublimated, as it were. The girl discovers that there are acceptable courtship and marriage conventions quite different from those of her family. Her sense of who she is and who she might become is enriched and enlarged. And though the older woman is perceived as a glamorous "free spirit" who contrasts sharply with the trivial and uncultured domesticity of the mother, in the role of mentor she remembers the pangs of her own adolescence and sensitively observes the line between freedom and restraint.

Unfortunately the objects of an adolescent crush are not always protective and caring persons. They may, in fact, have been chosen precisely for the allure of their narcissistic aloofness and grandiosity. Such women are delighted to bask in the golden light of idealization. In the adolescent girl's revering gaze they find a mirror for their narcissistic needs. And they are not at all beyond taking advantage of the vulnerable girl's temporary appeal to escape from the clutches of Mother. The girl has turned to such a woman seeking rectification for the disappointing relationship with Mother and probably for a number of disappointments in her father as well. Her disparagements of her own family have been generated by her attempts to transfer love-desire elsewhere. By attaching herself to this glorified woman the girl solves part of the problem of transfer and simultaneously restores the self-esteem that has been lost in her denigrations of Mother. But the extraordinary tribute and admiration that a revered narcissist exacts exacerbates what might have been merely the average expectable emotional tension between a mother and her adolescent daughter. The woman is not a guardian of youth. She cares only to recover the lost omnipotence and grandeur of her own infancy.

The confusion that follows these unfortunate crushes can have profound effects on the adolescent's future love choices, her sense of right and wrong, and her social ideals. The feminine identifications that are derived from the special friendships, crushes, and other idealized love relationships can be a source of new possibilities or they can reactivate the archaic dialogues of infancy.

When she tries to assume the roles of an adult woman, the girl who has identified during adolescence with a self-serving narcissist may find herself on a perpetually revolving stage. She turns from passionate idealized love affairs with self-centered, uncaring men (or women), and then, after the predictable disappointment, she turns back to the tender, affectionate, caregiving men who resemble her mother and father and who are bound, because they are merely human and not omnipotent divinities, to be let-downs when it comes to purified, narcissistic passions. As far as her actual choices for genital activity are concerned, the girl may or may not be "normally" heterosexual. But in her fantasies she is still a dependent nursling at the breast. This eternally childlike woman is stuck, not somewhere in infancy or childhood but in the transitional realm of adolescence. The adolescent crush succeeded in remobilizing the ordinary all-good/all-bad splits of the infantile period and transforming them into morbid propensities. This adolescent scenario is an example of how, in psychological life, the present can determine the emotional significance of the past. Infantile issues can acquire in the present greater intensity and often new meanings.

The eternal child-woman will seek from the idealized "free spirits" permission for any and all sexual catastrophe and moral transgression. Sometimes her transgressions are merely vicarious. She thrives on sharing the magical shimmer of the sexual exploits and moral delinquencies of her current idol. When the glamour wears off—as it inevitably does—she searches out a tender, ordinary homebody to nurse her wounds. From this person she hopes to regain the safety, restraints, prohibitions, and protection she had sought so hard to escape when she was an adolescent. The eternal child-woman has not grown up either sexually or morally. Her social ideals and moral standards are as fluctuating and subject to change as her sexual yearnings. That modicum of stability crucial to any chosen life was lost in a failure to resolve during adolescence the tangled strands of the infantile love dialogues.

Except in those societies in which a rite of passage or some convention institutionalizes the pubescent girl's identification with a mythical-divine woman or just plain Mom, in most modern societies girls are left pretty much on their own to solve the dilemma of what to do with their yearnings for Mother. The new identifications of adolescence tend to be personalized and drawn from one or two friendships and the crush. Such feminine solutions, though they are allowed by social conventions, are focused on personal identifications, not on group or social allegiances. In this respect, traditional female rites of passage have a similar emphasis.

On the other hand, in nearly every human society the messages of the incest taboo given to the boy are geared more toward bringing him into identifications with the larger social order. The stress is on a definitive severing of the ties with Mother and on establishing loyalties outside the domestic realm. The boy is charged with the necessity to give up his childhood ways. Even in the least chauvinistic and tenderhearted liberated men, dread of the tender trap continues as a prevailing undercurrent of relationships with women. The dread solidifies their bonds with other men.

Male bonding would appear to be a built-in feature of the average father-son relationship. True, father and son are rivals for the affection and caresses of Mother, but from infancy onward the father is also the boy's ally. Intruder though he is, Father is the hero who rescues the boy from the exclusive dyadic love affair with Mother. There are, of course, variations to this optimal turn of events. Some fathers and sons have difficulty getting into a harmonious alliance; they are mismatched temperamentally, or the father may have favored one child to the disadvantage of another, or the father may be domineering, seductive, weak. A father may be emotionally absent from the household. Occasionally a father may, in compensation for his conjugal disappointments, turn his erotic longings toward his son. This does not create a positive masculine alliance. It is a narcissistic exploitation that encourages a boy's envy and fear of women and encourages his passive-submissive wishes in relation to the father. Usually, however, by the time a boy reaches adolescence the father-son alliance is strong enough to weather the de-idealizations and uncompromising ideological warfare and rivalries of puberty. Moreover, the various opportunities provided by male bonding help the boy to resolve the dilemma of what to do with his erotic longings for his father.

Of course, even in male bonding, crushes do occur. And a crush will remain in the adult's imagination and fantasies as the embodiment of perfect manhood, a glorified image that a man will forever contrast with the less exciting, domesticated image of his father. Especially in periods of emotional crisis, a grown man will lament the glamorous, seductive, adventurous, delinquent, exciting person he might have become if only he hadn't settled into the domesticity of husbanding and fathering. But because the average boy also has a number of other replacements for his homoerotic strivings, the emotional residues of his adolescent crush are more subdued than the feminine variety. Only for the homosexual male does the adolescent crush have the intensity we attribute to female crushes. The homosexual male may devote his life to searching for the ideal man he adored during his adolescence.

Ordinary male adolescent friendships have out-in-the-open erotic overtones. Mutual masturbation, shared sexual exploits with prostitutes and "bad" girls, the frank ecstasies of the basketball court, exhibitionism and body inspection in the locker room, are socially acceptable practices of becoming a man's man. Such practices can come frighteningly close to homosexuality. If the homosexual components of these passionate activities begin to gain momentum, a friendship usually comes to an abrupt end. Even after he finally yields to the *ars erotica* of a young woman and makes a temporarily permanent commitment to her, a boy strives to be a man's man. Though a woman, even one who declares her liberation from men, is always more a man's woman than she will ever be a woman's woman, very few men will consider themselves to be a woman's man. The Don Juans and the Casanovas are no exception, since their womanizing is motivated by an ideal of hypermasculinity—"phallic narcissism," to use a technical term.

During adolescence male social groups, such as the team, the political club, the social club, the street gang, provide protection against the castrating father and the devouring, possessive mother. By asserting the dominance of the phallus such groups reinforce masculine identifications. They also neutralize homosexual inclinations. Boys who need to escape from the anxieties of castration and separation by becoming like Mother (or baby) borrow courage from the group to assert their masculinity and independence. In addition, the daring, risk-taking spirit of the adolescent group is a masculine strategy for dealing with fears connected with the mysterious and as yet unexplored female insides. The sharp differentiation between masculinity and femininity stressed in male groups is immensely reassuring to adolescent boys.

Throughout life, male groups of various sorts will continue to provide outlets for men's sexual and aggressive impulses as well as replacements for the idealizations that had been invested in the father. By investing them in the group, a man dilutes, as it were, his homoerotic yearnings and glorifications among a greater number of individuals and thus *im*personalizes them. This is one reason why men's social ideals tend to be more abstract than women's. Social conventions encourage women to invest their ideals in personal and domestic relationships, whereas boys are given social approval when they invest their energies in groups outside the family.

Group loyalties and group ideals *do* fill the void left by de-idealization of the father. Reverence for the leader and submission to his ideals and values, which are the standards and marks of distinction of the entire group, enable a man to transfer love of his father to love of the group. Male bonding deflects homoerotic currents. But in itself male bonding may do very little in the way of taming the conscience. A man can be just as submissive, fearful, absolutely adoring, and infantile in relation to a group or a leader as he once was with his father. Though they embody a form of social bonding, group loyalties often take on religious, military, political, or economic shapes that are energized by *amour-propre*. Feudalism, chivalry, Christianity, corporate life, professional affiliations—all employ those conventions that bolster masculine self-interest: vanity and petty pride. Man in his group compares himself to others. From the vantage of good standing in the group, a man may experience himself as better than those outside the group, and this in turn inspires him to line up to the ideals of his group. A group member may feel envy and jealousy toward those above him in the group hierarchy, but he balances this potential humiliation by feeling contempt for those below him or those outside the group.

When *amour-propre* is the guiding passion of his group loyalties, a man's ideals are likely to be as exaggeratedly infantile as when he looked to his parents as the sole source of love and protection. It is true that a man is bound to his brothers through their mutual identification with the values and interests of the group. But should a brother fall from grace by taking a misjudged step or exhibiting some human frailty, he will undergo the fate of the de-idealized parent.

In that sense, though a woman usually does not have the advantage of the wider group allegiances that would help her to impersonalize and sublimate her homoerotic strivings, she may have some moral advantage. Her more impassioned personal and domestic involvements may energize those compassionate sensibilities that are the hallmark of ethical ideals. But this is only so if the ideals by which a woman measures herself and others have been adjusted to human proportions.

The deflection of homoerotic yearnings for the parent of the same sex toward other persons and the larger social group in their desexualized, sublimated form is only one facet of the humanizing of conscience. Another entails the fate of the idealizations that had been invested in that parent—the narcissistic elements of the love relationship between daughter and mother, son and father.

To continue to measure ourselves and others by the stringent standards of perfection that are the residues of our archaic conscience leads to frantic attempts at self-glorification and self-aggrandizement. When the prime mover of our group loyalties, domestic or corporate, is *amour-propre,* we are the divided souls that Rousseau spoke of. Torn between our personal passions and our moral duties, we are neither true to our own selves nor are we true citizens. "Swept along in contrary routes by nature and by men, forced to divide ourselves between these different impulses, we follow a composite impulse which leads to neither one goal nor the other. Thus, in conflict and floating during the whole course of our life, we end it without having been good either for ourselves or for others." When we do not become the masters of our ideals, they master us. We slavishly serve whoever or whatever promises to raise us above our neighbor.

When we tame our ideals, we do not banish illusion or our hopes for human perfectibility. We acquire an enlarged vision of what it means to be human. We find out that we do not have to be saints or heroes in order to be true to our ideals. We find out that none of us are exempt from the sufferings that others suffer. We see in our own moral plight the plight of all humankind. Again Rousseau comes to mind: "In fact, what are generosity, clemency, humanity, if not pity applied to the weak, to the guilty, or to the human species in general?"

With his fuller appreciation of the evolution of the human

species, Darwin also thought to evaluate the progress of humankind in terms of the sympathetic regard of one human for another. In 1871 Darwin predicted that as feelings became more tender and affectionate they would extend to all humans, even to useless members of society, and finally to the lower animals. In 1920, echoing Darwin's sentiments, the psychoanalyst J. C. Flugel stated:

The increasing moralisation of the human character (in which the relationship between parent and child has probably played a leading part) has brought it about that at least some degree of attention is given in all civilised societies to the needs—material and mental—of those who are no longer able fully to support themselves or carry on their life without assistance. . . . This care of elderly, lonely or infirm parents by their children may perhaps legitimately be considered one of the most beautiful and touching expressions of the specifically human morality—a point in which Man has definitely risen superior to the conditions of a brutal struggle for existence.

Before she will be capable of a compassionate regard for the weak, the guilty, the human species in general, the adolescent has to come to terms with the fact that her parents are not the omnipotent beings they were once imagined to be. During infancy, personal omnipotence (love of oneself) is traded off for the advantages of sharing in the glory and power we attribute to our parents. We suffer the comparison of our now demidivine proportions in exchange for the protection and love of the divine parents. During adolescence, in order to acquire real power and the generosity of spirit that nourishes our ethical ideals, we must become reconciled to the imperfections of our parents, particularly that parent on whom our major identifications have been founded.

The new identifications with friends, admired adults, cultural idols, social groups help a young woman to bear the narcissistic injury of recognizing that the woman on whom she has modeled her own self is far from a divine creature fashioned in heaven. In the final reckoning, however, it will be a woman's more humanized identifications with her mother (a young man's more humanized identifications with his father) that will secure the viability and vitality of her social values and sense of ethics. Until she becomes a full-fledged member of her own adult generation and has had to accommodate her ideals to the down-to-earth perplexities of parenting, to the serious business of earning a living and supporting herself or contributing to her family, to the idiosyncrasies of colleagues, mentors, and bosses, we cannot expect a young woman to be able to evaluate the full extent of her own assets and liabilities or to appreciate the surprising ways in which she closely resembles her mother.

Though the definitive reckoning waits until she assumes the reins of adult responsibility, a young woman might be a reliably self-observing, self-analytic person long before. The more her social order provides opportunities for friendship, love, meaningful work and study, political and social responsibility, real power and real success, the less she will rely on the cockiness and self-glorification that make her feel so much wiser and superior to her mother. An older adolescent sees herself through a less dazzling mirror. Because she now has some self-compassion, she is able to have more compassion for the frailties of others. As removal proceeds, the exaggeration of mother's negative traits is no longer so imperative. As her own identity, her sense of who she is *and* who she is not, consolidates and becomes less stridently independent, the young woman begins to be able to reappraise her mother for what she really is and is not.

The reappraisal of the mother (and father) is helped along by youth's respect for the dimensions of historical time. When she was a young teenager, the burst of pubescent growth, the wave of vitality that expanded every appetite and interest engendered a frightening but nevertheless exquisite sense of freedom. The younger adolescent imagined herself in a realm of infinite possibility. She could become woman or man, poet, actress, computer programmer, astronomer, astronaut, nurse, secretary, doctor, princess, scientist, novelist. She was about to become an entirely new person. Time could go on forever.

As adolescence draws to a close, possibilities narrow. The young woman looks around her and realizes that the social world she has inherited is imperfect. Society is not an all-caring, magical mother or a rescuer who fulfills dreams and wishes. For the first time she experiences the existential anxiety of living a unique but ordinary life, which threads between a finite moment of birth and a finite moment of death. Past, present, and future begin to be strung together by the young woman's narrative of her personal history. The historical accounts of heroes and heroines, divine beings, famous lovers, artists, scientists which had enthralled her as a child and young adolescent can no longer compete with the autobiographical inspirations that now infuse her imagination. Now that the past has loosed its hold on the present, the young woman can look back and reevaluate what once was. Her retrospective interpretations of the baby-mother-father that once was is informed by her more practical, down-to-earth visions of the future.

Her respect for the finitude of time, the historical continuity of the self she has become, her sense that however much she is the master of her personal destiny, necessity and the caprices of fortune cannot be controlled—these developments will open her eyes to the historical realities and tragic dimensions of her mother. Now Melpomene, who knows that a child cannot appreciate the tragic, speaks.

The mighty mother is flawed, undone by the very traits that were once regarded as saintly and heroic. But this was when the child had no critical faculties with regard to parental achievement and no way to evaluate the manner of parental survival. Now, in adolescence, the original sources of the parental strength come to be recognized for what they were: pride, competition, apprehension, scrupulosity, impulsiveness. Moreover, the mother is not proof against fortune or necessity any more or less than anyone else.

The young woman regards her mother with clearer eyes—with judgment and forbearance. She sees a person with the quota of strengths and weaknesses that ordinary flesh is heir to. Yet it will take a while for her to realize the many significant ways she is like her mother. The veneer of Madison Avenue, Wall Street, secretarial school, Radcliffe just barely disguises the Ohio Valley twang. And when she tempts her own child with the delights of mashed artichoke hearts, somehow her coaxing voice and shamelessly seductive "Yum, yum" sound just the way baby's grandmother used to sound so many years ago. Quite unconsciously the love dialogues of infancy have managed to survive, though consciously and selectively the young woman will emulate those qualities of her mother she has grown to admire. Her sense of historical reality allows her to pick and choose from all the different mothers her mother has been for her: the twinkle of hope from the mother of her babyhood, the courage to launch a new career from the mother of her latency years, the mother's steadfast convictions about right and wrong which never surrendered to her adolescent's withering disparagements, the loyalty and devotion to family which were always somewhere in sight.

Finding love objects and losing them, reenacting old dialogues, mourning the losses, immortalizing the past—these are some themes of the adolescent narrative. Other dominant themes involve the legends of narcissism. It is one of the paradoxes of human existence that the forward-moving spirit of conscience, our belief in the moral perfectibility of the human race, should be energized by narcissism. By dipping back into the self-centered ways of infancy, the adolescent remodels infantile narcissism and accommodates it to the future. The structures of the past will be loosened so that each of the three currents of narcissism—bodily love, self-esteem, omnipotence—may from then onward contribute its energies to the future.

8
NARCISSISM I
The Autoerotic Excursion

BIOLOGICAL INTERLUDE:
Puberty

The adolescent can epitomize all that is offensively narcissistic. Her self-aggrandizing manner is infuriating. Although
contemporary parents have been prepared for the self-
centeredness, rebellion, and other unpleasantness of the
adolescent years, the reality always comes as something of a
shock.

In contrast to the innocent charm of infantile narcissism,
which parents usually enjoy and sometimes encourage, the
adolescent brand of narcissism is alarming and intolerable.
The self-centered toddler has no real power after all. But the
reappearance of profound self-absorption in an adolescent—who is growing to look more adult each day, who is
verbally ingenious, mocking, and inconsiderate—is regarded with circumspection. Adolescent narcissism challenges a parent's self-esteem and power.

Also, the adolescent is reevaluating her parents. She is
taking stock of all the marvelous qualities she had attributed
to them in those innocent days when they were her only
source of self-esteem and security. She is reaching out now
to take back what she had no choice but to give. She is
attempting to recapture her (imagined) infantile self-sufficiency. Adolescent narcissism is more consequential, more
threatening than the infantile version. The adolescent who
is as big or bigger than her parents can even seem physically
threatening.

Why this intensification of narcissism during adolescence? As removal gets under way, sexual hunger is turned

away from the parents and redirected. For a time, until she is able to invest herself in a sexual relationship with another person, the adolescent becomes preoccupied with, nearly consumed by an interest in her own body.

The dramatic upsurge of circulating estrogens and androgens intensifies sexual desire and stimulates the erotogeneity of the skin surfaces and body orifices. These hormones also have the effect of lowering the usual barriers against erotic stimuli. So while the pubescent child is besieged by sights, sounds, words, odors, and tactile stimuli that arouse erotic thoughts and feelings, she is not yet emotionally or physically prepared for genital sexuality. Hence the infantile eroticism of sucking, soiling, torturing, being looked at, being forcibly penetrated flourish in her sexual fantasies. And in her everyday behavior the pubescent girl endows her body, her room, her clothes, her possessions, and the bodies and possessions of others with infantile erotic qualities: she is greedy, messy, mean, exhibitionistic, intrusive. The civilizing trends of early childhood and latency are reversed.

As alarming as such outlandish behavior is to parents, teachers, and others, it is no less distressing to the pubescent girl herself, who must struggle with the temptations of gluttony, theft, flaunting her body in public. A chance phrase, a fleeting odor, might overcome her resistance to masturbating. Such unpredictable upsurges of desire are totally devastating to the adolescent's self-esteem, because they represent a challenge to her sense of control over her body and her destiny.

She will try to counter such threats to her narcissism by the typical rescue operations of adolescence, which are themselves extravagantly self-centered: spending hours before the mirror inspecting and pruning bodily imperfections, leaving her clothes and room in disorder, arriving in a disheveled state for dinner, arriving late for dinner, forgetting altogether about family appointments. Such defiant and inconsiderate acts are an adolescent's way of saying to grown-ups (and to herself), "I can do whatever I want, when I want." But she doesn't believe that for very long. Although there is some momentary sense of power in exciting parental tempers and reducing parents to stammering incoherence, the seeming triumph of her omnipotence diminishes an adolescent's self-esteem in the long run. She really feels powerless and at the mercy of these compelling and bewildering infantile impulses. In other words, the ways the adolescent tries to restore her power and self-esteem are likely to be as infantile as the humiliations they are meant to assuage. Infantile modes of power assertion and self-esteem regulation, many of which had been given up or at least partially restrained during latency, now infiltrate the present and assume a primitive quality.

Another reason for the increased self-centeredness of an adolescent is her susceptibility to humiliation. This brazen, defiant creature is also something tender, raw, thin-skinned, poignantly vulnerable. Her entire sense of personal worth can be shattered by a frown. An innocuous clarification of facts can be heard as a monumental criticism.

Fantasies of omnipotence are the order of the day. These fantasies are expressed in the adolescent belief that nothing is impossible, that she can do anything, be anything she wishes, solve any problem in the world, that she has total power and control over herself and her environment. Her grandiosity operates boldly and unblinkingly in the context of not finishing much of what she starts, of recognizing that her wished-for self-image is never quite the way she imagined it, of being unable to stick to her bright morning resolutions: not to eat too much, not to be messy, not to masturbate, not to be mean, not to covet what others possess. In her fantasies and wishes she is omnipotent. In reality she suffers deeply from the sense that she has no power at all. Socially she's useless. Her inability to resist temptation makes her feel like a moral imbecile. The loftiness of her plans and speculations are commensurate with her impotence and inability to get anything done. Wild flights of imagination and soaring speculations hold the adolescent in the realm of limitless potentiality. Ideas of limitation, reining in, focusing, coming to grips with one's actual potentials can hardly be expected to compete with the immediate gratifications afforded by feelings of omnipotence.

Corresponding to these overvaluations of her personal power is the adolescent propensity for idealizing the thoughts, values, physical appearance, and philosophies of specially selected members of the adult world. The adolescent regression to bodily preoccupation and omnipotence is accompanied by her unqualified adoration and desperate imitation of idols. Only now the idols are not the parents. Sometimes the idols selected for worship are pure and saintly types who represent the adolescent's longing to be virtuous and self-sacrificing. At other times the adolescent will revere and glorify ruthless and seductive men and women who represent the temptations the adolescent is struggling against. The new heroines and heroes make an appeal because of their glamour, sexual prowess, wealth, or prominence in politics, art, science, crime. Although they are held up as models of advanced moral qualities, these idols are in fact revivals or repersonifications of the sexual, worldly, and moral powers the infant had once attributed to her parents. Now that the authority and values of the parents are being questioned, the adolescent seeks again in the external world models of perfection that she can identify with. The stringent conscience and ideals by which the civilized schoolchild measured herself are weakened considerably. They are replaced by what appear to be extremely superficial values. In truth, many of the ideals of the younger adolescent are merely in the service of self-aggrandizement. Raw and vulnerable, she feels worthwhile and powerful only through her association, real or fantasized, with those she worships.

Her walls and closet doors will be covered with posters, photographs, and other mementos of her current superheroes and -heroines. One sure way for parents to know that an adolescent is finally on her way to more realistic self-aspirations and less glorified moral standards will be the gradual clearing of the wall space in her bedroom. At the termination of puberty and into young adulthood a few of the treasured possessions will remain. One or two of the heroines will be immortalized. The rest will vanish without a trace. As alarming as adolescent narcissism often seems to be, it will become a powerful resistance to clinging to the past.

The adolescent frequently supposes that she is breaking out of the confines of her mundane, schoolgirl existence simply in order to break rules and defy authority. She sheds the "shoulds" and "should nots" of her schoolgirl conscience. She rids herself of the "oughts" and the "musts" that convert every minor infraction into a sin of omission or commission. It certainly does not occur to her or to her family that by questioning the moral standards she erected as a child she is taking the first steps in her journey toward a firmer, more reasonable, less harsh, more ethical form of conscience.

The dependent, cared-for, loved, obedient, moralistic child is growing into the skin of an independent, self-protecting adult.

From the barely detectable elevation of a girl's nipples at age ten and a half to her capacity to produce mature ova requires about five years of physical growth. In the best of circumstances it takes nearly a decade of her narcissism to grow up. Even after a young woman becomes less preoccupied with her own body and is able to fall in love with another person, the narcissistic basis of her first love affairs must give way to a perception of the differences between actuality and the ideal. In order for her to invest herself in an enduring sexual relationship she must, sooner or later, recognize that disappointment is the normal fate of all love relationships. This extremely painful recognition becomes tolerable only if, somewhere along the way, the young woman has been able to reconcile her dreams of glory with the life of feasible possibility.

In the interlude her parents hold their breath and pray. Without benefit of ritual, wavering in their own moral resolve, parents stand by in awe, intimidated, unsteadied by the immense grandiosity of their moral changeling. They cannot scarify her body with the wisdom of the ages. They cannot carve her into the kind of womanhood with which they are familiar. They cannot enclose her in a hut until the gale blows over. Her mythic heroines are, to the parents, bizarre and unfriendly strangers. Her cosmic journey is something altogether different from the one they remember. Parents try, sometimes successfully, to steer a firm course. The moral waters are muddy and treacherous. The parents shudder at the corruption they see around them. With barely a caution the child sheds her schoolgirl conscience and plunges in. Will she reemerge? When will she return? Will she be unrecognizable? Will she drown?

Before she reappears she will expend an enormous amount of narcissistic energy reveling with false idols, worshiping superficial values. She will compare herself with others and be consumed with envy, hatred, jealousy. She might even lapse disastrously into promiscuity, thievery, vandalism, drunkenness. At the same time, with her friends and companions, she will be kinder, more altruistic, goodnatured, generous, compassionate, high-spirited, passionate than she ever could have been before. She is both witch and saint. She frolics with the vices and expands her soul on infinite virtue. Out of the chrysalis of her narcissistic regression the adolescent emerges as a young adult prepared to judge, criticize, and finally decide for herself, on the basis of experiences extending beyond the confines of her childhood family nest, that she has intrinsic merit. She is not a law unto herself. But neither is she dependent on accolades and tribute to inform her about what is wrong and what is right. The watchful eyes and cautioning voices are hers, friendlier and less accusatory than those of her childhood—perhaps.

But first all three currents of narcissism move backward to their original sources: libido is concentrated on one's own body. Self-esteem is regulated by identifying with idealized others. And although the adolescent has not achieved anything real, she flaunts her powers and imagines herself back in the realm of limitless possibilities. As adolescence progresses, the past and the future contend for primacy. The currents of narcissism once again flow forward. At the start they move sluggishly, tentatively, with many backward movements along the way, and then, with a rush, as the stumbling, inept, confused, raw youth seems all of a sudden to have become an adult. Boys and girls arrive at puberty, and in a few more years they become the caregivers and lawgivers to the next generation. Before we know it the future is here.

Puberty

In females the first outward signs of pubescence are the downy pubic hairs, the barely detectable elevation of the nipples, and the breast budding that follows shortly thereafter.

Around the same time as the initial signs of breast budding, other changes are also set in motion by the cooperative action of the adrenal and ovarian estrogens. The development of the vagina, the pudendum (the mons pubis, labia majora, labia minora, the vaginal vestibule, and clitoris), the Bartholin glands, and the uterus begins.

Lactic acid-producing bacilli replace the previously scanty bacterial flora of the vagina. The vaginal mucus changes from the childhood pH of 6-7 to the adult pH of 4-5, an increase in acidity that is favorable to fertility. The primary structural change in the vagina will be the increase in the thickness of the vaginal epithelium and a depositing of glycogen in it, which creates an environment favorable to the lactic-acid bacillus. The vagina increases in breadth and length. The mucous surface of the vagina reddens.

There are considerable changes in the pudendum. Fatty tissue develops in the pudendum area, thickening the outer, larger lips of the labia and causing them to grow over the smaller, inner lips. At no other period of life are the outer lips so close. This feature, combined with the rapid growth and fat accumulation on the hips and thighs, keeps the introitus and the vulva hidden.

The triangular apex of the small inner lips will protrude slightly and change from pink to a darker, brownish hue.

The pubertal growth of the clitoris is relatively about equal proportionately to the growth of the penis. And like the nipple and penis, the clitoris acquires the power of erectility. The Bartholin glands increase in size and produce a mucoid substance on excitation of the clitoris and other parts of the pudendum. This mucus lubricates the pudenda during masturbation, petting, and coitus.

The uterus, which is tucked into the pelvic cavity, grows almost threefold from its childhood size. Estrogen stimulation of the pubis and the lower part of the pelvis causes the pelvic cavity to tip forward and its neck to grow relatively shorter. As the uterus accommodates to the changing shape of the pelvis, its contours will change from cylindrical to pear-shaped. At the same time the uterine tubes grow longer and more opened. The thickness of the endometrium, the lining of the uterus, will increase greatly. As pubescence proceeds, the cells of the endometrium become more differentiated.

The time of the first shedding of the endometrium or *menarche* occurs at around thirteen years in the average American. The first menstrual cycles are anovulatory and irregular. At puberty, under stimulation of FSH, one egg-containing follicle will mature at each cycle. The released ovum passes into the Fallopian tube to await fertilization. The follicle lining, under stimulation of LH, forms the corpus luteum, an ovarian structure of about 1–1.5 centimeters. In the event of pregnancy, the corpus luteum enlarges. It will secrete progesterone, which helps to support the pregnancy. If fertilization does not occur, the corpus luteum for that ovum degenerates, leaving a scar tissue. It is believed that females do not achieve full reproductive capacity until the early- to mid-twenties.

In males the first outward sign of pubescence is the enlargement of the testes and scrotum. As the testes enlarge they secrete testosterone, which stimulates the growth of the penis.

Concomitantly with the growth of the penis the prostate enlarges and develops. It is situated just below the neck of the bladder, at the base of the penis. From a tiny, podlike structure, the prostate grows to the size and shape of a chestnut. Before pubescence the prostate consists only of ducts that terminate in buds. These buds are the growing points of future cells that are responsible for the secretion of seminal fluid. The rapid growth of the secreting cells is responsible for the increase in size of the prostate. At the time of the emission of semen, the prostate ejects a thin, milky, alkaline fluid into the urethra. This fluid provides the major liquid portion of the semen. Its alkalinity balances the acidity of the emissions from the seminal vesicles.

The two seminal vesicles lie above the prostate. They are expanded portions of the vas deferens, the duct that connects them to the testes. The cavities of the seminal vesicles serve as storehouses for the sperm from the testes. The walls of the vesicles are glandular cells that contribute the nutriment seminal fluid.

The other organ besides the testes, prostate, and seminal vesicles that may contribute to the composition of the ejaculate are the tiny Cowper's glands, which are believed to be analogous to the Bartholin glands in women and which lie behind the scrotum, at the base of the penis. The clear and slippery Cowper's-gland liquid is a preejaculatory mucus, which may exude from the urethral opening at the tip of the penis anytime during sexual arousal.

At the height of sexual arousal, contractions in the ducts of the testes and vas deferens cause expulsion of sperm into the urethra. The sperm then mix with the alkaline prostate fluids, the seminal fluid, and the mucus from the Cowper's glands. Together these products make up the semen that is discharged as ejaculate during orgasm.

The time of first ejaculation of seminal fluid, or *thorache,* occurs at around fourteen years in the average American. Nonspermatic emissions have usually preceded this event by several years. It will be another three or four years before the sperm are fully mature and the semen has an adult composition. It is likely that the onset of male fertility coincides with an increase in volume and a change in the consistency of the seminal fluid along with a sensed intensification of the ejaculatory spasms. Maximum fertility will not be reached until the early- or mid-twenties.

In the interval between giving up the love objects of infancy and finding an adult love dialogue, sexual hunger reverts to one's own body. Masturbation, the relief of sexual hunger through genital manipulation, occupies a crucial place in adolescent life. Masturbation is a way of linking infantile fantasy life with the life of actual fulfillment.

The literature on the subject of adolescent masturbation is almost exclusively on the male experience and male masturbation fantasies. It is believed that complete suppression of masturbation is a far more frequent occurrence in girls than in boys. This belief is buttressed by the theory that only a girl with a strongly bisexual constitution—"the active, rather than passive type"—will find it difficult to renounce masturbation. It is said that the more typical, passive girl will succeed in her struggle with masturbation. The view that nice girls do not actively seek erotic gratification, that they must be seduced into sexuality, is evident in most scientific discussions of adolescent masturbation.

According to statistical studies, adolescent boys achieve first orgasm by way of masturbation, whereas most girls achieve their first orgasms during sex play or petting. Almost all males reported masturbating during the adolescent years. Yet only about half the females studied report having masturbated. Moreover, when girls do masturbate, the frequency is considerably less than in boys.

On the other hand, more incisive clinical studies of the adolescent years reveal that most girls do masturbate and that in fact they achieve their first orgasms through masturbation. Though it is true that girls masturbate far less frequently than boys, they struggle with the temptation to masturbate no less than boys do. The significant dynamic issues are the adolescent's lonely and valiant struggles with masturbatory temptation and the eventual victory or defeat of genital desire. This does not mean that boys and girls have identical experiences with regard to masturbation or, for that matter, with any sexual experience. Their sexual fantasies are different. And so are their attitudes toward their genitals. For one thing, adolescent boys live with the reality of their erections, which are visible and difficult to control. This fact alone leads to uniquely male experiences of pride and humiliation. The penis is often regarded as a "thing" that has a life of its own.

Masturbating for a boy, then, is a way not only of experiencing sexual excitement but also of coping with the penis—controlling it. No doubt these ambivalent attitudes toward the penis contribute to the greater frequency of masturbation in males. Girls are far more secretive about their masturbatory activities, and they are more uncertain about the physical location of their erotic responses. But both sexes are reluctant to discuss their masturbation fantasies with anyone, even those trusted peers and adults to whom they might confide all else. Most of the information about the fantasies that accompany masturbation comes from clinical vignettes, novels, poetry, erotic art, and literature.

Despite the knowledge that almost all boys masturbate and that probably the majority of girls do also, many adults still regard onanism as an aberration—a breeding place for mental disorder and morbid physical conditions. Even among psychoanalysts, who were the first doctors and psychologists to seriously investigate the fantasy life associated with autoerotic behavior, masturbation continues to evoke mixed reactions.

In 1912 the Vienna Psychoanalytic Society published its symposium on onanism. The discussants were in agreement that the most significant set of issues concerned the fantasies that accompany masturbation. They concurred that it is primarily these fantasies and not the physical act itself that arouse shame and guilt reactions. The major disagreements in the symposium centered around the question "Are masturbatory activities in themselves physically or psychologically harmful?" Freud answered that question in the affirmative. The toxic effects of inadequately discharged instinctual energy could create a nucleus for psychoneurosis. Excessive masturbation produced symptoms of depletion—neurasthenia, constipation, headaches, fatigue. The anxiety states that led to these symptoms were a direct outcome of undischarged "coitus excitation."

Contemporary psychoanalysts do not subscribe to the toxic hypothesis. What they perceive as the primary danger of adolescent masturbation is that it might cement infantile sexual fixations. The return from fantasy back to reality, they believe, is made more difficult by the pleasures of masturbation. On the other hand, some psychoanalysts, especially those who have investigated the issues of adolescent narcissism, are tending to regard the masturbatory activities of adolescent boys and girls as potentially beneficial. Rather than representing an unhealthy fixation to forepleasure, genital masturbation and the forepleasure fantasies that accompany it can provide a feasible link between infantile desires and adult genital sexuality.

We could expect that, insofar as masturbation represents an aspect of narcissism and a preference for fantasy gratification over participation in the real world, it would be regarded as threatening to the needs of the larger social community. The magnitude of the taboos against masturbation is also a reflection of the ambivalence of adults toward not-yet-adult persons and toward sexuality in general.

With the advent of the industrial age and its requirements for a prolonged apprenticeship period between childhood and adulthood, adolescence became a phenomenon to be seriously reckoned with. The adolescent began to be thought of as the seed of the future, the hope of the human race. At the turn of the century in the United States and in western Europe the adolescent masturbator was therefore regarded with horror and suspicion. It was characteristic of sexual attitudes to think of masturbation as the plague of young men, while menstruation was viewed as the source of female insanity, neurasthenia, hysteria, fainting spells, criminality. Writers seldom mentioned the phenomenon of female masturbation. *Menarche* was viewed as the analog to *thorache,* the first menstruation as the parallel to the first seminal ejaculation. Then, as now, the incest taboo was directed primarily to the male, whose powerful body, seed, and sexual organs were viewed as the major threats to the social order. As always, the threat from the female was found in the dark mysteries of the monthlies and the suspicions and fears with which the recesses and insides of the female body are regarded. The father represented law and the social order, the no-saying principle of conscience. The regressive pulls to the mother and to things female were and still are understood as an undermining of law and order, society, nature, the cosmos.

The dread of adolescent masturbation at the turn of the twentieth century is attested to by the millions of pitiful letters received by quacks and sexual reformers from young men who were terrified by their involuntary emissions and by their losing battle with masturbation. In 1895 a single New York "broker" had acquired three million confidential letters written by boys and men to advertising medical companies and doctors. One typical youth "of good heredity" decided not to go to college, for he was ruined and must soon become insane. Another told the tale of having purchased a revolver. He planned, after a visit to his mother, to shoot himself if some relief for his torments could not be provided. Another always carried a strong cord in his pocket, awaiting the blessed day when he might muster the courage to hang himself.

Not infrequently the involuntary emissions and other typical adolescent growth phenomena were imagined to be damages that occurred as a result of the forbidden masturbatory acts. The quacks, whether because of similar innocence or informed guile, made certain to reinforce the body-damage theory in their circulars and recommendations.

The pamphlets and advertisements listed a mass of symptoms that could result from masturbation. Many were merely the wide range of normal variation in the male sexual organs: unequal descent and pendancy of the testes, laxity and pigment changes of the scrotum, position of the foreskin, length of the penis. Changes in vascularity of the scrotum were attributed to onanism, as were bad dreams, skin blotches, bashfulness, lascivious thoughts. Every detail of every organ might be described as a symptom of onanistic debility.

Bromides, tonics, and bread pills were the order of the day. They were recommended equally by reputable doctors and quacks. The reputable medical cures included ergots, blistering, section of certain nerves, circumcision. The quacks sold millions of bottles of Sexine tablets, Nerve Seed, Paris Vital Sparks, which promised both virility and abstention on the same package. Recommended for winding around the unruly penis were all manner of mechanical devices of rubber, wire, springs. Catheters and tubes of great variety were recommended for insertion in the penis. Many of these apparatuses were sold at exorbitant prices. Companies made fortunes on the sale of electric belts and suspension apparatuses. Ironically, it turned out that these apparatuses stimulated intense erotic fantasies. The patent office in Washington was deluged with proposals of mechanical apparatuses that cured onanism.

G. Stanley Hall stated: "One of the very saddest of all the aspects of human weakness and sin is onanism." However, as a sincere champion of youth, G. Stanley Hall condemned the scare tactics. He recommended instead plain talk and moral candor in dealing with the sin of onanism. Hall made detailed studies of the vice and found himself forced to admit that "wherever researches have been undertaken, the results are appalling as to prevalence and suggest that the Occident has little, if any, advantage over the sad records of the Orient, and that civilized man is on the whole, to say the least, no better, if not far worse, in this respect than his savage brother." Later Hall further admitted that "all we know points to the conclusion that it is far more common among civilized than among savage races."

As he set about investigating the causes of onanism, Hall stated his conviction that precocious mental development or too much psychic and not enough physical expression could be the major stimulant. The habit was very greatly favored by the sitting position. A long convalescence, piles, habitual constipation, idleness, laziness, weakness of will, and heredity factors could also play a considerable role in aggravating the insidious disease that acted upon "human nature like a worm upon fruit in producing premature ripeness and activity of the reproductive function." Springtime, he felt, was particularly dangerous, as was a warm climate or improper clothes, rich food, indigestion, nervousness, prolonged sitting, sitting cross-legged, spanking, too monotonous walking, straining of the memory. Hall went on: "In bright, nervous children, pubescence often dawns with almost fulminating intensity and sudden necessity and sweeps the individual into pernicious ways long before moral or even intellectual restraints are operative. Excessive danger here is one of the penalties man pays for that inestimable tool of his development on to the human plane—the hand."

In considering the results of onanism, Hall was reassuring. The brain will not be drained away. Dementia, idiocy, palsy, and sudden death are not imminent. The most common danger, he emphasized, is a sense of unworthiness, sin, and pollution, which takes away the joy of life and plunges the victim into utter despair. Yet, in all moral earnestness, Hall could not bring himself to condone self-abuse. He devoted himself to returning joy to youth by joining the battle against "the influences that seem to spring from the prince of darkness in his abode."

Although he recognized that the mental diseases resulting from onanism were not as serious as generally believed, Hall thought there could be direct connections between onanism and decline in physical health. According to Hall, spermine $(C5, H14, N2)$, for example, played a role in removing the products of bodily decomposition. Therefore, loss of spermine could be connected with the loss of concentration of albumin, lecithin, peptones. Loss of spermine could drain the body of vitality and lead to neurasthenia, optical cramps, intensification of the patellar reflex, purple and dry skin, lassitude and flaccidity, dry cough, clammy hands.

As for the moral effects of masturbation, Hall cited lying,

secretiveness, hypocrisy, timidity, cowardice, egoism, frivolity. With respect to the moral life, pity and sympathy for others was extinguished. "The masturbator's heart is weak like his voice." And apart from the moral and intellectual spheres, growth is stunted. There appear early signs of decrepitude and senescence—gray hairs, baldness, a stooping and enfeebled gait.

To prevent the disasters of masturbation and also to help to relieve the mental and physical tortures of the adolescent onanist, Hall humanely prescribed not the bromides or mechanical apparatuses more generally recommended by the less informed but devotion to the Christian life and a number of simple hygienic precautions. Cold, he said, is one of the best of all checks on onanistic excess. Cold washing without wiping has special advantages. The proper alimentation is milk, bread, cereals, and vegetables that are rich in protein and phosphorus. Little meat should be eaten except as it helped to provide salt for the skeleton, albumin for the muscles, fat for respiration. Of course, eggs, venison, aromas, coffee, and alcohol would serve only as exacerbations of already dangerous dispositions. Plenty of exercise, emulation, and rivalry were good.

Trousers should not be too highly drawn up by suspenders. They should be kept loose and lax. The irritation otherwise caused would act as a constant stimulus and temptation. Undergarments should be loose and not binding. All postures, automatisms, and habits that cause friction should be discouraged. Pockets should be placed well to the side and not too deep and should not be kept full. Habitually keeping the hands in the pockets should be discouraged. Hall mused that perhaps it might be best for boys to wear pants that open only at the sides.

Beds should be rather hard, the covering light. Too soft a bed leads to sensuous luxury and temptations to remain too long abed after awakening. Boys who lie abed late are not certain to be masturbators, but the habit of rising early is best for eyes, nerves, and morals. Each adolescent should have at least a bed for himself if not a room. But the room should not be too remote or too secluded from adult observation.

For the ultimate in good mental hygiene Hall proposed: "The ideals of chastity are perhaps the very highest that can be held up to youth during this ever lengthening probationary period. This is the hard price that man has to pay for full maturity. Idleness and the protected life of students increase temptation, so does overfeeding which also increases sterility, so that the enjoyment and the power of effective parenthood which God and nature united part company and at a certain variable period become inversely as each other."

Though he was a better-natured man and better meaning than most commentators on the problem of onanism, it is clear that Hall associated masturbation with the backsliding of the human race and an undermining of the Christian way of life. Hall was a first-rate psychologist, yet on this subject his evangelical tone is quaint and at times amusing. What he failed to understand was that, like any other feature of adolescence—idealizations, defiances, crushes—masturbation could as well advance as arrest the process of growing up. The problem is not masturbation as a general activity but rather its function in each individual case. Thus while there is something intuitively of merit in Hall's view that the adolescent requires a postponement of involvement with the forms of adult sexuality, Hall failed to appreciate that masturbation could be a hedge against precocious genitality. In fact, he apparently could not appreciate any form of sexuality that was unrelated to procreation and family life, and in this view he shared much of the official morality of his times.

Psychoanalysts have come to appreciate that what is crucial about masturbation is not the practice in general but the role it plays in the issues of adolescence. Thus masturbation can sometimes serve regression and impede the forward-moving aspects of adolescent development. By its very purpose of providing intense erotic pleasures without any of the conflicts attendant on relating to another person, masturbation can entrench the conservative, regressive tendencies that are so easily reinstated in a human history. Masturbation can become an indispensable, habitual regulator of tension. Masturbation and the accompanying fantasies can perpetuate the dominance of infantile sexuality. Masturbation may assume pathological proportions by consolidating rather than loosening and reorganizing infantile sexual modes.

When infantile fixations are consolidated, an adolescent forgoes the challenges of sexual rivalry. A boy's passive longings toward his father, which frequently culminate in a desire to take the mother's place with the father, can be reinforced through the masturbation fantasy. In the usual unconscious masturbatory fantasies that express these longings the boy pretends he has no penis so that he will not be regarded as dangerous. Fantasies of renouncing the penis may then go on to represent an even further retreat from genital sexuality. The boy desires only to be cared for, fondled, caressed, fed, cleaned, have his buttocks spanked, be given an enema or be breast-fed by a maternal figure. In an adult such fantasies foster a preoccupation with wishes to be passively indulged and cared for. He will expect and demand maternal protection and attention of the social environment itself. He will be unable to accept the sober necessities of independent existence. In order to be assured of gratification of his passive longings he willingly subjugates himself to any indignity his protectors might demand. He is slavishly dutiful to the powerful idol in whose emanating radiance he basks. The ideals by which he measures himself are the grandiose ideals of an infant. The watchful eyes and no-saying voices make sure that his passive gratifications have sufficient punishment in them to assuage any sense of inner shame and guilt. His social and moral lives are as infantile as his sexual life.

A young woman has no reason to reckon with others for a sexual partner when she finds all sources of pleasure within herself. She is not required to engage the problems of the anatomical differences between the sexes. She is not required to give pleasure or to tune her sexual rhythms and excitements to those of a love partner. In her masturbation fantasies she can be all things, both mouth and breast, both anus and penetrating object. She is not required, then, to solve the conflicts between passivity and activity, giving and receiving, which are priorities on the agenda for growing up. The adolescent agenda contains the problem of how the child who has been the cared-for one and the obeyer of the laws goes on to become a caregiver and a lawgiver. If an adolescent cannot learn how to get along without the old dialogues, then a primitive moral life prevails. Frightened by the possible frustrations and conflicts of independent existence, a girl might surrender her rights to genitality *and* moral authority. In her masturbation fantasies she can be both slave and master. In her relations to others she is like a helpless infant who imagines that she must sacrifice love in order to feel powerful and renounce power in order to feel loved.

To the extent that the masturbation fantasy represents an emotional surrender to the past, a passive surrendering of the body to the mother or the father, the masturbatory act becomes an expression of hatred toward the genitals and the genital self. Masturbation becomes linked to the wrath of a primitive conscience. It becomes difficult to integrate personal sexual desire with the requirements of the social order.

As with all other regressive activities of adolescence, and especially with those that reflect the inevitable temporary regression from love dialogues to narcissism, masturbation may become an expression of conflictual impasse. Or it may become symptomatic of a perverse attraction to infantile sexual gratifications. Or it may sponsor the substitution of fantasy existence for living in the real world: "I can just play at life; I don't have to live it." On the other hand, it may advance the forward thrust of development. Typically, for a time it combines in varying degrees all of such possibilities.

When the infantile attractions are too insistent, masturbation becomes yet another way of perpetuating outgrown modes of loving and hating. It becomes another form of emotional surrender, another detour from the path to adult sexuality. The gliding deeper and deeper into fantasy, the longings for passive gratification, the falling in love with one's own genitals, or the exclusive interest in the genitals of others prevents any emotional or physical investment in a real person.

When autoeroticism traces along these paths, however, it is merely one symptom among many of a generalized pathological trend and never *the cause* of the regression. The regression and the special path it has taken have been set in motion by the conflicts that surround adolescent removal and mourning *and* by fixations and arrests that originated in the infantile period. In fact, adolescent masturbation can advance development by allowing the still-emerging adult person to lay claim to her new body and to become familiar with the intricacies of genital arousal and discharge. It is one way of rescuing her body from childhood dependencies. As she removes herself from the caresses and tender gazes of her parents, the adolescent learns to love and understand her own body independently.

The adolescent is saying "This body is mine. I am in charge of where, how, and when gratification takes place." At the same time, the fantasies associated with genital arousal and discharge can bring the pubescent girl into the beginnings of a connection with the genital organs of the opposite sex. In her masturbation fantasies—which are primarily pictorial, with some accompanying verbal scenarios —the girl is both self and other. The self and the other are also disguised versions of the parents. In early pubescence the coital scenarios are versions of what a young child might imagine to be going on between her parents. Since she has been excluded from the reciprocities of genital-to-genital dialogue, what she has seen and heard or not seen and not heard of the mysterious goings-on between her parents will be translated into those erotic excitements she has participated in—being suckled, spanked, looked at, forcibly held down, thrown in the air and then caught in the nick of time.

It is not until puberty proper that the decision begins to

be made as to which are the permitted and which are the forbidden aspects of infantile desire. As the boy or girl approaches puberty, infantile versions of sexual behavior are gradually replaced by fantasies involving genital arousal and discharge. In contrast to latency and early pubescent masturbation fantasies, the fantasies of puberty contain images of partners engaged in genital coitus. The story line includes selected forepleasure possibilities, but these are subsumed under the theme of having mature genitals with a possibility of full genital discharge. Occasionally the fantasies are prolonged daydreams that resemble short stories.

Masturbation is a private sexual action, in which genitality acquires emotional meaning in the safety of one's private thoughts. It is a trial action, a way of testing which sexual thoughts, feelings, and gratifications are acceptable, which are not, which ones may or may not participate in genitality. Each adolescent will create a private arrangement in which infantile forepleasures and genital discharge become connected.

Genital masturbation is a phase-specific adolescent sexual activity that gradually divests the forepleasures of their independent erotic aims and progressively relegates these aims to arousal and initiatory roles. The genitals become the organs of discharge and consummation. As a physical act, genital masturbation is devoid of actual forepleasure. Nevertheless, in the fantasies there is the potential to represent every variety of forepleasure. Simultaneously, masturbatory activity encourages the eroticization of the testes, prostate, penis and clitoris, labia, and vaginal vestibule. Through masturbation, childhood wishes are tested in the context of having mature genitals. The final fully elaborated central masturbation fantasy contains the permitted infantile satisfactions and the main genital sexual identifications. Abstention from masturbation impedes the integration of infantile desires with genital desire and encourages an attitude of puritanical joylessness with regard to coitus.

In contrast to masturbation, early heterosexual activity can interfere with the rich elaborations of the erotic life, the slow work of fantasy that integrates infantile love-desires with adult genitality. Premature heterosexual performance often represents a personal dread of the regressive pulls of infantile sexual hunger—the horror that one will not be able to resist surrendering the body to the mother or father, the terror of homosexuality and perversion.

The growth spurt in general and especially the maturation of the genitalia are, for the boys and girls undergoing these physical changes, spectacular events that capture their attention and imagination. As the boy approaches puberty he is preoccupied with watching his penis and testicles grow in volume and in length, his scrotum becoming looser and more pigmented. His erections are becoming more frequent and they last longer. There is an increasing capacity for larger amounts of ejaculate in more frequent succession, events that are greeted with pride but also with an awesome fear of genital damage. These emotionally contradictory reactions create a kind of cyclical involvement with the genitals. Castration fears stimulate masturbatory impulses for reassurance, which then exacerbate castration fears. The boy is on guard, struggling to fend off temptation. Yet the sexual excitement seems to strike out of nowhere—like lightning. Genital arousal is frequent and intense, easily stimulated by a wide variety of images and thoughts, demanding immediate ejaculation and release. The long, careful masturbation rituals of latency and early pubescence are brought into conflict with the new wish to come as quickly as possible.

The ritual lubrications of the penis and planning for the disposal of the ejaculate, which had helped the younger boy to delay arousal and discharge, are obstacles to the wish for immediate gratification. The painful sensations of the full, hard penis during delays of discharge heighten the hypochondriacal fears that are so much a part of adolescent existence. The boy is peripherally aware of throbbings in the head, the frantic acceleration of heartbeat and breathing rate, feeling hot all over, the shrinking and hardening of his scrotum. As the orgastic rhythm accelerates and climaxes, the excitement is all-encompassing and entirely different from the ritualized, conventional, more controllable, less intense masturbation experiences of the latency years. Orgasm now brings dramatic relief but also intense letdown. The boy frequently interprets the ensuing lassitude as having drained his body of vital fluids and energy.

As her nipples grow firm and begin to project from the areola and breast mound, the pubescent girl experiences nipple erections. At times she may try to conceal her nipples under loose-fitting clothes. At other times she proudly exhibits them by wearing a tight-fitting sweater or blouse. She is preoccupied with perspiration odors, acne, the fat on her hips and thighs, the downy hairs on her legs, her underarm hairs. Even before she begins to menstruate, the pubescent girl becomes aware of the heightened eroticization of her clitoris, labia, vulva. Her masturbatory techniques during early pubescence are efforts to unite these more available erotic sensations with the mysterious sensations from the introitus. Thigh pressure and pressure on the pubic area are masturbatory techniques that attempt to unify the external genitalia and internal genital sensations. Fantasies of forced penetration of the introitus frequently accompany these techniques, but very few girls actually penetrate or enter the introitus with their fingers or other objects. Vaginal masturbation is rare, and when it does occur it is a temporary phenomenon.

When her ovulatory cycles begin, the uterine contractions and the chunks of tissue and blood awaken fears of being torn to bits, of having the inside of the body destroyed. In order to control these fears a girl might defensively attack her external genitals and try to enter the introitus during masturbation. Instead of passively submitting to the feared attack on her insides, she becomes the attacker. Soon afterward, as these initial fears abate, the girl usually returns to the more familiar and gentler methods of thigh tensing and voluntary contractions of pelvic muscles and sphincter. Pressure on the whole genital area with some direct stimulation of the clitoris and nipples become the central mastur-

batory techniques. But now these methods are used to prolong genital excitation and discharge, to experience the
gradual mounting of genital excitation, to shut off discharge, to begin again.

More varied forepleasure fantasies, such as seductions by
being looked at, sucked, and caressed, supplement those of
rape and forced penetration. But the rape fantasy is not discarded. It is amplified by other forepleasures.

The maintenance of a degree of continuous genital excitation is important to a girl's sense of control over her body.
The continuity of excitation helps to counteract fears that
her insides might fall out or be destroyed during the act of
intercourse. Occasionally this generalized low level of genital excitation mounts and becomes intense enough to produce a series of spontaneous orgasms. A frightening state of
nothingness, depletion, emptiness may follow such involuntary discharges. These alarming experiences of depletion
are also frequent aftermaths of the controlled masturbatory
discharges, particularly when they are especially intense
and pleasurable. The sense of depletion then creates a need
to be revived by outside stimulation. The girl becomes
hungry for sensation. She seeks thrills. She engages in dangerous activities. She becomes seductive with family
members and friends. She flirts, teases, and exhibits her
body. When her sexual advances are responded to in kind,
the girl withdraws. In general, her masturbatory efforts are
geared toward maintaining sexual excitation on a foreplay
level, inhibiting discharge as long as possible, and avoiding
the dangerous penetration.

Heterosexual petting and coital relations between pubescent boys and girls are bound to be fraught with tension.
The girl resents and fears the speed and freedom of the boy's
rapid discharge. The boy is confused and angered by the
girl's preference for foreplay excitation and slow, mounting
excitement. Both boys and girls are plagued by alternating
bouts of genital excitement and feelings of lassitude and
nothingness deriving from their masturbation conflicts.

Their comprehensions of the connections between foreplay and genital discharge are still uncertain. Unless they are pressured into early sexual competition and performance by peers and parents, or by certain prevailing social trends, young pubescent boys and girls will limit their sexual activities to mild petting that involves kissing and close body contact while fully dressed. It is the girl's hesitancy and fear of penetration that sets the limits to these sexual encounters and subdues the boy's sexual aggression. Most pubescent boys are relieved by the setting of these limits—even though they are angered by the insult to their masculine prowess and physically pained by the necessity to inhibit ejaculation. These early heterosexual relationships rarely lead to orgasm.

Heterosexual sex play will help the adolescent to become more familiar with the genitals and sexual rhythms of the opposite sex. Through these first sexual relationships boys and girls gain a tentative sense of reality about genital activity. They contrast these experiences with their masturbation fantasies. Nevertheless there are barriers stemming from the emotional differences between pubescent boys and girls which prevent the kind of true intimacy and mutual caring that will optimally develop later. Even after puberty proper, when petting becomes more elaborate and may lead to orgasm, boys use these sexual encounters to bolster their fragile sense of masculinity. They are resentful of any dependency needs. They are ashamed and fearful of any longings to be mothered or cared for. Girls, on the other hand, already yearn for dependency and prolonged intimacy. A boy wants real action and quick discharge. Sometimes a girl would just as soon think about true romance, fantasize about sexual fulfillment, elaborate her fantasies, which frequently involve caring and being cared for by a love partner.

During pubescence boys and girls seem to arrive at the most satisfactory emotional relationship to their emerging adult bodies by dealing with excitement and discharge in the privacy of their personal masturbatory activities and fantasies. After arrival at puberty proper, petting and petting to orgasm gradually supplement masturbation as the major forms of sexual arousal and discharge. Yet the masturbation itself continues to provide a certain degree of body-mind integration and a large degree of erotic pleasure. Its aftermath is guilt, anxiety about body damage, and the shame of once again not having been strong enough to resist. The ongoing fantasies continue to embody overtones of grandiosity and omnipotence. The aftereffects, however, are feelings of inferiority and self-accusations for the shameful thoughts and images.

Total absence of masturbation during adolescence indicates an inability to deal with erotic drives. In the mind of the adolescent, however, yielding to masturbatory urges signifies that she is ruled by sexual hunger and not in control of her body. The inner struggle against masturbation operates on its own and needs no external reminders of precautionary taboos. The conflict sponsors progressive development in that it results in a victory. The adolescent does not immediately or permanently achieve an ultimate victory over masturbation, but bodily love does achieve a victory over the archaic conscience. Some of the sexual prohibitions that arose during the construction of the infantile conscience are softened. Eventually masturbation, with the fantasies that accompany it and the inner conflicts they engender, helps the adolescent to lay claim to her body and herself as a lovable and loving adult who is entitled to the full expression of genitality. A grown-up version of the sexual act permits the expression of previously forbidden aspects of infantile sexual hunger.

For better or worse, contemporary adolescents, lacking the formal and consistent regulations of traditional societies, must reckon alone with their longing to return to infantile modes of being loved. Through her fantasy elaborations of the infantile love dialogues, an adolescent prepares herself for genital love; she has the opportunity to test the flexibility of her sexual responses. Will I give in to what I desire but must not allow? Am I permitted to become an adult, with adult genitals? Must I renounce my body and the sensations coming from it in order to be allowed to become an adult? Am I helpless in the face of my longing to return to the past? Am I in charge of my love fantasies or am I overwhelmed by them? Do my pubic hairs and breasts represent abnormality? Sinfulness? Which forepleasures may I enjoy when participating in sexual union with another person? Which must be relegated to fantasy? Which of my infantile pleasures must be renounced entirely? Is genitality permitted only if I refuse to suck, look, bite?

The masturbation fantasy is a lonely and courageous attempt to understand one's body, to love or hate one's own self and body in a controlled and organized way in an imaginary relationship to another person. By this means the adolescent slowly becomes able to love an actual person physically by lending the variety of infantile pleasures— looking, biting, touching, licking, fondling, sucking, caressing—to mutual genital contact.

9
NARCISSISM II
Ars Erotica *and Dreams of Glory*

Hall's suspicions of springtime and the erotic arousals of too much imagining, lying abed, luxurious slow walking, even the fit of clothing, are not without justification. However, much as such stimulants might lure an adolescent toward onanism, they also lure her into sexual union with another person. An adolescent's first love relationships are born of springtime, the morning time, the twilight time, the erections of her nipples, the insistent rubbing of her clothing against her soft, round, fleshy thighs as she strolls luxuriously down the street. Virtually everything conspires to bring her body into contact with the body of the boy of her dreams.

In their early teens most boys and girls are becoming familiar with their changing bodies, their genitals and emerging secondary sex characteristics. Girls are adjusting to the cyclical changes; boys are learning how to control or not control their erections. Masturbation conflicts are at their height. Boys are striving desperately to assert their masculinity; girls are trying to reconcile their femininity with their love for their mothers. Both sexes are struggling to resist the pull to the caregiving mother. Sex play between girls and boys is limited to "making out"—mild necking and petting—and it is still primarily masturbatory in spirit—that is, the eroticism is an attempt to become accustomed to the sensations aroused by one's own genitals.

This unsettling phase of expansive growth and self-preoccupation of pubescence is followed by the phase of clarification and integration brought on by puberty. Male-female gender differences and the differences between childhood and adult physical and emotional characteristics become more firmly settled and clearly delineated. Facial features, hair distribution, and body shape are adult in appearance. About 50 percent of adolescent boys have become adult in the physical sense at age seventeen. By twenty-one almost all boys have reached sexual maturity. By nineteen or twenty most girls have regular ovulatory cycles and have for several years been looking and behaving more like women. It is during puberty that the secondary sex characteristics of the opposite sex begin to become associated with mating desires, with longings for enduring love relationships, genital sexuality, procreation. Puberty is the springtime of childhood, the gateway to adulthood.

Traditionally and in nature it is the time known as the mating season. "In the spring a livelier iris changes on the burnished dove;/In the spring a young man's fancy lightly turns to thoughts of love." Life overflows with new colors. The air is filled with songs. New appendages appear on the bodies of animals heralding the season—combs, horns, erectile hairs, crests, nuptial plumage. Goats and apes develop beards. The glowworm acquires its love-light. The grass and air are resplendent with odors and noises. Insects buzz and stridulate. Birds open their wings to display their brilliant colors; the wings drum and rattle. Mammals strut and frolic. The animal world is consumed with the performance of love antics, love calls, love dances—the *ars erotica* of springtime.

Adolescents fall into a continuity with all this by exaggerating and modifying their sexual characteristics. The *ars erotica* of all humankind includes body mutilations, tattooing, shaving the hair or letting it grow as long as possible.

Each sex is keenly aware of and aroused by the secondary sex characteristics of the other: nipples, breasts, broad shoulders, narrow drooping shoulders, long lashes, arched narrow brows, hairy chest, downy arms and legs, dimples, prominent eyes, narrow slanted eyes, husky voices, sweet and lilting voices, lisps, dialects, rising inflections, curly hair, short frizzy hair, the tiny earlobe, the curve of the pinky finger, the arch of the foot. The diversity of erotogenic signals in the human species is endlessly variable.

This variability is enhanced by the long period of dependency on a mother and father with their own unique erotogenic displays—the special pouts, frowns, gestures, ways of laughing, crying, voice inflections, postures, walking strides, eye shape, hair color and texture.

From the vast array of human erotogenic possibilities a young woman will select which parts of her body to exhibit or conceal, exaggerate or diminish, decorate, mutilate—which gestures, frowns, postures, voice inflections; which ways of making up her face and wearing her hair. These will become the leitmotifs of her unique *ars erotica*.

The social order contributes its approved modes of dress and decoration: high ruffled blouses, low necklines, tight pants, baggy pants, parasols, handkerchiefs, bowlers, straw hats, long earrings, nose rings, ribbons, bracelets, ankle chains, armbands, headbands, feathers, mascaraed eyes, Cupid's-bow lip markings, no makeup, watch chains, teeth filled with gold. The adolescent generation will select from the prevailing styles those that set them apart as a new generation with unique erotogenic preferences. When the morals and manners of the social order are in a state of transition it becomes more imperative for youth to assert the generational differences. In such times they will invent more dramatic and flamboyant metaphors of body decoration.

During early pubescence, conformity to a generational dress code takes precedence over erotic display and individuality. After arriving at puberty each adolescent tries to assemble a more personal image of what it means to have an adult sexual body. Which items of dress or body decoration or ways of talking and walking mark me as a member of my generation? Which items ought to be included to appease the values of my family and social class? Which items declare absolutely that I am a woman and not a man? How daringly different may I be? Must I be?

No matter how deeply infused with the personal, the erotic displays of youth are meant to assert the arrival of adult sexuality, male-female differentiation, and generational difference. A young woman may wear pants and a man-tailored shirt. A young man may wear eye makeup, feathers in his hair, beads around his neck. An adolescent couple may obscure the gender difference between them by dressing, styling their hair, wearing their makeup, selecting their jewelry so that they look as much alike as possible. These youths are stressing the generational difference and mocking the sexual conventions of the adult social order. But there is no mistaking the frankly erotic nature of their postures, gestures, stride, dress and body decorations. Moreover, it doesn't usually require extraordinary powers of perception to ascertain that this one is a woman and that one a man.

Decisions about which parts of her body to exaggerate, diminish, mutilate, conceal also have been influenced by the forepleasure fantasies that the adolescent has been elaborating since early pubescence. At first these fantasies were constructed as a way of alleviating the anxieties connected with rapid growth. After arriving at puberty, the plot line and images become more closely interwoven with the facts of having adult genitals and adult desires for sexual partnership. In putting together her erotogenic display the young woman is signaling to her potential sexual partner which parts of her body are meant to be the landmarks of forepleasure. In addition, she is projecting an image of herself as a female, and she hopes to find this image mirrored in the gazes and love gestures of her sexual partner.

On much the same basis, the young man creates his personal *ars erotica*. Before a date with a woman he knows, or an encounter with one he only hopes to meet, the young man styles his hair, practices frowns, gazes, postures before the mirror, decides which clothes most effectively emphasize his masculinity—a T-shirt that reveals his broad shoulders, tight pants that call attention to his genitals, his buttocks, his thighs, and his calf muscles, a pair of dirty sneakers to demonstrate his liberation from social status. Yet he wears a golden necklace to insist upon his status. The young man hopes to attract a sexual partner, and he fantasizes that she will respond erotically to those parts of his body that are masculine and powerful.

During lovemaking the young man is relieved when he finds that he can depend on the foreplay signals of his partner. The male adolescent finds the step-by-step explorations of petting and forepleasure reassuring. These explorations give him time to discover the girl's mouth, nipples, vulva, buttocks, neckline. He confirms the differences between the outlines of her body and his. He is male. She is female. The young woman is also reassured about her femininity and her desirability as a love partner when her forepleasure signals have been appreciated and understood. Petting may serve as a preliminary to actual coitus. However, just as often, particularly among younger adolescents and in the initial phases of a sexual relationship, petting is an end in itself. Petting in and of itself, however limited, can bring erotic satisfaction to both partners.

Almost all mammals engage in sex play that never leads to coitus. In general, mammalian petting activities are initiated and performed by the male, who uses oral or manual stimulation on the surfaces of the female body and in and on her genitalia. In nonhuman mammals the mouth or snout region of the male is the primary organ used for sexual exploration. Whether by mouth, the hand, or body-to-body pressure, the physical stimulation most likely to bring about sexual arousal and response in mammals is any kind of touch contact. Whereas among insects the organs of smell and taste are the primary erotic receptors and among birds the organs of sight and hearing, in mammals the end organs of touch that are located just below the skin surfaces and in some of the deeper nerve centers of the body are the primary sexual receptors. Certain areas of the mammalian body, known as erogenous zones, are richly supplied with these end organs of touch. The areas that surround the penis head and vaginal vestibule are especially sensitive to touch stimulation. They serve as bridges between the nerve centers of the inner organs and the nerve zones situated in a more direct relationship to the outer world. Thus the entire skin surface of the human body is highly eroticized; the palms of the hands and feet, the earlobes, the nipples, the testes, under the arms, the pelvic area, the buttocks, the eyelids, under and around the jawline. With the appropriate accompanying fantasy, arousal sufficient to achieve orgasm can be accomplished through touch stimulation of any erogenous zone.

Petting techniques vary from society to society. These preferences depend to a large extent on male definitions of a female erotic zone and do not always or necessarily correspond to female desires. Breasts are favored in some cultures; the nape of the neck, the ankles, the buttocks, the inner surfaces of the thighs in others.

All the petting variations known to contemporary adolescents can be found in the ancient literature on human love and courtship. Even in the more sexually restrained Anglo-American societies of the late nineteenth and early twentieth centuries, sex-play activities known as toying, spooning, larking, bundling, smooching, dallying were widely practiced among young men and women. Contemporary adolescents tend to begin petting earlier than did previous generations. They are far more frank and accepting of petting activities. Petting in the nude and petting to orgasm are much more frequent.

In Anglo-American and Western countries the first petting experiences are likely to consist of general body-to-body contact, hugging, and simple kissing. Soon afterward most adolescents discover the pleasure of "soul kissing" and its seemingly endless variations: tongue to tongue, lip and tongue sucking, tongue licking of the inner surfaces of the lips, deep tongue explorations of the interior of the partner's mouth, licking, biting, sucking. Manual exploration of the various parts of the female's body by the male, especially her breasts and buttocks, is another preferred petting variation. And the male's manipulations of the unclothed or partially clothed female breasts and nipples with his tongue or lips has become an increasingly employed petting practice. Manual stimulation of the clitoris, labia, vaginal vestibule, and vagina are also common. However, oral stimulation of the female genitalia is still regarded as too close to "going all the way" and is acceptable only in certain social groups. Adolescent females are much freer than their mothers or grandmothers were to engage in oral and manual stimulation of the male's erogenous zones—his breasts and nipples, behind the ears, his buttocks, thighs, and skin surfaces. However, there is still some reluctance to handle the male genitalia, a resistance that is usually overcome by a request from the male.

Some form of petting to orgasm is the primary erotic accompaniment to the first falling-in-love experiences of youth. If the partners continue for any length of time in the love relationship, they may, depending on their educational, religious, and social backgrounds, go on to perform coitus. Nevertheless, even after coitus becomes more acceptable to the couple, petting and petting to orgasm often continue to be significant erotic activities.

The erotic arousal that characterizes these earliest sexual partnerships is heightened by the narcissistic quality of the love relationships. The lovers become entirely absorbed in each other. The relationship consumes them completely, whether it lasts several days or several months. They walk through the world together as though they were all alone and no one else existed. Merely looking into each other's eyes, or touching fingertips, or catching a whiff of the other's body perfumes, or feeling the same emotion at the same moment can arouse sexual desire. During lovemaking they rouse each other to the heights of ecstasy. After orgasm they remain united as though their two bodies were one. They hold each other as though there were no boundaries between them. With their eyes and every gesture, each mirrors a reflection of the other that says "You are perfect." And even when they are physically apart, each has the illusion that the other's presence pervades the world—clouds, trees, rocks, winds, sun, moon. The surf echoes the lover's love whispers. The stars blink the message that says "You are perfect."

All goes well with the lovers as long as they are able to mirror the state of absolute perfection, as long as they can capture the ecstasy of two bodies that merge into one, as long as the exquisite sympathy between them is not disturbed by the requirement for deeper, more complex understandings or by some indications that there might be a few differences of opinion between them. Despite this insistence on a perfect sympathy based on no differences in values, desires, wishes, opinions, one or both members of the love partnership will soon find it necessary to assert self-other boundaries, separateness and difference. The closeness of absolute perfection begins to resemble a frightening experience of smothering and entrapment. Nagging, arguing, complaining, tormenting become periodic accompaniments to the perfect relationship. Sometimes the furies of rage are like a life jacket that saves the lovers from drowning in the bliss of their all-too-perfect union. The lovers separate in fury. And then, magically, irresistibly, as the need arises, as they discover that no one else in the world is ready to mirror for them what they wish they once were, or are at present, or might become, they are drawn back to each other for another round of perfect love.

As long as the love partner can turn her adoring face in precisely the right way, at precisely the right moment, with precisely the right gaze, she will be idealized and adored. As long as he can be used as an all-giving, always-embracing partner, he is valued. Yet inevitably a perfect partner turns out to be an ordinary person in enough respects to frustrate desire, to fail to gratify magical wishes, and fail to mirror admiration and celebration; a person with faults, imperfections, her own opinions and ideas, a separate self whose comings and goings cannot be omnipotently controlled. In such an inevitability she might be abandoned without explanation. The search for some other perfect love is resumed.

Often these first love relationships are simply narcissistic exploitations. One or both lovers will get hurt. Feelings of betrayal, mistrust, despair, hopelessness are common aftermaths of the fiery ecstasies of first love. Despite the self-serving and sometimes devastating quality of adolescent first love, it is an honest outpouring and genuine expression of the stream that links the love-hates of the past with the future and with present living in the world. The lover might resemble some idealized version of Mother or Father, a sister or brother, some rendition of the golden self that was, or some blend of self-other that had once enabled the world to glow with beauty and perfection. This first love will reside in the memory of the adult, ready to emerge with nearly full intensity as the perfect love one might have had, the absolute sexual fulfillment one once had and then lost forever.

We usually try, with varying degrees of success, to forget the heartbreak of adolescent love and to remember only the delights. The human mind can be artful in its ways of preserving memory sweet. Some of the typical adolescent memories of infancy as the golden time, the time of innocence and joy, are very likely screens for the disappointments of adolescence. The falsifications of infancy make the heartbreak of an adolescent love affair more bearable. In fact there is good reason to believe that many of our memories of infancy were formed not during infancy and childhood but during adolescence. The childhood events the memories refer to may have happened, but when they originally occurred they were innocuous and unremarkable. The disenchanted youth will comfort himself by generating a memory of a magical day in childhood, a day of green hills, delicious black bread spread with butter and honey. There are yellow dandelions, two little boys frolicking with their favorite female cousin. The memory is a screen for the young woman he loved and lost. At the height of their love affair, which never went further than magical gazes and fingertip touches, she wore a diaphanous yellow dress the color of dandelions. She soon rejected his honeyed phrases for the bread-and-butter reality of the young man with a steady job and more promising economic and social prospects.

Our adult nostalgia for infancy, childhood, youth is partly based on the fate of the first love affairs of youth, actual or imagined, which do resemble the past while simultaneously representing a giant step into the future. They moved us from infantile love to adult love. They were an intermediate step in the removal of desire from the love objects of the past. They immortalized the past, perhaps not exactly as it was but as we wished it might have been.

No matter how grown-up we become, no love (not even a mother's love for her infant) can compete favorably with the ecstasies of the narcissistic, mirroring love of youth. And whenever fortune or necessity deals us a rotten hand, lowering our estimation of who we are, we may strive to recover our lost narcissism through a magical love affair. The diminishing of professional prestige, the loss of one's home through fire or hurricane, the loss of a job, a child's incurable illness, the empty nest that confronts us when our children leave home, the aftermath of the death of a parent— any of these can reactivate the quest for perfect love.

No one ever completely outgrows her yearning for a love that will mirror all the marvelous things she once was or might become. This is why some men and women base their entire existence on the pursuit of magical love, regarding the life they actually live as merely provisional. They harbor the fantasy that sooner or later they will be rescued from an everyday life that has grown dreary. Fantasy and illusion are what remodel and enrich everyday life. But in an adult the insistent fantasy of rescue from necessity converts everyday life into a prison, a deprivation. The fantasy devalues the pleasures that are there to be enjoyed, the successes one might be proud of, the loved ones who do care for us.

Eventually the pursuer of mirroring love comes face to face with the unloved, unlovable person she has become. She realizes that in her frantic quest for absolute self-fulfillment she has gradually abandoned, one by one, every possibility of love from husband, children, friends, colleagues.

And what of the rest of us, those who sensed that the pleasures of ordinary life are diminished by the personalized, eroticized quest for perfect love, those who consented to the idea that by living an everyday existence according to the rules we would someday be compensated for being deprived of the ecstasies of adolescent love? An everyday life, a family, a career, a calling, a profession begin as reparative alternatives to the love affairs of adolescence (real or fantasied) that had to come to grief because the dazzling mirror of narcissistic love is always only a temporary deception. Even in the earliest months of life a mother's mirroring of her infant's marvelous splendor never quite reflects the infant's dreams of glory and fantasies of omnipotence with unremitting endurance. The mother rations the fulfillment of desire; the mirror comes and goes.

The adolescent inherits from infancy the expectations and passions of mirroring love. But in adolescence something new is added to the infantile legacy. The bliss of mirroring love is heightened by the erotic intensities of genitality. Then what the adult inherits from the adolescent is an illusion of perfection potentiated by exquisite genital pleasure.

A young adult does not take on the responsibilities of caregiving and lawgiving merely as an acquiescence to the mandates of society. She does so with the fantasied hope of recovering through family life and work the magical possibilities that came to grief in those imagined or actual love affairs of adolescence. As the young adult accommodates the life of infinite possibilities to the life of finite possibilities, the projects of her everyday life, which were initiated as the alternatives to endless perfect love, go on to acquire a value of their own. But then this beloved and treasured everyday life of work and family devotions sooner or later is also doomed to be questioned, is also destined for disenchantment. On the agenda of every adult's life is still the reckoning with the fact that the determinations of her daily existence originated in an attempt at recovery from a narcissistic deprivation in adolescence. Everyday life can offer great fulfillment for a long time until such point as those projects inspired in adolescence, one by one, come to some termination or disenchantment, when the achievement of goals leaves only the toil by which they were pursued.

A woman arrives at the pinnacle of her profession only to realize that the fame and wealth she has acquired are not commensurate with her decades of driven ambition, nor do they compensate for her renunciation of motherhood. Another woman, whose daily existence was claimed by the joys and trials of family life and child rearing, discovers upon reaching middle age that the spoils for having sacrificed sexual adventure and a glamorous career are a couple of empty bedrooms, some photograph albums of children growing up, a closetful of baseball trophies and musty stuffed animals, and a husband who regards her as a dreary alternative to the dazzling girl of his adolescent dreams.

What happens then? The disenchanted adults look back to their adolescent years when everything did seem possible. They decide to have another go at youth. What we then see are grown-ups acting like adolescents—prancing at the discos, vying with their envied and resented teenage children for youthful sexual partners. At professional meetings we see such burned-out caricatures of youth sprawled in the lobbies of hotels, decked in feathers, T-shirts, Indian beads, headbands, jeans, and ethnic blouses, plunking guitars, chanting mantras. We see Father taking flight from the domestic trap, trading in his dreary menopausal wife for that golden flower child who will never grow old. We see Mother on the dance floor rocking ecstatically in the arms of her leather-jacketed Dionysus with heart of gold and supreme genital powers. Inspired by the reawakening of her sexual appetites, Mother takes off from her empty nest to find some of those possible lives she left behind when she consented to go along with the idea that by living an everyday existence according to the rules she would be compensated for her narcissistic deprivations.

An adolescent compensates herself for the deprivations of her infantile idealizations by regressions that simulate infancy: autoerotic excursions, adoring the saintly and humble, ruthless and seductive idols of her generation, falling in love with a mirroring partner. In a similar way, her middle-aged parents, when the projects they initiated in youth come to grief, go back to adolescence. In the first instance the regressions are temporary ones that support removal and prepare a once-powerless child to become caregiver and lawgiver; they also help to delineate and solidify the differences between the child and adult generations. In the adult regressions to adolescence the generational differences are dissolved, creating situations tantamount to symbolic if not actual violations of the incest taboo and signifying that something has gone seriously wrong in the state of Denmark.

But not all regressions to adolescence need be catastrophic. There is more in the adolescent legacy for the adult than eroticized narcissism. In the legacy is something of value that could provide a hedge against the small or large disenchantments of adulthood.

It has been said that the sexual and moral realms grow in tandem. Sexual puberty has in it several inspirations for the humanization of conscience.

Even in those long moments of recovering from the heartbreak of their first love affairs, some adolescents find a way to make the disappointing present a little easier to bear. They convert personal longing into a yearning for the perfectibility of humankind. The young woman nurses her wounds. Until her soul is healed she will not risk another personal romantic submersion. Yet her sexual hunger is insistent. So when her passions are no longer bound up in grieving for the glories she has lost, they are set free to be extended outward to the world. She embraces Humankind; she enters into mystical union with God, Nature, Music, Poetry, Politics, Painting, Dance, Theories of Evolution. In her love affair with the Universe, the adolescent expands herself lovingly into the world of others.

The sacred realm between the no-longer of childhood and the yet-to-be of ordinary adult life is a margin, a portal, a threshold, a passage in which the growing-up child partakes of the divine. Because she is incomplete, torn between what she once was and the uncertain someone she is about to become, youth yearns for those experiences that convey wholeness and unity. In themselves these yearnings have little to do with social ideals, religion, ethics. The adolescent is exploiting Politics, Art, Nature, God for her self-

enhancement. Such cultural obsessions are the shadowy outlines of the moral passions that bind individuals to their
species. But they are a step in the right direction. And they
have in them very often some new solutions to the dilemmas
of existence. They hint at possibilities that can be accomplished at some later point in life.

These displacements from eroticized narcissism to mystical and intellectual ecstasies are one source of the adolescent's compensations for disenchanted love. The growth energies of pubescence and puberty are another. These open
the floodgates of creativity, inspiring the adolescent to play
myriad parts in the human comedy. She begins numerous
projects, most of which she never completes. But some she
docs. She becomes a poet, a composer, takes up the flute or
the guitar, studies ballet or tap dancing, writes political
tracts, edits the art column of her school newspaper, builds
the sets for the school pageant, designs clothes, plays on the
soccer team, sings in the church choir, organizes a protest
against the spread of nuclear weapons.

Such alternatives are also part of our legacy from adolescence. Some adults, when the projects of their everyday
lives succumb to disenchantment, will finish the novels
they started in adolescence, refurbish the old Steinway and
strike up the old chords. Others might decide to resume the
social and moral causes they abandoned in youth, but now
they will act in the role of guardians of youth, elders who
communicate to those no longer powerless children who
are about to take over the reins a thing or two about the
relationship between personal power and ethical responsibility. Still others do nothing more remarkable than reread
the poets and philosophers who had once inspired them to
be just a little larger than ordinary life. New friendships are
made with renewed vitality, cultural pursuits are reinitiated
with adolescent fervor. A fresh capacity for nostalgia sets in.
There is another spurt of learning, with the possibility of an
increment in wisdom.

As another legacy from our adolescent years, most of us go
on believing that there is something more to life than sex,

work, procreation, and moral obedience. More often than not just what that something is eludes us. Let us say that it has to do with moral dignity, the capacity to remain true to ourselves, to somehow keep the visionary gleam alive even though what we wish for may turn out to be an impossibility, an illusion. Let us say that it is the conviction that we are permitted to set out for undiscovered territories, to become the architects of the flowering Edens that will stand in the place of the deserts, to return human and beast to the habitats they once had and then lost. The very heights of adolescent grandiosity! The question here is whether these visions are designed to extend the personal passions toward some larger community of others, or are they merely in the service of self-aggrandizement?

Very few of us are destined to be the actual architects of the future, but the inspirations of our adolescent years allow us to participate in the visionary acts of those who are. They enable us to remain faithful to our convictions—that there are some undiscovered truths, that the disappointing present might be made into something better. Yet such spirits may nowhere find themselves at home. They may lose their bearings, their connections with the everyday life that must sustain them and fortify their visions. Kierkegaard warned of the ways in which any of us might lose ourselves—in the infinite without finiteness or in the finite without the efficacy of work, marriage, profession, calling, political commitment, or sense of community. But if they are steadfast navigators, we will look to these visionary spirits for our opinions of ourselves and for our hopes of life itself.

DREAMS OF GLORY

The extraordinary thing about virtue is that in every human society it has been regarded as the mark of all that is best and noble in human character. The definitions vary: Plato's perfection of form, beauty, wisdom; Aristotle's courage, prudence, temperance, justice; the Roman manliness and valor; the chivalric code of chastity, valor, piety. But one theme, quite independent of these varieties of virtuous experience, periodically emerges: the paradox of identifying self-interest with the interests of all other humans. The basic formula recurs, here and there, throughout history. "No one is a believer until he loves for his brother what he loves for himself." The virtuous Upanishad is "he who sees all beings in his own self and his own self in all beings." Sometimes the message has political overtones, as when Lincoln said, "As I would not be a slave, I would not be master."

The paradox is implicit in most puberty rites. The changing status of the individual child is appreciated as both a social event and a cosmic one. As the girl is reborn as a fertile and whole woman, the boy as a fertile and whole man, they bring to the social order the gifts of civilization—medicine, crops, a method for baking corn cakes. But even more, henceforth they are supposed to be embodiments of the divine, of those elemental forces that reach beyond the personal and the social to affect the universal.

The paradox is evident in Rousseau's belief that the source of all our passions, the origins and principle of all the others—love of oneself—might, as an outcome of a wisely nurtured adolescence, be transformed into love of the species. Certainly Freud implied a similar transformation when he said, "What has belonged to the lowest part of the mental life of each of us is changed, through the formation of the ideal, into what is highest in the human mind by our scale of values."

Though contemporary psychoanalysts do not subscribe to the Lamarckian thesis embedded in Freud's provocative proclamation, they invariably refer to these words in their writings on that aspect of the superego called the ego-ideal. The ego-ideal is said to originate in the infant's primary narcissism and then go on in the adult to represent the highest attainments of humankind. In his description of the transformation of the ego-ideal during adolescence Peter Blos put it this way: "The ego-ideal spans an orbit from primary narcissism to the 'categorical imperative,' from the most primitive form of psychic life to the highest level of man's achievements." Or as Freud said, "What he projects before him as his ideal is the substitute for the lost narcissism of his childhood. . . ." The mature ego-ideal, which has its roots in the infant's original narcissism, serves even in the adult as an agency of wish fulfillment. In contrast, the other aspects of the superego, which originate in the infant's earliest experiences of unpleasure, will go on to function as agencies of restriction and prohibition. The superego has been likened to a Simon Legree, "with the power of the executive whip of anxiety as its persuader and forceful agency." On the other hand, the ego-ideal is like "the seductive, alluring smile of the Mona Lisa." By embodying our hopes, expectations, and aspirations, the ego-ideal eases the burdens of instinctual sacrifice and offers us compensations for our renunciations. Just as hallucinatory wishes of omnipotence and dreams of glory enable an infant to bear the inevitable disappointments and frustrations of being a powerless, helpless, entirely dependent creature, so the moral aspirations and social ideals of the adult enable her to reconcile herself to the tragic dimensions of life. By remaining true to her ideals the adult preserves her narcissism and at the same time strives toward the perfectibility of the human species. In this way love of oneself becomes identified with love for all other humans.

As we might expect, the identification of self-interest with moral aspiration can often lead to misinterpretations. Polonius' counsel to Laertes—"This above all: to thine own self be true,/And it must follow, as the night the day,/Thou canst not then be false to any man"—could have been a wicked piece of advice, a message of mere opportunism. Virtue does not follow from self-interest as easily as Polonius suggests. The moral complexity of his words could not possibly have been grasped by the self-absorbed, impetuous Laertes. Most probably the advice served only to confound the young man's moral plight. Polonius wasn't much help to Ophelia or Hamlet either. They were buds of promise. But there were no elders to guide them. The moral corruption in the state of Denmark was pervasive. All three—Laertes, Ophelia, Hamlet—floundered as they tried desperately to live up to their personal ideals of manhood or womanhood. Each was unable to wrench free of the past. Neither in their own families nor in the society at large were there edifying or functional ideals toward which they might strive. In the end they destroyed one another along with the older generation that had failed to provide adequate mentorship. Horatio did know a thing or two about the uncertain relationship between personal narcissism and ethical ideals. It is Horatio who is assigned to speak the lament of his lost generation to "the yet unknowing world." He will tell how self-interest and grandiose ideals can lead to "carnal, bloody, and unnatural acts,/[To] accidental judgments, casual slaughters,/[To] deaths put on by cunning and forc'd cause."

The ego-ideal, though it lures us with promises of perfection, can be as ruthless and harsh as the watchful eyes and prohibiting voices of the rest of the superego. The full story of the taming of conscience requires that we trace its evolution along two lines: the original, primary narcissism, and the secondary narcissism, derived from the infant's transfer of its own narcissism into idealization of the parents. During infancy, personal omnipotence is exchanged for the advantages of sharing in the glory and power we attribute to the parents. The adolescent, as we have already seen, must come to terms with the reality of who her parents are. And the mighty parents are always flawed. They are not omnipotent. They have the faults and weaknesses that ordinary flesh is heir to. The girl's desexualization of her relationship to her mother (the boy's to his father) allows for these homo-erotic-narcissistic energies to be invested in the social realm—as impersonalized ideals that might be realized in the future. Her compassion for both parents, her ability to forgive them for being less than she had once imagined them to be, will go a long way toward humanizing the standards by which she measures her own self and other people.

But what then happens to the original primary narcissism? Are we to assume that all the infant's narcissism is surrendered to the parents for the advantages of love dialogue and protection? Or does some of that original narcissistic energy remain invested in the self? On this score Freud was ambiguous. The fate of primary narcissism and its *direct* contribution to the moral life is one of the unsolved riddles of psychoanalysis. Freud, though he was never one to play down the trials of civilization and its inevitable discontents, did leave some room in life for wish fulfillment and illusion. Whereas the other aspects of the superego preserve civilization by demanding renunciation and sacrifice, the ego-ideal represents that other, more hopeful face of civilization, the benevolent visage we call culture. Though some of the moral content of the ego-ideal arises out of the secondary narcissism once invested in the parent, there is a portion of narcissism reserved for illusion. That portion derives from primary narcissism, the love of one's own self, which is never transferred over to the realm of love dialogue.

We seem to know from the very beginning that there is more to life than desire and lawfulness. Before we are anything else we are conjurers—jesters and poets who recreate the glory that was, the life of infinite possibilities, the life before contradictions, before the humiliating knowledge that we are forever separated from the universe.

Through her outlandishly narcissistic ways, and especially through her fantasies of omnipotence and dreams of glory, the adolescent is regaining contact with the time when she was absolutely true to herself. She is refinding the method that allowed her to preserve a sense of dignity and wholeness even while much of her original narcissism had to be given over to the realm of love dialogue. The method was there from the earliest moments of life.

Before an infant ever encounters the frustrations inherent in relating to others she has available to her an inborn method of conjuring a sense of personal power. The onslaught of the boundaried, finite world of light, sound, and sharply defined edges is countered by a newborn's innate capacities to ignore or to rid herself of these external disturbances through her own body movements. And even though inner excitations, which cannot so easily be ignored or removed, might temporarily belie her marvelous omnipotence of reflex and gesture, the tensions that these excitements give rise to lead to crying, thrashing one's legs, and the summoning of Mother. Sucking and head-turning gestures summon the nipple-in-the-mouth. Through her own gestures the infant conjures Mother, conjures the breast. And, though she is absolutely helpless, she has enlisted relief through her own body movements. This gives her a feeling of omnipotence. She experiences the first *post hoc, ergo propter hoc* in connection with her own actions. The forerunners and prototypes of adolescent fantasies of glory, of being all-powerful and able to convert reality into whatever one wishes it to be, are to be found in an infant's own activity at a time before she has any sense of an object out there upon whom she is really dependent for life, safety, relief of tension, a place for her passions to reside. Such primary experience of one's own self has its own history and also an energy of its own that is relatively independent of the energies of relating to another.

Of course the absolutely dependent, absolutely helpless newborn could not survive without an attachment to someone who cares enough to feed her, keep her warm, carry her about, and protect her from too many impingements from the outer world and from the strains and tensions of inner discomfort. The vicissitudes of love dialogue are there right from birth and from then on are interwoven with the fate of love of oneself. But from the point of view of the newborn, she is a law unto herself, complete and self-sufficient. Love for another, although it is the safety net of existence, can never be quite as satisfying as the powerful feeling of creating a nipple by wishing for it.

Mothers and fathers would seem to be the most suitable partners for enhancing an infant's narcissism, for mirroring back to her a feeling of omnipotence and total, unconditional love. After all, an infant is the extension of a parent's own narcissism. As parents we aspire to help our children to love themselves as much as we love them. When they are sad or disappointed we feel the hurts and longings as much as or perhaps even more than the child does. The child's fears and defeats become our fears and defeats. And no one outside the family nest will ever mirror perfection, will care so much or so generously overlook the child's imperfections and weaknesses as will a parent. But even such nearly perfect, nearly all-protecting self-other love is not tension-less. The two forms of narcissism—the parent's reflecting love and the infant's own version of love of self—do not articulate with seamless mutuality.

Insofar as our children are the extensions of our own narcissism, we frequently find it intolerable if they do not mirror back to us all those glorious and wonderful things we imagine we were, or wished we could have been, or might still become. In our children we keep alive the hope of recapturing our own lost narcissistic perfection. But since we are also civilized adults who comprehend the dangers of narcissistic self-absorption, we caution our children when they seem to love themselves too much. We admonish pride, impose modesty, limit illusion, require obedience to the moral values of the actual world, and put the brakes on desire. Only for the first few months of existence can a mother or father be a nearly flawless mirror for the infant's extraordinary love of self and sense of absolute perfection and omnipotence. Even then the fulfillment of desire is rationed; the mirror comes and goes.

For an infant the threat of being separated from the mirroring and powerful other can engender intense anxieties: one's whole being could be annihilated, one could fragment, fall forever, never be held again. These experiences of infinite helplessness and anguish could hold in check those aspects of self-experience that derive from the exercise of personal power and the freedom to use one's own body and mind as one sees fit. Therefore it is also to the good that the world of others is a disappointing world of delay, frustration, conflict, limitation, conditions, demands for renunciation. It is good that no mother can be there always, both inside and outside the skin like the seemingly limitless extent of placenta-womb, fetus-mother-amniotic fluid. The human condition is such that no mother can be a perfect mirror for her infant's omnipotence.

And so the child goes on perfecting her real skills in the real world. Her growth energies and individuation strivings ensure that her muscles and senses will become more and more powerful; she will reach out, grasp, sit up, creep away, stand up, walk, run, jump, speak the sentences and think the thoughts whose symbolic structures are the same for all human beings. As these innate human powers are enlarged and enhanced they will endow the child with some real power over the real world in which she lives. The exercise of real power is one residue of our primordial omnipotence. Another is the capacity to imagine the disappointing world as a better and more harmonious place than it actually is.

Whenever the trials and humiliations of renunciation become too much to bear, whenever our love dialogues disappoint us, whenever the reaching-out, running-jumping, exploring-puzzling become a strain, a confusing muddle of incoherences, we find a resting place. We create a world that is kinder and more congenial to our narcissism. We conjure and we continue to conjure even though our creations could turn out to be no better than the bitter and confounding reality. Conjuring lifts us into the realm beyond reality, beyond pleasure. And sometimes while there in that sacred intermediate realm we find our way back to trusting and loving, a few pieces of some inscrutable puzzle suddenly fit together with nearly perfect mutuality.

There is a corner of the world, a realm between the wishing life and the actual life, in which bridges are crossed and contradictions are held at bay. Even a ten-month-old knows how to conjure a resting place. She invents a security blanket, a humming sound, a rocking motion that banishes the frightening and humiliating discrepancies between the "me" world and the "not me" world, the animate and the inanimate, the self and the other. In place of discrepancy the humming sound recreates that primary experience of being held forever. The wish to be all-powerful is granted. Dignity is restored. A security blanket of some sort or other is the one thing that a baby can always fall back on. The blanket belongs absolutely to the baby. Her mother and father may admire it or give it a new name or pack it up in a suitcase as if it were merely a blanket, but only the baby can invest it with aliveness. The blanket is the baby's first personal possession. Nobody gave it to her. She invented it.

The very first conjuring gestures of turning-toward-the-nipple or shutting-out-too-much-light are mere gestures of the moment. The time space between wish and fulfillment is barely perceptible. In fact, when these conjuring gestures fail, as they must often do, the infant will simply hallucinate fulfillment. Hallucinations can't fill a stomach or bring enwrapping warmth or shut out light, but they will do very well for a while until real relief comes along. During these earliest days, what is conjured is not representable in the real world, as it is when a ten-month-old conjures a security blanket. The baby who once in a while prefers the illusion of her security blanket or rocking motion or humming sound to the actual presence of her mother has enlarged the realm of the conjured. She is on her way to making metaphors.

As infancy progresses, the resting place at which the broken world can be made whole again becomes more and more representable. The conjured becomes a communication, a link between the life of wishes and the life of lawful reality. As infancy progresses, the demands of the intermediate realm become more complicated. The distances between wishing and fulfillment become vaster. Security blankets are not adequate for resolving all the complex tensions between the wishing world and the world that dictates where, when, and how fulfillment is permitted. As the strains of relating the "me" world to the "not me" world intensify, the intermediate realm will be enlarged. In the context of desire's great debate with authority, omnipotence becomes a forerunner of moral dignity.

When the going gets rough a three-year-old may still seek a resting place in the familiar smells of her treasured security blanket. But the immense problems that challenge her self-esteem and sense of power cannot be represented by a metaphor of safety. At three, four, five years of age a child's management of her desires is still really dependent on the parents' presence and power. To have the fulfillment of one's desires—their acceptance or rejection—reside in some external authority, is humiliating. Even a young child finds such total moral dependency intolerable.

A child's personal dignity requires that she negotiate the distance between fulfilling her wishes and desires and her equally compelling need to come to terms with the moral order. For a three-year-old the moral order resides in the parents' authority. Although it is a struggle, a child will accept the authority of her parents because she loves and admires them. Moreover, the moral order is presented to the child via her parents in a highly personal manner that takes account of her idiosyncrasies. Nevertheless the acceptance of the parent's authority entails a certain amount of turning against what the child experiences as her innermost self. A child will obey those who love and protect her, but first she must save her integrity.

She finds a temporary remedy to the potentially humiliating situation of simply submitting to her parents' demands. Around this time many children begin to play with a unique companion. The companion usually has a definite name and a vividly characteristic appearance. But this marvelous friend is imaginary. Imaginary companions take various forms: animals, younger children, Peter Pans, Jiminy Crickets, superwomen or supermen. They come in odd shapes and sizes. In some households they sit at the dinner table or hide under the living room couch and play pranks on the grown-ups. They go for rides in the family car and attend family parties. Some of them take up residence only in the nursery or only in the bathroom or a closet. Perhaps there are many more of these marvelous creatures than we can ever get to know about. The most ingenious ones of all might be reluctant to get involved with the affairs of everyday life. Perhaps they exist as whispered or silent conversationalists, felt presences the child will never disclose.

Whether they are used primarily as protectors, scapegoats, impersonators of ideals, consciences, devils, or mother substitutes, these lively companions guard the narcissism of the child during the time when she is struggling to transform the power and authority of the parent into elements of her own conscience. In order to obey the parental rules she must come to terms with her own lack of power. She must begin to accept for herself the social unacceptability of some of her most pressing desires. The imaginary companion, or some other conjured equivalent, is a necessary intermediate step before a child can be obedient with inner conviction and pride.

The child is still uncertain about her ability to control her impulses and desires. Nor can she properly evaluate the extent of her parents' authority, which she imagines to be much greater than it really is. However, the child has total control over her companion's thoughts and actions and power. The companion's authority is acceptable and understandable. The companion can be counted on to soothe, mirror, and reflect the child's perfection and goodness. Or it can be very naughty indeed. Then the child has the delicious satisfaction of scolding the companion and teaching it how to behave in a civilized world. An imaginary companion is a Self with some of the qualities of an Other. It is a kind of self-other.

One little three-year-old named David, whose father, Donald, was a high school principal, invented a companion called Davdon. David was especially sensitive to any orders coming from his father. He usually found his mother more reassuring and comforting. But even her requests could make him tearful and grumpy. Family relationships improved considerably after Davdon made his appearance. It didn't take long for the parents to accommodate willingly to his presence. At mealtimes Davdon had his own chair. If the mother asked David to eat his eggs, David could now re-

spond with dignity, "I *must* first ask Davdon if I *should.*"
David would address his question in a loud voice to Davdon.
After some silence David would turn to his mother. "Davdon said I should eat those eggs." David became a much
happier child, less frequently tearful or sullen. But he
would never obey his parents directly. Only Davdon's sanc-
tions and commands brought compliance.

By adding a part of his father's name to his own, David
had created a companion partly derived from his own person and partly from the glory, omnipotence, and omni-
science he attributed to his father. Davdon was described as
being tall—"much taller" than the father. His voice was so
loud—"much louder than Daddy's"—that David sometimes had to hold his hands over his ears when Davdon is-
sued his commands.

Davdon could do other things beside issue commands. If
David's mother scolded him for a misdeed, David would
defiantly protest the injustice, proclaiming that Davdon had
given him permission. On the other hand, David would
sometimes cry and hang his head in shame for matters that
were quite mysterious to the parents. David was ashamed
for having displeased Davdon.

When David was five years old Davdon disappeared from
the household as suddenly as he had appeared. David now
spent a considerable amount of time playing teacher to an
imaginary dog who was a very poor student. David would
loudly and vehemently accuse this unnamed animal of the
most extraordinary, vile thoughts, impossibly stupid ideas.
The game ceased when David entered first grade, where he
became an avid reader and a spectacularly moral supervisor
of the schoolyard games.

Two children in the same family may sometimes share the
same imaginary companion. Adam and Elizabeth, siblings
aged two years and three and a half years, together created
an imaginary companion named Poop. Poop, as described
by Elizabeth, was a boy who was "very dirty and very bad.
He is thin," she said, "around three or four inches long. But
he grows bigger and fatter when he eats carrots or meat."

The name Poop and his special characteristics had originated with the little brother, Adam, who was in the throes of toilet training, but only Elizabeth was capable of introducing him to the rest of the family. Poop defied all the rules of the household and was held responsible for every breach of regulations. "Poop did it," was the bland, unblinking response to any reprimand. Poop was harshly punished by the children for his infractions, but conspiratorial lip service was given to his messiness and bad manners.

A year later Poop was joined by a sibling named Good Poop, an invention of Elizabeth's. According to Elizabeth, Good Poop was a neat, clean, obedient, exceptionally intelligent girl who wore a pretty pink pinafore. In Adam's fantasy, Good Poop was a very brave boy who could climb the tallest trees, a daring gymnast who was "bigger, stronger, and smarter" than Adam's father. Poop and Good Poop lived in harmony with each other, the latter gradually gaining in ascendancy. Finally, when Elizabeth went to school, both Poops vanished. And now left on his own, free from the somewhat intimidating presence of his older sister, Adam became a daring, exuberant four-year-old, very much like his own Good Poop.

In the first stage the companion of Adam and Elizabeth represented their forbidden desires. Later he/she became a companion with social and moral qualities. With the imaginary companion as her moral representative, a young child finds a way to continue to express her wishes and desires while simultaneously acquiring as her own the moral authority of the powerful figures who seem to control the ebb and flow of her gratifications. The companion is immensely flexible and can represent either side of the great debate between desire and authority. Remarkably, this childish invention sponsors the life of desire but then slowly transforms infantile wishes into moral aspiration. The companion bridges the distance between wish and fulfillment, confirming for the child that participation in the social order can be accomplished without surrendering one's power or moral dignity.

We become civilized through obeying commands and prohibitions, through yielding up our inborn omnipotence and bending desire to the contours of the social order. The civilized life is the daily life of rules and manners. As civilized beings we agree to modulate desire and accommodate narcissism to the requirements of living in the world. We thereby gain the ordinary satisfaction of relating to others, of being industrious, of belonging and being accepted, of being safe, as a part of the social community. Cultural life, on the other hand, derives from the inner guardians we conjure to preserve our moral dignity. Cultural life is composed of the daydreams, fantasies, metaphors that link past, present, and future on the thread of a wish.

With a mind that is drawn away from the structures and stability of the prosaic everyday life and a body relentlessly growing into its adult form, the adolescent is a mourner without rituals, unable to chart the territory of the resting place. The metaphors of security blankets, imaginary companions, family romance are simply not sufficient to the emotional trials of adolescence. In order to grow up into something more than just a larger, sexually mature schoolgirl, the adolescent must conjure new metaphors.

As they turn away from the childhood metaphors, adolescents are the incipient poets, the mad ones who defy the adult world to render sensible their undecipherable gestures and moods. They are the dreamers who must reject and devalue the dreams, clothing, realpolitik of the grown-up generation. The toddler must say "no" in order to find out who she is. The adolescent says "no" to assert who she is not. She does not belong to the parents; she belongs to her own generation. To pave the way for her own generational possibilities the adolescent must first undermine the utopia of childhood, with its frozen plots and confining bureaucracies. She will not be servile, she will not obey.

Adolescents will conjure their own world of dress, manners, language, and dance, their own tribal lore, their own idols for glorification and reverence. This conjured world will hold desire and soften the humiliations of being less than the all-powerful being they imagine they are supposed to be. They conjure their own resting places. They imagine they can rule over the life of desire. They pretend some power over nature. What adolescents conjure along the way into adulthood can rejuvenate the social order. The vitalities of growth that transform a child into a powerful, sexual, procreative being are associated with the general flowering and vitality of the society, nature, the cosmos.

In the Navajo Kinaaldá rite each girl becomes Changing Woman. She dresses and dances like her. She becomes the earth, the power of fertility in all things. She becomes the embodiment of upward motion, growth from the earth up to the sky. In her being she unites sun and moon, fiery sun with moist water.

In Greek mythology Kore the maiden, the virgin, the young girl, is carried off into the underworld; we know little of what happens to her there. But she returns as Persephone, reborn like the crops that emerge from the earth after a dark winter. Kore's sexualization, her becoming the fertile, productive, experienced whole Persephone, is synonymous with the springing forth of the fruits of the earth.

Among the tribes of the North American plains, boys were encouraged to seek personal power by temporarily escaping the hold of society. They would venture into hazardous regions where the protective laws of the tribe ceased to have any meaning. They would go to the breaking point of physical suffering in the hope of entering into communication with the sacred world. They put themselves adrift on rafts without any food; they isolated themselves on mountaintops where they fought wild beasts and exposed themselves to rain and cold; they would fast for weeks on end and aggravate their weakness by taking emetics. As Lévi-Strauss interprets such ordeals of adolescence: "In this unstable border area, there is a danger of slipping beyond the pale and never coming back, as well as a possibility of drawing from the vast ocean of unexploited forces surrounding society a personal supply of power, thanks to which he who has risked all can hope to modify an otherwise unchangeable social order.''

The adolescent has no control over her changing physiology—the endocrine secretions, the dramatic reapportionment of leg to trunk length, the expansion of every muscle and tissue, the pubic hairs, the erect nipples, the menstrual flow. But she expresses her power over these natural events by decorating (even mutilating) her body, chanting the sacred texts of her generation, participating in the secret language—all of which make apparent her incipient power and changing sexual status. When adolescents express their muscular power, sexuality, and reproductive potential in acceptable social modes of language and dance, dress and body decoration, they divest their awesome physiology of its threat to society. These metaphors become attached to components of the normal social order. By strengthening the emotional and physical bonds between peers, the adolescent metaphors reinforce the incest taboo. The wild haircuts, obscene body decorations, and clothing are an assertion of the generational difference and are intended to repel the adult generation. Adults, however, are stimulated by the vitality of the adolescent metaphors and are not entirely beyond emulating what they fear and envy.

But, as with security blankets and imaginary companions, the metaphors of adolescence must be protected from appropriation by the adult world. To retain their value they should remain the province of youth. After a while the sacred music, dance, texts, language, clothing, body decorations become part of the shared profane realm. Some metaphors will be absorbed into the stream of ordinary life. Others will retain their power and full vitality forever. But if the conjured realm should be controlled or appropriated by the adult generation, as so often happens in our competitive modern societies, then the current metaphors will be abandoned by youth and simply exchanged for others. The more the adult generation usurps what belongs to youth, the wilder and more ambiguous the new metaphors are likely to be.

In the texts that appeal to adolescents are meanings other than nostalgic longing for the golden days or lamentations for lost heroes and heroines. Scored with their brassy chords and plaintive rhythms, they tell of pain, of loneliness, of the confusion when a person departs from one phase of life and is about to enter another, of the divisions within the self, of the efforts to remain true to oneself.

> *I went to the holy man,*
> *Full of lies and hate,*
> *I seemed to scare him a little*
> *So he showed me to the golden gate.*
>
> *Can you see the real me preacher?*
> *Can you see the real me doctor?*
> *Can you see the real me mother?*
> *Can you see the real me me me me me me*
> *me me me me?*
>
> . . .
>
> *I've had enough of living*
> *I've had enough of dying*
> *I've had enough of smiling*
> *I've had enough of crying*
> *I've taken all the high roads*
> *I've squandered and I've saved*
> *I've had enough of childhood*
> *I've had enough of graves.*

They speak of the nightmarish uncertainty of what is almost here but still to come:

> *Dark star crashes*
> *Pouring its light into ashes.*
> *Reason tatters.*
> *The forces tear loose from the axis.*
> *Searchlight casting for*
> *faults in the clouds of delusion.*
> *Shall we go, you and I, while we can,*
> *Through the transitive nightfall of*
> *diamonds?*
>
> . . .

> *It's not yesterday anymore*
> *I go visiting . . . I talk loud*
> *I try to make myself clear*
> *In front of a face that's nearer*
> *   than it's ever been before.*
> *Not this close before*
> *Nearer than before*
> *Not this close before.*

The lyrics are mundane. We've heard them before, many times. Nevertheless they reflect the sense that the self is incomplete, the yearning for the powers or substances that might convey wholeness.

> *Love, reign o'er me.*
> *Love, reign o'er me, rain on me.*
>
> *Only love*
> *Can bring the rain*
> *That makes you yearn to the sky*
> *Only love*
> *Can bring the rain*
> *That falls like tears from on high.*

The pulsing beat warns of the enormous power of the powerless, and of what might happen if we don't take them seriously. And since we are all powerless sometimes, we move to the beat:

> *I'm a walking nightmare, a signal of doom*
> *I kill conversation when I walk into a room*
> *I'm a walking disaster*
> *I'm a demolition man.*
>
> *Tied to the tracks and the train is coming*
> *Strapped to the wings and the engine roaring*
> *You say this wasn't in your plan?*
> *Don't mess around with the demolition man.*
> *Tied to a chair and the bomb is ticking*
> *The situation is not of your picking.*

We create such metaphors, we conjure such illusions of power in order to bear living in an actual world of limited possibility. The world we actually live in is a world of actual others who are human as we are but different from us, each in his or her own way—a world of households, school-yards, offices, temples; a world of childhood, graves, crying, smiling; a world of those countless bonds that tie us to others and make us heavy, a world of real ambition and real power. Lionel Trilling in speaking of this actual world described it as a milieu with all "the inconveniences of undertaking to intercede, of being a sacrifice, of reasoning with rabbis, of going to weddings and to funerals, of beginning something and then at a certain point remarking that it is finished." Trilling did not intend to diminish the realm of infinite possibility or to dismiss the idea that there is something more to human existence than either desire or lawfulness. He, like Kierkegaard, was warning that none of us can be truly moral unless we respect and take into account the dimensions of the world we actually inhabit.

In that resting place, which is beyond the social, beyond pleasure, beyond reality, we still take into account the great debate between desire and authority. The imaginary companion allows the child to accommodate her desires to the moral requirements of the social order while at the same time preserving her moral dignity. She has not, then, submitted either to desire or authority. She has found a way to reconcile herself to the discontents that inevitably arise in the course of living in an actual world.

In order for any person to grow up and accommodate to the actual world, she must have an area of life reserved for conjuring. Whenever the energies of physical growth are intensified, whenever the psychological changes inherent in an individual life threaten to upset the social order, as in adolescence, the need for a resting place is intensified. The adolescent lives her life as though in constant interaction with her actual world. But a large part of her existence is lived in sacred time, held aloft, apart from the earth and its worldly concerns. It is here, in the intermediate zone, that the disharmonies of the half child, half adult can begin to achieve some inner unity.

Sooner or later the changing woman has to find her way back to the real world. During her residence in the underworld, or enclosed in a cocoon, or above in the cosmos, she has wrestled with her demonic and sexual desires. Still, if on her reentry there seems to be no "right" person for her sexual hungers to attach to, or any place for her powers to be expressed, she will wither and the corn crops will wither and the earth will become barren.

How a youth transforms mythic power into actual power depends in part on the social conventions and moral characteristics of the actual environment that is waiting to receive her. While in the transitional zone she may have come up with some innovative solutions, but if there is no corn for sacred corn cake, no pages for her poetry, no arenas for her dances, no schools for her to teach in, no temples worth praying in, no unknown territories for her to discover— what will she do then?

It is to be expected that youth will question the world that receives them, that reentry will be confusing and disillusioning. Yet as long as there is some form of civilization, some possibility for cultural life, there will always be cornfields, pages, arenas, households, schools, temples. The problem of youth is how to accommodate the life of infinite possibilities to the life of feasibility.

This personal problem has to be solved by each youth as he or she takes over the reins, to become caregiver and lawgiver. The other problems of reentry concern society at large and the older generation, with their conflicts about relinquishing power to youth, with their envy of the sexual and moral changelings who are about to be the next adult generation.

During adolescence, Rousseau said, "the blood ferments and is agitated; a superabundance of life seeks to extend itself outward." During adolescence imagination is boundless. The urge toward self-perfection is at its peak. And with all their self-absorption and personalized dreams of glory, youth are in pursuit of something larger than personal passions, some values or ideals to which they might attach their imaginations. Their energies are poised to transform personal narcissistic interests into a concern for the common good. Their physical power, their procreative and creative abilities, their visionary minds and imaginations are ready to be directed toward the future of civilization. As the renewers of the ethical possibilities of society, adolescents can be expected to resist the past and to assert their differences from the adult generation. At the same time, they would want to respect us, even emulate us, if what we offered them was consistent with their moral aspirations. Instead, our modern world is haunted by the tremendous waste of the moral potential of youth. The guardians of youth—parents and teachers, political and religious leaders—might do well to ponder whether what they represent and convey as social values and ideals will inspire virtue in youth or encourage those perversities of imagination and self-perfection that seem to be flourishing in our modern societies.

PART THREE

PROSPECTIVES
The Pursuit of Perfection

10

ANOREXIA NERVOSA
A Feminine Pursuit of Perfection

In the womb there are no reflections. The fetus-amniotic fluid-placenta-mother is complete in itself. And a newborn has no mirror other than reflexes, senses, muscles to tell her who or what she is. She takes in and reaches toward. She spits out, screens out, moves away. This marvelous omnipotence of gesture and action will be the template of her first psychological acts—those wishes that allow her to be whatever she wishes to be. She wishes away disturbance. She wishes for relief and satisfaction. And she obtains them—for a short while at least.

A newborn's only knowledge of herself is her tensions and excitements, her gestures of reaching toward and moving away. She searches. But she has no idea of what she is searching for until her movements bring her into contact with something that matches up with her searching body. She is a conjurer who creates magic without comprehending what she is conjuring: the nipple meets her searching mouth, her body fits into a yielding softness that smells just like her own body, the top of her head comes to rest against a boundary. The baby has the illusion that she has created the nipple, her mother's body, the edge of the world. This conjured world is her mirror.

At two months the baby has become aware that she is held together and protected from tension and excitement by some special events that go on outside her body. She senses a presence with odors, touches, heartbeats, body movements that are in perfect harmony with her own bodily states. The match between the mother's holding presence and the infant's gestures is good enough to sustain the baby's illusion that she is omnipotent. In the mother's presence she can still wish to be whatever makes her feel whole and marvelous.

Inexorably the baby is drawn into the safety net of her existence. Her excitements and tensions are tamed by her hunger for the holding presence that gratifies, screens out, rations, frustrates, introduces her to lawfulness. Now the baby begins to measure her own self as it is reflected in the gestures of the mirroring other. Sometimes that mirror comes pretty close to the magical days when the infant could wish to be and she was. The mother's trilling voice and glowing eyes telling the baby, "Oh, what a beautiful baby you are. How wonderful you are. How my soul lights up whenever I hold you in my arms" is almost as good as omnipotence. The baby looks deep into Mother's eyes, coos and gurgles in harmony with her voice, and sees herself mirrored as all the spectacular and powerful things she sometimes imagines herself to be. Mother's mirroring admiration is a caress that paints proud edges on the baby's body.

From then on, for the sake of sharing in the glory and power of the mirroring other, a baby will surrender much of the omnipotence of gesture and action with which she was born. From then on, the anxiety of being separated from the mirroring other holds the baby's omnipotence in check, prevents her from running away with herself. True, the comparison between her own limited power and the extraordinary power of the glorious others on whom she depends for love and safety engenders resentment and envy. But it's worth it. Because whenever she feels vulnerable, less than she would wish to be, reassurance is right at hand. If she doesn't reach out to grab the spoon and mess around with the mushy stuff, if she just opens her mouth and receives the spoon and swallows and coos, the mirroring eyes will light up: "What a wonderful baby you are. You are perfect." The dazzling mirror of self-other love can be a great deceiver.

A fourteen-year-old girl scrutinizes her reflection in the mirror. Her eyes are aglow with the marvel of her delicate face, her slender neck, shoulders, breasts, hips, thighs, calves, ankles. She beams with satisfaction at her luminous, soft skin, the sharp, angular outlines of her nearly flawless, fatless body. A flicker of worry dims her eyes. She has noticed a bulge of stomach. Aside from that one telltale omen the girl is momentarily reassured that she has silenced the *Fresslust* that dominates her existence.

On the other hand, what her mother and father see reflected in the mirror is a specter that bears hardly any resemblance to the wonderful daughter they once knew—a specter with dull, stringy hair; rough, blotchy, sallow skin; long, silky baby hair covering the trunk, back, arms, legs; brownish-hued finger- and toenails; fleshless bones; burning, sunken eyes. A cadaver, a walking skeleton. The parents decide that things have gone far enough with their daughter's crazy diet.

The girl condescendingly agrees to accompany her mother to the doctor's office. She bitterly resents her parents' attempts to undermine her accomplishment. Except for some occasional stomach cramps and the constipation she controls very nicely with laxatives and the numbness and tingling sensations in her hands and feet, she feels perfectly fine. She never felt better.

The doctor sees at once all the outward signs of cachexia, or physical emaciation. The girl is five feet two inches tall and weighs seventy-eight pounds. Her emaciation is near the life-threatening mark. Whatever the doctor's final diagnosis, unless the girl begins to eat immediately he will have to recommend hospitalization. The doctor's physical examination reveals subnormal body temperature, heartbeat less than sixty beats per minute, inflammation of the folds of skin bordering the finger- and toenails, swelling and blueness of the hands and feet, a diminished secretion of sweat and sebum, dehydration.

Laboratory tests will probably indicate an anemia of some sort—either an iron deficiency or possibly a deficiency in protein synthesis. There may be a decrease in the white blood cells, which help to maintain the body's resistance to disease, or an abnormal increase in these cells. The doctor expects a mild to severe bone-marrow deficiency, pancreas dysfunction and a 20 to 40 percent reduction from the girl's previous basal metabolism. Since her body weight has fallen low enough to reverse the hypothalamic-pituitary-gonadal feedback system, her menstrual cycle will have ceased, and X-ray studies would demonstrate a corresponding slowing down of skeletal growth rate. Pubescence has been brought to a halt.

A metabolic crisis leading to renal failure or cardiac arrest may be imminent. If the girl's physical deterioration is not reversed, if it should become chronic, there could be an irreversible shrinking of one of the internal organs—the heart, the kidneys, the brain. The girl might lose the capacity to bear children. If her emaciation proceeds, she will die.

Her mother reports that the household is well run and orderly. She works part time at her profession and is usually at home to supervise her children's homework and meal-times. The other daughter is now doing very well at an Ivy League college. There is no family dissension. The father leaves the management of household matters and child rearing entirely up to the mother. On neither side of the family is there any history of mental or serious physical illness. Until one year ago this scrawny, stubborn, irritable wraith had been a dutiful, obedient, beautiful, well-fed, chubby, high-achieving, 125–I.Q., ambitious, well-behaved child— in fact, the standard-bearer of their happy, harmonious household.

The mother complains that the deterioration happened so suddenly. Her daughter went on a diet. She asked her teacher for extra assignments. She gave up her calisthenics and ballet classes because they were not demanding enough and instead began to run several miles a day. But it wasn't until this usually obedient girl became argumentative, spiteful, stubborn, and began trying to rule over the family dinner hour that the mother thought something might be wrong. It was then the parents noticed that the girl who was planning the menus, supervising the cooking, setting the table, collecting recipes, instructing her father not to chew so loudly, was herself eating only two chicken livers and a slice of cheese for dinner. Nothing the mother or father said could induce her to eat more. Within four months after they initially took note of their daughter's loss of appetite, her weight had dropped from 110 pounds to its present 78.

The doctor is certain that the girl's dramatic weight loss and her idosyncratic behavior are symptomatic of anorexia nervosa. Although in his thirty years of practice he had never seen a case until the late 1970s, in the past two years he has already found it necessary to hospitalize four other girls. Nevertheless he methodically goes through the routine of ruling out those physical disorders that are also accompanied by significant weight loss, such as tuberculosis, adrenal-gland malfunction, spasm of the esophagus, stomach cancer, pernicious anemia. He also considers the possibility of those psychological disturbances in which refusal to eat and emaciation are the secondary symptoms of a broader clinical picture, such as certain forms of schizophrenia and the numerous depressive reactions that are so prevalent during adolescence.

In the last decade medical journals have alerted the doctor to the fact that there are also atypical versions of anorexia, uncomplicated by any other major physical or psychological disorder. These atypical anorexias are usually the result of adolescent dietary asceticism or coercive hunger strikes gone wild, and they are relatively easy to reverse in a short period of time. In view of his knowledge of this girl and her mother, the doctor does not have much hope for a diagnosis of atypical anorexia. Yet he still hopes for this. If that were the diagnosis, he would have the girl's cooperation in the treatment. She would be able to identify herself as a patient who needs help. She could herself complain about her weight loss and recognize that the specter in the mirror is not a beautiful nymph. She would not want to stay so thin and would, with only minor opposition, accommodate to the doctor's dietary recommendations.

What the doctor is holding out for is that this pathetic waif who glares at him so sullenly will show some sign of concern for her physical condition. However, their private interviews confirm the diagnosis of primary, typical anorexia nervosa. The girl's attitude and manner reveal all the distinguishing characteristics: a total absence of concern about her emaciation, her unshakable conviction that she is pursuing a sensible course of action, the vigor and stubbornness with which she defends her exquisite thinness. The girl stresses how well she feels, how she runs or takes strenuous walks of several miles a day, feels no fatigue whatsoever, needs to sleep only three or four hours a night. These proud assertions of her physical and mental well-being are all the more remarkable in view of her profound physical emaciation.

The girl insists that she eats quite enough and that she is never hungry. The doctor knows that she has lost all ability to recognize hunger and that, furthermore, she does not suffer from loss of appetite. For in primary anorexia nervosa the girl or young woman is obsessed with thoughts of food. "Anorexia," which generally means "loss of appetite" and literally "an-orectic"—"loss of the will to live"—is a misnomer on both counts. The girl's appetites are enormous and she does not wish to die.

The disorder was first given its medical label, "anorexia," by Ernest Lasègue in France in 1873 and by Sir William Gull in England in 1874. Gull stressed the generalized mental state that accompanied the seeming loss of appetite—hence *anorexia nervosa*. Lasègue, who believed the etiology was hysterical, called the disorder *anorexie hystérique.* Some years later another French physician, Henri Huchard, discounted the hysterical etiology and recommended the substitution of *anorexie mentale,* the term by which the disorder has been known ever since in Italy and France. In Germany the disorder is referred to as *Pubertätsmagersucht*—compulsive pubertal emaciation—a diagnostic label that is much closer to the observed facts.

The genuine anorectic complains of nothing except her parents' insistence that she try to eat. She goes along with their simpleminded notion that she has lost her appetite. But she knows full well that she often cannot control her appetite. She sneaks food into her bedroom. On occasion she binges until her stomach is bloated and then purges her body by vomiting or dosing herself heavily with laxatives. Her exquisite reed of a body is the sign that she is winning her battle against *Fresslust*. But in almost every other aspect of her life she feels arrested and dominated. She cannot rid herself of the inner experience that she always acts on the commands of others. Except for her dieting, running, and sleepless nights, she feels ineffective and worthless. Her emaciation is her triumph.

Medical historians tell us that prior to the late nineteenth century there were only sporadic, isolated descriptions of illnesses resembling anorexia: in the third century A.D. a Buddha in search of enlightenment; in the eleventh century a young prince suffering from melancholia; in 1613 a French girl who fasted for three years; in 1689 two cases described as a consumption of mental origins with emaciation, amenorrhea, constipation, overactivity, loss of appetite; in the late eighteenth century several cases in England, and in France the case of a girl that ended in death. That death was attributed to the pernicious influence of the mother.

From the 1870s onward medical descriptions of the disorder were to highlight the family constellation. Lasègue's classical paper, "On Hysterical Anorexia," warned: "Both patient and her family form a tightly knit whole and we obtain a false picture of the disease if we limit our observations to the patients alone." Gull recommended removal of the patient from the family. In 1895 Gilles de la Tourette, who also recommended separating the girl from her family, was the first to call attention to the fact that the patient did not suffer from loss of appetite. Refusal to eat and a distorted perception of her body, he claimed, were the hallmarks of the disease.

Except for the period between 1915 and 1935, when anorexia and nearly every other disease of subnutrition was attributed to Simmonds' disease, the pituitary marasmus dis-covered by Dr. Morris Simmonds, most experts have been aware that the physical emaciation was initiated, main-tained, and then escalated to the level of starvation by psy-chological forces. There was a consensus that the family constellation, especially the mother-daughter relationship, played a major role in the disorder.

As more and more cases came to their attention, physi-cians and psychologists were frustrated by their inability to solve the enigmas of the bizarre disorder, which in its pri-mary typical form was confined almost exclusively to upper-and upper-middle-class female adolescents. Speculations as to the underlying psychological dynamics of these self-starving girls and their families were rampant. Because the psychoanalysts and other investigators were attending to the most obvious and dramatic feature of the anorexia syndrome —the refusal to eat—their theories initially concentrated on the "oral" components of the disorder. Cannibalistic fan-tasies—the wish for oral incorporation of the mother, fear of swallowing the mother, the wish for oral impregnation by the father—were among the suggested central dynamics.

Interpretations to the patient based on these speculations did not swerve the anorectic from her fierce ambition. Of-ten the interpretations had the opposite effect of increasing the girl's determination not to eat. As some former patients described the therapeutic situation, they felt invaded and penetrated by the doctors' words and felt as dominated by the doctor-patient relationship itself as they did by their bodily functions. They would sullenly take in everything the doctor said and then vomit out the message by obliterating it from memory. The multiplication of theories did little to dispel the enigmas or to cure the anorectic. Until recently, when the death rate was lowered to 2 percent, it had re-mained at a steady 15 percent, and many girls went on to become chronic anorectics, living out the rest of their exis-tence on the border of starvation.

One fact is incontestable. In Western societies anorexia has been on a steady increase. Each year, over the past thirty years, about one new case per 200,000 population has been reported. In Scandinavia the increase has been fivefold. And in Japan, where prior to Westernization anorexia was so rare as to be considered nonexistent, the disorder has become nearly as prevalent as in the United States and in Great Britain. And whereas anorexia was once confined to white upper- and upper-middle-class girls, it has now spread across class and ethnic lines wherever upwardly mobile, ambitious families may be found. If the nonstarving, binger-purgers (bulimics) were to be included in the statistics, the incidence would be much higher. Despite the mounting frequencies, anorexia as of 1982 was still in the statistical category of "rare," about one out of every 250 teenage girls. Bulimia is estimated to occur in about 13 percent of this age group, with 30 percent exhibiting some bulimic symptoms.

Of course there is no way to estimate the undoubtedly enormous number of college students, dancers, models who are maintaining their "ideal weight" by vomiting after meals. The statistics also do not take into account the army of thin-fat people—those slim, slender, underweight, scrawny women whose image conforms to the Western ideal of beauty but who are starving the lusty being inside them and consequently are irritable, tense, nervous, compulsively orderly, controlling, emotionally needy, envious. As Heckel, the physician who in 1911 coined the term "thin-fat people," said, "un obèse amaigri [thinned]; mais il est toujours un obèse."

Within the last decade or so, as cases of anorexia multiplied at an alarming rate, it became apparent that the so-called oral features of the disorder were merely the tip of the iceberg. The experts began to pay attention to the other dominant aspects of the anorexia syndrome: the girl's distorted perception of her body and bodily functions, her fierce ambition, her perfectionism and overactivity. Psychologists of every therapeutic persuasion—orthodox psychoanalysts, behavior modifiers, family therapists, even the old-fashioned force-feeding, drug-oriented physicians—were to be increasingly impressed by the mirroring quality of the mother-daughter relationship and the psychological enmeshment of all the members of these supranormal, well-run, orderly, harmonious, ambitious families.

As psychologists became familiar with the details of the separation-individuation process, the infant-mother relationship began to be thought of as the key that would clarify the enigmas of anorexia. Gradually the oral theories were replaced by one version or another of separation-individuation dynamics. The usual format goes one of two ways: Some say that the anorectic is a girl who was unable during infancy to separate successfully from the mother. Now, at pubescence or puberty, when faced with the necessity to detach from Mother, the girl does not have the emotional wherewithal to engage the conflicts this move entails. Her alternative is to restore the state of oneness with Mother, "... her euphoria can be understood by assuming that unconsciously she was united with her nursing mother." These writers suggest that there has been an arrest at the symbiotic level of development: "the original mother-daughter symbiosis of infancy was not merely a predisposing factor but the beginning of a process that was continually active, in latent or manifest form, 'as long as they both shall live.'"

In the other typical version, clinicians focus on the love-hate struggle between the anorectic and her family, especially the mutual ambivalence between daughter and mother. The girl, they say, has regressed to the rapprochement subphase of separation-individuation; she clings to Mother and yet struggles to be free of her, much like a toddler in the throes of rapprochement. "Keeping mother and ridding oneself of mother are central to the struggle of the rapprochement crisis. . . . Paradoxically, this regression will afford at the same time autonomy, freedom from mother, the gain of self-determination, as well as its opposite, the retention of the omnipotent dyad."

Certainly there is some merit to these interpretations of the infantile etiology and ongoing dynamics of the anorexia syndrome. But when the symptoms are simply reduced to their infantile origins, they can and frequently do obscure the essential fact that in high-school and college-age girls anorexia is a solution to the dilemmas associated with becoming a woman. True, we are led to assume from the girl's present behaviors and fantasies that there had been inadequacies in the subphases of separation-individuation *and* in the infantile Oedipal scenario and that these deprivations predisposed her to react to pubescence and puberty with inordinate anxiety. Evidently the girl brings to the expectable trials of adolescence a unique fragility of personality. And if we observe the girl after the starvation has taken possession of her life we must conclude that there has been a regression; the love dialogues of infancy have infiltrated the solutions of adolescence. However, none of this is true enough, for if we forget that initially, in pubescence, the girl made a heroic effort to obey certain paradoxical imperatives of the incest taboo, we will not be involved in a full understanding of her situation. She is not an infant struggling with issues of separation-individuation but an adolescent trying to come to terms with genitality.

The anorexia solution is a warning about the precarious position of the adolescent. Sometimes the inevitable temporary regressions we have noted can take over the adolescent's life and prevent any further movement into the future. In those young people who are so predisposed, such solutions as dietary asceticism, compulsive masturbation, promiscuity, perversions, drug addiction, alcoholism can in and of themselves lure adolescents further into the past. Some slip beyond the pale. They never find their way back.

The anorectic does not start out her dietary misadventure with the unconscious wish to return to the omnipotence of infancy. She starts out with the unconscious question "Shall I renounce genital desire and remain faithful to the past? Or shall I direct my desires away from my family and give up my idealizations of the past?" In the choice between remaining bound to her parents in a nongenital, infantile way or affirming genital vitality and her commitment to ongoing life, the average adolescent decides in favor of giving up the past. Similarly, the anorectic wants to wrench free of the past and assert her independence. But in her case the past, which even under ordinary conditions does not willingly lend itself to be given up, is especially tenacious. In such a predisposed girl the archaic past is insistent in its demands to be reinstated. But the second burst of individuation gives the girl a chance to rectify the humiliations of infancy. She does not simply surrender to the past; she tries to find a way to be loyal to it and still assert her selfhood and autonomy. Her solution, as awesome and horrifying as it is, is an ingenious compromise.

Looking backward to the infancy of their anorectic patients, an infancy that they have reconstructed from parent interviews and from the patients' remembrances, reports, transference experiences, and fantasies of those early months and years, clinicians, as we have seen, are bound to be impressed with a separation-individuation gone awry. From the retrospective reports the picture that consistently emerges is that of the intelligent, compliant baby who all too easily and willingly surrendered her omnipotence and precious love of her own self for the self-esteem of becoming a narcissistic extention of Mother.

Yet, looking ahead from infancy to adolescence, no sensible clinical observer would be so arrogant as to predict from observation of a girl's relationship to her mother during infancy an anorectic solution during adolescence. In the intervening years, changes in the family's emotional constellation—the birth of another child, the father becoming a more active participant in the household, the mother's melancholic reaction to the death of her own mother, a move to a new neighborhood, the father's loss of professional prestige—and, more important, the flourishing during latency and early pubescence of temperamental, artistic, and intellectual qualities dormant during the infantile period could have the effects of alleviating, modifying, potentiating, or exacerbating the possibilities set in motion by the deprivations of infancy.

Examining the enigmas of anorexia from the point of view of adolescence, we find one central dynamic identified repeatedly. Most clinicians concur with Hilde Bruch's general formulation, which she arrived at in the late 1960s, that anorexia represents a desperate striving to attain a sense of personal identity, an urgent need to claim possession over one's body and mind in order to become an autonomous self. Embodied in Bruch's formulation is the premise that the anorectic girl, like any other adolescent, is trying to become independent of her family. The enigmas concern the forces that oppose the anorectic's strivings to attain this sense of personal authenticity.

The primary danger of adolescence is the reawakening of the love attachments of infancy. As we have seen, the major conflicts concern removal as an effort to detach from the past. The anxieties aroused by saying farewell to childhood are more than the anorectic can manage. Indeed, her symptoms could be viewed as a mourning process that failed—a melancholia. Freud was close to a truth when in 1895 he spoke of anorexia as "a melancholia where sexuality is undeveloped." Why does the anorectic find it so hard to relinquish the past? As Bruch recently observed, the self-starvation is but the final step in a long-standing developmental disorder. Preceding the starvation and then escalating in intensity as co-symptoms are the girl's excessive ambition and perfectionism. Like other girls her age, the anorectic starts out by striving for individuation and autonomy. Her downfall is her excessive ambition, her desperate quest for perfection. Thus anorexia is a pathology of the ordinary issues of the adolescent passage.

From the vantage point of a neatly framed, undistorted mirror, this scarecrow, this walking cadaver, bears no resemblance to the average teenage girl; she looks so freakish that surely she is beyond the limits of ordinary human experience. What could the anorectic tell us about normal adolescents contentedly munching away on their Rocky Roads, pizzas, hot dogs? But looking at her through her own mirror, we would have to concede that she has achieved the glory that every adolescent merely dreams of: goodness, purity, perfection of mind and body, chastity, valor, wisdom— in short, absolute virtue. Whereas most adolescents are destined to fail in their pursuit of perfection, in her own way the anorectic has succeeded. Whereas the average adolescent moves from childhood to adult ways of thinking, imagining, experiencing, feeling, and acting via arduous circuitous pathways employing the slow, gradual method of success, relapse, trial and error, and temporary reversal, the anorectic attempts to wean herself of desire overnight; hoping to bypass grief, anxiety, struggle, conflict, she opts for a shortcut to instant virtue. The dazzling gleam of her mirror deludes her into believing that she has arrived at the future, that she has found "the way," that soon she will be reborn as a new and better person.

The solution she has chosen is extraordinary, but the dilemmas she is attempting to solve are identical to those of the garden-variety adolescent. The dilemmas entail desire, love dialogue, authority, and all three currents of narcissism—bodily love, self-esteem, omnipotence. Above all else, the anorectic endeavors to remain true to her own self. But her ordeal of perfection has obscured the distinctions between vanity and self-regard, pride and power. Her conjuring has blinded her to reason and necessity. She is alone, lost in the infinite, lost in her imagination, without the efficacy of real work, love dialogue, companionship, social concern, a sense of community.

How did she get lost? How did her heroic efforts to become a new and better person bring her to the verge of death? With anorexia, as with any other adolescent solution, the sexual and the moral intertwine. Everything else grows up around them.

The anorectic's dramatic and abrupt descent into the ways of infancy, her exotic behaviors, which at first glance seem an amazing replica of the subphases of separation-individuation, can easily blind the observer to the source of the anorectic's immediate anxieties: dread of emotional surrender to the caregiving mother *and* dread of incest. When the girl is brought to our attention after the starvation has taken hold of her personality, she has already lost her emotional connections with adolescence. But if we had caught her a few months earlier, just as she was poised to embark on her fanatical search for perfection, we would have observed exaggerated renditions of the typical adolescent strategies whose primary goal is *removal.*

By the time the potential anorectic arrives at pubescence or puberty she is so thoroughly enmeshed in the family web, so much a mirroring extension of her mother that she must put up a more determined and valiant struggle with her incestuous desires. It is the exaggerated quality of the adolescent strategies that signals the extent of the pull to the past. In the burst of panic that follows on the girl's foreboding sense that she is not worthy enough, not good enough to fight off the lusts that are invading her body, the girl musters every adolescent strategy, sometimes all at once: bodily asceticism, uncompromising ideals, flight from the family, reversal of love-desire into hatred. With every weapon at her command she tries to ward off desire and sever her attachments to her family.

The anorectic is a wild creature driven mad by appetite, lust, desire. With the anorectic, asceticism takes over. She is unrelenting in her war on bodily pleasure; what starts out as an ordinary adolescent dietary fad eventuates in a perversity of starvation. She dresses in the equivalent of sackcloth, runs seven miles a day, sleeps only four hours a night. She is totally uncompromising in her thinking and attitudes. Rules, obedience, duty are all that count. The blending of opposites or the possibility of assenting to the harmony between opposing points of view are intolerable to her. Thus she struggles to protect her mind from the ugly temptations of the body. The vitalities of genital awakening inspire the girl to play all parts in the human comedy. But she is terrified to play any part but a mirroring extension of someone else. She listens only to the voices of infancy and childhood, which demand a narrowing of roles, renunciation, sacrifice. The role she is most suited for is that of a saint.

But fighting off desire is not enough. The anorectic will quickly enlist other adolescent strategies that aim at loosening her passionate attachments to her family. Ordinarily the detachment of libido from the parents takes the gradual course of a piece-by-piece relinquishment. To an anorectic such a slow and potentially hazardous method is intolerable. She must take recourse to more dramatic and immediate tactics. Before the starvation diet takes over, some not-yet anorectics force themselves to become emancipated and independent, much the way they forced themselves to be undemanding, good little babies. Their attempts to flee from the family nest in a trip to Europe or a year at boarding school serve instead to precipitate the anorexia. Away from home they become frightened, alone, vulnerable, unsure of who or what they are supposed to be. The girl returns from her precipitous misadventure with freedom looking like a scarecrow. Having failed, the girl must now enlist the aid of reversal of love-desire into hatred. As the girl retreats more and more into the web of family hatred she becomes less and less available to the transfer of love-desire outside the family.

And as it typically happens, because an adolescent cannot tolerate for long such destruction directed at her parents, the eventual outcome of reversal is that the destructive wishes initially directed toward the parents get turned around toward the self. Self-denigration and severe forms of self-abasement are the common elaborations of the series: love-desire reversed into hate-desire becomes self-hatred.

As the anorectic's self-destructive emaciation gets under way, she is convinced that all adults are persecutors—oppressors whose sole aim is to rob her of her achievement of perfection. The physiological effects of emaciation now combine forces with the anorectic's all-out desperate strategies for removal. She becomes a law unto herself, totally absorbed in the functioning of her body, bolstering her self-esteem, asserting her power over her lusts. The pathetic irony of the anorectic's flight from incestuous desire is that she ends up by returning to the past. She will struggle to the bitter end, even to death. But her frantic gestures of removal pull her deeper and deeper into the past. The words she speaks are a parody of her parents' values, of their great pretense at moral perfection. Her emaciated body is a caricature of the mirroring baby her mother needed her to be— a baby without desire, in absolute control of her bodily functions.

What we see, then, in the anorectic are the subtle interweavings of past and present. First and foremost she is an adolescent striving to extricate herself from the web of family desire. Past and future have contended for her soul. The past has temporarily, perhaps permanently gained the day.

The narratives of human existence consist always of the interweaving legends from various phases of a life history. As the conjugator of childhood and adulthood, adolescence is always the battleground on which the past and future contend. Onset of primary anorexia in females is virtually nonexistent before the age of eleven and infrequent in women over twenty-five. Since babyhood the girl predisposed to anorexia has been relatively precocious in her physical and intellectual development. Pubescence and menarche are likely to commence about one or two years earlier than the average. But whether her pubescence begins early, at age ten, or late, at age fourteen, the potential anorectic is not an anorectic until she tries to cope with the dilemmas of becoming a woman.

If the biological changes of pubescence had not taken place, the dormant illness of infancy might not have revealed itself. The self-starvation, ambition, perfectionism of anorexia could be understood as the guiding themes of an adolescent fantasy, which, when projected backward onto the past, expose the infantile love dialogues for what they were. If it were not for the trials of adolescence, we might never have known that this best of all little girls, living in the most affluent of social environments, endowed by nature with nearly every physical and temperamental advantage (except probably sufficient individuation aggression), provided by her well-intentioned family with every advantage of money and power, had been deprived of the omnipotence, bodily love, and self-esteem that most ordinary babies can take for granted.

If she could have remained in the never-never land of childhood, this dutiful girl might have turned out to be the model citizen of a utopia. Her forte is controlling her bodily functions. She would do everything within her power to decipher the inscrutable expectations of the authorities and then live up to them. She would enthusiastically accept the drab uniform and number assigned to her. She would flourish on regimentation. Her excessive ambition could have been unobtrusively satisfied by obeying the rules better than anyone else. Since everybody would be the same, she would not suffer so from *amour-propre,* from comparing herself to the others. The banishing of the poets would suit her very nicely.

The onset of pubescence drives the girl out of the schoolyard, inspiring her to escape from her well-run, orderly, harmonious, smothering, domestic cocoon. Pubescence is her chance to rewrite the scripts. Like most upper- and middle-class adolescent girls growing up into womanhood in a modernized society during the closing decades of the twentieth century, the potential anorectic has been granted permission to use her talents, to advance her intellectual ambitions. She has been given a license to pursue her sexual desires in any way she sees fit with any person she deems desirable. All this freedom of opportunity is overwhelming. Perhaps it would be overwhelming for any girl or boy. Surely it is for a girl whose babyhood and childhood were guided by absolute obedience and submission to the exacting rules and regulations of the nursery dialogue.

The best little girl in the world was deprived of the narcissistic advantages that are the birthright of every human infant, and of the *inner* authority to regulate her own desires. One reason for these deprivations is the ease with which the girl became a mirroring extension of her mother. Another is the relative absence in her infancy and early childhood of a fathering presence. It is as though the girl never went much further in her sense of goodness and badness than to be successful in controlling her eating and her bowel movements, but without the experience that her body and mind belonged to her. It was a matter of pleasing Mother or displeasing her—even with a governess or nursemaid left in charge of the actual nursery duties. And the father did not offer an alternative to the infant-mother dialogue. At the conclusion of infancy he did not make his presence felt. He did not interrupt the daughter-mother love affair. He did not introduce his daughter to the authority of the social order. She was left with the permissions and prohibitions of nursery morality.

All babies enter the world with their own temperaments: some are more easily comforted than others; some are quietly persistent, others more fiercely demanding; some are smarter, quicker to comprehend how to please their caregivers; some cannot bear frustration of any kind; others will tolerate all kinds of restrictions and prohibitions with remarkable equanimity. As a general rule, girl babies are more compliant, more able to withstand frustration, more easygoing, more accommodating to the demands of civilization, more content to be a mirroring extension of Mother. They are easier to wean and toilet train than boys. Parents are more accepting, more tolerant of a boy baby's wildness, aggression, motoric energies, exploratory rampages. When it comes to asserting their differences and separateness from Mother, most boys have the inner sense that they are more like Father than like Mother, that Father is an ally. Throughout infancy, when differentiation is the central thrust of life, the father's primary emotional role is to help his child to differentiate self from Mother, Mother from other, femininity from masculinity. Usually a daughter's attachment to her father lures her out of the exclusively mirroring relationship with mother. The father's emotional presence diverts some of the child's Mother-possessiveness toward himself. His masculinity complements his daughter's incipient femininity. With a father as an active presence in her daily life a girl baby begins to experience the possibilities of feminine identity outside the exclusive relationship with Mother. Being a girl or a woman doesn't mean being Mommy.

During these early months and years the father is experienced by his children as an intruder, the one who represents the emotional wedge between Mother and child. Boys and girls will frequently divert their longings for Mother toward the father. They turn to him for fun and games, for comforting, for compensation for some of the disappointments and frustrations in the infant-mother dialogue. Then Mother is the intruder. "Enough of this fooling around. Time for bed." "Time to come in to dinner." Through her gestures of gratifying, rationing, dosing, frustrating, the mother introduces her infant to the basic rules of law and order. She is both the primary giver of pleasure and the primary principle of reality in the family. The father comes to represent the law and order of society, the voice that says, "Enough of this mother-baby mirroring. I am the law. Mother belongs to me—not to you. You are the child. We are the grown-ups."

Eventually, during the Oedipal phase, the incest taboo as represented by the "voice of the father" brings the dialogues of infancy to a definitive close. Then the child becomes the outsider, the intruder. In this later, more conclusive, triangle the parents acquire a new version of power. For the first time the child has the experience of being left out of the love dialogues, which now go on between the parents. Imagination, wishing, fantasy are her only clues to what is going on in these exchanges between grown-ups. Her imagination is informed only by what she has known— feeding, toileting, the excitements of her immature genitals. This bitter reminder that she is small, vulnerable, deficient in her capacity to participate in grown-up desires, motivates a child to become like her parents in every way she can. She is compensated for her defeat by acquiring for her own self some of the moral power and authority of the parents. Also, selected aspects of their ways of talking, walking, thinking become aspects of her own self-experience. Their interests, attitudes, values, prohibitions, and permissions become her own inner experience. In exchange for banishment she gets the right to participate actively in the principles of law and order that govern the social world in which she will grow up.

When the Oedipal triangle is weakly articulated, a child is deprived of the opportunity to own her conscience. She is ruled by a conscience of weaning, absence, toilet training, controlling bodily functions. The parental prohibitions and commandments then will continue to be experienced as coming from outside the self, or as alien inner voices. One of the major complaints of the anorectic is that she cannot rid herself of the sense that she always acts on the commands of others. "There is another self, a dictator who dominates me. . . . A little man screams at me when I think of eating."

Not every girl deprived of the law-giving influence of the father is destined for anorexia. But "father absence" in its largest sense does affect every feature of a child's emotional and intellectual life. The differences between femininity and masculinity are blurred. For the girl to become feminine, she becomes a caricatured version of Mother. For the boy, becoming a man is mysterious and awesome. He either becomes a pretender to manhood of some sort or feels that he must surrender his genitals to Mother as he once surrendered his body contents. Essentially the child's body and mind are experienced as possessions of the mother. When one's own genitals belong to Mother (or to Father) conscience never grows up either. In its infantile form conscience is a list of isolated rules, regulations, prohibitions, cautions.

With such a conscience as one's sole guide to lawfulness, a child is forced into a robotlike obedience, following each rule to the letter, imitating literally and concretely some behavior that has been prescribed as the right way, but never grasping the more general social and moral implications of the behavior. No distinctions are attained between flexibility and transgressions. In some children this primitive form of lawfulness leads to overexacting obedience. In other children it could lead to literal forms of disobedience. Whereas the average child is able to derive enormous satisfaction from the sense that she has some inner authority to regulate her hungers and desires, the child who has been deprived of the voice of the father begins to approach every action as preordained by some ruthless and implacable tyrant. She becomes a slave to desire, a slave to the commandments of conscience, a slave to perfection. She becomes a caricature of goodness, confused about her body and its functions, plagued by an all-pervasive conviction that she is basically ineffectual, undeserving, unworthy, never quite good enough. "Enough means when you collapse, when your body just won't give up any more of itself."

It is not incidental that the fathers of anorectic girls are usually fiercely ambitious in their professional roles and remarkably passive and unavailable when it comes to domestic issues. They expect polished performances from their children and wives but are content to let their efficient wives rule the roost and dominate the trivialities of the nursery. Nor is it by chance that anorectic girls are reported to have been especially good babies, the mother's pride and joy and a source of great satisfaction to the father's vanity. The "best little girl" role is easy to learn if one is intelligent, if one is not too aggressive, demanding, or possessive of a mother's time and energy, if one is fairly adept at reading what one's audience wants and then mirroring it back. The rules that govern the role are relatively simple. One looks into the other's face and emulates what one is supposed to be. The best little girl is supposed to please her mother and father, achieve what they want, talk early, walk early, do her puzzles in jig time, nap for the prescribed two hours and then wait patiently to be picked up, diaper her dollies, never get too hungry, show off for company, be self-sufficient, never look sad or angry. Sometimes she is supposed to be like a caregiver to Mother, a kind of nurse who soothes her mother into feeling happy and good by being herself happy and good. Sometimes she is supposed to mirror her mother's ambitions for smartness and perfection of body and mind, all things that Mother had wished to become but didn't quite succeed at. "Be my golden girl. Shine with good cheer and brilliance. But do not be greedy. No cuddling or rocking. No lingering in the bathtub, no sucking, no sweets, no messing with glue and mud and dirty crayons. Just so many hugs, no more from my alabaster arms." In other words, no omnipotence, not too much bodily love, but lots of mirroring admiration when you do what makes Mommy feel happy and worthwhile.

J. B. Watson, the American psychologist who in the 1930s tried to teach parents how to stamp out a child's unruly desires, might have nodded his approval of this particular mother-infant relationship.

There is a sensible way of treating children. Treat them as though they were young adults. Dress them, bathe them with care and circumspection. Let your behavior always be objective and kindly firm. Never hug and kiss them, never let them sit on your lap. If you must, kiss them once on the forehead when they say good night. Shake hands with them in the morning. Give them a pat on the head if they have made an extraordinarily good job of a difficult task. Try it out. . . . You will be utterly ashamed of the mawkish, sentimental way you have been handling it.

Watson and the other early behavior modifiers wanted to prepare a child for civilized living. They didn't know that among the more efficient ways to ensure lawlessness and narcissistic self-preoccupation are squelching an infant's omnipotence and bodily love and attempting to do away with desire. These methods can be as corrupting to the moral sense as exaggerating omnipotence and overgratifying desire. With a Watsonian scenario as its leitmotif, the infant-mother dialogue is sparse in the ordinary sensuality and sentiments that are the heartbeats of parental love. But desire is born anyhow, and once born, desire fights for its rights. It knows how to appease, how to disguise itself, how to wait patiently for its day to come. In the meantime the superego is devouring, tempting, watching, a sadistic tyrant stilled only temporarily by masochistic measures. At the same time, the ego-ideal is ruthless. Nothing less than absolute perfection will do.

Childhood for the perfect child becomes an ordeal of living up to someone else's expectations, an anguish of never feeling good enough in comparison to others. Because she is a proficient mirrorer of what her parents expect, there are few occasions for punishment or harsh words. No whips are necessary. There is much care, concern, and parental investment in this special child. But the girl cannot grasp what her parents are really thinking or feeling behind their smiling, approving faces. At any moment she might take the step, speak the words, display the emotions that could sour her parents' faces with rejection and denigration.

The parents themselves are pretenders, performers who are preoccupied with the images that others have of them. In order to reassure her parents and preserve the peace, the girl becomes an expert at pretending. She often feels sad, but she puts on a cheery smile that makes her parents feel that they are worthwhile. She may become angry about all this submission, but she does not talk back or act stubbornly. She is as out of touch with her emotional states as she is with her bodily functions. The mind's job, she supposes, is to control the unruly body, to mask the awkward stammer of her emotions. Later on, after she becomes anorectic, her body will rule her mind. With the anorectic, nothing is as it seems to be. There is no loss of appetite. Desire is on a rampage. The girl is a deceiving pretender to goodness.

Outside the family web, even when surrounded by friends, the girl is an emotional isolate. Accustomed as she is to finding out who and what she is supposed to be in the gaze of her parents, the potential anorectic has no self-conviction, no firm sense of her own individuality. During her latency years she conceives of herself as a blank tablet, a piece of wood on which the other girls may carve out the sort of friend they want, a nice friend with suitable clothes, suitable likes and dislikes. The girl has only a few friendships, usually one at a time. With each new friend the girl acquires a new self, with brand-new interests and attitudes. The girl is a great emulator but is never sure she is doing exactly the right thing. "There wasn't a person inside at all. I tried with whoever I was with to reflect the image they had of me, to do what they expected me to do."

Lacking the inner emotional yardsticks, the personal standards by which she might evaluate herself, the potential anorectic during latency is absorbed by *amour-propre*. She incessantly compares herself to others, and no matter how outstanding her performance or how much praise she gets from parents and teachers, she finds herself wanting. In school she scrutinizes the faces of the other girls and boys. She tries to figure out whether they are learning more or less than she. If the other girls in her class are preoccupied with clothes, she tries to dress like all of them. Her mother, who usually makes all the decisions but who also wants her daughter to look happy and be popular, goes along with the girl's "bizarre" requests—the specially pleated skirt, the plastic beads, the patent-leather boots, the riding jodhpurs, the wooden barrettes. But Mother draws the line at "those barbaric earrings." For the girl, getting dressed in the morning is an ordeal. She changes three or four times, never sure whether she will pass muster among her peers. "What will they say about me?" "Will they like me?"

The peculiar feature of this ambitious child's *amour-propre* is that she is not so much interested in rising above her peers as being merely okay, acceptable, right. It is only later on, about a year before the dieting starts, that the girl gives up trying to be like others. She withdraws from the challenges of friendships. She becomes a social isolate. Now her inflexible judgmental attitudes, which she had once applied so pitilessly to her own self, are employed to demean others. "They are so childish, so superficial in their values. . . . All they think about is boys and clothes." The literal rules for getting along in the world which had been serviceable during childhood do not work in the strange new world of adolescence. As she becomes more and more distanced from her age-mates, the pitiless inhumanity of the girl's moral life takes over, sometimes in the guise of humanitarianism. "I feel that I can't live on just an ordinary scale of human endeavor. I feel I have to make this world better and do as much as a human being is capable of doing. What I have to achieve is something that absolutely squeezes the last drop out of me, otherwise I haven't given enough. Only when everything has been given and I can give no more will I have done my duty."

As she approaches pubescence many a school-age girl is susceptible to shame concerning her slightly overweight, plump body. She tries to curb her appetites. She goes on crazy diets. She indulges in food fads. She becomes a vegetarian. What distinguishes the potential anorectic from the other chubby fourth-graders is the intensity of her ambition. She is the girl who gets the A's, prepares the neatest and best-organized science projects, is chosen to dust the books, erase the blackboard, hand out the test papers, run errands for her adoring teacher. "She's marvelous! If only all the kids were like her, teaching would be a joy." Some teachers are not impressed. "She's just fine when it comes to following the rules, answering the questions in just the right way, memorizing the facts. But she falls apart when she tries to understand abstract concepts. Questions that require imagination and inventiveness seem to go over her head." "She does not participate in the give-and-take of classroom discussions. She either gives the 'right' answer immediately or waits until we all get to the right answer. Then she recites it like a parrot." "Let me call attention to one little spelling mistake or change the seating arrangement or daily lesson schedule, she gets teary-eyed."

The potential anorectic is a perfectionistic schoolchild. She cannot bear to be wrong or inaccurate. She is extremely sensitive to criticism. If the rules fluctuate, if the customary structures of her life are altered, if someone corrects or criticizes her, she is overcome with an unnameable dread.

Changes in routine, embarrassments, disappointments, minor criticisms, rejections, slights, a joking reference to her chubby face will have a decisive impact, a catalytic effect on an overly sensitive, highly ambitious, perfectionistic girl at that time in her life when she is also trying to confront the biological changes and psychological dilemmas of adolescence. The potential anorectic will react to menstruation, to erect nipples, to the slightly raised areola and breast mound, to the increase of fatty tissue on her calves, hips, thighs, breasts with a deep sense of fear and foreboding. This girl, who since babyhood has been the stringent overseer of her bodily functions, now feels utterly helpless. The physical changes take over her body like a rapist. She is haunted by the fear that everything could go out of control. Perhaps I cannot quiet my hungers? Will I be overcome with lust? The irrevocability of femaleness, the idea that she must now become a woman and nothing else is a shock, a profound insult, an awesome reminder that no matter how strong, how clever, how good, she cannot control nature. Her possibilities are limited.

The girl is bereft. She dare not expose how frightened she is. "What's wrong with me? . . . Why am I such a weak, bad person? . . . What can I do to make myself more attractive and likable?" The girl sets about to rectify this terrifying and humiliating situation. She cannot control nature, but she can throw herself into schoolwork, exercise more, work harder at everything. And if these moves don't allay her anxieties, eating is an activity that can be controlled. Dieting is something you can do all on your own without asking anyone for help, without admitting that you feel frightened, vulnerable, alone. Her friends try to diet and don't succeed. Her mother is perpetually diet-conscious. Her father struts his lean, tough body. The whole world is jogging, running, exercising, on one diet or another. Dieting is a good thing—an act of virtue.

The diet begins as part of a resolution to become a better person, a strong, self-sufficient person, an admired, superior person. At first the girl seems like any other dieter. She talks enthusiastically about her regime with anyone who will listen to her. She limits the starches and the sweets and steps up her exercising. Then she eliminates beef, and lamb, and eggs, all but one or two vegetables. Soon she is down to a few raisins for breakfast, two chicken livers and some carrot slices for dinner, perhaps four to six Cheerios, a sliver of cheese or apple now and then during the day. These meager meals are sprinkled with vinegar or pepper to give them an exotic flavor. Within a few months the girl has advanced from simple dieting to semistarvation. She is on her way to emaciation. By the time she has lost her first twenty or thirty pounds, starvation is the master she serves. If the Well-doers and Big Brothers were to encounter her then, they would strip her of her number and uniform; they would exile her along with the recalcitrant poets and the saints. Her lofty self-sufficiency, her intimacy with passion has transformed the dutiful citizen into a menace to society, more dangerous than any ordinary juvenile delinquent who can be brought to submission by gentle persuasion, brain washing, torture, body mutilation. Once she gets going, nothing can deter the anorectic from her pursuit of perfection. If they hospitalize her, she begins to know more about the methods of reeducation than her captors. She defeats them all: the forced feeding by mouth or nasogastric tube; the insulin therapy designed to bring about sweating, anxiety, dizziness, hunger; intravenous hyperalimentation; the chlorpromazine designed to reduce her fear of eating; the electroconvulsive therapy; the behavior-modification regimes that will permit running only after eating and weight gain; even the neurosurgery, the leucotomy that gets her to eat but turns her into a bulimic and secret vomiter.

Anorectics are isolated, reserved, pretentious, evasive, not very truthful, foxy. Only to their diaries or to a trusted therapist will these secretive and intelligent girls speak their minds: "I do not think the fear of becoming fat is the real obsession, but the *continuous desire for food*. The desire, the greed for eating must be the primary cause. The fear of becoming fat acts like a brake. I see in this 'Fresslust' the real obsession. It has fallen over me like a beast and I am helpless against it."

Hunger is a beast, a persecutor, a sinister power, a curse, an evil spirit, an ever-pursuing demon, a fanged hound straining at the leash. Some girls who start out with the goal of achieving a thin and delicate body yield to the beast— but not entirely. They learn, sometimes quite by accident from a schoolmate or a magazine article, that there are some easy techniques for outfoxing the hound. Bulimia is one solution.

Even after a large meal a bulimic is often overcome by a sudden craving for food. Within two hours she will consume four cheeseburgers, two quarts of ice cream, a dozen jelly doughnuts, five candy bars. After her stomach is bloated to the bursting point the girl purges her body by self-induced vomiting or laxatives and diuretics. The anorectic turns away from food. The bulimic, who is just as concerned with acceptance and approval, turns toward food to alleviate her anxieties. For the bulimic food is safe, secure, dependable. The bingeing anesthetizes her fears, numbs the anger and loneliness. She eats for emotional comfort. Soon, however, she begins to fear that she will gain too much weight and thus become vulnerable to the disapproval she is escaping from. Purging becomes an integral aspect of her emotional crutch. The binge-purge ritual becomes more and more frequent, taking over like an addiction. The binge numbs the emotions; the purge flushes them away. So relieving, so cleansing is the act of purging that the entrenched bulimic begins to eat for the sake of purging. The physical complications of the purging are serious—irreversible damage to the esophagus, bursting blood vessels in the eyes, loss of tooth enamel, tooth decay, heart arrhythmia, heart failure. The bulimic is unable to lose weight consistently or to maintain a diet. She is easily overcome by craving and impulses. Between eating binges, if she can afford it, she goes on shopping sprees. If funds are short, she steals what she craves. She becomes adept at wheedling money from her parents to support her habits. She uses book money and faked tuition fees to pay for her binges. Bulimics also surrender to their lustings for body contact, cuddling, warmth, approval, admiration. Some are sexually frenzied, desperately searching for the enfolding arms, the nourishing admiration they crave.

While her sisters under the skin succeed only in appeasing the beast, the anorectic seems to have triumphed over *Fresslust,* possession lust, genital lust. Occasionally the anorectic might steal a shiny trinket to adorn her body or hoard food in her bookcase. Many anorectics indulge in episodes of kleptomania or bingeing and purging. But, as their thin, delicate bodies testify, they are 99.99 percent pure, above desire or hunger. Let them speak and we hear another story.

"I am really ruining myself in this endless struggle against nature. Fate wanted me to be heavy and strong, but I want to be thin and delicate."

"I used to be hungry and I couldn't concentrate on things. I don't remember any of the books I read when I was starving; I don't remember the movies I saw at that time. I never used to think about anything except food."

"I learned the trick to allow myself to enjoy food tremendously. I would eat only food I enjoyed, only the smallest amount. It was not refusal to eat. It was refusal to gain weight."

"It was as if I had to punish my body. I hate and detest it. If I let it be normal for a few days, then I had to deprive it again. I feel caught in my body—as long as I keep it under rigid control it can't betray me."

The anorectic's pretended victory over desire is her downfall. Her sisters, the overweight girls, the thin-fat ones, even the bulimics before the binge-purge cycles take over, however desperate and unworthy they feel, are engaged in life. They study, they work, they have friendships, sexual partnerships, some immediate sense of belonging to the social order and contributing to it. Not so the anorectic. She is a lone wolf. Before she reaches the stage of emaciation she is aware of her isolation. She longs for closeness, for conversation, for approving looks, the handshake, the human warmth. "I see other people through a glass wall, their voices penetrate to me. I long for being in real contact with them. I try, but they don't hear me."

Dread of appetite, sexual hunger, or desire, is one major ingredient of anorexia. The other ingredient, the one without which the self-starvation would not be possible, is the quality of the anorectic's conscience. Even the purest anorectic has moments of weakness. But once she has made up her mind to do something, her conscience ensures nearly absolute obedience. Because the anorectic has enormous will power, because she is intelligent, ambitious, persevering; because the fierce watching eyes and the harsh prohibiting voices have never become tamed, she obeys them without hesitation. Because the ideals by which she measures herself are so exquisite, so perfect, so unrelenting and stringent, she bows down before them in an attitude of divine worship. Her conscience is savage, double-dealing, corrupt.

Only when the incest taboo asserts its moral dilemmas does the anorectic's moral duplicity rise to the surface from its wellsprings. The duplicity has been fulminating since infancy behind the screen of a family structure and a social order that applaud her ambition, her power strivings, her self-righteous obedience to duty. Her all-out warfare on desire is a grand deception. It looks as though all sensual and erotic tendencies have been eradicated. But the anorectic has worked it out so that she is totally engrossed with eroticism, with *Fresslust* especially. Desire is her constant companion.

With more devotion and commitment than any ordinary teenager, the anorectic is continually reckoning with desire. She weighs it, she apportions it, she flames the fires, she makes sure that desire will not abate in its claims for attention. Though she keeps desire hidden, the anorectic knows full well that it is always there, waiting for the opportunity to erupt, break through, rush in, take over. Her conscience, never softened by the group loyalties of latency or the passionate friendships and allegiances of the early adolescent years, is an implacable tyrant, modeled entirely on the template of her desires; it devours, it probes, it scrutinizes, it tempts, it torments: "I felt as though a slave driver were whipping me from one activity to the other." Desire and authority are partners in crime. With the silencing of the great debate between desire and authority, narcissism flourishes without restraint.

The girl is preoccupied with food, bowel movements, sex, but tenderness and affection have been banished. To make absolutely certain that she will not be lured back into the web of family love-desire, the anorectic has reversed love-desire into hate-desire. Now she does not have to leave home. The force of her hatred and persecutory fantasies keeps her safe. Consumed by lust and hatred, she invests these hungers almost entirely in her body. With the same magical gesture of self-starvation she whips her body into a frenzy of perfection and simultaneously slaughters it. Her body is a reproach. She remains at home, "very literally as a permanent skeleton at the feast." She is omnipotent, so she cannot die even if her body should wither away. This time no one will wrest her power from her. "They wanted me to gain weight so that they wouldn't have to see how unhappy I was. Well, I wouldn't! Because I was! You know, they're so happy. And they have this good little girl, they want her to be pretty and happy too. They wanted me to be an ornament. Well, I wouldn't."

The girl eats herself up with spite. Her vengeance on her captors is like a satisfying meal. "You see how obedient I am. I do not overeat. I do not demand. I have absolute control over my appetites. This is what you wanted. The perfect child with the perfect body. Now, you've got it—for all the world to see."

Now that affection and tenderness have been banished, now that her conscience is self-sufficient, outside, beyond morality, the anorectic's wrath knows no bounds. Before she will descend from her lofty heights and rejoin the human race the girl has a score to settle. The slave and the master are bound together as long as they both shall live: "She is me, I am her. By destroying myself, I destroy my mother also." The obedient slave rattles her chains. The fat on her thighs, her rounded breasts, and menarche are her enemies, but the wave of fresh vitality that expands every appetite and desire also unlatches the structures of the past. Though she is as lustful as an infant, a law unto herself, the anorectic is not simply reverting to the ways of the past. The best little girl in the world is rattling her chains.

The girl's whole life has been a grand performance. As she will sometimes confess later in an uncharacteristic outburst of honesty, it was "the greatest put-on of all times." Her death-defying act of self-starvation, her emaciation, is the girl's Academy Award performance, the triumph of emulation she has been rehearsing since babyhood. The audience is horrified yet spellbound, which in turn produces in the hunger artist a delusional elation of power. From her point of view she is the consummate artist. Only afterward, when her body weight returns to near normal and she concedes the insanity of her artistry, does she tell us that there was a small voice inside that begged her to stop, an observing part of herself that viewed the act with as much horror as we did. But for the most part, as long as she remains in a state of emaciation, she is devoted to her performance. The longer the illness lasts, the more self-absorbed the girl becomes.

Soon she forgets about her audience. Narcissism takes over completely. The anorectic is demanding back her mind and her body, claiming them as her own; she is asserting the omnipotence she had once so completely relinquished in exchange for mirroring admiration. No mirroring admiration, no prohibiting looks from Mother or Father can swerve her now. She is her own mirror. She stands outside herself, both observer and observed. "I got my wish to be a third sex, both girl and boy. Standing in front of the mirror, I saw a lovely, attractive woman. My other self, the body outside the mirror, was a lusting young man preparing to seduce the girl in the mirror. I was having a love affair with myself."

She is on the alert, on the go, sleeping only three or four hours a night. Gone are the days when she would spend hours doing extra homework, being the star of her swimming class, lecturing her bored classmates on the theory of relativity. She is dizzy, faint with elation, with the sense of her absolute attunement to the world of time and space. Contradictions between "me" and "not me," animate and inanimate, are held in abeyance. There are no separations here. In her mystical unity with her physical surroundings the girl needs no others. She has reached a transcendental peak. She has endless endurance, enormous mental acuity. Though she can no longer concentrate on books and words, lectures and classroom nonsense, she is foxy when it comes to the preservation of her soul.

The high that she now gets from her near-starvation and ceaseless physical movement is like a jolt of morphine. "You feel outside your body. You are truly beside yourself—and then you are in a different state of consciousness and you can undergo pain without reacting. That's what I did with hunger. I knew it was there—I can recall and bring it to my consciousness—but at that time I did not feel pain." Theologians are familiar with the moral excesses of such ecstasy, the spiritual delusions of the starving state and its sexual overtones. "The awareness of spiritual power is increased and with it *the danger of losing sight of what is assigned to each one of us, the limits of our finite existence, of our dignity and our abilities.* Hence the dangers of pride, magic, and spiritual intoxication."

Experiencing herself as ineffectual in almost every other pursuit, through her acts of starvation and hyperactivity the anorectic achieves immense power—much more than she bargains for. As the starvation escalates, the physical side effects potentiate and verify the anorectic's dreams of glory. She has not sought ecstasy, only control over the invading physical forces. Sainthood has come to her as an accidental by-product of her starvation. Now she lusts for hunger as she once lusted for food. The high of her fasting state is her victory over the passions of the body, her triumph over her masters. Once outside her body she is true to her own self, to her voices, her powers.

Voluntary suicide is rare in anorexia. Only if the girl should fail in her battle with *Fresslust* or be forced to yield to her captors will she attempt suicide. But her belief in her omnipotence deceives her. She is unaware of her precarious physical state. The starving anorectic can be overtaken by her body with resulting cardiac arrest, metabolic crisis, circulatory collapse. It is said that just before she dies the anorectic takes on a look as though she were aware that her self is slowly passing out of her body. Her gaze is distant, "fishlike," out of contact with the world. She is escaping from her imprisoned existence.

11

THE IMPOSTOR
A Masculine Pursuit of Perfection

When adolescent boys set out to prove themselves, they are
not likely to choose the method of self-starvation. Anorexia
is exceedingly rare in males, and when noneating and emaciation do occur, they are most often secondary symptoms
of some other mental condition, such as schizophrenia or
severe depression. It is true that many male athletes, models, dancers, actors are periodic self-starvers, that some
adolescent boys are weekend bulimics, that many men are
thin-fat people preoccupied with keeping their weight
down by running, jogging, exercising, dieting, while allowing themselves well-controlled episodes of gourmandising
and bingeing. But very few males are afflicted during adolescence or later with severe eating disorders such as anorexia
or bulimia.

Males account for, at most, 10 percent of all cases of *primary* anorexia. During their latency years the young boys
who do become anorectic have many of the same personality characteristics as the potentially anorectic girls. They are
high achievers in school, compliant and obedient at home.
Like the girls, the boys suffer from a sense of inadequacy
and ineffectuality. They are overly ambitious, perfectionistic,
overactive, and extremely sensitive to criticism. However,
despite their similarities, there are a number of important
differences between male and female primary anorectics, to
the extent that some writers question the appropriateness of
the anorexia label for males. Males are less clandestine with
regard to their *Fresslust*. Most will admit to being hungry.
Some speak openly of pining away for food. Typically with
the males, periods of vigorous food refusal will alternate
with monumental eating binges, which are then followed by
self-induced vomiting. The major point of difference is that

the onset of the disorder is earlier in males, occurring usually in prepuberty, between the ages of nine and thirteen. The boys so afflicted do not develop sexually until cured. In fact, many a potentially anorectic boy has been rescued by puberty. The growth spurt and the influx of androgens flood the boy with aggressive vitalities and genital strivings which encourage the self-assertion he could not get in touch with during infancy, early childhood, and latency.

Rather than directing an actual attack on their bodies, pubescent boys are likely to try to prove themselves by attacking their environment with exaggerations of the power of masculinity. They take risks in the world at large. In males, rates of serious delinquent offenses, such as vandalism, theft, assault, threatened assault, shoplifting, armed robbery, and joyriding, rise fairly consistently from age eleven, peak at fifteen, then abate somewhat at eighteen, and continue to decline to age twenty-three. During this age span, serious criminal offenses by girls, though they also peak at age fifteen, are far less frequent. At fifteen, for example, girls are committing far fewer serious crimes than either eleven-year-old boys or twenty-three-year-old men. Even when the less serious, so-called status offenders are included in the statistics—the runaways, truants, alcohol and drug abusers—boys outdo the girls.

As many psychologists observe, adolescent boys act out their personal dilemmas in and on the larger social environment. They tend to act in groups, from which they receive a great deal of peer approval and narcissistic enhancement for their acts of aggression and defiance.

Adolescent girls, as we have seen, express their dilemmas within personal relationships; mother, father, siblings, teachers, friends bear the brunt of the girl's reactions. Girls form crushes, take flight in sexual promiscuity, steal as a substitute for love. Girls manage the vulnerabilities of becoming a woman by aggrandizing their bodies. They indulge in secret crimes—gossiping, concocting romantic alliances, lying, bingeing, and vomiting. Girls are more inclined to act in their imagination and on their own selves and are less inclined toward acting out on the larger social environment.

In adulthood men go on to become victimizers of a sort—killers, robbers, burglars, muggers, flashers, peeping Toms —who are confined to prisons for their antisocial behaviors. Women, on the other hand, are the victimized—the self-destroyers, the ones who are sexually enlisted by men, the ones who succumb to depression and hysteria rather than behave with outwardly directed aggression and sexuality. If women steal, they are merely the accomplices of men or the solitary kleptomaniacs who steal for love. When women are sexually promiscuous or overtly aggressive, they are not imprisoned for criminality. In previous eras such behavior was given religious significance and women were burned at the stake. Now they are carted off to mental hospitals by their distraught parents and spouses. When men and women become psychotic, the men will be the violent paranoids, the women the silly, self-mutilating hebephrenics.

We are told that even in their choices of suicidal methods men and women behave along gender lines. Men are the more violent: they hang themselves, shoot their brains out, hurl their bodies from rooftops. Women prefer more passive, gentle methods, such as sleeping pills, drowning, and gas. In the case of neuroses, men are the obsessive-compulsives, women the hysterics. In selecting their sexual partners women search for mirrors of their narcissistic ambitions. Men are more likely to choose loved ones who will fulfill "real" needs and desires. Women suffer from shame, men from guilt. Women are masochists, men are sadists.

In these popular notions on gender differences for crime and emotionality, fact and fancy mingle. When groups of men and women are studied statistically these differences between the sexes seem to be supported. In studies of individual cases, however, the distinctions begin to fade, and we find that men and women do not differ quite so sharply. Men are also masochistic, depressed, hysterical. Women can be sadistic, obsessive-compulsive, and violent. Nevertheless there is still some merit in the idea that males and females *tend* to express their conflicts, vulnerabilities, and despairs through different types of emotional disorders, personality traits, and behaviors. Commentaries on the differences will always invite a variety of interpretations of the relative influences of nature and nurture. Some commentators stress that males and females are made differently; hormones and anatomy determine the predilections for acting in or acting out. Others hold that social conventions determine that women will be the passive, self-destroying victims, and men will be the violent, acting-out victimizers.

There are some facts. We do know, for example, that from the moment parents become aware of the sex of their newborn they begin to behave in subtly different ways, depending on whether the baby is a girl or a boy. The wide range of neonatal temperaments, physical characteristics, and mental endowments stimulate in parents a great variety of fantasies and behaviors. But with all the variety, there is always a concordance between the sex of the baby and some unconscious parental script for femininity or masculinity. In every society there are numerous scripts for sex-gender concordance on which a parent's fantasies about her baby might be based. Even the most nontraditional parental script expresses some socially valued ideal of femininity or masculinity.

Every child is to some extent a reflection of the parents' narcissistic ambitions. And in infancy she or he will mirror the mother's hopes, wishes, aspirations. In turn the mother's aspirations for that infant will be influenced by its own unique characteristics—its temperament, its physical and mental endowments, and its *sex*. A girl baby, no matter what her temperament, will stimulate in a mother some script for femininity; a boy baby will stimulate a script for masculinity. However, when a child is still an infant the mother's fantasies are necessarily limited to infantile ego-ideals, and these are not meant to be a child's only rendition of femininity or masculinity.

With each stage of separation-individuation the infant-mother dialogue undergoes modification, and with each stage the sex-gender script also undergoes some revision.

From the beginning a father provides an alternative to the infant-mother dialogue, so that his fantasies will also influence the child's gender inclinations. The nursery texts are then supposed to acquire around them the more advanced ideals imparted by both parents in their roles as the primary representatives of the moral authority of the larger social order. These later enlargements of the scenarios for femininity and masculinity are associated with the moral attainments of the Oedipal and latency phases of childhood. The sexual life and the moral life evolve in tandem.

As representatives of society, the parents are supposed to interrupt the nursery dialogue. The father's presence in the mother's life and the mother's presence in his should make it evident to the child that there is a great deal more to sexuality and morality than absence, weaning, controlling one's body functions. The triangle of mother-child-father announces the intimate connection between male-female anatomical differences and the fact that there are profound and unalterable differences between child and parents—the generational differences. The mother's and father's genitals have something to do with making babies; there are those secret pleasures that Mother and Father share for which the child has no anatomical capacity. This Oedipal defeat carries the child out of the nursery with its primitive morality of absence and weaning, and into the lawfulness of the social order, as now represented by the incest taboo.

The parents' intentions in enforcing the incest taboo are to protect the child from precocious involvement in adult sexual behavior. The child, however, experiences such protection as a commentary on his genital inferiority. He attributes his exile to his various physical, emotional, and moral inadequacies. Among his moral delinquencies are his genital strivings for his mother and father. Though he must postpone to the future any actual realization of his genital wishes, the child compensates for his humiliation by identifying with the parents' moral authority. The moral standards the child adopts from the parents are subject to his own rigid interpretations of good and bad. But these standards have an enormous advantage over nursery morality in that they are relatively independent of external authority. The child acquires the moral dignity to be his own prohibitor and observer. He also acquires values and aspirations that encourage him to look forward to the time when he will be a grown-up, with adult genitals and adult social and moral prerogatives.

When the scripts for sex-gender concordance are dominated by nursery ideals and nursery morality, the outcome is very likely to be some caricature of femininity or masculinity—especially if the prevailing social values encourage these stereotypes. Technically, anorexia is a disorder of desire, a malady of *Fresslust* and sexual appetite. But as we have seen, it is also a disorder of the moral life, arising out of deprivations in the love dialogues of infancy: one of the deprivations was the overwhelming quality of the mother's narcissistic investment in this female child; the other was an absence of the father. The primitiveness of the anorectic's conscience is decisive in the etiology of the disorder. And until adolescence brings her the opportunity to revise the scripts, the girl has been dominated by a nursery scenario for femininity, a caricature that also plays a considerable role in her ruthless pursuit of self-starvation.

There is another disorder that comes to fruition in puberty, a form of criminality that is typical of males. Figuring prominently in the etiology of this disorder is a kind of mirroring relationship to the mother and an absentee or emotionally unavailable father. Whereas in anorexia the mother's sex-gender concordant text was for a caricature of femininity, in this disorder the mother has conveyed a caricature of masculinity. We will be discussing the impostor, a person who assumes a false identity for the sole purpose of deceiving others. With the rare exception of Pope Joanna, who is said to have reigned as pontiff in the ninth century until she gave birth while riding in a religious procession, so far as we know, all *full-fledged* impostors are males. Imposture flourishes during the closing stages of puberty as the young man attempts to reconcile the inadequate person he supposes himself to be with the exalted masculine ideal conveyed to him during infancy.

Though he sometimes manipulates others for financial gain or social advantage, the impostor is not a mere criminal. Nor is he a simple show-off or poseur whose obvious pretentiousness deceives no one for very long. The impostor assumes completely false identities because he must hide from himself and from everyone else the inadequacies of his actual self. True, he is a liar and a cheat and a manipulator. But as Phyllis Greenacre, one of the few psychoanalysts who have investigated the character of the impostor, tells us, he is "a very special type of liar who imposes on others fabrications of his achievements, position or worldly possessions. This he may do by misrepresenting his official (statistical) identity, by presenting himself with a fictitious name, history or other items of personal identity either borrowed from some actual person or fabricated according to some imaginative conception of himself."

There are different forms and varying degrees of imposture, but only some of them lead to full-fledged imposturousness. The arch impostor has a vast repertoire of accessory behaviors in which he resembles other men who in their talents, character structure, and/or sexual orientation also have a certain degree of imposturousness. The blatant impostor may forge, plagiarize, counterfeit, and swindle, and in these behaviors he resembles the men who make careers of such pursuits. Like magicians, gurus, mediums, occult healers, who also have a considerable talent for dissembling, the impostor appreciates that his acts of conjuring depend on the suspension of disbelief in his audiences. The victim is his abetting audience, the unconscious conspirators who are as hungry as the perpetrator to consummate the illusion. The impostor is frankly exhibitionistic; he changes costumes frequently and also has a voyeuristic relationship to his audience.

Some of these accessory behaviors, such as the forgeries and the counterfeiting, are props for the impostor's artful deceptions. Others, such as the exhibitionism and voyeurism, while they serve the deception, are also direct expressions of the impostor's shaky masculine identity. The impostor's sexual orientation is as infantile as his moral life, and so he is predisposed to acquiring actual perversions such as transvestism, fetishism, exhibitionism, voyeurism. Impostors also suffer from potency problems, so that when they do engage in heterosexual pursuits they are pseudogenital. That is, while they employ their genitals heterosexually, they emphasize scoring, performance, the imitation of fantasized ideal males, orgasm in the partner not as the giving of pleasure but as a vanquishment and defeat, and they view erection as risk, enmity, deception, survival. Thus the impostor may court, seduce, and marry many women—with or without the formality of divorce—many of whom are much older or much younger than he and therefore not of his own generation.

With respect to his pseudomanhood the impostor resembles the Casanova, the bigamist, the supermacho male. In his enormous grandiosity and with the fanatical ploys with which the impostor fends off disclosure, he resembles certain paranoid characters, such as the founders of religious cults and members of secret male societies. The men who suffer from these other disorders—the perversions, the pseudogenital pursuits, the grandiose paranoias—have some features in common with the full-fledged impostor. They are pretenders to adult sexuality. They feel entitled to be treated as moral exceptions and thus assume license to achieve power over others through acts of dissembling.

In some persons, men *and* women, the degree of imposture may consist of relatively minor, restricted episodes of dissembling identity or falsifying achievements. In these less pervasive versions we inevitably discover that the dissemblers are very much like the arch impostor in that his or her sexual and moral immaturities are hidden beneath a cloak of narcissistic entitlement. And in their childhood histories we usually find the two basic elements in the etiology of the full-fledged impostor: the person was expected to mirror the exalted ideal of one parent, and the other parent was an emotional or actual absentee.

After World War II, and particularly since the early 1960s, the number of men and women suffering from narcissistic disorders of one kind or another has grown at a steady rate. Though those persons who populate our so-called "culture of narcissism" are not full-time impostors and represent a wide range of character types, they all present tendencies toward dissembling their identities and achievements and demonstrate perversions of the sexual and moral life. The seeds of these now commonplace disorders can be found in infancy and early childhood, but they do not come to fruition until the person confronts the sexual and moral dilemmas of adolescence.

If we were to include in our statistics the all-too-willing audience, the vast army of abettors who want nothing more than to shine in the reflected glory of the enchanting narcissist, we might conclude that most of us, to some degree or other, are facilitators of a social environment in which imposturous tendencies flourish. Throughout the ages, impostors of various sorts—the alchemists, divine healers—have depended on their audiences for success. These days the audiences appear to be as hungry for magical salvation as any lord or serf of the Middle Ages.

The demi-impostors—the gurus, magicians, faith healers, swindlers, forgers, plagiarists, exhibitionists, transvestites, Casanovas, bigamists, grandiose paranoiacs, and occasional dissemblers—all different from one another in motives and behavior, share some characteristics with the genuine impostor. They might not, however, feel compelled to impose their false identity or achievements or social positions on others except on occasion. Only when such a desperate compulsion is the primary force behind the act of deception is magician, plagiarist, bigamist entitled to the rank of full-fledged impostor. Nevertheless the fate of the impostor reveals the common fate of all the demi-impostors and of all those who strive to fulfill the exalted ideals of infancy rather than face up to the inevitabilities of an actual ordinary life.

The full-fledged impostor suffers from a profound impairment of his sense of identity. He knows that he is not the person he pretends to be, but he feels that he *must* be some person greater or more magnificent than the ordinary mortals he sets out to deceive. His behavior is driven and repetitious. His very existence depends on the success of his trickery. To be a full-fledged impostor is a full-time occupation rather than a ploy for social or material gain.

A boy does not graduate to the rank of full-fledged impostor overnight. He starts out as the spoiled darling of the nursery, becomes a liar and a cheat in boyhood, and then in early adolescence is an arch manipulator. The average adolescent boy often experiences himself as a pretender. It is not at all unusual for a boy on the verge of manhood to try to prove himself by assuming grandiose postures and roles. Every teenager and adult, male or female, will occasionally manipulate others to advance his or her psychological cause. But for the potential and eventually full-fledged impostor, lying, cheating, manipulating are a way of life. The impostor lies even when there is no immediate practical gain. His shaky identity is held together by the false images he imposes on others.

Here the statistics are hard to come by. Unless the boy is apprehended for some criminal offense incidental to his manipulations, such as forgery or plagiarism, he is unlikely to come to the attention of law-enforcement agencies. And his disorder is such that he has no motive for requesting psychological help. In fact, the con artist is anxiety-free only when he is engaged in acts of deceit. The parents of the potential impostor are taken in like everyone else. Consciously or unconsciously, they support his fraudulence. Many adults admire the boy for his facile charm and clever antics. But if you were to ask a teacher or other school official to describe the type of adolescent boy who most confounds her, she would not point to the rowdies and teacher tormentors, the vandals and thieves, the drug abusers and alcohol abusers, all of whom are expressing the serious but identifiable problems of teenage boys and most of whom commit these delinquent acts in groups, with the approval and sponsorship of their peers. After giving the matter thought, most teachers would begin to talk about the manipulators, the con artists, the boys who operate alone, outside of any group loyalties, but who very often subtly incite delinquencies in the other boys and girls.

The adolescent con artist is bewildering because the adults in his environment can never be entirely certain that the boy is being untruthful. A boy like this will lie, cheat, plagiarize, but it is extremely difficult to gather any hard evidence of his delinquencies. Even when the facts speak for themselves—the twenty-page paper copied word for word from an old, dusty thesis—the boy deftly pulls out his trumps: an unblinking profession of innocence, a wrathful protestation of injustice, a perfectly rational explanation, an excuse of illness in the family, or, if absolutely necessary, an admission, an apology, a promise never to do it again. And since all those involved want to believe him, they do.

The really smooth manipulator doesn't simply falsify the facts; he devises ways of protecting his act. He is the model of virtue in every class but one. He confines his cheating to that one setting so that the teacher who might catch him in his fraud manages to look the fool to all the other school personnel. He steals his mother's jewels and his father's cash, but away at boarding school he is everybody's darling. Or he does it the other way around: he is an angel at home and a liar, risk taker, and falsifier at school. The manipulator, smooth as he is, of course is neither saint nor daring hero but an angry, frightened boy who must dissemble in order to cloak the pathetic nobody he imagines himself to be. His deceptions aim at enhancing the illusion that he is a powerful person, so powerful, in fact, that he can fool the grown-ups who are in authority. In a broad sense he is trying to do away with the genital and generational differences that make him feel so inadequate. Fooling the authorities and thereby exposing their weaknesses and vulnerabilities is one of the central motives of the imposturous boy.

The teacher who sees through the boy's veils of illusion

and blows the whistle is not respected by the boy or by the other adults. Those duped, even when they suspect they are being tricked, seem thrilled to go along with the duper. They resent those fanatics whose exposure of the impostor deprives the audience of the excitement of complicity. In spite of their better judgment, teachers and parents find themselves once again, for the fifth, tenth, or fiftieth time, believing in and forgiving this mercurial and rather fascinating chap. As the gurus, mediums, and occult healers well know, the emotional susceptibility of the audience is essential to their act. Deliverers of emotional salvation have more certainty, larger bank accounts, and considerably more adulatory followers than those truer prophets who turn humanity's eyes toward the importunate realities of fate and necessity with all the perplexity that such reality entails.

The impostor—liar, cheat, manipulator—is foxy, so foxy that his deceptions can rarely be exposed. He is a lone wolf, thoroughly absorbed by the role(s) he is playing, dominated and compelled by his pursuit of perfection. The impostor's driven behavior follows a script that is one of several versions of a family-romance fantasy that must be enacted over and over again. This universal childhood fantasy has as its central theme the idea of being a foundling in a family of provisional parents. Most young children construct such a fantasy as a defensive maneuver to soften the humiliations and allay the anxieties generated by the Oedipal drama. The average child merely imagines that he is a foundling reared by foster parents who are the temporary substitutes for his absent biological parents. He merely fantasizes that he is an unacknowledged aristocrat in a mundane world. When he arrives at puberty he relinquishes the idealizations of infancy and childhood and in the process also gives up his family romance. But by the time he arrives at puberty the liar, cheat, manipulator has become absorbed in his fantasy. He must now live out the scenario of his childhood family romance. He becomes an impostor.

The more typical family-romance scenarios are reflected in the Frog Prince, Dick Whittington, Snow White, Cinderella myths, in which a child has been temporarily reduced to a lowly and demeaned status, but because of his or her patience, honesty, industry, obedience, kindness, innocence, and underlying if not actual beauty, the child is at last rescued and restored to his or her legitimate status of king or queen, prince or princess. In these common family-romance prototypes there are often a few siblings who compete for the parents' favors but who because of their meanness, laziness, dishonesty, ugliness, or greed, are eventually punished for their wicked ways and banished from the kingdom—unless the humane and compassionate prince declares a general amnesty and forgives his less fortunate brothers and the witch who had once upon a time treated him with so little pity or generosity.

A different sort of fairy tale is the model of the impostor's family romance. One of these tales is "The Master Thief." Here a young man, whose real family is poor and humble, disguises himself as a rich nobleman and returns to the kingdom of his birth after many years of wandering the earth as a master thief. He acepts the three challenges of the king: to steal his favorite horse from the stable; to steal the bed sheet from under the king and queen while they are asleep and to remove the wedding ring from the finger of the queen; and, third, to kidnap the parson and the sexton from the king's chapel. The penalty for failure to rob the king of his most prized worldly, sexual, and moral treasures is the gallows. No prize is ever mentioned. The master thief risks the gallows simply to prove that he is cleverer than the mighty king. In accordance with fairy tale tradition, he succeeds in pulling the wool over the king's eyes with three incredible and masterful deceptions. But does the master thief get to marry the princess? Is he restored to the kingdom of his birth? No. The king pays tribute to his clever antics but wisely sends the master thief on his way. "You are an arch thief and you have won your case. This time you shall get off with a whole skin, but never set foot in my kingdom again. If you do, you can count on your place on the gallows." The arch thief goes once more into the wide world and is never heard of again. Since fairy tales are the morality legends of childhood, warnings to the wicked and the greedy, an obvious master thief may be admired for his cleverness, but he must not be rewarded.

The other fairy tale prototype for the impostor's family romance, the one that comes even closer to his wishes than "The Master Thief," is the familiar tale of "Jack and the Beanstalk." Here the thief is well disguised as an innocent, dutiful boy whose thievery is not only moral but an act of justice and rightful retribution. This version of fooling the grown-ups captures the essence of the impostor's childhood humiliations and the illusory victory that dominates his life. Jack, we may remember, lives with his poor, hardworking mother in a humble cottage. His father is dead and thus neatly out of the way as a competitor for the mother's affections. Soon Jack and his mother are so destitute that they are forced to sell Milky White, the cow who has at least given them a daily quota of milk. Jack's mother trustingly sends him to town to sell their precious cow, their last remaining worldly possession. Little Jack, believing himself to be a capable and clever boy, is all too easily hoodwinked into trading Milky White for a mere handful of "magical beans." He returns triumphantly to show his mother the evidence of his superior tradesmanship only to face the humiliation of being told that he is a much less clever man than he had thought. His mother is furious. She hurls the beans out the window and sends Jack to bed. Jack goes to sleep in a mood of profound dejection.

Lo and behold! When Jack looks out his window later that night he discovers that he was right after all. The beans were indeed magical. Outside his window is an enormous beanstalk that reaches up to the sky and into the clouds. The deception has been converted into a victory. Now Jack can really prove himself worthy of his mother's trust and admiration.

Act II is Jack's vengeance on those who deceived him. He decides to climb the beanstalk and enter the kingdom of the Giant. Climbing and climbing and climbing, he reaches the castle of the Wicked Giant who eats up all those who dare to trespass on his kingdom. He especially relishes little boys the age of Jack, whom his wife always cooks in new and interesting ways. But clever Jack hoodwinks the Giant, who for all his loud and terrifying mutterings turns out to be nothing but a lazy, foolish, gullible show-off. With the assistance of the Giant's wife, who for some reason makes an exception of Jack (the excitement of complicity, perhaps) and is also hoodwinked by him, Jack robs the Giant of his most precious possessions—not once, but three times. First he steals his bag of gold, then the goose that lays the golden eggs, and finally his singing Golden Harp. The Golden Harp sings out to warn the Giant, but it is too late. Jack scrambles down the beanstalk carrying his loot. The Giant follows in hot pursuit. Just in the nick of time Jack reaches the safety of home. He grabs his hatchet and chops down the beanstalk. The mighty Giant comes crashing to the earth. Now that they have the bag of gold, the goose that lays the golden eggs, and the Golden Harp, Jack and and his mother need never worry again. The look of admiration returns to his mother's eyes.

Every imposture is an enactment of a Jack and the Beanstalk legend, the redemption aspect of the family romance. The impostor must impose his false personality and achievements on others again and again in order to maintain the illusion that he is not small and insignificant, that he is worthy of his mother's admiration, that, moreover, he is entitled to trick the father, overthrow him, and rob him of his powers. Though many adolescents engage in reenactments of infantile emotional scenarios so as to rectify the injuries of the past, the impostor's role playing is designed to actualize an illusory victory. The impostor is the master thief who has given himself the moral permission to do wrong because he has been wronged.

The psychology and childhood history of the impostor has been pieced together from a few dozen treatment cases of full-fledged impostors, the far more numerous case histories of episodic or demi-impostors, the biographies of notorious

impostors, and from fictional accounts of impostors or im-
posturouslike characters. Because many creative artists
sense some affinity with the divided soul of the impostor,
they have been intrigued with his personality. Of the literary sources, Thomas Mann's *The Confessions of Felix Krull,
Confidence Man* is the most acclaimed and incisive fictional
rendition of the impostor. As Mann said of his novel, "It is in
essence the story of an artist; in it the element of the unreal
and illusional passes frankly over into the criminal." That
Mann—a writer unusually absorbed with the deceptions in
art, the artful camouflages of nature, the artist's attraction to
corruption and disreputability, the insidious influence of
magicians, gurus, faith healers, deliverers of political salvation on their susceptible audiences—should have captured
so precisely the mentality of the impostor is, after all, not
surprising.

Without benefit of official psychological theory and rely-
ing mainly on the sketchy memoirs of the Romanian rogue
Manolescu, Mann composed a portrait of the childhood, adolescence, and early manhood of an impostor that bears a
remarkable likeness to the clinical picture painstakingly
constructed by the few psychoanalysts who have worked
with such patients. The only reservation registered about
the Krull narrative (which was written in the first person) is
that a genuine impostor could not have had such accurate
insights into his own psychological dyanmics. The impostor's dishonesty and superficiality, his drive toward incessant repetition, his intolerance of frustration, his shaky
sense of reality would nullify any capacity to review and
reconstruct his own life history. The loss of emotional connection with his actual past is a *sine qua non* of impostor
mentality. Of course, as one reads Krull's account of his
childhood and manhood, one is never entirely certain if the
events actually happened or if they are a fantasy attempt to
make a victory out of a humiliation. As we shall see, Krull
and Jack of the beanstalk are fully deserving of the title
"full-fledged impostor."

According to psychoanalytic construction, the character

of the impostor arises out of either of two prototypical infantile scenarios that, though different in most external details, nevertheless eventuate in identical impairments of identity and conscience. Impostors from either of these two childhood backgrounds have an attitude toward life that declares: "Nature has done me a grievous wrong. Life owes me a reparation, and I shall see that I get it. I may do wrong because wrong has been done to me." A vengeful attitude such as this might be anticipated from one of the types, those impostors who were born with physical and/or mental defects and who were ignored, deprecated, rejected, and otherwise unfairly treated by one or both parents. A few of the more notorious impostors have had just such a childhood history.

One famous impostor, Titus Oates, one of the instigators of the Popish Plot, in the reign of Charles II, the man whom the pope proclaimed as damned to universal fame, was born deformed, with one leg shorter than the other, and was afflicted with convulsions. His mother, a midwife, considered the birthing of her own child the worst she had ever known, and the father, "a clergyman with scoundrelly tendencies," thought Titus so ugly that he refused ever to look at him. Another impostor, the Tichborne Claimant, an illiterate young man from Australia who in the late nineteenth century achieved fame, fortune, and imprisonment by pretending to be the long-lost heir to the Tichborne fortune, was the youngest child of a poor, "violent" butcher and a "decent" mother and was born with a genital deformity. He was pseudohermaphroditic.

Without further recourse to theories on conscience development and masculine-gender identity, our common sense allows us to appreciate how such early and prolonged insults to his bodily integrity and omnipotence might motivate a boy to seek restitution by rising above his ignominious beginnnings through becoming a person or persons other than the miserable one that had been dealt to him by chance. Even his penchant for revenge might strike a compassionate chord. Do we not sympathize with Jack as he steals from the Giant? For who among us has not at some moment or other reproached nature or destiny for not having conferred on us greater advantages? We feel entitled to right the wrongs that have been done to us. We sympathize, thus, with Gloucester, soon to become the villainous Richard III, as he laments his fate, "Cheated of feature by dissembling nature,/Deform'd, unfinish'd, sent before my time/ Into this breathing world, scarce half made up,/And that so lamely and unfashionable/That dogs bark at me as I halt by them."

Far more frequently, however, the reported cases of the impostor resemble the advantaged childhood history of Felix Krull. "Often enough," says Krull, "I heard from my parents' lips that I was a Sunday child, and although I was brought up to reject every form of superstition, I have always thought there was a secret significance in that fact taken in connection with my Christian name of Felix . . . and my physical fineness and attractiveness. Yes, I have always believed myself favoured of fortune and of Heaven, and I may say that, on the whole, experience has borne me out." The type of impostor we know most about is like Felix, the favored child of fortune, the beautiful one, the prodigal son, the infant boy who is the entire focus of his mother's adoring gaze. About the only external circumstance he would seem to have in common with the outwardly less advantaged impostors is the actual or emotional distance between himself and his father. Why would a boy endowed by nature with every physical and mental advantage, the indulged darling of his mother's existence, want, during adolescence and thereafter, to assume the identity of another person? What circumstances surrounding his apparently remarkable good fortune would have led the boy to declare "I have been wronged and therefore I am entitled to do wrong!"?

In this second, more prevalent prototype the boy's character is initially patterned by an overly close attachment to a doting mother whose seductive, possessive love of this marvelous, well-endowed infant impairs his ability to establish a firm sense of separateness from her. He remains not so much an extension of his mother but rather a mirroring reflection of her exalted ideal of masculinity. Contributing to the boy's difficulty in separating from the mother is an absentee or emotionally ineffectual father. Some impostors are posthumous infants—born shortly after a father's death. In other instances the father died during the boy's infancy, or was a deserter, or was continually away on business trips, or preferred his older male children, or was denigrated by the mother, or was himself a shabby pretender to social and financial importance. As the boy emerges from infancy the father is still unavailable to him as an object for affection and identification. For one reason or another the boy then spends his infancy and early childhood in an emotionally "fatherless" household. No one comes along to intrude on the mother-infant relationship and assert the principles of social law and order. The "voice of the father" is dimly heard at best. When neither father nor mother represents for a child the moral principles of the social order, his moral sense, expectably, will continue to be dominated by the concrete prohibitions and permissions of the nursery. Nursery morality, when it is not subordinated by the child's more encompassing identifications with parental authority, values, attitudes, and interests, is easily and inevitably corruptible. Moreover, as we might suspect, the impostor's corrupt moral sense is more pervasive and even less available to the corrective influences of puberty than is the conscience of the anorectic.

For a boy child "absence of the father" usually has more disastrous consequences than for a girl. Though the anorectic's ideal of femininity is a caricature of her mother's feminine ideals, prohibitions, permissions, she at least has had the benefit of an emotionally meaningful relationship with the parent of her own sex. She has some basis for comparison between the real mother and the ideal the mother has conveyed. But when a boy knows only shreds and patches of his father, he can construct only a patchy image of some masculine self; without a father in his life to identify with, he must base his entire gender identity on a masculine ideal conveyed to him by his mother.

The point is not that there is such a thing as a bona fide ideal of masculinity and that it can be conveyed only by a father. Rather, when the mother has a problematic sense of masculinity the absence of a father becomes a complication to the boy's acquisition of a sense of gender difference. A sense of masculinity conveyed by the same parent (the mother) who conveys a sense of femininity is bound to be a different acquisition from masculinity conveyed by a father. For example, the common ideal of transgression as masculine—to be a boy is to be naughty—when conveyed by a father will lead a child into a peer group whose ideal is the commission of mischief. Questionable as this may be, it does advance the boy's participation in the social world. However, such an ideal of masculinity conveyed by a mother leads to lone-wolf delinquent activities such as imposturousness, with an arrest of socialization.

It is likely that in the absence of a father figure, many perverse, criminal, and grandiose men have also identified with some exalted maternal ideal of masculinity. But for the future impostor, whose masculine identity is already destined to be a fragile one, there is an additional feature, the one that most directly foreshadows the specific orientation toward imposture. The mother especially—but sometimes also grandparents, siblings, nursemaids—encourages the little boy to believe that he is the most enchanting creature in the world. This infant phenomenon is constantly applauded for his talents at mimicry and imitation—capacities natural to most two- and three-year-olds. The tiny charmer delights his susceptible audience with his "cute" caricatures of powerful grown-ups, of soldiers, policemen, royalty, movie stars, and other grand personages. Felix Krull describes himself as an imaginative child whose feats of mimicry gave his family much entertainment and pleasure:

Sitting in my little go-cart, which my nurse would push around the garden or entrance hall of the house, I would draw my mouth down as far as I could so that my upper lip was unnaturally lengthened and would blink my eyes slowly until the strain and strength of my emotions made them redden and fill with tears. Overwhelmed by a sense of my age and dignity, I would sit silent in my little wagon, while my nurse was instructed to inform all whom we met who I was, since I should have taken any disregard of my fancy much amiss. "I am taking the Kaiser for a drive," she would announce, bringing the flat of her hand to the side of her head in an awkward salute, and everyone would pay me homage.

As for the other skills that infants and toddlers derive enormous satisfaction in perfecting, such as eating by themselves or dressing themselves, these are actively discouraged. His lordship is pampered and indulged, treated as a marvelous toy that is expected to do no more than open its mouth to be fed, to surrender its adorable body for cleansing and adornment. Mother and everyone else anticipates his physical needs and desires, making sure to fulfill them before the boy has a moment to experience any dissatisfaction or longing. He need not move a muscle or exert any initiative or autonomy. In this atmosphere of slavish devotion, in which everything is given unconditionally without the expectation of anything in return, narcissism and passivity are bound to flourish.

In comparison to his absentee father, the boy is led to believe that he is more glamorous, powerful, exciting, adorable, admired. Gradually the boy accepts the general household impression that he rather than the father is capable of satisfying his mother's emotional and sexual requirements. Without the tests of reality, the boy imagines that he has vanquished the father. There is no contest, no rivalry, no competition. Without moving a muscle, simply by existing and going along with the mother's image of who he is, the boy has magically and in effect robbed the father of his powers. The reality, of course, is that when it comes to matters genital the boy is wholly inadequate. Whether or not he is more admired and valued than his father, a little boy simply does not have the anatomical wherewithal to become his mother's sexual partner.

This defeat is not taken lightly by our little kaiser. It is a rude awakening, a devastating deflation of his high-blown narcissistic ambitions. An ordinary boy suffers a far less dramatic fall from grace, and he has the compensation of being able to adopt as his own at least some portion of his father's authority and values. The future impostor's hostility toward his father (dead or alive, absent or present) is aggravated by the impossibility of any positive identification with him. In some reported cases the boy is able to imitate and emulate selected aspects of his father, not his principles of authority but those outward and superficial manifestations of his power —his loud, tyrannical voice, his pretense to grandeur, his contempt for ordinary humanity, his supersalesmanship, his exhilaration at putting one over on the customers, his bragging self-aggrandizement—the very characteristics that would sponsor the boy's later impostures.

Through his identification with (or, more properly, imitation of) the aggressor, the boy manages to allay some of the enormous anxiety that is inevitably generated by his illusory usurpation of the father's power. But essentially his plight must be solved by more extraordinary means. His narcissism depends on retaining his supremacy, but his wish to replace the father, who because of his emotional absence is imagined to be a ferocious, devouring giant, potentiates the separation and castration anxieties that are typical of this age and churns them up into unmanageable proportions. The only viable option for the doubtful hero is to reinvoke in fantasy the omnipotence of his infancy days when he was the uncontested winner, the mirroring extension of his mother's exalted ideals. In that way he presents no real challenge to his father while at the same time he is able to retain the illusion that he is still a little king.

Thus the family romance that will come to dominate his existence now salvages the boy's narcissism and protects him in fantasy from the anxieties that would otherwise accompany any real competition or rivalry with the father. Through his pseudoheroic conquering of the Giant, the impostor will return time and again to the conditions before the Oedipal awakening when the mother was an Olympian and the boy shared in her special privileges and unconditional love. As an adolescent he will feel whole, intact, completed, safe only when he can succeed in getting the world to respond to him—not according to any real achievements—which he neglects to pursue—but according to his exalted ego-ideal. He will be a clandestine rival who never has to face the real challenges of manhood; he can play at life eternally and never have to really live it.

Underlying the boy's later manipulations and impostures are exceptional imbalances in the three strands of narcissism. Omnipotence particularly undergoes a disastrous fate. The omnipotence of gesture and action that might have fueled the boy's ambitions to perfect his real skills in a real world were actively discouraged by his doting mother. On the other hand, the magical gestures of mimicry and imitation, the boy's talent for being whatever and whomever his mother wished him to be, were stimulated and enhanced. Usually an infant's omnipotence and the mother's mirroring exaltation of his marvelous power do not slide into place with seamless mutuality. Although every infant is to some extent a mirroring extension of the mother, most mothers and fathers appreciate the dangers of narcissistic self-absorption. They will caution their children against loving themselves too much. They admonish pride, limit illusion, require obedience to the moral values of the real world. Only for the first few months of life can a mother be a mirror for an infant's extraordinary narcissism. And even then her love is not unconditional. The mirror comes and goes.

But when the mirror of one's exalted omnipotence is all one has, when one's entire existence and safety depend on merger with the all-powerful other, then the threat of being separated from the mirroring other will engender intense anxieties. These terrifying feelings of helplessness will hold in check those aspects of self-experience that derive from the exercise of one's inborn initiative and autonomy. It is better to play it safe, to conjure oneself into a mirroring extension of the other. Thus the impostor's infantile omnipotence never had much chance to be toned down by the expectations of hard reality.

As far as his bodily love and self-esteem are concerned, his mother's seductive coddling, her flirtations and flattery rouse him to greater and greater heights of exhibitionism. His body is a delicious sweetmeat (just the kind that giants like to eat), a marvelous tower of perfection designed for the sole purpose of being fed and admired and adorned. How shall a little boy, who must discover sooner or later that in comparison with grown-up men his own body is but small, insignificant, vulnerable, reckon with all this fantastic encouragement of his omnipotence and bodily adoration?

The discrepancy between the person he is supposed to be and the person he actually is becomes too vast to reconcile. He regards his miniature penis, which is supposed to be more enchanting and magnificent than his father's, and is mortified at how small and puny it really is. Whether or not he has an actual bodily deformity, the potential impostor grows up with the entrenched conviction that his body, especially his genitals, are inferior and defective. However, once again fantasy comes to the little kaiser's rescue: "I could not conceal from myself that I was made of superior stuff, or, as people say, of finer clay, and I do not shrink from the charge of self-complacency in saying so. If someone accuses me of self-complacency, it is a matter of complete indifference to me, for I should have to be a fool or a hypocrite to pretend that I am of common stuff, and it is therefore in obedience to truth that I repeat that I am of the finest clay."

Encouraged as he has been in his role as the Olympian extension of his mother, the little boy soon catches on that truth and facts, the real appearances of things, can be, in fact should be, ignored and supplanted by fantasies and illusions. The premise for getting along in the world is to put one over in an act of deception, to fool the audience, who itself welcomes the elation of having the wool pulled over its eyes. When one is adored for being the self one is not, the self one might have been gets lost in the shuffle and never has a chance to grow up. The impostor goes through life with two incompatible self-images: the shabby, poorly knit real self and the illusory self that cloaks it. The experience that one's entire existence hangs on the ability to be false to oneself generates enormous hostility and resentment toward the mirroring other. Much as the boy hates his father for having robbed him of his rightful position, even more does he despise his adoring mother for her cruel deception. It is not long before the message "Fool the audience" becomes translated into "Make fools of your audience."

Artist and impostor have some qualities in common: special gifts of mimicry, the tensions between the real, ordinary self and the magical conjuring self, a fascination with dissembling. But in their regard for reality and in their attitudes toward their audiences, artist and impostor are quite different from each other. The artist is exquisitely attuned to the sights, sounds, movements of the natural world, and he employs them as the medium of his artistic productions. The impostor denigrates the real. He mimics solely to falsify and has no interest in representing what is real. After an infancy devoted to falsification and illusion, he barely comprehends the rules that govern reality. Like Jack the Giant Killer, he takes risks that a sensible, ordinary boy knows better than to attempt.

The impostor's sense of reality is as defective as his identity. With respect to his audiences, the artist regards his marvelous simulations as a gift of love to the world; the impostor, on the other hand, longs solely for the narcissistic exhilaration of putting one over. The impostor, whose hatred and contempt for his audience is only barely disguised, has one single driven aim, to regain his rightful position, to overthrow and displace his father again and again. As he was once robbed of his Olympian stature, so he will now rob the Olympians of their power—but not through the perilous and potentially humiliating path of real achievement or real skill.

Unfortunately for the impostor-to-be, whose life circumstances rarely change in the direction of closer contact with a reliable and authoritative father figure, the deceptions of his nursery days continue unabated throughout the latency years. The role of Mother's precious darling is perpetuated. His contempt for her is quite unconscious. He will speak of her as a marvelous, beautiful creature. He does everything he can to please her. He may even imitate her clothing and hairstyles. But whenever he has the opportunity, he deceives her. He pawns her jewelry to buy expensive jackets, boots, skis, tennis rackets, baseball gloves—any gadget or possession that will impress the other boys with his fantastic wealth and high social standing. He has no real or stable friendships, only fluctuating groups of susceptible admirers. He compensates himself for his extraordinary loneliness by convincing himself of his superiority.

The other boys of the town seemed to me dull and limited indeed, since they obviously did not share my ability and were consequently ignorant of the secret joys I could derive from it by a simple act of will, effortlessly and without any outward preparation. They were common fellows, to be sure, with coarse hair and red hands, and they would have had trouble persuading themselves that they were princes—and very foolish they would have looked too.

When he has to go to school he is prepared to adopt almost any role that might please or impress his teachers except that of a boy who does real work. He is restless, driven to show off, totally unable to submit to the rules of the classroom. Rather than face up to the competition of schoolwork and examinations, he feigns illness and loafs about the house, where he is assured of approval and admiration. His mother winks conspiratorially at his excellent mimicry of stomachaches and sore throats. The family doctor, who might have to recognize his own incompetence to diagnose the boy's mysterious ailments, willingly goes along with the deceptions. Very often such a boy has to get his basic education at home from well-paid tutors or from his indulgent mother. He gets through grammar school by cheating, bribing the other kids to do his homework, ingratiating himself with his teachers, playing truant, and forging absence notes.

He is forgiven for all his faults and failures. Though his schoolwork is dismal and he makes no effort to improve, he is praised and admired. He uses his intellect, imagination, and talents, which are often considerable, to perfect his forgeries and deceptions.

With the advent of puberty, the prospect of having to prove oneself as a real man looms like an ominous cloud. Whereas most adolescent boys are at least partially reassured by the signs of their approaching manhood, the manipulator, potential impostor, is understandably reluctant to relinquish the fantasies and daydreams that have until now so superbly sustained his narcissism and held together his shaky sense of identity. Whereas the average adolescent boy will begin to give up the family romance that softened his disillusionment with his real parents and helped him to bear the humiliation of Oedipal defeat, on arriving at puberty the potential impostor not only clings more desperately to this fantasy but elaborates and refines it. He begins to enact the scenario in his everyday life.

The liar and the cheat, the manipulator, is on his way to becoming an impostor. It is the persistence of the family-romance fantasy and its pervasive infiltration into the solutions of adolescence that are the hallmarks of the impostor. Puberty compels an irreversible remodeling of sexual desire in which the parents must be relinquished as its objects. The infantile idealizations that enshrined their power must also be given up. As he arrives at puberty the impostor too is alerted to the messages of the incest taboo. They are brought home forcibly in the physical realm. The growing body, with its pubic hair, enlarging testicles and penis, seminal ejaculations, heralds adult sexuality and the possibilities of procreation. The hormonal awakenings encourage adult genital desires and genital erotic fantasies. The social order subtly but definitively proclaims that it does not tolerate violations of the taboo. In the average course of things, for the average adolescent, reality slowly but surely gains the day. But the impostor, who has never paid much heed to the messages of reality, has no intention of giving up the past, though he too must find a way to obey the incest taboo.

With a few flourishes here and there and some minor alterations of the story line, the family-romance fantasy that once rescued him in early childhood becomes the impostor's major strategy for the problem of removal. Usually the romance is an expression of a child's longings for the happy vanished days when his father seemed to him the noblest and strongest of men and his mother the dearest and loveliest of women, and it also serves as an elegant compromise between a child's incest strivings and the incest taboo. The child's awareness of his own parents as sexual beings is defensively disguised by the desexualized nobility who are his "legitimate" parents. At the same time, by becoming a stranger to his own family, the boy protects his father from his aggressive, rivalrous wishes and himself from his father's retaliation while clearing the way for the survival of his unconscious sexual wishes toward his mother.

No doubt a sort of compromise was also achieved by the impostor's childhood fantasy. But his fantasy served a more regressive solution. The impostor had to enter a premature but abortive pseudo-Oedipal phase, with a quick retreat from the emotional challenges of any actual Oedipal relationships—a kind of ingenious sidestepping of the incest taboo. The compromise succeeds in making him a stranger to his real family: "I had to conclude that I did not owe much to heredity; and unless I was to assume that at some indefinite point in history there had been an irregularity in my family tree whereby some cavalier, some great nobleman, must be reckoned among my natural forbears, I was obliged in order to explain the source of my superiorities to look within myself."

The impostor's fantasy allows him to renounce any actual rivalry or competition with his father in favor of a return to his original position as the uncontested little kaiser in the kingdom without a father. The fantasy also banishes the wish to claim the mother sexually by replacing that wish with the innocuous desexualized wish for reunion with her exalted masculine ideal. This fantasy is not to replace Father as Mother's sexual partner but merely to overthrow him and rob him of his treasures—thereby symbolically robbing him of his genital superiority. But the impostor has no further use for the spoils. Mere acquisition is enough.

Now, in adolescence, by acting out the fantasy the impostor continues to sidestep the incest taboo and to avoid the emotional challenges of removal. Each imposture announces "I am a stranger to my own family." With each imposture he regains his rightful place, robs his father of his powers, and shapes himself according to the image he loves best—the exalted ideal conveyed to him by his mother. His symbolic flight from his real family does not eliminate the incestuous longings, it merely short-circuits them.

No matter how far he roams, how many times he assumes another identity, falsifies another achievement, how many women or men he seduces, how many times he charms and overpowers his audience, how often he robs his teachers and bosses of their powers, he can remain the nursery innocent who need not reckon in any real way with the differences between the sexes or the differences between his own and his parents' generations.

The average adolescent is nostalgic for the land of lost content—the happy highways he traveled and cannot pass over again—but the impostor's life is itself an endless journey along the happy highway of his infancy. He need never experience sadness, grief, anxiety, nostalgia, nor need he recognize the irreversible nature of the loss of his infantile past. Since the acting out of his fantasy succeeds in substituting narcissistic aggrandizement for genital desire and in symbolically removing the actual parents as the objects of desire, the impostor, technically speaking, has avoided incest. But he has also given up the possibility of transferring love-desire anywhere else. His numerous love affairs with women or men are reenactments of his family romance and nothing more. And his audience is only too ready to confirm his fantasy. One of Krull's passing lovers implores him to steal the jewels given to her by her powerful but denigrated husband, M. Houple, the manufacturer of Strassburg bath-

room toilets. "Oh," she says, "how much more precious to
me is the thief than what he took!"

For the impostor there is no possibility of an enduring
love relationship. His life is given movement and direction
solely by his repeated acts of fooling the audience and making fools of them. In this sense he is very much like those
other unfortunate souls, the paranoiacs, who have forgone
the anguish and grief of removal by reversing love-desire
into hatred and contempt. The impostor can be banker, general, corporate executive, judge, psychology professor, politician, philosopher (all of these, perhaps). However, deprived of his imposturous roles the impostor would be
revealed as the humiliated, wrathful, impotent, powerless
infant—the tormented self that never had a chance to grow
up. Except for his daydreams and the repeated moments of
exhilaration and triumph when he is living out his exalted
ideal of manhood, the impostor is an emotional hermit, totally isolated from the advantages of ordinary life. It is true
that he is free of those countless bonds that tie us to others
and make us heavy. He glides above the world of real ambition and real power. He need not deal with "the inconveniences of undertaking to intercede, of being a sacrifice, of
reasoning with rabbis, of going to weddings and funerals, of
beginning something and then at a certain point remarking
that it is finished." But his burden, which is to be larger
than life, must be borne alone, with no relief or comfort
from others; for his burden is precisely his secrecy.

During adolescence the impostor is a lone wolf. He has no
group allegiances, no responding excitements to the *ars erotica* of a young woman, no involvement with social ideals,
no concern or compassion for others. Krull, of course, finds
a way to make a virtue of his loneliness: ". . . in my early
youth an inner voice had warned me that close association,
friendship, and companionship were not to be my lot, but
that I should instead be inescapably compelled to follow my
strange path alone, dependent entirely upon myself, rigor-
ously self-sufficient."

The extraordinary narcissism of the impostor throws into bold relief the narcissistic strategies employed by the average adolescent boy in his quest for manhood. In the process of de-idealizing his father the adolescent boy will select for worship a variety of new idols that can bolster his self-esteem—the pure and saintly types as well as the ruthless and seductive ones. Now that he is tearing down the standards and authority of his father, the boy overvalues and exaggerates the powers of his current idols. As he dances to their music, reads their sermons and poetry, watches their triumphs on the playing field or TV screen, an ordinary young man merges his own self with these glorious personages and thereby restores the omnipotence and self-love he lost when he began to see his father's imperfections. He identifies with these seductive, exciting, glamorous, powerful idols and temporarily feels a little bit better about the inadequate person he imagines himself to be. Eventually, he accepts his father as he really is, and he begins to have some compassion for himself and for others. The exalted ego-ideal of infancy has been tamed—carved, as it were—into its human proportion.

But the impostor can never tame his ego-ideal, because his very existence depends on acting out its demands. He sometimes idealizes others, but his driven ambition is to outwit and trick them. Each time he fools his audience, the mother's ambitions and his ambitions coalesce in a single gesture. The impostor's father can never be de-idealized, because he must forever be cast in the role of the terrifying but gullible giant of the nursery.

Because the adolescent is tender, raw, thin-skinned, and poignantly vulnerable, he invests his energies in dreams of glory and fantasies of omnipotence. These dreams and fantasies allow him to believe that nothing is impossible, that he can do anything, solve every problem, have total control over himself and his environment. The loftiness of his plans and speculations are at times commensurate with his inability to get anything done. His pretensions to absolute power are of the same magnitude as his sense of impotence and inadequacy. The influx of genital vitality prompts the boy to act every part in the human comedy. Since he can be anything he wishes to be, he does not limit his vision of who he is to the vulnerable, limited person he supposes himself to be. In several respects, then, the average adolescent is as much a pretender to fame and glory as an impostor.

For most boys, however, these narcissistic strategies are temporary ones which enable him to bear the emotional stresses of bidding farewell to childhood. True, his strategies are conjuring acts that hearken back to infancy, to the days in the Garden of Eden. But in these adolescent conjurings are also a boy's visions of the future. The typical adolescent looks forward to growing up. His nostalgia is an expression of all that he must leave behind on his way to manhood. He yearns for the past because he has begun to recognize that time is irreversible and that the past is irrevocably gone. These longings for the lost state of perfection will often heighten an adolescent's social awareness and evoke some musings on how to improve the human lot. Though past and future contend for mastery, the future, by and large, wins out. The idealizations of infancy are impersonalized and transformed into social ideals.

For the impostor and others like him there is no contest. The battle between the past and the future is simply not engaged. The imaginary life is more palpable than the real one. Nothing the actual world can offer will ever compare favorably with the masculine ideal conveyed to him in infancy. Besides, real competition and real achievement are too risky, much riskier than swindling, forgery, counterfeiting, stealing, hoodwinking the powerful Giant. One might have to start at the bottom. One might come out second or third or perhaps even fail now and again. And following all that hard work and industry one might not win the Nobel Prize or become President.

Though he does not become an impostor, many a young man has been arrested in his pursuit of manhood by his Nobel Prize complex. These young men had also been the darlings of the nursery. A mother's aspirations for her son can enrich his emotional capacities and inspire his intellect and creativity. But all too often a little boy's conviction that he is the object of his mother's entire love, the emblem of her own unfulfilled "masculine" ambitions, the center of her existence, can deprive the boy of his alliance with the father. Whether or not the father wishes to be an emotional absentee, whether or not the mother actually demeans the father, he might become in the little boy's mind a devalued, inconsequential figure simply as a result of the mother's exaggerated investment in this boy.

The boy grows up resenting his father for not having rescued him from his infantile dependencies. Later on, during adolescence, the devaluation and resentment of the father erupt as a devaluation of the entire society. The man's world, the world of his father, is rejected in favor of continuing to live out the mother's exalted ambitions—ambitions that preclude real achievement. The youth becomes one of the uncommitted, a genius without portfolio, a Raskolnikov, a nihilist, a young man whose contempt for convention and social responsibility prevent him from fulfilling his real talents and intellectual potentials. He opts out.

These sorts of arrests on the way to manhood are reinforced when the prevailing values of the social moment correspond to those conveyed to the boy in his infancy. The content of parental ideals is to some extent always imposed by society. A mother's and father's fantasies about their child will always match up with the various sex-gender concordant scripts supplied by the society. Social institutions always channel individual narcissistic trends toward some common ideal. But when the social order nearly duplicates the exalted ideals of nursery life by valuing glory, prestige, power, self-fulfillment, personal aggrandizement over real achievement and a commitment to impersonal ideals, a young man or woman has very little motive to modify his or her dreams of glory. Yet to become caregiver and lawgiver of the next generation, every youth must first solve the personal problem of how to accommodate the life of infinite possibility to the life of feasible possibility. Some of the problems of arriving at manhood or womanhood are personal ones that have arisen in connection with the various love dialogues of family life from infancy to adolescence. The other problems that youth must contend with are those that stem from the values and ideals of the social order, which may be as false to that being we call our true self as any deception of nursery life.

12
THE LEGACIES OF ADOLESCENCE

The anorectic and the impostor are lone wolves. They imagine that they are exceptions who are entitled to act outside the moral authority of the social world in which they live. Their mission is not antisocial, it is merely personal. They have no room in life for the kinds of sentiments that might bind them to other human beings. They float above the ordinary world, lost in the realm of infinite possibility where the uncertainties of commitment to the actual world need not trouble them. They can play at life forever. They need not grow up to assume the sexual and moral responsibilities of adulthood. From the point of view of personal history, their lonely fate is largely a matter of *amour-propre,* the driven vanity of the envious soul. The exalted ideals conveyed to them in infancy were never tamed, never carved into human proportions and brought into harmony with the life of feasibility.

Yet at the same time, the anorectic and the impostor speak to us of their humanness. With their solipsistic grandiosity they are announcing their distinction from the beasts below them on the *scala naturae.* For what else have they done but assert those two ineluctable faculties of the human mind—imagination and the urge toward perfectibility—the very dynamics of civilization that may destroy as they create, corrupt as they improve, ruin as they civilize?

According to Rousseau, all other animals but the human one are safe from the perils of imagination and therefore subject to the commands of nature. Imagination is the light of human reason. It guides us out of the darkness in which nature has enveloped us. On the other hand, imagination can be an immense adversary to human happiness. Imagination enlarges our natural appetites into insatiable longings. It endows the objects we desire with attractions far greater than nature designed. By inciting desire, imagination impels us to compare ourselves to others. We find it humiliating that others should have certain pleasures and possessions that we do not. And the disparity between the actual world, with its practicalities and conditions, and the world of the imagination, which has no boundaries, increases our miseries and makes us resent our responsibilities to others.

In the privacy of imagination we may feel passions without the consequences of those passions; we may play at life without taking any risks; we revel in feelings without committing our sentiments. Imagination absolves us from direct experience; it becomes a surrogate for action. Finally, imagination may so inflame our longings for perfection that we lose our souls in pursuit of our ambitions and ideals: "our souls have been corrupted in proportion to the advancement of our sciences and arts towards perfection. Can it be said that this is a misfortune particular to our age? No, gentlemen: the evils caused by our vain curiosity are as old as the world. . . . Virtue has fled as their light dawned on the horizon, and the same phenomena has been observed in all times and in all places."

Rousseau was referring here to the loss of social concern among those enlightened minds that were responsible for the advances of civilization. "We have physicists, geometers, chemists, astronomers, poets, musicians, painters; we no longer have citizens." In all times and in all places, the single-minded pursuit of perfection is associated with the alienation of the self, not only from its own nature but also from the sentiments that bind individuals to a community of others. With the Enlightenment, as artists, scientists, philosophers were just beginning to grope toward the ideas and visions that could encompass the cataclysmic revolution that was almost upon them, Rousseau was the first to identify *alienation* as the common plight of humanity. He predicted that European civilization was on the verge of a political, social, and technological upheaval that could bring all of humanity to "the edge of the abyss," and in that context he used the word *moderniste* as it would come to be understood in the twentieth century. The chronic plight of alienation would become acute. The question of how the self might survive the shock of modernization would become the central moral dilemma of the modern world. The perversions of imagination and self-improvement that Rousseau portrayed would multiply and become the prototypical maladies of the modern world.

From the point of view of social history, then, the anorectic and the impostor are not exceptional. They are emblematic of all those divided souls "always appearing to relate everything to others and never relating anything except to themselves alone." They are more or less like any victim of modernization: "floating the whole course of our life, we end it without having been able to put ourselves in harmony with ourselves and without having been good either for ourselves or for others."

To be human is to be prey to the ravages of imagination. To be human is to strive for perfectibility. The dilemma for the modern world is how to enlist these faculties of the human mind toward the common good. Imagination may transform self-interest into social virtue. The ideals we strive for may become commensurate with moral dignity. As Rousseau knew, these same human faculties had allowed man to "rise above himself; soar intellectually into celestial regions; traverse with giant steps, like the sun, the vastness of the universe; and—what is even grander and more difficult—come back to himself and study man and know his nature, his duties, and his end."

Compassion itself, from which flows all our social virtues—generosity, clemency, justice—is inconceivable without imagination. The most significant act of imagination is our capacity to experience what others experience. Humans alone, among all creatures, can put themselves in the situation of other beings, feel what others feel, suffer what others suffer, and even grasp the meaning of that suffering. This imaginative leap from self-experience to other-experience is the inspiration of the paradigmatic golden rule that instructs us to mirror the suffering of others as our own suffering. "One pities in others only those ills from which one does not feel oneself exempt."

To be human is to be dependent on others. Other-love is the safety net of human existence. Soon after birth, love dialogue becomes more important to us than the gratification of physical needs. So we yield up our inborn omnipotence and bend desire to the contours of the social order. "Every attachment is a sign of insufficiency. If each of us had no need of others he would hardly think of uniting himself with them. Thus from our very infirmity is born our frail happiness." Such dependency can be experienced as a humiliation, a slavelike submission that rankles the soul and directs us away from our common humanity. However, imagination offers us compensations for our loss of absolute freedom. By directing our sentiments, passions, and reason toward the common human plight, imagination grants us the advantages of a moral existence. What we surrender of innocent love of self is exchanged for the safeties and pleasures of belonging to a larger whole. We are born dependent, but only imagination can bind our passions to other human beings.

Imagination also grants us moral dignity. Whenever the humiliations of renunciation become too much to bear, imagination enables us to conjure up a world more congenial to our love of self. It lifts us into those realms beyond reality, beyond pleasure, where bridges are crossed and contradictions are held at bay. We imagine the disappointing world as a better and more harmonious place than it actually is. Without imagination and the ideals of perfectibility it nourishes we would not willingly suffer the sacrifices entailed in belonging to the world of others. We could submit only with resentment. When there is nothing more to life than sex, work, procreation, moral obedience, nothing beyond the realities and pleasures of the moment, no past glories to conjure up, no future ideals to project ourselves toward, the inevitable ambiguities existing between the individual human spirit and the demands of civilization become irreconcilable antagonisms.

As Rousseau predicted, the ambiguous relationship

between the individual and civilization has become the central dilemma of the modern world, and alienation the universal malady of modern men and women. Many modern writers—Kant and Nietzsche, Marx and Kierkegaard, Trilling and Lévi-Strauss—have grappled with these predicaments. In *Civilization and Its Discontents* (1929) Freud took account of the obstacles to human happiness. He listed three inescapable sources of our common miseries: the feebleness of our bodies, which are doomed to decay; the natural world, "which may rage against us with overwhelming and merciless forces of destruction"; and the restraints that bind us as members of the family, the state, and the social order. Most of us accept the inevitabilities of the first two sources of our unhappiness. We appreciate that the advances of civilization have allowed us to alleviate the sufferings of our bodies and to mitigate those that afflict us from the indifferent external world. It is the third source of our misery, the relations that bind us to others, that confounds us. The emotional price we pay for these mutual relationships seems to outweigh their benefits by far. Our liberties are curtailed, our passions and desires are restrained, and some of them must be renounced altogether.

We consent to the idea that by living an everyday life according to the rules we will be compensated for our renunciations. We expect to recover through family life and work some of the imagined possibilities we surrendered for the advantages of belonging to the world of others. At the least, we expect that civilization will protect us from the impersonal violences of nature and the selfish brutalities of our neighbors. But these days the common complaint is that civilization itself is the cause of all our miseries, that we would all be much happier if we entrusted ourselves to the impersonal laws of nature.

The history of the modern world speaks to the individual's increasing hostility to civilization. By now the complaints are familiar enough. With every step toward improving the lot of humanity, civilization has put us further at odds with nature. In our present century the great scientific

discoveries that set in motion the processes of modernization seem at last to have alienated us from our own human
nature. The discoveries of Darwin and Einstein radically altered our relationship to the cosmos. All that was sacred has
been profaned. We cannot reconcile ourselves to the humiliating fact that we are forever separated from the universe.

The industrialization of production has converted scientific knowledge into the instant currency of technology. The
laws of nature are employed to sever us from our earthly
environment. New urban environments are created at a cataclysmic pace, while whole tribes, ethnic groups, nations
have been wrenched from their ancestral homes and dis-
persed into the lands of strangers. The tempo of life has
accelerated to a frenzied commotion. We have lost the
rhythms of season and generation. History is compressed
into decades. We measure our lives according to the day,
the hour, the minute. Even the continuities of daily life are
disrupted by perpetual upheavals in our personal relations.
All is uncertainty and agitation. As Marx saw it in the nineteenth century, "All our inventions and progress seem to
result in endowing material forces with intellectual life and
stultifying human life with a material force."

For the maladies of our physical state, civilization has substituted the mental anguish of its own designs. Medicines
and medical technology have alleviated and cured diseases,
significantly reduced infant mortality and the infections of
childbirth in women, and extended the life-span. But if it
were not for the overrefined diets, cramped urban housing,
sedentary and stultifying occupations, insatiable consumer-
ism, narcotizing leisure of modern life, we would have less
need of doctors or their medicines. As Rousseau observed in
the eighteenth century, we have given ourselves "more ills
than medicine can furnish remedies."

The tools that our imagination has inspired us to invent
represent the improvement of our limited natural senses and
muscular power: spectacles, hearing aids, the telescope, mi-
croscope, telephone, automobile, aircraft. This is what led

Freud to declare that "Man has, as it were, become a prosthetic God." And he observed that such mechanical extensions often bring new forms of suffering rather than the self-
improvement our imagination anticipated.

Civilization, in its frenzy to exploit the resources of the
natural world—to cultivate the soil, build towns, fashion
implements from the minerals below the soil, eliminate the
wild beasts, breed the domestic ones—has turned out to be
what Lévi-Strauss depicted as "the most effective agent
working towards the disintegration of the original order of
things and hurrying on powerfully organized matter towards
ever greater inertia, an inertia which will one day be final."
The exploitation of nature has allowed us to become lords
of the earth and at the same time to extinguish the great auk,
the bison, the wild ass, the mammoth, the woolly rhinoceros, the Irish elk, and also the hunter-gatherer peoples of
our own species.

It is evident that compassion alone, without justice, cannot protect the weak from the brute force of the powerful.
To ensure the mutuality of the relations of one person to
another and bind individuals to other members of the species, civilization establishes customs, laws, and regularized
systems of justice. So that no person should have to be at the
mercy of another, we all sacrifice portions of our personal
liberties. Yet, even more than impersonal nature or human
selfishness, custom and law may as often serve to increase
the power of the powerful as to diminish the inequalities
among individuals. Too often, also, the equalities established by law may be absurdly unjust, as when rich man and
poor man alike are forbidden to sleep under bridges. Rousseau described these paradoxes of justice as "the multitude
oppressed from within as a consequence of the very precautions it had taken against that which menaced it from without."

Thus, in exchange for protection from nature and the regulation of social relations, civilization requires enormous
renunciations, sacrifices, and restrictions of personal liberty, which in turn seem to lead merely to further curtail-

ments of our already flimsy possibilities for happiness. We resent our bonds. Our resentment inclines us toward a perception of the ills and injustices of civilization and a disparaging view of its benefits.

We demand from civilization some recompense over and above its utilitarian designs. Beauty, cleanliness, and order, for example, are not essential to civilized existence, but all human societies have customs to assure the elaboration of these aesthetic benefits of civilization, however unbeautiful, unclean, or disorderly they might seem to our more "civilized" modern minds. We demand of civilization that there be room in life for our higher mental endeavors— intellectual, scientific, artistic—and especially our strivings toward "a possible perfection of individuals, or of peoples or of the whole of humanity."

Though he paid tribute to the compensatory extras of civilization, Freud was reluctant to assign a special increment of value to these cultural pursuits. "I scorn," he said, "to distinguish between culture and civilization." Freud might even have consented to the spirit of Rousseau's commentary on culture: "While government and laws provide for the safety and well-being of assembled men, the sciences, letters, arts, less despotic and perhaps more powerful, spread garlands of flowers over the iron chains with which men are burdened, stifle in them the sense of original liberty for which they seem to have been born, make them love their slavery."

In the end, however, Freud as much as Rousseau would have opposed the contention that civilization and its cultural compensations were fundamentally antagonistic to the individual spirit. They would have agreed that we suffer not because we are civilized but because we are human. And both looked within the human passions to find the sources of our ruination—and our deliverance.

Freud's lament on the tragic dimensions of human civilization led him to hypothesize an aspect of living organisms that could abolish the whole of civilized human life. Against this menacing force the benevolent visage of civilization—

with its cultural aspirations—might count for very little. Freud raised the specter of the death instinct with its sole aims toward inertia, decay, disunity, simplification, fragmentation, entropy. In the face of this destructive energy the antagonisms between the urge toward personal happiness (egoism) and the urge toward union with others (altruism) melt away. Freud admits to a possible reconciliation within the individual toward civilization, and perhaps even in civilization toward the individual, since it might eventually do its work in a manner less oppressive to personal liberty and pleasure. Humanity's antagonist is neither self-interest nor civilization—both of which are manifestations of the binding and unifying powers of eros—but the instinct of aggression and self-destruction that is to be found in every form of living organization from the single cell to the family to the state.

The last paragraph of *Civilization and Its Discontents* begins with a question for the human species. To what extent, Freud asks, will civilizations "succeed in mastering the disturbance of their communal life by the instinct of aggression and self-destruction?" In its original version the response and final sentence was Freud's cautiously hopeful plea that eternal Eros might assert himself in the struggle with his equally immortal adversary, the death instinct. Two years later, as the menace of Hitler became apparent, Freud appended another sentence: "But, who can foresee with what success and with what result?"

Our understanding of adolescence in the modern world does not require an examination of the destructive instinct, a theoretical issue of considerable dispute. Nevertheless, whether or not some destructive force is at work in the human mind, in civilization, in nature itself, we do know that human aggression in its crude, untamed form is fundamentally antagonistic to individual life and to civilization. We also know that whenever something is given up for something else, whenever passion is about to be deployed to another person, another realm, another order of existence, the event always begins as a variation on violence.

The danger is that once unleashed, the violence will assume its own momentum, get out of hand, run its course toward final dissolution before our sexual and moral passions can exert their binding and unifying influences. Whenever a dramatic historical change is about to take place, whether in a human life or in society, "there shows itself, juxtaposed and often entangled with one another, a magnificent, manifold, jungle-like growing and striving, a sort of tropical tempo in rivalry of development, and an enormous destruction and self-destruction, thanks to egoisms violently opposed to one another, exploding, battling each other for sun and light, unable to find any limitation, any check, any considerations within the morality at their disposal." This is Nietzsche, the prophet of the New Man, extolling our remarkable abundance of possibilities and warning of the absence and emptiness of the moral values that might contain them.

Adolescence itself begins with crudities, simplifications, primitivizations of aggression and narcissism—a breakdown of controls, an eruption of unruly passions and desires, a dissolution of the civilizing trends of childhood. One of the trials of any revolution, whether in the individual or in the social order, has to do with what is conserved and what is destroyed. In fact, it is this very consideration that determines whether a revolution is advancing a new cause or merely reinstating the tyrannies of the past in a new guise. Adolescence is an unsettling of the established order in favor of an impassioned determination of new and as yet untested ideals.

But adolescence is also a narrative on the unifying tendencies of eros. We learn from adolescence that new ways of thinking, feeling, imagining cannot be acquired overnight, fully formed. The adolescent does not relinquish the past without a struggle, without grief, without anxiety. The purpose of adolescence is to revise the past, not to obliterate it, and in this revision, as the past is reconciled with the future, the moral life achieves a force and prominence that rescues narcissism from isolated self-interest and aggression from mere destruction. Adolescence entails the deployment of family passions to the passions and ideals that bind individuals to new family units, to their communities, to the species, to nature, to the cosmos. Therefore, given half a chance, the revolution at issue in adolescence becomes a revolution of transformation, not of annihilation.

At the beginning of adolescence the antagonisms between individual passions and civilization are exacerbated. A burst of growth expands every appetite and interest; a wave of fresh vitality agitates imagination, intensifies self-absorption, galvanizes erotic desire. Then the adolescent encounters the incest taboo. The adolescent must direct her sexual passions and narcissistic ambitions outside the family and toward the larger social units. During infancy, desire and love of self are not antagonistic to the purposes of civilization. The appetite for dialogue draws us into our first human community, and imagination awakens in us an erotic hunger for the person who is our first caregiver. Loving another person entails conditions, and because we are helpless and dependent, we obey those conditions. Little by little we submit to the demands of nursery morality. The urges to suck, swallow, be held, caressed, rocked, are granted, but only in terms of "so much," "in this place," "at that time." We submit to delay, frustration, and the rationing of pleasure. Finally, the law and order of family life declare that when it comes to genital gratification, the child is an outsider. Desire is not rationed or dosed, it is entirely forbidden.

In compensation for the Oedipal defeat we acquire the authority to regulate our own desires. Though we have been banished from the Garden of Eden, our banishment liberates us from the humiliating moral dependency of the nursery. We are ready, willing, and able to accept our position in the larger community: we go to school, learn to read and write, to program computers, and we endeavor to become obedient, civilized human beings, all the while keeping alive the fantasy that one day—if we are good enough, clever enough, beautiful enough, when we finally grow up—the humiliations of infancy will be rectified. We will be restored to the Garden of Eden.

But our childhood fantasies do not come true. At adolescence the relationship between the passions of family life and civilization becomes highly equivocal:

> It expresses itself at first as a conflict between the family and the larger community to which the individual belongs. We have already received that one of the main endeavors of civilization is to bring people together into larger units. But the family will not give the individual up. The more closely the members of the family are attached to one another, the more often do they tend to cut themselves off from others and the more difficult it is for them to enter into the wider circle of life.

Once again we have a paradox, one of the few that Rousseau did not propose. If it were not for the formation of the powerful erotic attachments of infancy we would not undergo during adolescence the wrenching struggle to relinquish them; nor, at the same time, would there be motives for the perversities of imagination and self-improvement that result in the anorectic and the impostor. When family passions go awry, imagination is set free to do its worst. What we see then are not the binding and unifying tendencies but an enormous destruction and self-destruction without limitation, check, or "any considerations within the morality at their disposal." On the other hand, the weakening of family attachments undermines the emotional basis for those social and moral passions that bind us to others and often unleashes worse forms of self-destruction and tyranny.

One of the major trends of modernization has been the increasing privatization of the family. The cocoon that was meant to protect the individual from the indignities of the machine became an iron cage that isolated the family from the realities of the larger social community. The aversion of family life to community life is, of course, no new phenomenon. Utopian visionaries have always reckoned that it might be necessary to weaken, perhaps even eradicate family attachments in order to assure obedience to communal values. What has changed in the picture within the past three centuries is the gradual undermining of the sense of community by the perversions of narcissism flourishing in the bosom of the family. By the middle of the twentieth century self-fulfillment and individuality had ascended as the reigning values of family life. The family became a mirror of the machine.

Finally, by opposing all interests that might intrude on the self-interests of its members, the nuclear family brought about its own demise. It disintegrated into what became the prototypical family of the sixties and seventies—a temporary accommodation to necessity, barely bound by the vagrant passions of its adult members; a free-for-all quest for personal liberation in which each family member, including the child, was more or less on his or her own. It appeared as though we were poised to return to the medieval ideal, in which, like the little Prince, we might be "free of the weight of human relationships," free at last of "those countless bonds" that tie us to others and make us heavy. But in this modern go-around there will be few cultural compensations for our bondless existence. The individual will be really alone. In that darkest of all ages preceding the Enlightenment, there was at least a sense of community, the magic and spirituality that connected the individual, albeit loosely and diffusely, "to God, saints, parents, children, friends, horses, dogs, orchards and gardens."

The day is late, but it is still too early to know exactly where the modern family is headed. Just as everybody was ready to accept the death of the family, it began to stir again. The violent egoisms of the past few decades may have been a revolution of transformation, not annihilation. In 1979 the National Organization for Women convened a national assembly whose topic of study was "The Future of the Family." Here it was announced that the feminists of the eighties were moving on to a new frontier—the family. One prominent feminist proclaimed: "I think, in fact, that the woman's movement has come just about as far as we can in terms of women alone—we are finding that it's not so easy to live with—or without—men and children solely on the basis of that first feminist agenda."

The panelists were unanimous in the view that women needed children and men, men needed women, and in fact that everybody needed everybody else. There was also a consensus that participation in family life was the best bulwark against the modern work ethos that turned men and women into dehumanized corporate automatons. The conference indicated that there was a pervasive longing for intimacy and for the restoration of the binding commitments of family life. One was reminded of that innocent and hopeful voice of the psychoanalyst J. C. Flugel, who, in 1921, asserted that all schemes from Plato onward that had set out to destroy familial attachments had failed and would continue to be doomed to "practical failure, because these feelings are too strong, too intimate and essential a part of human nature to be successfully and permanently inhibited by alteration of the environment; moral failure because the development of certain of the most important aspects of human character are, in their origin and first appearance, bound up with family feelings and would probably fail to ripen if these feelings were abolished."

As one of the leaders of the new feminism proposed at the 1979 conference, "Maybe the greatest challenge now is to find a way to keep independence while also committing ourselves to the ties that bind people, families and ultimately societies together."

Turning to the next generation of caregivers and lawgivers, what can we expect of them? Is it true that the yearnings for attachment and unity with others are too powerful to abolish forever? Will Eros stand up against the forces of decay and dissolution? Amid the immense dilemmas that confront the youth of our modern world, would it be a Pollyannaish deception to hold out even some small measure of hope? For it does seem that the slow march of progress has accelerated to a frantic race toward the apocalypse. Against the prevailing values of modernity—that frenzy of self-improvement and rampant imagination—dare we pose the legacies of adolescence? Might we take our measure of hope from that burst of energy, that wave of fresh vitality that unlatches the structures of the past and gives us the opportunity to rewrite the scripts?

In all times and in all places, adolescence is the time of life when, as Erikson cogently put it, "the life history intersects with history: here individuals are confirmed in their identities, societies regenerated in their life style. This process also implies a fateful survival of adolescent modes of thinking in man's historical and ideological perspectives." The vitalities of growth that transform a child into a powerful, sexual, procreative, morally responsible being have always been associated with the general flowering and vitality of society, nature, and the cosmos. One of the major challenges to the youth of the modern world is the obscure relationship between their own personal historical moment and social or cosmic history.

In hunter-gatherer and traditional societies a youth could find the larger meaning of his or her personal transition into adulthood by identifying with some larger temporal rhythm. What a youth would undergo personally automatically coalesced with a cosmic plan, with human destiny, with the history of a nation, tribe, military or religious order, kinship group. The articulation between personal time and natural or social time was more or less explicit. Now the linkage between the adolescent present and the larger temporal units is uncertain. The ambiguity challenges the newly awakened sensibilities, intellectual powers, and imagination of the adolescent.

It should not surprise us that a challenge of such magnitude might provoke a sense of fragmentation and hopelessness in some young people, especially when they cannot locate in the social environment any historical units that extend beyond the present—beyond the decade, the hour, the minute. The flattened historical perspectives of the modern world can often inflame a youth's antagonisms to civilization and exacerbate her solipsistic grandiosities.

But with all its uncertainty and agitation, its ceaseless growing and striving, modern civilization, by virtue of its relative absence of fixed structures and finally determined solutions, also sponsors certain countertendencies that facilitate the full flowering of the moral life. The value placed on innovation, for example, though it can lead to opportunistic exploitations, even annihilations, has a potentially constructive side. Innovation implies the feasibility of remedy, repair, corrective alteration, the value of solving rather than enduring the predicaments of existence. Social reformation—another prominent force of the last three centuries— incites the imagination of youth to convert the rhetoric of amelioration into universal practice. And pluralism, by affording alternatives to the isolating experience of deviance, enhances the experience of sociability and liberates the capacity to surpass self-absorption and egocentricity. Along with this goes a greater diversity of role opportunity and the viability of alternative terms for adjustment and adaptation. Such modern forces potentiate the unifying, constructive aspects of imagination, encouraging adolescents to transcend the personal and the immediate, to soar intellectually, to explore within themselves the wide reach of human possibility, and then to return to everyday life with outgoing energies prepared to grapple with the dilemmas of existence, to know our nature, our duties, our end.

In one way or another, even though the precise words may elude them, adolescents ask themselves, "Can my personal ambitions find a place in society?" "How will my personal future mingle with the future of the world I live in?" "Is there something outside or beyond my personal everyday life that I might believe in?" "Are these beliefs worthy?" "Can I trust them?" What we hear, if we listen, are young lives in search of something larger than ordinary, everyday existence—some ideals or values to which they might be true. And as we know, even in those tribal rites that fully sponsor a youth's personal quest for meaning, these searches have in them "the danger of slipping beyond the pale and never coming back."

The casualties of youth are on the increase. Some—those who retreat totally or partially from the ordeals of growing up—the suicides, the psychotics, the addicted, the succumbers to perverted imagination such as the anorectics and the impostors—are as much the consequences of the aberrations of modern family life as they are reflections of the alienating narcissistic ideals of the modern world.

Other calamities that afflict our youth, though less absolutely destructive to the individual, are as ruinous in the moral sense. They arise in direct connection with the easy corruptibility of adolescent imagination, which demagogues of various political and religious persuasions—be they Nazis, representatives of the Reverend Moon, Maoists—can so easily harness to their own grandiose purposes. A cynical and ruthless narcissist will not hesitate to exploit the expectable tendencies of adolescents to de-idealize their parents while hungrily attaching themselves to other more exciting and romantic idols. The youth are told that they are the "true leaders" of the future, that they are "destiny's children," that they have the right to rule over the decadent adult generation, that in fact it is their moral obligation to denounce the transgressions of their parents and if necessary to participate in a parent's actual or spiritual execution. In such perversions of imagination, the youths can become more obedient and submissive, more slavishly adoring of their new idols than they were as helpless, vulnerable infants in relation to their parents. A youth who wants desperately to believe in something or someone is highly vulnerable to the promises of the false prophet. And in those dim periods when people lose their connections with the past and when the future seems to have no meaning, the false prophet finds his most susceptible audiences.

Some of the casualties of youth are so commonplace that they might escape our notice. These, the garden-variety results of the miscarriages of youthful imagination, are the legion of "silly kids," the adolescents who become replicas of the caricatures we design for them. But even such a seemingly "mindless teenager" as the kid on line for a Superman movie, the beachboy, the Dionysus of the dance floor, the Atari addict, the Val girl, the punk, is searching for something or someone to be true to. And when their adolescence is over, some are destined, like Icarus, to fall from the heavens or from whatever narrow or wide reach of imagination they have dared, right into the conformities of everyday existence, without making so much as a ripple.

A young person's quest for meaning has more chance of ending in a mundane failure when the collective values of a society are shaped *solely* by the objectives of the present. Because it has become more pervasive and considerably more insidious than obvious corruption or the temptations of a false prophet, the bureaucratization of modern life, with its emptiness of value and narrowness of historical perspective, may be the gravest danger to youth. When the future loses its dimension as a meaningful temporal unit and the past is efficiently consigned to an unrememberable oblivion, the present moment assumes an urgency that robs youth of the full flowering of the moral life that is the purpose of adolescence.

The cult of immediacy, with its emphasis on sensation, simultaneity, and impact, saps the vitalities of the young, incites their sexual passions to precocious consummation, stultifies their intellect, trivializes their imaginations. They can only feel that what they might aspire to as individuals has no place in any larger scheme of things. They suppose that society doesn't really need them, that they have no future. They sow their wild oats and then quickly grow out of their awkward and annoying ways to become the adults who have no option but to submit to the benevolent tyranny of "the assistant postmaster." Soon there is little left to them but the renunciations of civilization. What few recompenses they are granted—order and cleanliness, some moments of beauty, a token religion—are scanty indeed. The more they submit the more they resent the bonds of civilization and the less willing they are to sacrifice self-interest for the common good. "Why should they?" They cling to the safeties of everyday life, with some time off for titillating excitements.

This last mundane variety of adolescent casualty is certainly not unique to the modern world. But its current prevalence should make us wonder if we haven't begun to invent a mythology of adolescence that will accommodate to a new version of civilization. Every society attempts to preserve itself by inventing the adolescence it requires. Four decades ago some writers and artists were already proclaiming the eclipse of modernity. We were said to be entering the post-Modern era. No one as yet is sure exactly what post-Modernism is. But whatever it is, it seems to entail a considerable disillusionment with the hopeful and visionary aspects of Modernism. The old dialogues are running out, and there are no new ones to replace them. The dialectical vibrancy of Modernism—its fiery ecstasies, its violent egoisms searching for a morality that might contain them, its spirit of innovation, challenging ambiguities, speculative possibilities, and generous diversities—has petered out into a chilling mood of futility and finality, a resigned acceptance of the absence and emptiness of value.

When all that is sacred has been profaned, when God is dead and the emperor has been banished and there is nothing else to believe in, the revolution could end in a frozen plot that simply reinstates the tyrannies of the past in a new guise. Aggression and narcissism will have been quelled but not abolished. What we will see is an army of obedient citizens who harbor a secret romance life that continually fans the flames of desire. The Big Brothers and the Well-doers will know exactly what they are up against. They will keep the citizens under constant surveillance, program their sexual appetites, and trivialize the inspirations and beauties that might otherwise awaken their souls.

We have not come to that baleful utopia yet. If the casualties of adolescence seem to be on the increase, many still survive the ordeals of growing up. They engage in and face the challenges of finding a sense of personal continuity in a world of narrowing historical perspectives. They even triumph over the small and large disappointments of modern life. They command their hearts. They are capable of self-legislation and those acts of moral freedom that enlarge the boundaries of the human spirit. Remarkably, they have accomplished these consequential revisions of their inner life without benefit of ritual or formalized convention, and all too often without much guidance or support from the adults who care for and educate them. Given half a chance, youth will continue to be the bearers of cultural renewal. They will ensure the survival of adolescent modes of thinking in our historical and ideological perspectives. They will continue to leave some legacies that advance us all a little further toward an enlightened humanity. The pity is that so many young lives are allowed to slip beyond the pale. The hope is that we will heed the legacies of adolescence and extend to more young people the privilege of moral responsibility.

The central legacy of adolescence is the transformation of family passions into those sublime passions that bind us to our species. We humans are not born with a moral sense. If it were not for the transformations of adolescence, no one of us would willingly sacrifice private desire for public duty. The union of desire with duty, which Kant called true culture, does not come naturally, but nature does provide the means by which our moral education can be consummated.

In the human, the parts of the brain responsible for advanced intellectual functioning have a chance to grow and develop before the parts that initiate pubescence have been given the "signal" to commence functioning on an adult level. Human children have the opportunity to learn to cooperate in family and group life before being forced to negotiate the complex demands of genitality and the prolonged parenting required of our species. Puberty brings them to a second birth, in which hitherto unexpressed talents, emotions, and intellectual capacities come to light, while many childhood capacities are given fresh vitality and range. Now, as the genital passions awaken, morality can surpass an unquestioned submission to the laws of reason. Morality requires the energy of a passion to bring it to its full flowering. Genitality provides that passion, and imagination unites private desire with public duty.

Because of the inverse relationship between civilization and the free development of sexuality, genital sexuality can never yield that final satisfaction we long for and remember from infancy. During adolescence the longing to reinstate the love dialogues of infancy is countered by the incest taboo. The incest taboo is not a law of nature, but nature has provided humans with those faculties of mind by which passions from one realm of experience can be deployed to another. By endowing us with imagination, nature has given us the means to transform natural acts into cultural aspirations. All other animals are safe from the perils of imagination and therefore are subject entirely to the commands of nature.

In contrast to other animals, for whom the sexual act is a purely physical one, human sexuality exists largely in the imagination—which is why the erotic attachments of the human infant are so much more tenacious than in any other primate species; which is why at puberty, imagination can sublimate sexual passion into those moral passions that are the highest expression of our common humanity; which is why the sexual and moral revolution that takes place during adolescence can become a revolution of transformation and not annihilation. During adolescence, past, present, and future are strung together on the threads of imagination.

Thus another legacy of adolescence is the capacity to construct a narrative of our personal life history. It is not speech or toolmaking that distinguishes us from other animals, it is imagination. Just as imagination inflames the erotic passions that bind us to other human beings, it also inspires us to conceive of a future that might be better than the disappointing present. Of what use are speech sounds and tools without an inspiration toward perfectibility, without a sense that we can create a future or construct a history?

We are the only animal species that possesses and is possessed by a history, personal and social. During adolescence, as the past must be reconciled with the future, the inspiration to construct a personal history springs to life. We become capable of recognizing that actual time is irrevocable, that our life threads between a finite moment of birth and a finite moment of death. In youth, after the adolescent has experienced the full sorrow of all she is leaving behind, an appreciation of the longed-for past develops in conjunction with the conviction that it will never come again. The bittersweet emotion of nostalgia is born. Our nostalgia for the golden days of infancy evokes in us some inspirations for the future. Imagination transforms our idealizations of the past into social ideals that might be realized at some later point in life.

Now Melpomene speaks. As adolescence draws to a close, the epiphyses of the long bones fuse, possibilities narrow. We begin to comprehend the historical continuities of the self we have become and the inevitable limitations to what we might become. Our eyes open to the historical realities and tragic dimensions of our parents. The mighty parents, those omnipotent gods of our childhood, are flawed, undone by the very traits that were once upon a time regarded as saintly and heroic. Now the idealizations that were once invested in the parents can be impersonalized and humanized, set free to be invested in social ideals. At the same time, a young person enlarges her affectionate and tender ties to her parents. She forgives them for being somewhat less than she had once imagined them to be. Children, even infants, are capable of sympathy. But only after adolescence are we capable of compassion.

During adolescence the history of the individual intersects the history of the tribe, nation, species. The adolescent modes of thinking, feeling, acting, imagining, and constructing history are passed on from one generation to another, not by the laws of genetic inheritance but once again by the means that nature has granted us. We come into our earthly human existence with an innate love of self, a primary narcissism that we endeavor to preserve even as we must bend desire to the contours of the social order in which we live. This primordial passion, "the source and principle of all the others," embodies our hopes, expectations, aspirations. Before an infant ever encounters the frustrations inherent in relating to others, he has a method for conjuring personal power. Before we are anything else we are wish-fulfilling conjurers, jesters, and poets, who can re-create the glory that was, the life before contradiction. Just as an infant's hallucinatory wishes and security blankets—or a young child's imaginary companion or an older child's family romance—enable him to bear the inevitable frustrations and renunciations of being a powerless and dependent creature, so the moral aspirations and cultural ideals of an adult enable her to reconcile herself to the tragic dimensions of civilized existence.

During adolescence, what has belonged to the lowest part of the mental life is changed into what is highest in the human mind by our scale of values. The method—omnipotence of gesture, love of self, primary narcissism—is there from birth. But not until adolescence are our personal aspirations, our dreams of glory transposed into those aspirations that might serve all of humanity. When our personalized dreams of glory are impersonalized, they kindle in us a wish to preserve the species as we once preserved our own love of self. Adolescents are the bearers of cultural renewal, those cycles of generation and regeneration that link our limited individual destinies with the destiny of the species.

More than birth, marriage, or death, adolescence entails the most highly elaborated drama of the passage from one realm of existence into another. It is then that the individual passes from family life into cultural existence. The puberty rites of the hunter-gatherer peoples were a dramatization of this passage. A young person became a responsible member of the social and moral order by *actively* participating in the drama of her own passage into adulthood. Even more, the drama imparted to her existence from then on—however mundane and limited it was destined to be—was an aura of something larger than life. And those who listened to the tales or sang the songs with her remembered all they once knew and then forgot. In a performance that may have extended for a week, a month, a season, several years, the metaphors of existence were brought into play—music, dance, song, the recitation of the sacred texts and tribal lore, masks, jewelry, body decorations, symbolic enactments, scarifications and mutilations that mature a child into an adult, the legends of losing old dialogues, finding new ones, refinding the old ones.

Modern adolescence, when it is not trivialized or aborted by some deformity of family life or social convention, is an inner drama no less encompassing in its metaphorical reach. By temporarily abandoning the modes of ordinary existence the young person enters a sacred zone in which time is eternal and limitless, in which experience is reversible and recoverable. Time is regenerated; the past is reactualized and transformed into a future mode; the forging of a personal life becomes connected with the possibilities of a new society, a new humanity. In modern societies the drama does not end with everything returning to the beginning. We can no longer expect that young people will undergo their personal ordeals and then return to us with an unqualified acceptance of things as they are. When things are rotten in Denmark the young will be quick to sniff out the decay and corruption. Modern youth resist the idea that they, or the social order, are hopelessly determined by the past. They counter our conservative, reductionist tendencies with their inspirations—exploration, innovation, aspiration. In finding out who they are and who they are not, adolescents mobilize the energies of the archaic past and use them to extend the cultural dimensions of the future.

The sacred world they pass through, which is outside time, outside the order and protection of civilized life, can be a lonely and frightening place. The demons they encounter there are not masked representations of evil and violence and crude sexuality but their own internal demons—their unruly desires, their untamed consciences that afflict them with threats of defilement, castration, mutilation, starvation, exile. Adolescents encounter within themselves elemental passions in their raw, simplified forms. These encounters, frightening and emotionally painful as they are at the time, will later allow for a more generous and humane appreciation of the human plight.

In the interval between giving up the old dialogues and finding new ones, there are long periods of time when there is an absence of love dialogue. The dread of loss of dialogue, a loss that is like a falling-away into an eternal nothingness where one will never be held again, can make submissive cowards of us all. But adolescents risk it. They risk also the loneliness and fear of departing from one realm of existence and entering a new but as yet unknown realm. They come to know within themselves the hopelessness when there is no place for desire to go, no person to love, no ability to divert sexual hunger into friendship or activity. They learn what it means to lose the past and to recognize that it will never come again.

Most adults do not care to be reminded of these anguished emotional states. In late adolescence and young adulthood some youths have not forgotten; they are still close enough to such experiences to feel compassion for those who suffer as they once did. They see their beloved, once vigorous, productive grandparents now aging, decaying, moving closer to that finite moment of death. "Is this what life is all about?" they ask. "A frantic race with time and then a long eventless ending?" Young people, those who allow themselves to remember the loneliness and grief of their recent years, have more compassion and tenderness toward the elderly than most middle-aged adults. Nothing—not avarice, not pride, not scrupulousness, not impulsiveness—so disillusions a youth about her parents as the seemingly inhumane way they treat her grandparents.

It has been said that one of the most touching expressions of our specifically human morality is the care of elderly, lonely, or infirm parents by their children. But in the modern world we grown-ups run from the elderly as we might run from a plague. Their very presence is a nagging reminder of the despair and stagnation that might await us. Our own dread of the finitude of time overwhelms our compassion. We leave the entire matter to "the assistant postmaster," who will efficiently dispense the welfare checks and arrange for tidy housing. The elderly, except perhaps for those with wealth or power, are treated as castoffs, leftovers that in the most charitable of circumstances we confine to their retirement communities.

Youth, because they are facing forward toward a new life, can endure what it means to grow old. They can still recall the violence and disorder of spirit, the grief, the loneliness, the loss of dialogue when a person must depart from one realm of existence and enter another. They have an emotional grasp that enables them to engage in a meaningful dialogue with the aged. The young, for example, are certainly more appreciative than we are of the nostalgic "ramblings" of their grandparents. And they often find in these retrospective accounts a certain wisdom that we too often ignore. A young person's willingness to listen keeps alive the memories of the golden days. Her compassionate gestures counter the dread of loss of dialogue. The descent into nothingness is halted. Even though they are soon to be forever separated from the universe, the elderly are reminded of regeneration and renewal. In the presence of a youth they feel held. For the moment, at least, they sense that life is not a meaningless passage of time, that their own individual destinies are linked to some larger, eternal human destiny.

In this we see another legacy of adolescence: the sense that departure from one realm to another need not entail a severing of bonds but rather may offer an expansion and renewal of our common humanity.

Soon after a newborn has been severed from the womb he enters into his first human dialogue, a dialogue that reminds him of that fetus-placenta-amniotic fluid-mother he once knew. In order for him to become a person with his own unique selfhood, he must depart from that realm of human oneness and enter a new realm of humanness. He undergoes the separation-individuation of his first three years of life. In the process he will expand the range of his emotional capacities, release himself from the humiliating dependencies of nursery morality, and extend himself into the law and order of family life. His separation-individuation does not sever his attachment to his mother; it enlarges the meaning of that attachment. In a similar way, the adolescent's second psychological birth leads to expansion of a child's emotional and intellectual reach, a quickening of the tender and affectionate bonds to the parents, a humanizing enlargement of the sexual and moral passions.

Yet we have come to view the adolescent opportunity to grow up and achieve a new level of identity as a time for rupturing the bonds of family attachment. Even the experts have become prey to this version of things. In fact, the intensity of an adolescent's resistance to growing up may be gauged by how desperately and how far he must flee, actually or emotionally, from the intimacies of family life in order to preserve his sense of self.

A young child releases himself from the bondage of nursery passions by taking in, internalizing, what he then imagines to be parental inhibitions, authority, ideals. These early internalizations of the parents allow the child to become a relatively civilized human being who can regulate and manage his desires. He has achieved at least a certain degree of independence from external authority. But his new internal masters are exceedingly harsh and demanding. For a child to become a responsible adult these exaggeratedly idealized versions of the parents must undergo some revision. And the infantile desires that are attached to the parental idealizations must also undergo revision so that they can be transferred outside the family.

As we know, whenever passions are about to be deployed to another person, another realm, another order of existence, the event always begins as a variation of violence. An adolescent, however, is not trying to get rid of the parents or to demolish the existing order of things. She may look like a wild, untamed creature, but her adolescent madness is a sign of her warfare on desire and her attempts to transform the infantile idealizations into something more humane and less exalted than they once were. In this way she enlarges her passions and is able to extend them into new relationships with peers, lovers, children, grandparents, *and* her parents, who can now be forgiven for being less perfect than they were once imagined to be.

If into the bargain the adolescent extracts permission to aspire toward values and ideals that go beyond the realities of everyday life, it will be the result of a personal inner struggle, a struggle that cannot be ordained by any social order. But the formation of that inner structure of the mind we call the adult ego-ideal can be fostered only in a social order that confirms the intimate cogwheeling of generations—a society that sponsors the connections between sexual dialogue and moral dialogue at every phase of the life cycle.

The way it now stands, the interests of civilization are served if a person simply leaves the childhood family unit to procreate a new family, works at an assigned job, obeys a few uncomplicated moral commandments. When infant-parent love attachments are thought to be necessary to the preservation of society, some societies do what they can to protect the family unit. But even in our contemporary Western societies, with their narrowness of historical perspectives and trivialized moral values, some adolescents, employing all the means that nature has given them, do become adults who are more concerned with expanding the boundaries of human existence than with preserving the social order exactly as it is. They may move us all a little further into the light.

The articulation of an individual life with its environmental niche is like a kaleidoscope with infinite flecks of colored glass which might be turned a million times and still not produce all its potential designs. The moral potential of the retarded primate is not infinite, but it is much vaster than we have yet dared to imagine. This eminent anthropoid who need not give up searching, who need not return to the beginning and always repeat the past, who has within her flexible responses, inventive solutions, limitless curiosity, will always have to reckon with the forms of civilization that are the safety net of her existence. She may have it within her to control nature, to uproot the earth she inhabits, to dominate and even extinguish all the animals below her on the *scala naturae,* to achieve power over the helpless and the powerless, to fly off to the distant galaxies, but she must still preserve civilization or her species will die out. At the same time, in order to make life on this harsh and confusing planet more bearable, she must find a way to preserve the resting places, beyond society, pleasure, or reality. Organized human societies could last a while without cultural aspirations, but no society has survived for long without them.

Civilization itself can be preserved and be passed on from one generation to another without change. Even so, there are always metaphors, rituals, temples, and tribal lore that will express the idea of "no change." Adolescence can be a great drama of passion and upheaval in which at the end everything returns to the beginning. Even so, the green light beckons. We are born with an irresistible urge to push on, to strike out for the territory. When obedience to the authority of the social order leaves no room for the expression of personal power or a sense of moral dignity, we feel less than we might be—we feel false to ourselves.

An actual human history is bound and finite. We will have made only one life, leaving our other possible lives by the wayside, dimly remembered, haunting the life we actually lead. Sometimes we will imagine that our real life is the life we didn't lead, or we will sense nameless feelings coursing through our breast. There is a realm of existence in which the history of infinite possibilities continues. We call it the resting place, the transitional zone, the intermediate realm, culture, metaphor, illusion. Here we temper the sense of the finite, unbolt the breast, and become aware of life's flow and hear its winding murmur. And though the adolescent becomes an adult who will live but one finite life, for a time she has lived in the realm of infinite possibility. Another legacy the adult inherits from her adolescent years is the inner experience that once she might have played all parts in the human comedy, that once she was true to herself and to her powers.

When adolescence is over, the young adult's character is etched with the inner struggles she has undergone. The changing woman has not been a passive recapitulator of infancy; she has been an active reviser. Her strategies, her losses, her defeats, her triumphs, her new solutions leave their imprint on the adult form. Later in life she may further humanize her conscience, she may find some more extended ways of loving and caring, she may even rediscover the powers she merely imagined during adolescence. It is part of her species-specific inheritance that no matter how set or rigid her character, there is always some flexibility, always some curiosity to be reawakened. But for an adult to change her ways requires immense effort and risk and a great expense of spirit. In adolescence the forces of growth are a spur to innovation and moral renewal. Adolescence is the conjugator of a human life. When it is over, who we are and what we might become are not as open to change. We are never as flexible again.

Some youths conclude their journey by settling back into the familiar civilized routines. They reinstate, albeit with a few new flourishes and minor alterations, the frozen plots of childhood. They are ruled again by the inflexible dictates of should and ought, dominated by seeking and finding sexual gratification—but only this way and not that way. They try to assuage dread by returning to the safety of the school-yard. They never quite yield up the wish to be totally cared for and protected by some all-powerful idol, even if that idol should turn out to be a tyrant. They are forever young. But they have lost their youthfulness.

It could be said that the number of adults who have faltered in this journey out of childhood is exceedingly large. But this is the case only when we measure what we became against the possibilities that were there. This is a harsh and primitive way to evaluate a human life. Every now and then, when a woman is pregnant, when a newborn leaves the womb to enter the world, when a child reaches puberty, when someone is married or someone dies, there is a resting place. We go to weddings. We go to funerals. We begin something. We remark that it is finished. We look back on our youthful years as the hopeful time when it did seem possible to radically change the course of our personal fate. We forget the loneliness, the pain of loss, the narcissistic anguish, the wrestlings with desire, the torments of our unruly, unlovely, disobedient bodies. We dimly remember the return of exquisite passion, the longings that loosened us from the confining safety of childhood.

NOTES

INTRODUCTION

The clause "past, present, and future are . . . strung together" is a paraphrase of Freud: "Thus, past, present and future are strung together, as it were, on the thread of the wish that runs through them," in "Writers and Day-Dreaming," *Complete Psychological Works of Sigmund Freud,* Standard Ed. (London: Hogarth Press, 1955), 9, 148. Hereafter references to Freud will appear as SE plus volume number and page(s). (See above, e.g.: SE, 9:148.) Here Freud was referring to fantasies and daydreams. By bringing back a memory of an earlier experience in which a wish was fulfilled, the fantasy creates a situation in the present relating to the future in which the wish will be fulfilled.

The interpretation of the scarification designs refers to the Tiv of Nigeria and appears in Bruce Lincoln, *Emerging from the Chrysalis* (Cambridge, Mass., and London: Harvard University Press, 1981), p. 98: "Tiv scarification posits such contrasts as line/circle, lineage/ age, ancestors/descendants, and, most important, past/future. This last opposition is resolved in the emergence of a present moment that is capable of drawing on the past as it creates the future. The present thus understood is not a hairline between 'was' and 'yet-to-be' but a totality filled with history and potentiality, and it is in such a total presence that the initiand stands." The Tiv scarification is part of my composite on puberty rites, Chapter 1.

The Ernest Jones paper appears in Ernest Jones's *Papers on Psychoanalysis* (Boston: Beacon Press, 1961), pp. 389–412. A further discussion of Jones's position is to be found in Chapter 3.

A few psychoanalysts tried to lay the recapitulation myth to rest, especially with regard to adolescence. A notable contribution is Leo A. Spiegel's paper "A Review of Contributions to a Psychoanalytic Theory of Adolescence," in *The Psychoanalytic Study of the Child* (New York: International Universities Press, 1951), 6:375–393. Spiegel has this to say on the issue: "Adolescence is not a simple repetition of the oedipal and post oedipal period. For the first time, the psychic apparatus has at its disposal genital sexuality with adequate discharge for sexual tension. The complete meaning of this change is unknown but it alone is sufficient to stamp the phase adolescence as something new and not a duplicate of an earlier age" (pp. 375–376).

Spiegel is writing about the sexual changes of adolescence. Erik Erikson, in *Young Man Luther* (New York: Norton, 1958), high-lights the concomitant moral advances of adolescence, specifically that aspect of the superego—the ideal—that points toward the fu-ture. In this connection he discusses the persistence of recapitula-tionist thinking in psychoanalysis. "In its determination to be spar-ing with teleological assumption, psychoanalysis has gone to the opposite extreme and developed a kind of originology. . . . I mean by [this term] a habit of thinking which reduces every human situa-tion to an analogy with an earlier one, and most of all that earliest, simplest and most infantile precursor which is assumed to be its 'origin.'. . . In other words, psychoanalysis tends to look deter-minedly backwards, into the past; whereas the superego in its capac-ity of posing the ideal, the goal toward which we strive, looks con-sistently to the future" (p. 18).

For complete references to the writings of Rousseau and Hall see notes to Chapter 2.

Freud's statement on the mental life is from *The Ego and the Id*, SE, 19:36.

1.   ADOLESCENCE: TRIVIALIZATIONS AND GLORIFICATIONS

PUBERTY RITES: The sections on puberty rites are based primarily on Arnold van Gennep's classic work *The Rites of Passage*, trans. Mo-nika V. Vizedom and Gabrielle L. Caffee (Chicago: University of Chi-cago Press, 1960; original text, *Les Rites de Passage*, pub. 1908); Monika Vizedom's monograph *Rites and Relationships* (Beverly Hills, Calif.: Sage Publications, 1976); Victor Turner, *The Ritual Process* (Chicago: Aldine Publishing Co., 1969), and *The Forest of Symbols* (Ithaca: Cornell University Press, 1967); Audrey Richards, *Chisungu: A Girl's Initiation Ceremony Among the Bemba of Zambia* (first pub. London: Faber and Faber, 1956), with intro. by Lean La Fontaine (London and New York: Tavistock Publishing, 1982); and Bruce Lincoln, *Emerging from the Chrysalis*, (Cam-bridge, Mass., and London: Harvard University Press, 1981), were also major sources for the descriptions and interpretations of male and female puberty rites.

The descriptions of body mutilations and the interpretations are primarily from van Gennep, pp. 71–72. The specific idea of treating the body like a piece of wood appears on p. 72: ". . . the human body has been treated like a simple piece of wood which each has cut and trimmed to suit him: that which projected has been cut off, partitions broken through, flat surfaces have been carved . . ."

The scarification interpretation is Lincoln's; see the notes to the Introduction for his exact quote, which I have here paraphrased. As Lincoln points out (p. 36), the significance of the scarifications is not alluded to by the Tiv, who do not think of the act as a rite. They insist that the only purpose of the scars is to make the woman more attractive. The Tiv scarifications occur after menarche and are enlarged and elaborated throughout a woman's lifetime.

Turner speaks of the referents of ritual symbols which tend to cluster around opposite semantic poles, the *normative*, or moral norms and principles governing social structure and the *oretic*, or grossly physiological. In *Ritual Process* he says: "Such symbols then unite the organic with the sociomoral order, proclaiming their ultimate religious unity, over and above conflicts between and within these orders. Powerful drives and emotions associated with human physiology, especially with the physiology of reproduction, are divested in the ritual process of their anti-social quality and attached to components of the normative order, energizing the latter with a borrowed vitality and thus making the Durkheimian 'obligatory' desirable" (p. 53). His data are primarily from the Ndembu of northwestern Zambia. In *Forest of Symbols* Turner expresses the relationship between the physiological and the moral: "Norms and values, on the one hand, become saturated with emotion, while the gross and basic emotions become ennobled through contact with social values. The irksomeness of moral constraint is transformed into the 'love of virtue'" (p. 30).

The ceremonies for the boys are a composite from van Gennep, Vizedom, and Turner; those for the girls are from Lincoln, Richards, and Vizedom.

Van Gennep stresses that initiation does not always coincide with puberty and that the boy is not always permanently separated from his mother. But with boys and girls, "These are rites of separation from the asexual world, and they are followed by rites of incorporation into the world of sexuality and, in all societies and all social groups, into a group confined to one sex or the other" (p. 66).

Van Gennep derives the novitiate idea from the initiation of magicians and religious novices among the Carib and the Barundi of Tanganyika (Tanzania) (pp. 108–110) and then applies the concept to all initiands (pp. 110–115). Turner describes the neophyte status on pp. 96–110 of *Forest of Symbols*.

The idea of a woman being likened to a child, with her puberty binding her to a home place, is stressed by Lincoln and Vizedom.

Inserting nettles and grass into the vagina to "cause" bleeding: Vizedom, pp. 38 and 41. It refers to the Arapesh of New Guinea.

Rubbing the girls' breasts: Bruno Bettelheim, *Symbolic Wounds* (Glencoe, Ill.: Free Press, 1954), p. 34. The custom is found among the Arunta and the Central African Cewa.

Molding the girl into womanhood: Lincoln, pp. 20 and 94–95. This appears in his description of the Navajo Kinaalda ceremony.

Painting a circle around the nipples: Bettelheim, p. 135. He is referring to the Arunta.

Enlarging the lips of the vagina and the interpretation attached to large labia: Bettelheim, p. 143. He is referring to the Dahomey tribe. He describes similar rites among the Bagandi and the Suaheli peoples. Vizedom also refers to the elongation of the labia minora among the Yao of Central Africa (p. 41).

Girl growing into womanhood: Richards, p. 121. "The *chisungu* is danced they say, to make the girl grow (*ukumukushya*); to teach her (*ukumufunda*) and 'to make her a woman as we are' . . . What does the word *ukumukushya* mean? It is the causative form of the word 'to grow.' In other words, 'We do the rite to grow the girl' " (p. 121).

Richards (and most anthropologists) distinguish between the puberty ritual proper—that is, acts that take place immediately after the first signs of puberty—and nubility or fertility rites that are a prelude to a marriage ceremony. The latter may occur at any age. Sometimes, as among the Tiyyar of North Kerala, India (described by Lincoln), the nubility rites may occur when the girl is eight or nine years of age. Among the Bemba an individual nubility rite is preceded by a short puberty ceremony proper; these occur when a girl knows that her first period has come: Richards, p. 54.

Enclosing the girl in a seclusion chamber: The Bemba girl is hidden under a blanket in an initiation hut (Richards, passim). According to Lincoln, the Kinaaldá rite (first menstruation or house sitting) occurs after a girl's first menstruation. The girl is first ritually transformed inside the family hogan. During the course of the rite the family hogan becomes a sacred space as a result of the songs that are sung (p. 18). Among the Tukuna of the northwest Amazon the ceremony performed for girls at menarche is spectacular. The preparations for the official ceremony take three months or longer, during which time the initiand (*voreki*) is kept in seclusion in a chamber inside her family dwelling. The chamber is two meters in diameter and is furnished only by the hammock in which the girl sleeps (p. 53). As the girl emerges from isolation the following words are sung: "Like a caterpillar our *voreki* was placed in seclusion by us." "The chamber," says Lincoln, "is thus compared to a cocoon into which the girl went as a caterpillar, immature, plain and terrestial and from which she emerges a butterfly, mature, beautiful, and celestial." During her time of seclusion the *voreki* is thought to be in the underworld (p. 55).

Identification with a mythic heroine: Lincoln, referring to the Navaho Kinaaldá in which the girl becomes Changing Woman (pp. 17–33). See his interpretation, pp. 95–97. "As each initiand assumes the role of these figures, the mythic events are repeated and the gifts of civilization reappropriated. Initiation thus is expected to benefit not only the individual initiand but society as a whole and beyond this the entire cosmos. . . . The girl *becomes* the goddess or culture heroine, and forever after her life partakes of the divine." (p. 96).

Cosmic journey: Lincoln, referring to the Tukuna Moca Nova ceremony (pp. 50–70) and also to the Eleusinian Mysteries, which he interprets as a female initiation rite derived from the Persephone myth (pp. 71–90). "The cosmic journey makes the immature girl into a woman whose proper field of activity is the cosmos, who has transcended the bounds of her mundane existence and has become truly a cosmic being, jolted out of her immediate locale and introduced to the universe at large" (p. 97).

Neophyte as a blank slate: Turner, *Ritual Process,* pp. 96–110. "The neophyte in liminality must be a tabula rasa, a blank slate on which is inscribed the knowledge and wisdom of the group. . . . They have to be shown that in themselves they are clay or dust, mere matter, whose form is impressed upon them by society" (p. 103).

Treatment of the neophyte: van Gennep, p. 81; and Turner, "Betwixt and Between: The Liminal Period in Rites de Passage," in *Forest of Symbols,* pp. 93–110. "They are at once no longer classified and not yet classified. In so far as they are no longer classified the symbols that represent them are in many societies drawn from the biology of death, decomposition, catabolism . . . The other aspect, that they are not yet classified, is often expressed in symbols modelled on processes of gestation and parturition. The neophytes are likened to or treated as embryos, newborn infants or sucklings" (p. 95).

Double series of separations: van Gennep. "In short, there is a double series: rites of separation from the usual environment, rites of incorporation into the sacred environment; a transitional period; rites of separation from the local sacred environment, rites of incorporation into the usual environment. But as a result of this passage through the sacred world, the initiate retains a special magico-religious quality" (p. 82).

Passage, thresholds, portals, margins: van Gennep, in the chapter "The Territorial Passage," pp. 15–25.

Deflection of emotional energies: Yehudi A. Cohen, *The Transition from Childhood to Adolescence* (Chicago: Aldine Publishing Co., 1962), p. 110.

Pretense that society controls the natural processes: Vizedom, p. 38. She refers here to Lévi-Strauss, *The Savage Mind* (Chicago: University of Chicago Press, 1966). The sequences and interpretations of puberty rites were also informed by S. N. Eisenstadt, "Archetypal Patterns of Youth," *Daedalus* (Cambridge, Mass: Journal of American Academy of Arts and Sciences) (Winter 1962), pp. 30–33.

VIRTUE: "In all times and in all places" is from Jean-Jacques Rousseau's *First Discourse,* in *The First and Second Discourses,* ed. Roger D. Masters and trans. Roger D. and Judith R. Masters (New York: St. Martin's Press, 1964), p. 40. The sequence of societies is intentionally not chronological. I chose hunter-gatherer societies that still existed as of 1960 and "civilized" societies that no longer existed as of that date. The universality is not based on documentation from these societies. Rather, the phrase is in the spirit of Rousseau's *First Discourse.*

Definitions and interpretations of virtue: The *New Columbia Encyclopedia* (New York and London: Columbia University Press, 1975) contains remarkably concise and accurate accounts of both virtue and ethics. My other references were *The Ethics of Aristotle,* trans. J. A. K. Thomson (London: Penguin Classics, 1955), and *The Divine Comedy of Dante Alighieri,* trans. Carlyle Wicksteed (New York: Modern Library, 1944). The Introduction to the "Purgatorio" by C. H. Grandgent was particularly helpful.

Youth movements: The association of youth with the emancipation of the working class is from Annie Kriegel's article "Generational Difference: The History of an Idea," *Daedalus* (Fall 1978), pp. 23–28.

IMAGES OF ADOLESCENTS: The alternating victim and victimizer images of adolescents are from E. James Anthony, "The Reactions of Parents to Adolescents and to Their Behavior," in *Parenthood: Its Psychology and Psychopathology,* ed. E. James Anthony and Therese Benedek (Boston: Little, Brown, 1970), p. 311.

Trivializations of teenagers and youth: These are common enough not to require documentation. I had in mind certain film treatments in which adolescents, although portrayed as appealing and captivating, finally emerge as caricatures. My thoughts here were also influenced by Reuel Denney's essay "American Youth Today: A Bigger Cast, A Wider Screen," *Daedalus* (Winter 1962).

Identification with the aggressor: The dynamics of this defense are from Anna Freud, *The Ego and the Mechanisms of Defense* (New York: International Universities Press, 1946), pp. 109–122.

New image of adolescence: The Offer report, *The New York Times,* July 9, 1981, C:1 (interview with Dr. Howard, professor of psychology at Northwestern University on C:2); "Goodbye, Holden Caulfield," *The New York Times,* July 13, 1981, p. 30; "An average American adolescent is walking down a street, licking a cone of Rocky Road, carrying a Frisbee. A full set of teeth, a full head of hair, the right number of pounds, heading for Superman II." The tone of the editorial is ambiguous. Is it mocking the Offer portrayal? See Daniel Offer, Eric Ostrov, and Kenneth I. Howard, *The Adolescent, A Psychological Self-Portrait* (New York: Basic Books, 1981).

In her review "The Awkward Age," *New Republic,* Oct. 28, 1981, pp. 36–39, Ann Hulbert criticizes the Offer report. The "clone" idea is from her review. The idea of adolescents as saints, monsters, and heroes expressed at the conclusion of this chapter and subsequently is also from Hulbert's review.

The earlier Offer work is *The Psychological World of the Teenager* (New York: Basic Books, 1969). Here Offer lamented "the state of affairs in society which seems to encourage rebellion . . . we in the social sciences likewise glamorize the rebellions that offer us change" (pp. 188–189). As he observed the turmoil of the 1960s, Offer, like many other social scientists, was to try to rectify the stereotyped image of "rebellious youth." However, in his efforts to do justice to the "other" adolescents, the ones who were not manifestly in conflict with the older generation, Offer and others like him ended up by diminishing the inner psychological realities of adolescents.

INVENTION THEORY: Those researchers who, like Offer, wanted to dispel the stereotypes of the rebellious adolescent contributed some significant correctives to our views on adolescence. However, their questionnaires and interviews could not tap the inner dynamic changes, which, though tumultuous and stressful can occur without making a sound. If, on the other hand, as some of these researchers claim, the manifest accurately reflects the inner substance, the question then remains: Are not these "emotionally adjusted," bland, harmonious, "ordinary" young persons being deprived of the opportunity to revise the past? I cite below some of the significant and valuable contributions to our revised versions of adolescence. I do not disagree with the observations of these researchers, merely with their interpretations. It does not follow from their observations that adolescence, as we know it, is a myth or an arbitrary social invention.

William A. Westley and Nathan B. Epstein, *The Silent Majority: Families of Emotionally Healthy College Students* (San Francisco: Jossey-Bass, 1969). "They were, in moral terms, good, honest people living conventional lives, struggling to meet their problems, and giving no trouble to anyone. Ordinarily we know little about such people precisely because they present few problems and mind their own business" (p. 17).

Elizabeth Douvan and Joseph Adelson, *The Adolescent Experience* (New York: Wiley, 1966). (The data was collected in the 1950's.)

Most contemporary comment on adolescence focuses on two conspicuous but atypical enclaves of adolescents, drawn from extreme and opposing ends of the social class continuum, and representing exceptional solutions to the adolescent crisis. . . . The extremes are alike in showing an unusual degree of independence from the family; they are alike in disaffection, in acting out or thinking out a discontent with the social order; they are alike, above all, in that they adopt radical solutions to the adolescent task of ego synthesis.

We want to suggest that one cannot generalize these processes to the adolescent population at large . . . The great advantage of the survey technique is that it allows us to study these adolescents who make up the middle majority, who evoke neither grief nor wonder, and who all too often escape our notice. [pp. 350–351]

F. Musgrove, *Youth and the Social Order* (Bloomington, Ind.: Indiana University Press, 1964). Other commentaries on adolescence with similar perspectives are: Joseph Adelson, "The Political Imagination of the Young Adolescent" and David Bakan, "Adolescence in America: From Idea to Social Fact," *Daedalus* (Fall 1971), pp. 1013–50 and 979–995. The Bakan essay, an exceptionally thoughtful presentation of the social realities that surround our myths of adolescence, was the prototype for my discussion of "the invention theory." Again, though I agree with much that Bakan says, I do not agree with his interpretation of adolescence. He, like other writers, cites the dictionaries and Musgrove and Mead to advance his arguments.

Margaret Mead, *Coming of Age in Samoa* (New York: Morrow, 1928). Fifty-five years later, in 1983, Derek Freeman published his *Margaret Mead and Samoa—The Making and Unmaking of an Anthropological Myth* (Cambridge, Mass. and London: Harvard University Press, 1983), which contradicted Mead's bucolic vision of growing up in Samoa. The controversies aroused by Freeman's book were summed up in the following manner by Bradd Shore, professor of anthropology at Emory University: "But, if she suppressed the dark elements, Freeman painted all the dark elements in his book. She generated a myth out of opposition to eugenics, he generated a distorted picture out of opposition to Margaret Mead," *The New York Times,* Jan. 31, 1983, C:21.

David Bakan is the social idealist I refer to. His article, cited above, is my source for the idea of exposing the discrepancies between our professed aims to protect children and our insidious suppression of them. A more optimistic view of the relationship between adolescence and sociopolitical reform appears in the following essays from the Winter 1962 issue of *Daedalus*, entitled *Youth: Change and Challenge*: Reuel Denney, "American Youth Today: A Bigger Cast, a Wider Screen"; S. N. Eisenstadt, "Archetypal

Patterns of Youth"; Kenneth Keniston, "Social Change and Youth in America"; Kaspar D. Naegele, "Youth and Society: Some Observations"; Talcott Parsons, "Youth in the Context of American Society." And although the pendulum of opinion began to swing by the 1970s, in the Fall 1971 issue of *Daedalus* such psychologists as Peter Blos, Robert Coles, Jerome Kagan, and Lawrence Kohlberg continued to stress the positive and unique contributions of the adolescent phase of life.

Ariès and *Centuries of Childhood*: Though I am critical of some of Ariès' contentions on the quality of life for children and adolescents during the Middle Ages, *Centuries of Childhood: A Social History of Family Life*, trans. Robert Baldich (New York: Vintage Books, 1965), offers a brilliant historical interpretation of the history of childhood. My concern with Ariès' interpretations is that they were taken over literally by those who wished to document the idea that adolescence is a mere social invention.

". . . a transition made by means of an initiation": *Centuries of Childhood*, pp. 411–412.

My primary sources for descriptions of life in the Middle Ages are: Barbara W. Tuchman, *A Distant Mirror: The Calamitous Fourteenth Century* (New York: Alfred A. Knopf, 1978), and Frederick B. Artz, *The Mind of the Middle Ages A.D. 200–1500: An Historical Survey*, 3d ed., rev. (New York: Alfred A. Knopf, 1958).

"People lived in a state of contrast": *Centuries of Childhood*, p. 414.

Ariès' essay, "The Family and the City," appeared in *Daedalus* (Spring 1977), pp. 227–237: "like an animal or bird," p. 227; "It was a game in which the venturesome boy," pp. 227–228; diffuse feelings, p. 229.

The quotation from *The Little Prince*, by Saint-Exupéry, is cited by Ariès at the opening of his concluding chapter to *Centuries of Childhood*, p. 411; "the birch, the prison cell," p. 413.

History of childhood since the seventeenth century: The Victorian-Calvinist child is from P. Coveny, "The Image of the Child in English Literature," in A. Skolnick, ed. *Rethinking Childhood* (Boston: Little, Brown, 1976), pp. 62–67. The overidealization of filial piety and the later alterations of conscience formation are from P. Muller, *The Tasks of Childhood* (New York: McGraw-Hill, 1969), p. 15. The Christopher Lasch quotation and his ideas on twentieth-century family life are from *Haven in a Heartless World* (New York: Basic Books, 1977), p. 35.

POLITICS OF NATURE-NURTURE: The spurious quality of the political categories of right and left, the role that the Western image of childhood plays in the left-right controversies are ideas from Joseph Featherstone, "Rousseau and Modernity," *Daedalus* (Summer

1978). The left-right alliances and misalliances on the subject of adolescence can also be found in *Daedalus* Winter 1962 and Fall 1971 issues, referred to earlier in this chapter.

2. THE "INVENTORS" OF ADOLESCENCE: JEAN-JACQUES ROUSSEAU AND G. STANLEY HALL

JEAN-JACQUES ROUSSEAU:

Emile, or On Education, trans. and with introd. and notes by Allan Bloom (New York: Basic Books, 1979).

Discourse on the Sciences and Arts (First Discourse) and *Discourse on the Origin and Foundations of Inequality (Second Discourse)* as they appear in *The First and Second Discourses,* ed. Roger D. Masters, trans. Roger D. and Judith R. Masters (New York: St. Martin's Press, 1964).

Confessions, trans. and with introd. by J. M. Cohen (New York: Penguin Books, 1953).

COMMENTARIES ON ROUSSEAU:

Roger D. Masters, *The Political Philosophy of Rousseau* (Princeton, N.J.: Princeton University Press, 1968).

Frederick B. Artz, *The Enlightenment in France* (Oberlin, Ohio: Kent State University Press, 1968).

Peter Gay, *The Party of Humanity* (New York: Alfred A. Knopf, 1964).

Thomas Davidson, *Rousseau and Education According to Nature* (New York: Charles Scribner's Sons, 1898; repub. St. Clair Shores, Mich.: Scholarly Press, 1970).

Joseph Featherstone, "Rousseau and Modernity," *Daedalus* (Summer 1978).

Bronislaw Baczko, "Rousseau and Social Marginality," in *Daedalus* (Summer 1978). This issue is titled *Rousseau for Our Time.*

Benjamin R. Barber, "Rousseau and the Paradoxes of the Dramatic Imagination," *Daedalus* (Summer 1978).

Rousseau's writings will be cited by title and page; commentaries will be cited by author and page.

Rousseauean attributions are a composite impression and not exact quotations from Gay, pp. 213–215, 232–233, 242–244, 253–255, 264–265, 281, and Davidson, pp. 224–244, and Bloom's introd., pp. 3–7, 28, and *Daedalus* (Summer 1978), passim.

Mme. de Staël's comment: Artz, p. 29.

Rousseau as the victim of modernity: Baczko, pp. 27–29.

". . . the paradox is not that Rousseau understood imagination to be at war with innocence, and self-improvement to be at odds with simplicity, as if these were competing dispositions within human nature vying for dominion. Rather it is that imagination and self-improvement, as ineluctable facets of human nature and thus human history destroyed as they created, corrupted as they improved, ruined as they civilized": Barber, p. 81. Barber cites his translation of the *Second Discourse.*

Rousseau's childhood, adolescence, manhood, from *Confessions:* "all that sorry nonsense," p. 23; "the shame and pain," p. 25; "managed in very short time," p. 39; "the heat in my blood," p. 90; "that dangerous means of cheating Nature," pp. 108–109; "No; I tasted the pleasure," p. 189; "change your string," p. 271.

Rousseau's children: *Confessions,* p. 333.

Rousseau's description of Thérèse: *Confessions,* p. 311.

Rousseau's position among the *philosophes:* Artz, pp. 130–150 and Gay, pp. 211–225.

Rousseau's inspiration: Artz, p. 136.

Voltaire's attack on the *Second Discourse:* Artz, pp. 139–140.

"Italy had a Renaissance": Artz, p. 66.

Voltaire: Gay, pp. 7–32: Voltaire's denunciation of Rousseau: Gay, p. 78 (Gay's portrait of Voltaire is more generous than my interpretation).

Interpretations of the relationship between *Emile* and *The Social Contract* are from Masters, Bloom's introd. to *Emile,* and Madeleine B. Ellis, *Rousseau's Socratic Aemilian Myths* (Columbus: Ohio State University Press, 1977).

From *Emile:* "But let mothers deign," p. 46; "a paradoxical man," p. 93; "It is clean, it is useful," p. 201; Rousseau on Plato, pp. 362–363; "natural and purely physical knowledge," p. 207; "The first sentiment," p. 220; "Command your heart," p. 445.

From the *Second Discourse:* love of oneself, p. 222; self-love, p. 222. (*Note:* Masters translates *amour-propre* as "vanity." For clarity, in this book "self-love" will appear as *amour-propre* or "vanity"; "love of oneself" will appear as *amour de moi* or as it is in English.)

From *Emile:* "second birth . . . foreign to him," p. 212.

G. STANLEY HALL:

Adolescence, 2 vols. (New York: D. Appleton and Co., 1904).

Life and Confessions of a Psychologist (New York: D. Appleton and Co., 1923).

BIOGRAPHY:

Lorine Pruette, *A Biography of a Mind* (New York and London: D. Appleton and Co., 1926).

Louis N. Wilson, *G. Stanley Hall* (New York: G. E. Stechert and Co., 1914).

From *Adolescence:* "last great wave . . . second birth," I, 48; "for those prophetic souls," I, 50; "higher and more completely human traits," I, xiii; "without any sin," I, 587; "ephebeitis," I, 588; "spice of conscious flattery," II, 374.

From *Life and Confessions* (Hall's account and Wilson's place his date of birth as 1846. However, the accepted date is 1844 [Pruette, p. 263].) Hall's pedigree, pp. 22-86; "eighth generation," p. 23; "Reckoning back," p. 26; "content with simple ways," p. 82.

Climbing of Mount Owen: "It was resolve": Wilson, pp. 23-24. Wilson retells the experience from Hall's "Note on Early Memories" (1899).

From *Life and Confessions:* balance-wheel," p. 65; "On the whole," p. 85; "Hard as it was for them," p. 85. The effect of his relations with his father: "respect and even awe for him," p. 86; "the dirty place," p. 131; Hall's farm duties, p. 131; "rigged an apparatus," p. 132; the fear of leprosy, p. 132. "I was always rather a boy's boy," p. 135; "They awoke capacities," p. 221.

Death of Cornelia and Julia: Pruette, p. 95; pagan and puritan strains in Hall's character: ibid., pp. 29-78; Hall's two favorite words: ibid., p. 75.

From *Life and Confessions:* Hall's studies with Mark Hopkins: pp. 164-170; the exact quotation from Hall is "in the highest study of mankind, which is man," p. 170; "wild electives," p. 190; "But, the only whole-hearted scheme," p. 22; "*enfant terrible*," p. 9; "fool of the Parsifal order," p. 9.

Opinions about Hall, reactions to his work: Pruette, pp. 187-204; "Darwin of the Mind": Pruette, p. 208, and *Life and Confessions,* p. 360; "word 'evolution' . . . was music": *Life and Confessions,* p. 357.

From *Adolescence,* Vol. II: "ancient period of storm and stress," p. 94; "plants dream of the sun," p. 94; "superanthropoid," p. 95; "every nubile function," p. 120; "apex of individuation," p. 120; on Rousseau's noble savage, pp. 320 and 718-719; "adolescents of adult size," p. 649; mistreatment of "higher races," pp. 650-654 and all of Chap. XVII, "Adolescent Races and Their Treatment"; extinction of animals, p. 650; "stocks and breeds," p. 651; conclusion of *Adolescence,* p. 748.

3.   THE STEPCHILD OF PSYCHOANALYSIS: THE RECAPITULATIONIST MYTH

Therapists' rationalizations are from E. James Anthony, "The Reactions of Parents to Adolescents and to Their Behavior," in *Parenthood: Its Psychology and Psychopathology,* ed. E. James Anthony and Therese Benedek (Boston: Little, Brown, 1970), p. 313.

Adolescence as the stepchild: Jeanne Lampl-de Groot, "On Adolescence," in *The Development of the Mind* (New York: International Universities Press, 1965), p. 308.

Freud as the "Darwin of the Mind": *The Life and Work of Sigmund Freud,* III, ed. Ernest Jones (New York: Basic Books, 1957), 304.

Freud on the inheritance of acquired characteristics: "The Ego and the Id," SE, 19:38.

"What has belonged to the lowest part": SE, 19:36.

The analysis of the Haeckelian influence is from Stephen Jay Gould, *Ontogeny and Phylogeny* (Cambridge, Mass.: Belknap Press of Harvard University Press, 1977), pp. 115–166. The three quotations in the text are cited by Gould: "the child is naturally": from Havelock Ellis, *The Criminal* (New York: Charles Scribner's Sons, 1910)—Gould, p. 124; "the atavism of the criminal": from C. Lombroso, *Crime: Its Causes and Remedies* (Boston: Little, Brown, 1911)—Gould, p. 123; "the woman stage of character": from E. D. Cope, *The Origin of the Fittest* (New York: Macmillan, 1887)—Gould, p. 130.

The wholesale adoption of evolutionary biology by psychoanalysts ("In nothing is the courage"): Gould (p. 156) cites W. M. Wheeler, a biologist who studied social instincts.

From Ernest Jones, "Some Problems of Adolescence" (1922), in *Papers on Psychoanalysis* (Boston: Beacon Press, 1961), pp. 389–412: "distinctly more pronounced in the male sex," p. 396; "But before these important changes," p. 397–398; "adolescence recapitulates infancy," p. 399.

From Lampl-de Groot, "On Adolescence": "The patient brings us a wealth of infantile material," p. 311; "One can smile at a little child's," p. 312; adolescent experience of adult vulnerability, p. 314; "They are invulnerable," p. 315.

Discussions on the status of adolescence in psychoanalysis appear in Richard A. Isay, "The Influence of the Primal Scene on the Sexual Behavior of an Early Adolescent," *Journal of the American Psychoanalytic Association* (1975), 25:535–554, and Charles I. Feigelson, "Reconstruction of Adolescence and Early Latency in the Analysis of an Adult Woman," *Psychoanalytic Study of the Child* (New Haven: Yale University Press, 1976), 31:225–236.

For full details on separation-individuation see Margaret S. Mahler, Fred Pine, and Anni Bergman, *The Psychological Birth of the Human Infant* (New York: Basic Books, 1976), and Louise J. Kaplan, *Oneness and Separateness* (New York: Simon and Schuster, 1978).

Intentionally I have taken the infant-adolescent analogy quotations from two highly respected psychologists whose writings otherwise demonstrate a profound appreciation of adolescence. The phrases "structure formation" and "second stage of omnipotence" are from Ruthellen Josselson, "Ego Development in Adolescence," in *Handbook of Adolescent Psychology,* ed. Joseph Adelson (New York: Wiley-Interscience, 1980), pp. 193 and 194 resp.; "low-keyedness" and "Granted of course" are from Aaron H. Esman, "Adolescent Psychopathology and the Rapprochement Process," in *Rapprochement,* eds. Ruth F. Lax, Sheldon Bach, and J. Alexis Burland (New York and London: Jason Aronson, 1980), p. 286. Esman, a personal friend and colleague, was immensely helpful to me during the initial phases of *Adolescence.* He and I have had the analogy dispute before.

Peter Blos, "The Second Individuation Process of Adolescence," *The Adolescent Passage* (New York: International Universities Press, 1979). In a footnote Blos says: "In speaking of the second individuation of adolescence it is understood that the separation phase of infancy (in Margaret Mahler's sense) is not involved in this higher-level process of psychic differentiation" (p. 412, n.).

Lévi-Strauss's views on Rousseau and Rousseau's modern view of evolution are found in Robert Wokler, "Perfectible Apes in Decadent Cultures: Rousseau's Anthropology Revisited," in *Daedalus* (Summer 1978). "He [Lévi-Strauss] has expounded this view of Rousseau's contribution not only in an article devoted specifically to the subject and in the passage from *Le Totemisme aujourd'hui* which is cited here, but similarly at points throughout his major writings from *Tristes tropiques* to *L'Origine des manières de table* where—in the last case—splendid citations from *Emile* are employed to introduce the theme of nearly every chapter" (p. 107).

Freud's views on the distinctive contributions of puberty are delineated in "The Transformations of Puberty," Chap. III of *Three Essays on the Theory of Sexuality* (1905), SE, 13. The inverse relationship between civilization and sexuality appears in "The Tendency to Debasement in Love," SE, 11:188–190. "The very incapacity of the sexual instinct to yield complete satisfaction as soon as it submits to the first demands of civilization becomes the source, however, of the noblest cultural achievements which are brought into being by ever more extensive sublimation of its instinctual components" (p. 190); "as a result of the diphasic onset of object choice, and the interposition of the barrier against incest, the final object of the sexual instinct is never any longer the original object but only a surrogate for it" (p. 189).

The infantile and the primitive: I owe these very important and often neglected distinctions to my discussions with my husband, Donald M. Kaplan, who referred me to Freud's paper "The Claims of Psychoanalysis to Scientific Interest," SE, 13. The quotation appears on p. 286.

The descriptions of the regressive and progressive tendencies in development are from Anna Freud, "Regression as a Principle in Normal Development," in *Normality and Pathology in Childhood* (New York: International Universities Press, 1965), pp. 93–107. The differences between the prospective and retrospective accounts of a life history are from Louise J. Kaplan, "The Developmental and Genetic Perspectives of a Life History," *Contemporary Psychoanalysis,* 16, No. 4 (Oct. 1980), 565–580.

4. THE RETARDED PRIMATE

CONCEPT OF THE RETARDED PRIMATE: Stephen Jay Gould, "Retardation and Neoteny in Human Evolution," *Ontogeny and Phylogeny* (Cambridge, Mass.: Belknap Press of Harvard University Press, 1977). *Neoteny,* or the retention of juvenile characteristics in adults, as it operates synergistically with protracted maturation, produces developmental and evolutionary processes nearly diametric to the processes of *recapitulation*—the repetition of ancestral adult stages in embryonic or juvenile stages of descendants.

Gould (p. 401) cites W. M. Krogman, *Child Growth* (Ann Arbor: University of Michigan Press, 1972), p. 2: "This long-drawn-out growth period is distinctively human; it makes of man a learning rather than a purely instinctive animal. Man is programmed to learn to behave, rather than to react via an imprinted determinative instinctual code." Gould also presents the view (which he attributes to "Schelling, the philosophical mentor of German romantic biology") that "higher organisms strive to delay as long as possible the onset of sexual maturation. . . . Lower organisms fail in this quest and find themselves locked into low positions on the *scala naturae.* Higher organisms postpone this inevitable fate and reach higher levels of organization" (p. 401).

THE ONSET OF PUBESCENCE: Herant A. Katchadourian, "Medical Perspectives on Adulthood," *Daedalus* (Spring 1976); M. M. Grumbach, "Onset of Puberty" and J. C. Job et al., "Effect of Synthetic Luteinizing Hormone-Releasing Hormone (LH-RH) on the Release of Gonadotropins (LH and FSH) in Children and Adolescents. Relation to Age, Sex and Puberty," in *Puberty,* ed. S. R. Berenberg, proceedings of a conference of the Josiah Macy Jr. Foundation and the International Children's Center Paris, Dec. 9–11, 1974 (Leiden: H. E. Stenfert Kroese B.V., 1975).

Footnote on the melatonin "trigger" for the onset of pubescence: Gina Kolata, "Puberty Mystery Solved," *Science,* Jan. 20, 1984, 223:272.

Biologists differ about the precise ages of onset of pubescence and arrival at puberty. The timing of these events will of course vary from one child to another. The ages I have selected represent a consensus based on Western estimates.

Descriptions of the hypothalamus, the gonads, and the pituitary are from Grumbach, Job et al. and from *The Color Atlas of Human Anatomy,* ed. Vannio Vannini and Giuliano Pogliani, trans. and rev. Dr. Richard Jolly (New York: Beekan House, 1980; original, *Nuovo Atlante Del Corpo Umano,* Milano: Gruppo Editoriale Fabbri S.P.A., 1979).

Some anatomical details in Chapter 4 and in succeeding biological interludes are from Henry Gray's classic work, *Anatomy Descriptive and Surgical* (1901) ed. T. Pickering Pick and Robert Howden, with new introd. by John A. Crocco; rev. American ed. from 15th English ed.

DIFFERENCES BETWEEN INFANCY AND ADOLESCENCE: "The floodgates of heredity": Hall, *Adolescence* (New York: D. Appleton and Co., 1904), I, 308.

The precise quotation from Paul Ricouer appears in *Freud and Philosophy: An Essay on Interpretation,* trans. Denis Savage (New Haven and London: Yale University Press, 1970), p. 175:

Dreams look backward toward infancy, the past; the work of art goes ahead of the artist; it is a prospective symbol of his personal synthesis and of man's future, rather than a regressive symbol of his unsolved conflicts. But it is possible that this opposition between regression and progression is only true as a first approximation. Perhaps it will be necessary to transcend it, in spite of its apparent force. The work of art sets us on the pathway to new discoveries concerning the symbolic function and sublimation itself. Could it be that the true meaning of sublimation is to promote new meanings by mobilizing old energies that were initially invested in archaic figures?

The Rousseau quotation is from *Emile, or On Education,* trans. and with notes and intro. by Allan Bloom (New York: Basic Books, 1979), p. 212. (*Note:* Bloom sometimes translates *amour de moi* as "self-love" and sometimes as "love of self." In this book I refer to *amour de moi* as "love of self" or "love of oneself" and self-love as *amour-propre* or vanity.)

The idea of desire's great debate with authority is from *Freud and Philosophy.* Ricouer says every history or narrative is subordinated to "the history of desire in its great debate with authority." He is alluding particularly to the resonance of the Oedipal myth but also to earlier losing and refinding of the love object.

5. LOVE DIALOGUES I: DESIRE'S GREAT DEBATE WITH AUTHORITY

DESIRE: The process by which libido is developed in conjunction with object relating is delineated by René Spitz, in collaboration with Godfrey Cobliner, *The First Year of Life* (New York: International Universities Press, 1965). Spitz often makes the point that libido must be brought into existence. He refers to this process as "the emergence of the libidinal object."

AUTHORITY: The functions of the superego are from Sigmund Freud, "The Dissection of the Psychical Personality," in *New Introductory Lectures on Psychoanalysis,* SE, 22:66. The interpretation of Freud's passage is from Paul Ricouer, *Freud and Philosophy: An Essay on Interpretation,* trans. Denis Savage (New Haven and London: Yale University Press, 1970), pp. 184–186.

The contents of the child's superego are from Freud's "Psychical Personality," SE, 22:67: "Thus a child's superego is in fact constructed on the model not of its parents but of its parents' superego; the contents which fill it are the same and it becomes the vehicle of tradition and of all the time resisting judgements of value which have propagated themselves from generation to generation." In this passage Freud is undoubtedly hinting at the inheritance of acquired characteristics. My intention is to highlight the sense of the imperishable past and the primitive mental functioning of the unconscious mental life.

UTOPIA: The concept of utopias as exaggerated versions of the latency period is from Martha Wolfenstein, "Looking Backward from *A Clockwork Orange,*" *Psychoanalytic Study of the Child* (New Haven· Yale University Press, 1976), 31.535–553. Though Wolfenstein's interpretation flies in the face of our commonsense notions of a utopia, I have always been impressed with the accuracy of her interpretation of latency in western European societies and of the utopian genre. Almost all the examples, data, and interpretations are from Wolfenstein's paper.

The connections between More's utopian vision and the intellectual climate of the sixteenth century is from J. Bronowski and Bruce Mazlich, *The Western Intellectual Tradition* (New York: Harper and Row, 1960; Harper Torchbooks, 1962): negative numbers, pp. 54–55; comparison with the order of Saint Benedict, p. 51.

Rousseau's utopian visions: Utopias as *chimères* is from Frank E. Manuel, "A Dream of Eupsychia," *Daedalus* (Summer 1978). Manuel describes the tensions in Rousseau as tensions between the *moi* and the *moi commune.* From *Emile, or On Education,* trans. and with introd. and notes by Allan Bloom (New York: Basic Books, 1979): "our passions are the principal instruments," p. 212; "So long as his sensibility," pp. 219–220.

Schoolyard games: Lili E. Peller, "Libidinal Phases, Ego Development and Play," *Psychoanalytic Study of the Child* (New York: International Universities Press, 1954), 9:178–199.

Family romance: The scenario is from Sigmund Freud, "Family

Romances," SE, 9:236–241. (See also notes to Chap. 11, "The Impostor.")

PUBESCENCE: The biological interlude on pubescence, particularly the sequences of breast development and pubic hairs, are from: J. M. Tanner, *Growth at Adolescence* (Springfield, Ill.: Charles C Thomas, 1962), and William A. Schonfeld, "Adolescent Development: Biological, Psychological and Sociological Determinants," *Adolescent Psychiatry*, Vol. I, ed. S. Feinstein, P. Giovacchini, and A. Miller (New York: Basic Books, 1971). The following definitions appear in the notes to the Schonfeld paper: "Puberty: from the Middle English *puberte,* derived from *pubertas,* noun derived from *puber,* 'one who can procreate,' and *pubertas,* 'state or condition of being able to procreate,' because they contain the root *pu,* 'to beget.' However, *puber* and *pubes* are also defined as 'the signs of manhood, i.e. with hairiness' and *puberty* as 'the time of the coming of hair.'"

MOURNING THE PAST: Giving up the past, the messages of reality: Sigmund Freud, "Mourning and Melancholia" (1915), SE, 14:244–245.

Reality testing has shown that the loved one no longer exists, and it proceeds to demand that all libido shall be withdrawn from its attachments to that object. This demand arouses considerable opposition. . . . Normally respect for reality gains the day. Nevertheless, its orders cannot be obeyed at once. They are carried out bit by bit, at a great expense of energy and in the meantime the existence of the lost object is psychically prolonged. Each single one of the memories and expectations in which the libido is bound to the object is brought up and hypercathected, and detachment of the libido is accomplished in respect of it.

6.   LOVE DIALOGUES II: MOURNING THE PAST

REMOVAL: The term "removal" and the descriptions of the specific displacements entailed were first discussed by Anny Katan in "The Role of Displacement in Agoraphobia," trans. Gertrud Kurth, *International Journal of Psychoanalysis* (1937), 32:41–50. Most psychoanalysts follow the tradition of referring to such displacements as "removal" or "object removal." The term, however, can create confusion, especially if understood as a removal of the actual parents and not a re-moval of libido from their images. The definition of removal is on p. 43.

Adolescent strategies: Anna Freud, "Adolescence," *Psychoanalytic Study of the Child* (New York: International Universities Press, 1958), 13:255–278. I have tried to present these strategies or defenses as they appear in Miss Freud's text, but for the sake of clarity a number of changes and deletions were necessary. An important defense, "defense by withdrawal of libido to the self," I have deferred to the ensuing chapters on narcissism, but even there I do not present the entire range of pathology indicated by Miss Freud. "If anxieties and inhibitions block the way toward new objects outside the family, the libido remains within the self. There it may be employed to cathect the ego and the superego, thereby inflating them. Clinically this means that ideas of grandeur will appear—fantasies of unlimited power over other human beings or of major achievement and championship in one or more fields. Or the suffering and persecuted ego of the adolescent may assume Christ-like proportions with corresponding fantasies of saving the world" (p. 272).

Three axes of failed solution: Katan, pp. 43–45.

Adolescent mourning: The adolescent mourning process is not exactly like mourning a lost loved one, but I have borrowed some of Freud's phrases from "Mourning and Melancholia" (1915), SE, 14:244–245 (passage cited in notes to Chap. 5). Descriptions of adolescent mourning: Martha Wolfenstein, "How Is Mourning Possible?" *Psychoanalytic Study of the Child* (New York: International Universities Press, 1966) 21:93–126; contrast with the adult mourner, pp. 113–116.

GROWTH SPURT: J. M. Tanner, *Growth at Adolescence* (Springfield, Ill.: Charles C Thomas, 1962). See also notes to Chap. 3 and G. Stanley Hall, *Adolescence,* 2 vols. (New York: D. Appleton and Co., 1904).

NOSTALGIA: Comparison with the child's sense of the past and the section on nostalgia are from Wolfenstein, "How Is Mourning Possible?" pp. 109–115. The poets she refers to are Wordsworth and A. E. Housman (p. 115).

The lyrics in the nostalgia section are all by Paul Simon: "April Come She Will," copyright © 1965 by Paul Simon, used by permission; "Me and Julio Down by the Schoolyard," copyright © 1971 by Paul Simon, used by permission; "Bookends," copyright © 1968 by Paul Simon, used by permission; "Kodachrome," copyright © 1973 by Paul Simon (Kodachrome® is a registered trademark for color film), used by permission; "Mrs. Robinson," copyright © 1968 by Paul Simon, used by permission; "America," copyright © 1968 by Paul Simon, used by permission; "American Tune," copyright © 1973 by Paul Simon, used by permission; "Slip Slidin' Away," copyright © 1977 by Paul Simon, used by permission; "The Sound of Silence," copyright © 1964 by Paul Simon, used by permission.

REENACTMENT: The descriptions of the reenactments of adolescence are from Peter Blos, "The Split Parental Imago," in *The Adolescent Passage* (New York: International Universities Press, 1979). The personal environment that Blos describes as an "autoplastic milieu" (in contrast to an alloplastic milieu, in which the individual effects changes in an actual external environment) appears on pp. 83–86; the differences between splitting and the ordinary good-bad dichotomies of adolescence, p. 76; the lack of memory of these quasi relationships, p. 85. Blos's remarkable chapter is one of the best protrayals of how the infantile past can infiltrate the adolescent present (and later sometimes even the adult present), not as a recapitulation but as the reinstatement of a primitive mode of functioning. Splitting in an infant is the outcome of normal and expectable developmental issues, with some evocation of primitive functions.

Some of the descriptions of infantile "splitting" are from Louise J. Kaplan, *Oneness and Separateness* (New York: Simon and Schuster, 1978).

The immortal past: Infantile love dialogues are ne er really lost: Roy Schafer, *Aspects of Internalization* (New York International Universities Press, 1968), pp. 221–222: "the object loses or gains importance, it takes on new hostile or loving significance or becomes more neutral . . . it nevertheless appears to retain a fundamental sameness, this sameness reflects the subject's unchanging fundamental wishful tie to the object." (Schafer is talking here only of the primary process. Two other ways of immortalizing the object are identification and changes in the self-representation.)

7. THE BRIDGE BETWEEN LOVE DIALOGUES AND NARCISSISM: LOVE FOR THE PARENT OF THE SAME SEX

THE FORMATION OF THE ADULT EGO-IDEAL IN ADOLESCENCE: In his 1914 paper "On Narcissism: An Introduction" Freud wrote: "Large amounts of a homosexual kind of libido are drawn into the formation of the narcissistic ego-ideal and find outlet and satisfaction in maintaining it," SE, 14:96.

I am indebted to Peter Blos for his creative elaboration of Freud's 1914 thesis and for his conceptualizations on the role of adolescence in the formation of the adult ego-ideal, the structure of the mind that represents the most humanized and foward-looking aspects of the superego. Blos' writings in *On Adolescence* (New York: The Free Press, 1962) and *The Adolescent Passage* (New York: International Universities Press, 1979) are the primary sources for this chapter. In fact, it was Blos who, many years ago, inspired me to investigate the unique contributions of the adolescent phase of life to the moral dimensions of human existence. In this regard it is noteworthy that the two psychoanalysts who have become identified with the psychoanalytic theory of adolescence, Blos and Erik Erikson, both singled out the centrality of moral development— Blos, the ethical ideal, and Erikson, virtue. Other writers, such as Robert Coles, Lawrence Kohlberg, Kenneth Keniston, Rousseau, and

G. Stanley Hall, have also stressed the moral dimensions of adolescence. It is Blos, however, who first called attention to the role of the relationship to the same-sexed parent in the humanization of conscience.

The chapters from *The Adolescent Passage* that most influenced my thoughts were "The Initial Stage of Male Adolescence," "The Child Analyst Looks at the Young Adolescent," "Preoedipal Factors in the Etiology of Female Delinquency," "When and How Does Adolescence End?," and particularly "The Genealogy of the Ego Ideal." From *On Adolescence* the most influential chapters were "Phases of Adolescence" and "The Ego in Adolescence." Subsequent references to Blos in this section will cite chap. title, book (*OA* or *TAP*), and page nos. if necessary.

Other writings that had a significant influence on this chapter but to which I do not refer directly are Jeanne Lampl-de Groot, "Ego Ideal and Superego," in *The Development of the Mind* (New York: International Universities Press, 1965); John M. Murray, "Narcissism and the Ego Ideal," in *Journal of the American Psychoanalytic Association* (1964), 12, No. 3: 477–511; and Edith Jacobson, *The Self and the Object World* (New York: International Universities Press, 1964).

Early adolescence in boys: "The Initial Stage of Male Adolescence," *TAP*; the boy's relation to the caregiving mother, his feelings about women: "Phases of Adolescence," *OA*, pp. 63–65; girl's relation to the caregiving mother: ibid., pp. 66–68, and "Preoedipal Factors in the Etiology of Female Delinquency," *TAP*, pp. 104–108. The boy's reactions to the growth of the testicles is attributed to Anita Bell in "Scientific Proceedings: Prepuberty and Child Analysis," reported by Eleanor Galenson (pp. 601–602) in *Journal of the American Psychoanalytic Association* (1954), 12, No. 3: 600–609. Comparison between girls and boys in the initial stages of adolescence: "The Child Analyst Looks at the Young Adolescent," *TAP*, pp. 196–202.

Differences between girls and boys in the evolution of the adult ego-ideal: "The Genealogy of the Ego Ideal," *TAP*, pp. 329–335. Considerably more than I do, Blos emphasizes the girl's gender-related difficulties in forming an abstract, impersonalized conscience. While I do not mean to minimize the role of penis envy in female development, I do not believe that penis envy interferes with the ethical sensibilities in the direct, gender-specific way that Blos does. In my experience with patients, male and female alike, the central issue is *amour-propre*, the vanity and self-aggrandizing tendencies that are common to both sexes. That women frequently attach their ideals to individuals rather than to groups is certainly true, but I have found this tendency to be related more to conflictual issues arising at all stages of development than to penis envy per se.

The feminine crush: Most of the material is from my clinical work with adolescents and adults. I was alerted to the impact and significance of the adolescent crush in feminine development by Blos, "Phases of Adolescence," *OA,* pp. 80–87. Blos uses Mann's story *Tonio Kröger* as an example of a masculine crush (pp. 80–82). A classic example of the betrayal of adolescent ideals is Dora's crush on Frau K (see "Fragment of an Analysis of a Case of Hysteria," SE, 7:7–122). The crucial dynamics of the case concern Dora's early relationship to her mother and her later one to Frau K.

Role of male societies: pp. 137–138 of Judith Kestenberg, "Phases of Adolescence, III," *Journal of the American Academy of Child Psychiatry* (1968) 7: 108–151.

Rousseau on moral development: "Swept along": *Emile, or On Education,* trans. and with introd. and notes by Allan Bloom (New York: Basic Books, 1979), p. 41; "In fact, what are generosity": *Second Discourse,* in *The First and Second Discourses,* ed. Roger D. Masters, trans. Roger D. and Judith R. Masters (New York: St. Martin's Press, 1964), p. 131.

Quotation from J. C. Flugel: *The Psychoanalytic Study of the Family* (London: Hogarth Press, 1921), p. 140. Flugel refers to Darwin's predictions on p. 239.

The young adult's generational love: Tender relationship to the same-sexed parent: "Phases of Adolescence," *OA,* pp. 129–148; exaggeration of mother's negative traits becoming redundant in late adolescence: Kestenberg, p. 136; young adult's relationship to parents and society: "Phases of Adolescence," *OA,* pp. 148–158; autobiographical sensibilities of the older adolescent: Kestenberg, p. 136; young adult's realization of the finitude of time, her sense of the tragic dimensions of her parents: "The Genealogy of the Ego Ideal," *TAP,* pp. 365–369, and "The Ego in Adolescence," *OA,* pp. 184–197. In "When and How Does Adolescence End?" (*TAP,* p. 415) Blos says: "This is the time when he forms his own view of his past, present and future. The past is retrospectively subjected to a kind of historical reality testing. Here we witness the ascent of self-conscious man who, as never before, has become aware of his unique, yet ordinary, life that lies between birth and death. So-called existential anxiety cannot be experienced before adolescence; the same is true for the sense of the tragic."

8.   NARCISSISM I: THE AUTOEROTIC EXCURSION

THE NARCISSISTIC REGRESSION: Peter Blos, "The Second Individuation," in *The Adolescent Passage* (New York: International Universities Press, 1979), and Edith Jacobson, *The Self and the Object World*

(New York: International Universities Press, 1964), pp. 177–193.
Fantasies of omnipotence: Eugene Pumpian-Mindlin, "Vicissitudes of Infantile Omnipotence," *Psychoanalytic Study of the Child* (New York: International Universities Press, 1969), 24:213–226.
Idols selected for worship: Jacobson, pp. 178–80.
Clearing off the posters: Blos, "The Second Individuation": "It should not surprise us that the bedroom walls, plastered with posters of collective idols, become bare as soon as object libido becomes engaged in genuine relationships" (p. 156).
Three currents of narcissism: Vann Spruiell, "Three Strands of Narcissism," *Psychoanalytic Quarterly* (1975) XLIV:577–595. Spruiell identified the three strands as self-love, self-esteem, and omnipotence.
ARRIVING AT PUBERTY: J. M. Tanner, *Growth at Adolescence* (Springfield, Ill.: Charles C Thomas, 1962); Judith Kestenberg, "Phases of Adolescence, III," *Journal of the American Academy of Child Psychiatry*, 7:108–151; and William A. Schonfeld, "Adolescent Development: Biological, Psychological and Sociological Determinants," *Adolescent Psychiatry*, Vol. I, ed. S. Feinstein, P. Giovacchini, and A. Miller (Basic Books, 1971). Descriptions of the genitals: William H. Masters and Virginia E. Johnson, *Human Sexual Response* (Boston: Little, Brown, 1966).
MASTURBATION: "the active, rather than passive type": Jeanne Lampl-de Groot, "On Masturbation and Its Influences on General Development," *Psychoanalytic Study of the Child* (New York: International Universities Press, 1950), 5:153–174: "It is the girl with a strongly bi-sexual constitution who fails in the masturbation struggle" (p. 172), and "Thus the active type of girl like the boy does not succeed easily in renouncing masturbation" (p. 175). Jacobson also comments that conscious masturbation conflicts are not as prevalent in girls (p. 162). Jacobson is probably correct that the conflicts are less *conscious* in girls.
Differences between boys and girls: I thank Dr. Irving Steingart for reviewing the material on masturbation and for his suggestions.
Masturbation from Infancy to Senescence, ed. Irvin Marcus and John Francis (New York: International Universities Press, 1975). Virginia Lawson Clower's essay in this volume, "Masturbation in Women," was particularly helpful: "All adult women unless severely inhibited by cultural taboos or neurosis masturbate on occasion" (p. 640).
A. Kinsey, W. B. Pomeroy, and S. I. Martin, *Sexual Behavior in the Human Male* and *Sexual Behavior in the Human Female* (Philadelphia: Saunders, 1948 and 1953, resp.).
"Die Onanie" (On Masturbation), 14 Beiträge zu einer Diskus-

sion der Wiener Psychoanalytischen Vereinigung (Wiesbaden: J. F. Bergmann, 1912). The minutes to the 1912 meeting were printed in Vol. II of *Zentralblatt für Psychoanalyse* (1911–1912). There were fourteen members who met on nine evenings, from November 22, 1911, to April 24, 1912. See Freud, "Contributions to a Discussion on Masturbation," SE, 12:241–254. Freud remarks in his discussion and summary that he disagrees with Stekel and others who felt that masturbation was not toxic. Freud reminded the members to distinguish between infantile, adolescent, and adult masturbation. Freud related masturbation toxicity to the so-called actual neurosis.

In the chapter "Masturbation," in *On Adolescence* (New York: The Free Press, 1979), Peter Blos summarizes the harmful and beneficial aspects of masturbation. Many of the ensuing details are from this chapter, pp. 159–169.

Hall on masturbation: Turn-of-the-century advertisements, scare literature, and recommended cures are described by Hall in *Adolescence,* 2 vols. (New York: D. Appleton and Co., 1904), I, 453–463: "One of the very saddest," p. 432; "wherever researches have been undertaken," p. 435; "all we know points," p. 453; "like a worm upon fruit," p. 463; "In bright, nervous children," p. 438; "the prince of darkness," p. 440; Hall's reports on the physical and mental effects of onanism, pp. 435–463; formula for spermin, p. 442; "the masturbator's heart," p. 443; Hall's prescriptions, pp. 463–471; "the ideals of chastity," p. 453.

PSYCHOANALYSTS' VIEWS ON MASTURBATION: Victor Tausk's paper "On Masturbation" (considered a classic) was his contribution to the 1912 Vienna conference. In 1951 it was translated and reprinted for *Psychoanalytic Study of the Child* (New York: International Universities Press, 1951), 6:61–79: "the individual has no reason to compete with others for a sexual object since he finds all sources of pleasure easily within himself" (p. 74).

Annie Reich, "The Discussion of 1912 on Masturbation and Our Present Day Views," *Psychoanalytic Study of the Child* (New York: International Universities Press, 1951), 6:80–94. Reich discusses Tausk's paper and describes the swinging of the pendulum from 1912 to 1950 in the psychoanalytic evaluation of the dangers of adolescent masturbation.

Moses Laufer is one of the psychoanalysts whose many years of intensive clinical work with adolescents (at the Hampstead Child Therapy Clinic and in private practice in London) has enabled him to evaluate and describe the potentially positive contribution of masturbation to adolescent development. "The Central Masturbation Fantasy, the Final Sexual Organization, and Adolescence," *Psychoanalytic Study of the Child* (New Haven: Yale University Press, 1976), 31:297–316: the evolution of the central masturbation fantasy, p. 300; "During adolescence oedipal wishes are tested within the context of mature genitals . . . a compromise between what is wished for and what is allowed" (p. 298).

Laufer, "The Body Image, the Function of Masturbation and Adolescence," *Psychoanalytic Study of the Child* (New York: International Universities Press, 1968), 23:114–137: In normal adolescence perverse fantasies are unconscious and a heterosexual fantasy predominates. Disturbed adolescents do not experience masturbation as a trial action and usually the perverse fantasy predominates and is experienced as real and dangerous (p. 134).

Laufer, "The Psychoanalyst and the Adolescent's Sexual Development," *Psychoanalytic Study of the Child* (New Haven: Yale University Press, 1981), 36:181–193: the fantasy of offering the mother a body without adult genitals (p. 185). Laufer sees this fantasy as "a giving in in a hopeless way to a mother who they believe has destroyed their genitals and robbed them of it."

Tausk expressed a similar idea with regard to the father in his 1912 discussion: "Masturbation is a spiteful rebellion against the father" (p. 78); "By virtue of making the genitals dominant he loses his inner relation to the total personality of the woman" (pp. 75–76).

The idea that absence of masturbation during adolescence is a poor prognostic sign appears in much of the contemporary literature on adolescence, even in the more conservative papers. K. R. Eissler, "Notes on Problems of Technique in the Psychoanalytic Treatment of Adolescents: With Some Remarks on Perversions," *Psychoanalytic Study of the Child* (New York: International Universities Press, 1958), 13:223–254. Eissler, although recognizing that absence of masturbation in boys is a worrisome sign, speculates that perhaps girls react differently (p. 243).

MASTURBATION FANTASIES: Descriptions of masturbatory activities and their fantasy interpretations appear in "Masturbation: Panel Report," John J. Francis, reporter, *Journal of the American Psychoanalytic Association* (1968), No. 1, 16:95–112.

My primary reference in this section was Kestenberg, "Phases of Adolescence, III": the masturbatory activities of girls, pp. 125–129; the masturbatory activities of boys, pp. 126–128; the unsteadiness of heterosexual relations during early puberty, pp. 130–131.

Vann Spruiell, "Narcissistic Transformations in Adolescence," *International Journal of Psychoanalytic Psychotherapy,* ed. Robert Langs (1975), 4:518–536: early success seems to interfere with the rich possibilities of an elaborated erotic life, p. 535; the self as lovable, p. 527; a lonely and courageous attempt to love or hate oneself, p. 527.

9.   NARCISSISM II: *ARS EROTICA* AND DREAMS OF GLORY

AGES OF ARRIVAL AT FULL SEXUAL MATURITY: Judith Kestenberg, "Phases of Adolescence, III," *Journal of the American Academy of Child Psychiatry,* 7:134.

ARS EROTICA: G. Stanley Hall, *Adolescence,* 2 vols. (New York: D. Appleton and Co., 1904): "Life overflows with bright colors"—the plant and animal kingdom, II, 110. Descriptions of secondary sex characteristics, body decorations, facial expressions, clothing, pp. 113–115.

"In the spring": Alfred Lord Tennyson, "Locksley Hall," *The Poems and Plays of Alfred Lord Tennyson* (New York: Modern Library, 1938), p. 170.

Relations between the sexes during early puberty and foreplay during late puberty: Kestenberg, pp. 138–140, and Edith Jacobson, *The Self and the Object World* (New York: International Universities Press, 1964), pp 164–167. Foreplay as an assurance of masculinity and femininity: Kestenberg, pp. 138–139.

PETTING: A. Kinsey, W. B. Pomeroy, and S. I. Martin, *Sexual Behavior in the Human Female* (Philadelphia: Saunders, 1953): mammalian and nonmammalian petting activities, pp. 229–230; cultural definitions of erotogenic zones, p. 259; the variety of petting variations—toying, spooning, etc., p. 231; current petting practices (1953), pp. 251–259.

It should be understood that any research findings on sexual practice among adolescents, particularly those from the Kinsey reports, which were based on group statistics and interviews with women and men who came of age between 1930 and 1950, many of whom were presenting retrospective accounts of their adolescent years, cannot possibly be an entirely reliable and valid representation of current adolescent practice. I have included only that data from the Kinsey reports that correspond to my own and my colleagues' impressions of adolescent sexual behavior in contemporary western European societies.

Robert E. Sorenson, *Adolescent Sexuality in Contemporary America* (Cleveland: World Publishing Co., 1973), reports that 59 percent of all boys and 45 percent of all girls, ages thirteen to nineteen, have had sexual intercourse. On the other hand, Kenneth Keniston, "Youth: A 'New' Stage of Life," *American Scholar,* 39, No. 4 (Autumn 1970), reports:

In modern Western societies, as in many others, the commencement of actual sexual relationships is generally deferred by middle-class adolescents until their late teens or early twenties: the modal age of first intercourse for American college males today is around twenty, for females about twenty-one. Thus, despite the enormous importance of adolescent sexuality and sexual development, actual sexual intercourse often awaits youth. In youth, there may occur a major shift from masturbation and sexual fantasy to interpersonal sexual behavior, including the gradual integration of sexual feelings with intimacy with a real person.

Ruth Bell et al., *Changing Bodies, Changing Lives: A Book for Teens on Sex and Relationships* (New York: Random House, 1980), renders what I feel is a realistic assessment of current sexual attitudes and practices among middle-class American adolescents. As one learns from this book, which consists of interviews with thirteen to nineteen-year-olds, the range of sexual attitudes and practices is much wider than is usually reported. Nevertheless the adolescents interviewed by Bell and her colleagues were agreed on some matters. They were careful, for example, to distinguish between "making out," which is an activity that goes beyond simple kissing and hugging, and "petting" or "fooling around," which entails manual exploration of the genitals—the penis and clitoris. And, apparently in this age group, oral sex and "going all the way" are not as frequent as some adults (and some adolescents) might imagine. True, many of the boys and girls interviewed by Bell did feel pressured by the code of sexual permissiveness. The males especially were worried that their "virginity" might be a sign of deviance.

Sorenson, commenting on his own results, is far from sanguine about the interpretation of his statistics. "Most adolescents are giving themselves little time for beginning sexual activities and move directly to sexual intercourse. One reason for this is that in our society sexual intercourse is widely considered the only valid expression of sexual love. Another reason may be the unwillingness of many parents to consider advanced sexual beginnings as different from sexual intercourse" (p. 375).

There appears to be some consensus among the experts and among adolescents themselves that in pubescence and early puberty boys and girls are more comfortable with what Sorenson calls "advanced sexual beginnings" and adolescents refer to as "fooling around" than with sexual intercourse. In my own account of the sexual activity of youth (nineteen to twenty-three and onward) I have tried to put the emphasis on the quality of the sexual relationship rather than on the practice.

The narcissistic quality of these earliest love affairs has been stressed by many authors. Vann Spruiell, "Narcissistic Transformations in Adolescence," *International Journal of Psychotherapy,* ed. Robert Langs (1975), 4:518–536, has commented specifically on the mutually exploitative quality of young love (p. 528).

SCREEN MEMORIES: The screen memory reported here is a variation on the memory described by Sigmund Freud in "Screen Memories," SE, 3:301–322. It is generally accepted that the childhood memory was

Freud's and that it was formed during Freud's own adolescence in order to screen out the disappointment of an adolescent love. In Freud's paper the specific details of the memory—the yellow flowers, the black bread—are interpreted differently. The emphasis is on the young man giving up an ordinary bread-and-butter life for his career. There is in Freud's interpretation a sense of longing for the ordinary life he might have lived had he not surrendered to his calling.

Sören Kierkegaard, *Fear and Trembling,* trans. and with introd. and notes by Walter Lowrie (Garden City, N.Y.: Doubleday Anchor Books, 1954). The dilemma is explicated on pp. 64–77. The interpretation is from Paul Ricouer, *Symbolism of Evil* (Boston: Beacon Press, 1969), p. 312.

DREAMS OF GLORY: The examples of the golden rule are from Erik Erikson, "The Golden Rule in the Light of New Insight," *Insight and Responsibility* (New York: W. W. Norton and Co., 1964), pp. 220–221.

Narcissism and the ego-ideal: "the source of our passions": *Emile, or On Education,* trans. and with intro. and notes by Allan Bloom (Basic Books, 1979), p. 212; "what has belonged to the lowest part," Freud, SE, 19:36; "the ego-ideal spans": Peter Blos, "The Genealogy of the Ego Ideal," *The Adolescent Passage* (New York: International Universities Press, 1979), p. 368; "On Narcissism," SE, 14:94; Simon Legree–Mona Lisa images: John M. Murray, "Narcissism and the Ego Ideal," *Journal of the American Psychoanalytic Association* (1964), No. 12, 3:478; lessens the instinctual sacrifice: My thoughts on the relationship between the ego-ideal and cultural aspiration were influenced by Paul Ricouer's distinctions between culture and civilization in *Freud and Philosophy: An Essay on Interpretation,* trans. Denis Savage (New Haven and London: Yale University Press, 1970), pp. 248–250. The three tasks of culture, Ricouer says, are to lessen the burden of instinctual sacrifice, reconcile the individual to renunciations that are ineluctable, and offer compensations for those sacrifices (p. 250).

The commentary on Polonius' counsel to Laertes is derived from Lionel Trilling, *Sincerity and Authenticity* (Cambridge, Mass: Harvard University Press, 1972), p. 3.

Comparisons between ego-ideal and superego: Murrary, "Narcissism and the Ego Ideal" and Jeanne Lampl-de Groot, "Ego Ideal and Superego," in *The Development of the Mind* (New York: International Universities Press, 1965).

Culture, infantile prototypes: the benevolent visage: Ricouer, *Freud and Philosophy,* p. 250.

Environment of primary love: Michael Balint, *The Basic Fault* (London and New York: Tavistok Publications, 1968; rpt. 1979): "it has hardly any structure, in particular no sharp boundaries towards the individual; environment and individual penetrate into each other . . ." (p. 66).

The *post hoc, ergo propter hoc* first appears in Sandor Ferenczi, "Stages in the Development of the Sense of Reality," in *Sex in Psychoanalysis* (New York: Basic Books, 1950). René Spitz, in *The First Year of Life* (New York: International Universities Press, 1965), refers to Ferenczi's idea on infantile omnipotence, relating it to causality and illusion: "In this achievement of enlisting the mother's help for his needs through screaming, the human being for the first time experiences the *post hoc, ergo propter hoc* in connection with his own action. Of course, this is a forerunner only and not the principle of causality proper." The principle branches later in two directions. "One of them will remain in its crude form as a basic mode of functioning of the primary process. The other will become progressively refined until it becomes one of the most potent ideational tools of man in the form of the principle of determinism" (p. 153).

"Foetus, amniotic fluid and placenta are such a complicated interpenetrating mix-up of foetus and environment-mother": Balint, p. 66; the threat of being separated from the love object: Balint, pp. 69–71.

We create a world that is kinder: "This latter may entail as a first step a regressive withdrawal from objects found too harsh and frustrating, to the harmonious mix-up of earlier states which is then followed by an attempt to create something better, kinder, more understandable, more beautiful and above all more consistent and more harmonious than the real objects proved to be": Balint, p. 68. THE SECURITY BLANKET: Donald W. Winnicott, "Transitional Objects and Transitional Phenomena," *International Journal of Psychoanalysis*" (1953), 34, Pt. 2, pp. 89–97:". . . the third part of the life of a human being, a part that we cannot ignore, is an intermediate area of experiencing to which inner reality and external life both contribute. It is an area which is not challenged, because no claim is made on its behalf except that it shall exist as a resting place for the individual engaged in the perpetual human task of keeping inner and outer reality separate yet interrelated" (p. 90).

The humiliation of moral dependency: Anna Freud, *Normality and Pathology in Childhood* (New York: International Universities Press, 1965): "To have fulfillment of one's wishes and desires, their acceptance and rejection lodged in some external authority equals moral dependency and as such is the hallmark of the immature" (p. 170). Miss Freud did not associate the remedy with the creation of an imaginary companion.

IMAGINARY COMPANION: The varieties and functions of the imaginary companion: Humberto Nagera, "The Imaginary Companion," *Psychoanalytic Study of the Child* (New York: International Universities Press, 1969), 24:165–196.

The Davdon scenario is adapted from the Rudyman character described by Otto E. Sperling, "An Imaginary Companion, Representing a Prestage of the Superego," *Psychoanalytic Study of the Child* 9: 252–258.

The Adam and Elizabeth scenario has been adapted from Sheldon Bach, "Notes on Some Imaginary Companions," *Psychoanalytic Study of the Child* (New York: Quadrangle Press, 1971), 26: 159–171.

ADOLESCENT TRANSFORMATIONS: The adolescent who says "no" is from my interview with Peter Blos, Oct. 18, 1981.

Kinaaldá and Kore rites: Bruce Lincoln, *Emerging from the Chrysalis* (Cambridge, Mass., and London: Harvard University Press, 1981); North American plains rites: Claude Lévi-Strauss, *Tristes Tropiques* (Librairie Plon, 1955; New York: Atheneum, 1974), p. 40.

"The Real Me," "I've Had Enough," and "Love, Reign O'er Me" were written by Peter Townshend. Copyright © 1974 Fabulous Music Limited. All rights in the United States, its territories and possessions, Canada, Mexico, and The Philippines are controlled by Towser Tunes, Inc. All rights reserved. International copyright secured. Reproduced by kind permission of Peter Townshend, Fabulous Music Limited, and Towser Tunes, Inc.

"Dark Star," copyright © 1971 Ice Nine Publishing Company. Music by Jerry Garcia, Mickey Hart, Bill Kreutzmann, Phil Lesh, Bob Weir, and Ron McKernan; words by Robert Hunter. Reprinted by permission.

"New Feeling" was written by David Byrne. Copyright © 1977 Index Music Inc/Bleu Disque Music, Inc. (ASCAP). Excerpt reprinted with permission. All rights reserved.

"Demolition Man" was written by Andrian Lee and Toyah Willcox. Copyright © 1981 Dick James Music Limited and Sweet 'n' Sour Songs, Ltd. Used by permission. All rights reserved.

Actual world of limited possibility: "the inconveniences of undertaking to intercede": Trilling, p. 174; "the blood ferments": Rousseau, *Emile,* p. 220.

10.   ANOREXIA NERVOSA: A FEMININE PURSUIT OF PERFECTION

The portrait of the anorectic is a composite, a prototype that does not take into account the range of personality disturbances in which the symptom might occur. The prognosis, for example, in the more neurotic anorectics is more hopeful and the underlying family dynamics are usually less aberrant. The father is a more active voice in the family.

MAJOR REFERENCES ARE:

Hilde Bruch, *Eating Disorders: Obesity, Anorexia Nervosa and the Person Within* (New York: Basic Books, 1973), and *The Golden Cage: The Enigma of Anorexia Nervosa* (Cambridge, Mass.: Harvard University Press, 1978).

John Sours, *Starving to Death in a Sea of Objects* (New York: Jason Aronson, 1980).

Mara Selvini Palazzoli, *Self-Starvation: From Individual to Family Therapy in the Treatment of Anorexia Nervosa* (New York: Jason Aronson, 1977).

Center for the Study of Anorexia and Bulimia, "The Eating Disorder Bulimia" and "Anorexia Nervosa" (New York: Institute for Contemporary Psychotherapy, 1982).

Jack I. Ross, "Anorexia Nervosa—an Overview," *Bulletin of the Menninger Clinic* (1977), 41 No. 5: 418–436 (Topeka, Kans.: Menninger Foundation).

Charles Chediak, "The So-called Anorexia Nervosa," *Bulletin of the Menninger Clinic* (1977), 41 No. 5: 453–474.

Rosemary Dinnage, "The Starved Self," *The New York Review of Books,* 26 No. 2, Feb. 22, 1979, 6–9.

Joyce McDougall, *Plea for a Measure of Abnormality* (New York: International Universities Press, 1980).

Medical signs and laboratory findings: Sours, pp. 295–305.

Historical account: Sours, pp. 207–217; Bruch, *Eating Disorders,* pp. 211–215; Ross, pp. 418–419.

Quotation from Lasègue, "De l'anorexie hystérique," *Archives Gènèrales du Mèdecine* (1873), 2: 367–369, as translated in *Evolution of Psychosomatic Concepts,* ed. M. R. Kaufman and M. Herman (New York: International Universities Press, 1964): quoted in Selvini Palazzoli, p. 5.

Effects of the oral interpretations: Ross, pp. 424–426; Bruch, *Golden Cage,* pp. 122–125.

Rates in Western societies: Sours, pp. 280–286.

Statistics among high-school and college-age girls: Center for the Study of Anorexia and Bulimia; Sours, pp. 280–286.

Thin-fat people: quotation from Heckel, as cited by Bruch, *Eating Disorders,* p. 195.

Symbiotic interpretation "as long as they both shall live": Sanford Gifford et al., "Anorexia Nervosa in One of Identical Twins," in *Anorexia Nervosa and Obesity,* ed. C. V. Rowland, *International Psychiatric Clinics* (Boston: Little, Brown, 1970), 7 No. 1:139–228 (p. 153); rapprochement interpretation: Chediak, p. 461. Sours stresses separation-individuation issues for his categories I and II (pp. 338–347), but he also identifies adolescence as the precipitating cause.

Bruch's formulation: *Eating Disorders,* pp. 251–253.

Freud's statement: SE, 1:200.

Precipitating events: Bruch, *Golden Cage,* pp. 57–71, and *Eating Disorders,* pp. 255–261.

Age of onset in females: Center for the Study of Anorexia and Bulimia; Sours, pp. 336–338; and Bruch, *Eating Disorders,* pp. 255–261.

Infantile sexual differences: Louise J. Kaplan, *Oneness and Separateness* (New York: Simon and Schuster), pp. 211–213.

"There is another self": paraphrase from Bruch, *Golden Cage,* p. 55.

"Enough means when you collapse": Bruch, *Golden Cage,* p. 148.

Watson quotation: *Psychological Care of Infant and Child* (New York: Norton, 1928), p. 70.

Parents as pretenders: Sours, p. 326.

Description of the perfect childhood, pp. 38–56; "There wasn't a person inside," p. 49; and "I feel that I can't live on just an ordinary scale," p. 53—all from Bruch, *Golden Cage.*

Quotations from classroom teachers are a composite and paraphrasing from sections of Bruch (*Eating Disorders* and *Golden Cage*), Sours, and Center for the Study of Anorexia and Bulimia.

Taking over the body like a rapist: Selvini Palazzoli, p. 69.

Hospital treatment procedures and the anorectic's reactions: Sours, pp. 360–377; Bruch, *Golden Cage,* pp. 91–105.

"I see in this 'Fresslust' ": Bruch, *Eating Disorders,* p. 220. Bruch's quotation is from the case of Ellen West as reported by L. Binswanger in "Der Fall Ellen West" in 1944. Ellen West had been diagnosed as a multiple personality and was likely to have had a schizophrenic disorder in which anorexia was a secondary symptom. Her case was constructed by Binswanger largely from her diaries and writings.

Bulimic symptoms and personality characteristics: Center for the Study of Anorexia and Bulimia, "The Eating Disorder Bulimia." Sours identifies bulimia as a Category IV type of anorexia (pp. 349–350). Most writers are uncertain about whether bulimia and anorexia do represent distinct disorders or whether, in fact, most anorectics are also sporadic binge-purgers.

The anorectic speaks: "I am ruining myself": Ellen West, in Bruch, *Eating Disorders,* p. 221; "I used to be hungry": Bruch, *Golden Cage,* p. 17; "I learned the trick": ibid., p. 19; "It was as if I had to punish my body": Bruch, *Eating Disorders,* p. 279; "I see

other people through a glass wall": Ellen West, in *Eating Disorders,*
p. 222; "I felt as though a slave driver": Bruch, *Golden Cage,* p. 20;
"a permanent skeleton at the feast": Gifford et al., "Anorexia Nervosa in One of Identical Twins," p. 153; "They wanted me to gain
weight" and "You see how obedient": paraphrased composites from
clinical and literary sources; "She is me, I am her": paraphrase from
Bruch, "Transformation of Oral Impulses in Eating Disorders: A Conceptual Approach," *Psychiatric Quarterly* (1961), 35: 458–481
(p. 477); "the greatest put-on": Bruch, *Golden Cage,* p. 54; "third
sex": paraphrase and construction from Bruch, *Eating Disorders,*
p. 98; "You feel outside your body": Bruch, *Golden Cage,* p. 18.

"The awareness of spiritual power": Selvini Palazzoli, p. 75.
The description of the dying anorectic: Sours, p. 308.

11. THE IMPOSTOR: A MASCULINE PURSUIT OF PEFECTION

MAJOR REFERENCES ARE:

Karl Abraham, "The History of an Impostor in the Light of Psychoanalytic Knowledge," *Psychoanalytic Quarterly* (1935), 4:570–587.

Helene Deutsch, "The Impostor. Contribution to Ego Psychology
of a type of Psychopath," *Psychoanalytic Quarterly* (1955),
24:483–505.

Phyllis Greenacre, "The Impostor," in *Emotional Growth I,* and
"The Relation of the Impostor to the Artist" and "The Family Romance of the Artist," in *Emotional Growth II* (New York: International Universities Press, 1971).

Phyllis Greenacre, "Conscience in the Psychopath," in *Trauma,
Growth and Personality* (London: Hogarth Press, 1953).

Thomas Mann, *The Confessions of Felix Krull, Confidence Man,*
trans. Denver Lindley (New York: Vintage Books, 1969).

Sigmund Freud, "Some Character Types Met with in Psychoanalytic Work I, The Exceptions," SE, 14: 311–315; "Family Romances," SE, 9:236–241; "Moses and Monotheism," SE, 23:11–15.

Lionel Finkelstein, "The Impostor: Aspects of His Development,"
Psychoanalytic Quarterly (1974), 43: 85–114.

Edith Jacobson, "The Exceptions," *Psychoanalytic Study of the
Child* (New York: International Universities Press, 1959), 14:135–154.

Joyce McDougall, *Plea for a Measure of Abnormality* (New York:
International Universities Press, 1980).

Though I do not refer directly to the life of Thomas Chatterton,
who was more artist than impostor, the following books on his work
and life history influenced my formulations:

W. Macneile Dixon, "Chatterton," Wharton Lecture on English

Poetry, British Academy (London: Humphrey Milford Amen Houses E.C., 1930).

John Cranstown Nevill, Thomas Chatterton (London: Frederick Mullen, 1948).

Descriptions of the male anorectics: Hilde Bruch, *Eating Disorders: Obesity, Anorexia Nervosa and the Person Within* (New York: Basic Books, 1973), pp. 285–305; John Sours, *Starving to Death in a Sea of Objects* (New York: Jason Aronson, 1980), pp. 269–273.

Statistics on juvenile delinquency: Martin Gold and Richard J. Petronus, "Delinquent Behavior in Adolescence," *Handbook of Adolescent Psychology,* ed. Joseph Adelson (New York: John Wiley and Sons, 1980): male-female trends from ages eleven to twenty-three, pp. 504–507; categories for typing juvenile offenders, p. 509. The data that Gold and Petronus cite are from the National Survey of Youth, 1972, and Youth in Transition study, 1977 (Ann Arbor, Mich.: Institute for Social Research).

The formulation for the sex-gender concordance script was arrived at in discussion with my husband, Donald M. Kaplan.

The information on Pope Joanna: Greenacre, "The Impostor," pp. 107–108.

"a very special type of liar": Greenacre, "The Impostor," p. 93; the forms and degrees of imposture: Greenacre, "Relation of the Impostor to the Artist," pp. 535–536.

Driven and repetitious behavior of the full-fledged impostor: Greenacre, "The Impostor," p. 95.

The family-romance interpretations are based on Greenacre, "The Impostor," "Relation of the Impostor to the Artist," and "Family Romance of the Artist."

The Jack and the Beanstalk inspiration is from my daughter, Ann Elizabeth Kaplan.

"it is in essence the story of an artist. . . ": Thomas Mann's Preface to *Stories of Three Decades,* trans. H. T. Lowe-Porter (New York: Modern Library, 1936).

"Nature has done me a grievous wrong": paraphrase from Sigmund Freud, "The Exceptions," SE, 14:314–315.

The two types of impostors: a composite description from Greenacre, "The Impostor," and Deutsch, "The Impostor. Contribution to Ego Psychology."

Deformities of Titus Oates and Tichborne: Greenacre, "The Impostor," pp. 105–107; early childhood of Oates and Tichborne: ibid., pp. 101–102.

The quotation is the opening soliloquy from *Richard III,* as cited by Freud, "The Exceptions," SE, 14:314.

"A Sunday child": *Felix Krull,* p. 7.

"Cuteness" of the impostor's imitations, praise he receives for his achievements of walking and talking, comparison with other two- to three-year-olds: Greenacre, "The Impostor," p. 103.

"Sitting in my little go-cart": *Felix Krull,* pp. 7–8.

The impostor's relationship to his father: Greenacre, "The Impostor," Finkelstein, "The Impostor: Aspects of His Development," and Deutsch, "The Impostor. Contribution to Ego Psychology," passim.

The impostor's genital humiliation during infancy: Greenacre, "The Impostor," p. 102.

"I could not conceal from myself": *Felix Krull,* p. 9.

The shabby, poorly knit real self and the illusory self: Greenacre, "The Impostor," p. 98.

Comparison of artist to impostor: Greenacre, "The Relation of the Impostor to the Artist" and "The Family Romance of the Artist."

Relationship of the impostor to his mother during childhood and early adolescence: Finkelstein, "The Impostor: Aspects of His Development," passim.

The impostor's lonely plight, from *Felix Krull:* "the other boys of the town," p. 8; "I had to conclude," pp. 60–61; and "more precious to me is the thief" p. 175; "the inconveniences of undertaking": Lionel Trilling, *Sincerity and Authenticity* (Cambridge, Mass.: Harvard University Press, 1972); "in my early youth": *Felix Krull,* p. 102.

Nobel Prize complex: Helen H. Tartakoff, "The Normal Personality in Our Culture and the Nobel Prize Complex," *Psychoanalysis, A General Psychology,* ed. R. Lowenstein, L. Newman, M. Schur, and A. Solnit (New York: International Universities Press, 1966), pp. 236–249.

Rejection of the man's world, the world of his father: Helene Deutsch, *Selected Problems of Adolescence* (New York: International Universities Press, 1967), p. 61; the uncommitted youth, p. 63.

Social institutions channel narcissistic trends toward a common ideal: paraphrase from Peter Blos, "Genealogy of the Ego Ideal," in *The Adolescent Passage* (New York: International Universities Press, 1979), p. 364.

12. THE LEGACIES OF ADOLESCENCE

Analysis of imagination: Benjamin R. Barber, "Rousseau and the Paradoxes of the Dramatic Imagination," *Daedalus* (Summer 1978). Barber's interpretations are derived primarily from his personal translations of the *First Discourse* and the *Second Discourse* and *Emile.*

"our souls have been corrupted": *First Discourse,* in Jean-Jacques Rousseau, *The First and Second Discourses,* ed. Roger D. Masters, trans. Roger D. and Judith R. Masters (New York: St. Martin's Press, 1964), p. 39.

"we no longer have citizens": *First Discourse,* p. 59.

Rousseau as the herald of modernity: Marshall Berman, *All That Is Solid Melts into Air* (New York: Simon and Schuster, 1982); Joseph Featherstone, "Rousseau and Modernity," and Robert Wokler, "Perfectible Apes in Decadent Cultures," *Daedalus* (Summer 1978).

"always appearing to relate everything" and "floating the whole course": *Emile, or On Education,* trans. and with introd. and notes by Allan Bloom (New York: Basic Books, 1979), p. 41.

"rise above himself": *First Discourse,* p. 35.

"One pities in others" and "Every attachment": *Emile,* pp. 224 and 221.

Freud, *Civilization and Its Discontents,* SE, 21: 86–107.

The quotation from Marx is from "Speech at the Anniversary of the *People's* Paper," in Robert S. Tucker, *The Marx Engels Reader,* 2d ed. (New York: W. W. Norton, 1978), as cited by Berman, *All That Is Solid,* p. 20.

Effects of industrialization and urbanization: Berman, introd.

"more ills," *Second Discourse,* p. 109.

"prosthetic God," SE, 21:91.

Claude Lévi-Strauss, *Tristes Tropiques* (Librairie Plon, 1955; New York: Atheneum, 1974), p. 413; the extinction of the great auk: G. Stanley Hall, *Adolescence,* 2 vols. (New York: D. Appleton and Co., 1904), II, 650.

"the multitude oppressed from within": *Second Discourse,* p. 175.

"a possible perfection": Freud, *Civilization and Its Discontents,* SE, 21:94.

Freud on culture and civilization, in *The Future of an Illusion,* SE, 21:6: "Human civilization by which I mean all those respects in which human life has raised itself above its animal status and differs from the life of beasts—and I scorn to distinguish between culture and civilization—presents as we know two aspects to the observer." The two aspects in Freud's account are knowledge and the mutual relations of human beings.

"garlands of flowers": *First Discourse,* p. 36.

The death instinct: The final sections of *Civilization and Its Discontents* (Chaps. V–VII) contain Freud's rationale for hypothesizing a death instinct. The concluding paragraph is on p. 145. The idea that the disputes within the economics of libido (personal happiness-narcissism) and union with others (object relations) are not irreconcilable appears on pp. 140–141.

Friedrich Nietzsche, *Beyond Good and Evil* (1882), as cited by Berman, *All That Is Solid,* p. 22.

Freud, *Civilization and Its Discontents,* SE, 21:103.

The description and citations from the 1979 assembly are from *The New York Times:* "Women's Movement Sets Its Sights for the Future of the Family," Nov. 20, 1979, B:11.

J. C. Flugel, *The Psychoanalytic Study of the Family* (London: Hogarth Press, 1921), p. 220.

PERSONAL AND SOCIAL TIME: Erik H. Erikson, "Youth, Fidelity and Diversity," *Daedalus* (Winter 1962), p. 23. In my discussions of the obscure relationship between personal and social time I have relied also on S. N. Eisenstadt's "Archetypal Patterns of Youth," in the same issue of *Daedalus;* cult of immediacy: David Riesman, *The Lonely Crowd* (Garden City, N.Y.: Anchor Books, 1953); values of sensation, simultaneity and impact: Daniel Bell, "The Disjunction of Culture and Social Structure," *Daedalus* (Winter 1965), p. 213; "the assistant postmaster": originated with the philosopher Stephen Toulmin and is cited in Eisenstadt, "Archetypal Patterns," p. 44.

Union of desire and duty is attributed to Kant in Allan Bloom, "The Education of Democratic Man," *Daedalus* (Summer 1978), p. 47. The idea of nature providing the means (passions) for transforming the personal into the social is the focus of some sections of Bloom's paper. Nevertheless the direction I have taken derives primarily from concepts I have elaborated in previous chapters of *Adolescence, The Farewell to Childhood.*

I owe some of my thinking on the relationship between drama and puberty rites to Richard Schechner, who suggested that puberty rites may have been the first form of theater.

"One's real life is so often the life one does not lead," Oscar Wilde, *L'Envoi to Rose-leaf and Apple-leaf* (1882), in *Oxford Book of Aphorisms,* chosen by John Gross (Oxford: Oxford University Press, 1983), p. 57.

"nameless feelings coursing through our breast," "unbolt the breast and become aware of life's flow and hear its winding murmur": Matthew Arnold (1852), *The Buried Life* (London: Oxford University Press, 1945), pp. 170, 171.

We go to weddings. We go to funerals: paraphrase of Lionel Trilling, *Sincerity and Authenticity* (Cambridge, Mass.: Harvard University Press, 1972), p. 174. Chap. 10 of *Adolescence* contains the full quotation.

INDEX

Abraham, Karl, 381
acquired characteristics,
 inheritance of, 78, 82, 83,
 361*n*
Adelson, Joseph, 355*n*–56*n*
Adolescence (Hall), 69, 70,
 78–80, 359*n*–60*n*, 384*n*
Adolescent, The (Offer, Ostrov
 and Howard), 40–41
Adolescent Experience, The
 (Douvan and Adelson),
 355*n*–56*n*
adolescents, adolescence:
 acting out in, 155–57, 159–
 160
 adult imitation of, 14, 38–
 39, 81, 223–24, 241
 adult misperceptions of, 149
 adults threatened by, 14, 37,
 116, 146, 154, 185
 antidesire warfare in, 136–
 137, 142, 263–64, 344–
 345
 casualties of, 334–36
 class differences and, 11,
 36–37, 41
 consensus of views on, 27
 consequences of absence of,
 21
 cultural differences and, 11
 cultural and moral
 aspirations of species
 reborn in, 13, 145, 239–
 240, 343–47
 denial of, 13, 15, 17, 37,
 38, 81
 dilemmas and resolutions of,
 15, 18–21, 89, 113–246,
 259, 261, 262–65
 diversity of, 27–28, 108–9
 as emotional battleground,
 14, 19, 40, 41, 342
 etymology of, 42
 as fiction, 40–41, 49
 images of, 13–14, 17, 25–
 112, 354*n*–55*n*
 innovativeness of, 153, 347
 invention of, 13, 16, 17,
 42–48, 49–50, 51–80, 81,
 355*n*–57*n*, 358*n*–60*n*
 legacies of, 13, 22, 222–26,
 318–48, 383*n*–85*n*
 as mourners, 19, 117, 140,
 146, 150, 366*n*, 367*n*
 narrowing of possibilities in,
 183, 339
 negative image of, 13, 37,
 39
 nostalgia of, 150–53, 367*n*
 privileges of, 36–37
 as prototypical experience,
 11
 puberty vs., 27, 28, 42
 rebellious image of, 13, 37
 recapitulationist theory of,
 15–17, 18, 78, 81–100,
 349*n*–50*n*, 360*n*–63*n*
 revolution of transformation
 in, 116, 327–28, 338
 as second birth, 17, 18, 69,
 70, 96, 99, 337–38, 344
 "splitting" mechanisms of,
 158–59
 as stepchild of
 psychoanalysis, 15–16,
 81–100, 360*n*–63*n*
 time in, 14, 19, 98–99, 115,
 116–17, 150, 151, 182–
 183, 265, 332–33
 trivializations and
 glorifications of, 13, 14,
 17–18, 27–50, 80, 81,
 350*n*–58*n*
 as victims vs. victimizers, 37
 visions of, 123
 as work of art, 21, 109

ABOUT THE AUTHOR

Dr. Louise J. Kaplan, critically acclaimed author of *Oneness and Separateness*, has published extensively on child, adolescent and adult development. She is also coauthor, with Donald M. Kaplan and Armand Schwerner, of *The Domesday Dictionary*. She has been associate professor in the Graduate Clinical Psychology Programs at both New York University and the City College of the City University of New York, and is the former Director of the Mother–Infant Research Nursery at NYU and former Director of the Child and Adolescent Clinic of the Psychological Center at CUNY. During the years Dr. Kaplan was writing *Adolescence*, she was on the faculty of the Seminar College of the New School for Social Research. Dr. Kaplan is a member of the Professional Advisory Committee of The Margaret S. Mahler Research Foundation.

Dr. Kaplan lives in New York City with her husband, Donald, and is the mother of two grown children, Ann and David.